JAPANESE VERBS

by

Roland A. Lange, Ph.D.

Formerly Associate Professor of Japanese Language and Linguistics
Columbia University, New York

BARRON'S

BARRON'S EDUCATIONAL SERIES, INC.
New York • London • Toronto • Sydney

All inquiries should be addressed to:
Barron's Educational Series, Inc.
250 Wireless Boulevard
Hauppauge, New York 11788

Library of Congress Catalog Card No. 90-46167

International Standard Book No. 0-8120-4525-4

Library of Congress Cataloging-in-Publication Data

Lange, Roland A.
    Japanese verbs / by Roland A. Lange
       p.   cm.
    Adapted from 501 Japanese verbs.
    Includes index
    ISBN 0-8120-4525-4
    1. Japanese language—Verb. I. Lange, Roland A. 501 Japanese
verbs. II. Title.
PL585.L34 1991   90-46167
495.6′82421—d c 20   CIP

PRINTED IN THE UNITED STATES OF AMERICA
1234 5500 98765432

CONTENTS

INTRODUCTION

IN ORDER TO LEARN A FOREIGN LANGUAGE efficiently students must follow a series of organized, graded lessons which cover the essential points of grammar, pronunciation, vocabulary, and usage. They must not only *study* such material to learn new words and grammatical constructions, but also *practice* what they have already learned in drill sessions with native speakers of the language.

This handbook of Japanese verbs is not designed to provide students with a complete course in Japanese. Rather, it is a reference work which gives a concise, easy-to-understand description of Japanese verbal inflection and derivation, together with tables showing all the necessary forms of 301 important and widely used Japanese verbs.

Japanese Verbs should be of help to both beginning and advanced students. For beginners, it constitutes a valuable aid in learning basic verbal inflection. Most textbooks only provide students with a few examples to illustrate the principles of inflection. This means that students are hampered because there is no way to check a given form of an unfamiliar verb. With *Japanese Verbs* students will be able to quickly verify the form in which they are interested. By presenting the full array of verbal inflection and derivation in tables, this book also enables beginning students to see the language as a system, rather than as a haphazard collection of stems and endings.

More advanced students will also profit from this systematic view of the language, because it will help them to organize the many verb forms they have learned into a systematic body of data. Such formalization is especially necessary for anyone who plans to teach the language some day.

PRONUNCIATION

A detailed treatment of the Japanese sound system is beyond the scope of this work, but it is necessary to give some explanation of the value of the letters used in our romanization. In the following explanation, italics represent our romanization while English sounds and words used as examples are enclosed in single quotation marks.

I Vowels

	Symbol	Nearest American English Equivalent		
	a	'o'	in	'cot'
	i	'ee'	in	'steep'
	u	'u'	in	'put'
	e	'e'	in	'pet'
	o	'o'	in	'post'

NOTE: All *Japanese vowels* are short and tense in comparison with their *English equivalents*. In Japanese the lips are not rounded and the vowels do not glide off into dipthongs. When occurring between voiceless consonants, *i* and *u* are whispered.

II Consonants

Symbol		Nearest American English Equivalent	Special Remarks
k	before *k*	'ck' in 'sick-call'	held for full beat*
	before vowels	'k' in 'kangaroo'	
g	as word initial	'g' in 'goat'	
	elsewhere	'g' in 'goat' or 'ng' in 'singer'	
s	before *s*	'ss' in 'grass-skirt'	full beat*
	before *i*	'sh' in 'sheep'	further forward in mouth than
	before *a, e, o, u*	's' in 'sip'	English sound
z	before *i*	'j' in 'jest'	further forward
	before *a, e, o, u*	'z' in 'zest'	further forward
t	before *t*	't-' in 'hot-toddy'	full beat*
	before *i*	'ch' in 'cheat'	tongue touches
	before *u*	'ts' in 'tsetse fly'	teeth

*See description of the Japanese 'syllable' below

II Consonants, (Continued)

t	elsewhere	't' in 'teen'	tongue touches teeth
d		'd' in 'deep'	
n		'n' in 'cone'	tongue touches teeth
ñ	before *k, g*	'n' in 'angle'	full beat*
	before *p, b, m*	'm' in 'mine'	full beat*
	before *z, t, d, n, r*	'n' in 'pun'	full beat*
	elsewhere	no English equivalent	made by raising tongue toward, but not touching, roof of mouth and humming through nose. Before *o*, sounds like *ñ + w + o*; before *e*, sounds like *ñ + y + e*
h	before *i*	'h' in 'heap'	with more friction
	before *u*	'wh' in 'whom'	made by puffing air between lips
	before *a, e, o*	'h' in 'holly'	
p	before *p*	'p-' in 'hip-pocket'	full beat*
	elsewhere	'p' in 'compare'	
b		'b' in 'combine'	
m		'm' in 'mince'	
w		'w' in 'went'	
y		'y' in 'yacht'	
r		no American equivalent, but similar to the 'r' of 'very' in clipped British pronunciation	made by single flip of tongue tip against ridge behind teeth

*See description of the Japanese 'syllable' below

III Consonant Clusters

Symbol	Nearest American English Equivalent		
ky	'c'	in	'curious'
gy	'g'	in	'angular'
sy	'sh'	in	'sheep'
zy	'j'	in	'jest'
ty	'ch'	in	'cheer'
ny	'n'	in	'menu'
hy	'H'	in	'Hubert'
			(in those American dialects in which the 'H' is not silent)
py	'p'	in	'pure'
by	'b'	in	'bureau'
my	'm'	in	'amuse'
ry	flapped 'r' followed by palatalization.		

The Japanese equivalent of the English syllable is not really a syllable but a mora, a unit of relative meter like a beat in music. People may speak quickly or slowly, but within a given stream of speech each mora will occupy the same length of time. This is true regardless of the type or number of sounds which make up each mora. For instance, the five words

sa.ku.ra	'cherry'
a.o.i.	'blue'
hi.ñ.i	'quality'
ki.p.pu	'ticket'
ryo.ka.ñ	'inn'

each consist of three mora (with the division indicated by dots) and each takes the same length of time to say. These examples serve to illustrate all the possible mora types in Japanese: a single vowel, a vowel preceded by a single consonant, a vowel preceded by a cluster of consonants plus *y*, and a single consonant. Only five consonants occur as independent mora: *k* (only before *k*), *s* (only before *s*), *t* (only before *t*), *p* (only before *p*), and *ñ* (in all occurrences).

The system of syllable division in Japanese can be summed up in two simple rules:

1. *THERE IS NEVER MORE THAN ONE VOWEL IN A SYLLABLE*. This holds true whether the vowels are of the same type or of different types. A word like *oi* 'nephew' is pronounced as *o + i*, not as the 'oy' in the English word 'boy'. A word like *yooi* 'preparation' is pronounced as *yo + o + i*. In some romanization systems two *o, a,* or *u* which occur in juxtaposition are treated as a single 'long vowel' and are written as *ō, ā,* and *ū,* respectively. In this book, however, they are written as *oo, aa,* and *uu*.

2. *EXCEPT FOR THOSE CONSONANTS WHICH OCCUR AS INDEPENDENT MORA (ñ in all occurrences and k, s, t, and p before themselves) CONSONANTS ARE ALWAYS PRONOUNCED WITH THE VOWELS WHICH FOLLOW THEM*. Thus the words *beñkyoo* 'study', *hañnoo* 'reaction', and *hakkiri* 'clearly' are pronounced as *be.ñ.kyo.o, ha.ñ.no.o,* and *ha.k.ki.ri*.

Japanese does not have a stress accent like that of English in which some syllables of a word are given special prominence by being pronounced louder than others. Instead, Japanese has a pitch accent system. This means that syllables are all pronounced with about the same force (sometimes giving a rather monotonous impression to the stress-accent oriented American) but some are pronounced on a higher pitch than others.

There is considerable variation in pitch accent depending upon regional dialect, but in the Tokyo accent, which is the standard for education and public discourse throughout Japan, there are three possible patterns, each of which is illustrated in one of the following words. (The solid line above the words indicates relative pitch.)

koomori 'bat' a high-pitched syllable followed by low-pitched syllable(s)

tomodati 'friend' a low-pitched syllable followed by high-pitched syllable(s) *mizuumi* 'lake' high-pitched syllable(s) preceded by a single low-pitched syllable and followed by low-pitched syllable(s)

As seen above, there is always a change in pitch between the first and second mora of a word. (This example also illustrates why the romanization used in this book uses *oo* rather than *ō*. If *ō* were used it would be impossible to show the change in pitch between the first two mora of *koomori*.)

What is most perceptible to the human ear is the contrast between a high-pitched mora and an immediately following low-pitched mora. Therefore, words such as *tomodati* which do not have this contrast sound flat, and are said to be unaccented or to have a "flat accent." There are also words such as *imooto* 'younger sister' which have what might be called a latent accent in their final syllable. When spoken by themselves they sound as flat as *tomodati*, but their accent is revealed when they become part of a longer pause group. For instance, when the particle *ga* is added to *tomodati* the resulting *tomodati ga* remains flat, but when this same particle is added to *imooto* it produces *imooto ga*, revealing the latent accent by providing a following low-pitched syllable.

When indicating pitch accent in this book we shall use the mark ´ above a vowel to indicate a high-pitched syllable immediately before a low-pitched syllable. Thus the above examples would be rendered: *kóomori, tomodati* (unaccented, so no mark), *mizuúmi,* and *imootó*.

It should be mentioned that Japanese pitch accent patterns operate for pause groups, each of which will have one of the three patterns described above. When a word is uttered in isolation it forms a pause group of its own, so its intrinsic accent pattern will be apparent. But when it is incorporated into a larger pause group the accent may shift. For example, the copula *désu* has what might be called a recessive accent. It appears in isolation or when preceded by an unaccented word, but it is lost when following a word with its own accent. The following examples show this clearly.

>*kore* + *désu ka* gives *Kore désu ka.*   'Is it this?'
>but   *dóko* + *désu ka* gives *Dóko desu ka.*   'Where is it?'

SPEECH LEVELS

Languages are arbitrary systems used for communication within the societies which develop them. Since societies differ in their view of the world, one can expect that languages will differ not only in vocabulary and pronunciation, but also in their fundamental grammatical categories. When native speakers of English confront the Japanese verb this expectation is fully borne out. Instead of the familiar (to them) distinctions involving number and person, they find distinctions between levels of formality and deference which serve to indicate the speaker's relationship to the person spoken to or about.

Proper use of these grammatical categories requires keen judgment as to the relative social status of speaker, listener, and referent, the complexities of overlapping in-group/out-group status, and whether an occasion or relationship is formal or informal. These judgments must be in line with *JAPANESE* social views, so students' success or failure will depend upon their knowledge of Japanese social customs and attitudes. Within the scope of this book we can only give some explanations regarding the working of these categories as a linguistic system.

Formality

The two sentences *Otya o noñda.* and *Otya o nomimasita.* both mean 'I (you, he, she, it, we or they) drank tea,' but the second is more formal (and polite) than the first. While the formal sentence with *nomimasita* could be used under any circumstances without giving offense, an adult Japanese would use the sentence with *noñda* only on informal occasions when speaking to persons of lower social status or to persons of the same status with whom he or she was on close terms, such as members of one's immediate family or close friends at school or at work. While formal and informal sentences are used by both men and women, in general, women's speech tends to be more formal and polite than that of men. (Women also tend to make greater use of the honorific and humble deference levels which are discussed below.)

The style of speech is usually kept uniform throughout a conversation, and is determined by the form of the final verb, adjective, or copula in a sentence. It is this which expresses the general tone of the occasion and of *the relationship between the speaker and the person spoken to*. Since it is the final verb (adjective or copula) which sets the style, other verbs (adjectives or copula) which may occur earlier in the sentence are usually of the shorter, informal type, even in formal speech. For example, the sentence *Kare ga otya o noñda kara, watakushi mo nomimasita.* 'He drank tea, so I drank tea too.' is in the formal style even though it contains the informal *noñda. Students must be familiar with both forms of the verb, but should use only the formal sentence style* until they have learned to whom and under what circumstances they may use the informal style without offending the person spoken to or appearing ludicrous.

Deference

While the formality style expresses the speaker's attitude toward *the person he is speaking to,* the deference level expresses the speaker's attitude toward *the person he is speaking about*. As far as verbs are concerned, the deference level shows the speaker's attitude toward the subject of the verb (even though the subject of the verb may not be mentioned explicitly in the sentence). There are three basic levels: honorific, plain or neutral, and humble when the subject is a person, and another 'neutral-polite' category when the subject is inanimate. The plain level is the most common, with the honorific and humble levels being used when the speaker wishes to express special deference or respect toward someone. The categories of formality and deference operate independently of each other so that each verb form can be classified according to both systems as in the following table, which shows a partial paradigm of the verb *kak.u* 'write.'

	INFORMAL	FORMAL
Honorific	okaki ni naru	okaki ni narimasu
Neutral	kaku	kakimasu
Humble	okaki suru	okaki simasu
	okaki itasu	okaki itasimasu

In addition to indicating respect, the use of the humble or honorific level serves to vaguely identify the subject because one does not use the honorific to refer to oneself, or the humble to refer to the person to whom one is speaking.* So while *kakimasu* could mean 'I (you, he, she, it, we, or they) write.' *okaki ni narimasu* could not mean 'I (or we) write.' nor could *okaki simasu* mean 'You write.' In the absence of other context the honorific level will refer to an action of the listener, and the humble level will refer to an action of the speaker.

As with the category of formality, the best guide to proper use of deference levels is a thorough knowledge of Japanese social custom. Until the student gains this he can follow the general principle that honorifics are used most often in reference to actions performed by the listener or members of his family, and humble forms are most often in referring to actions performed by the speaker.

INFLECTION AND DERIVATION OF JAPANESE VERBS

Japanese has two main classes of verbs: those with stems ending in *i* or *e* and those whose stems end in consonants. We

*An exception to this is the humble presumptive in which the person spoken to is sometimes covered in an inclusive 'we.' For example, *Takusii de mairimasyoo ka* may mean 'Shall we (you and I) go by taxi?'

shall call them Class I and II respectively. The following is a list of basic inflectional endings (informal) using *ake.ru* 'open' and *kat.u* 'win' as examples. Here the dot shows the division between stem and ending, but it will also be used at times to mark the division between the infinitive of a verb and an infinitive-based ending.

	Class I	Class II
Infinitive	ake	kat.i
Indicative	ake.ru	kat.u
Imperative I*	ake.ro	kat.e
Presumptive	ake.yoo	kat.oo
Provisional	ake.reba	kat.eba
Gerund	ake.te	kat.te
Past Indicative	ake.ta	kat.ta
Past Presumptive	ake.taroo	kat.taroo
Conditional	ake.tara	kat.tara
Alternative	ake.tari	kat.tari

Comparing the endings for the two verb classes, we find that in the last five categories they are the same (-*te*, -*ta*, -*taroo*, -*tara*, and -*tari*) but in the first five categories they differ as follows:

	Class I	Class II
Infinitive	-zero	-i
Indicative	-ru	-u
Imperative	-ro	-e
Presumptive	-yoo	-oo
Provisional	-reba	-eba

*This form is used only by male speakers when speaking harshly. Otherwise it is replaced by more polite informal imperative expressions. Two common ones which we will label informal imperatives II and III are infinitive + *nasai* (imperative of *nasar.u* 'to do') and gerund + *kudasai* (imperative of *kudasar.u.* 'give to me'). Of these the second is the more polite and is the one preferred for general use in making requests.

Except for the discrepancy between the vowels in the two imperative endings, the differences between the endings can be accounted for by a rule to the effect that the initial vowel of a suffix is lost when the stem ends in a vowel (Class I), and the initial consonant of a suffix is lost when the stem ends in a consonant (Class II). For example, *kat-* + *-i* = *kat.i*, but *ake-* + *-i* = *ake*; while *ake-* + *-ru* = *ake.ru*, but *kat-* + *-ru* = *kat.u*.

Turning now to the verb stems, we find that both Class I *ake-* and Class II *kat-* remain constant throughout the ten categories. This behavior is typical of Class I verb stems, but not of Class II verb stems. *All Class II verb stems which do not end in -t- undergo a change when attached directly to one of the five suffixes which begin with -t- (-te, -ta, -taroo, -tara, and -tari).*

These changes differ according to the final consonant of the stem, but all Class II stems which end in the same consonant undergo the same change. All of the possible changes are illustrated in the following list of examples. (*-te* is used as an example, but the change would be the same before any of the other four *-t-* endings.)

kas- + -te	becomes kasi.te	(kas.u 'lend')
kak- + -te	becomes kai.te	(kak.u 'write')
kag- + -te	becomes kai.de	(kag.u 'sniff')
yob- + -te	becomes yoñ.de	(yob.u 'call')
yom- + -te	becomes yoñ.de	(yom.u 'read')
sin- + -te	becomes siñ.de	(sin.u 'die')
kar- + -te	becomes kat.te	(kar.u 'cut')
kaw- + -te	becomes kat.te	(ka(w).u 'buy')*

This concludes our outline of inflection, but Japanese verbs have many more forms which are the result of derivation or the addition of various auxiliary endings. Up until now we

---

*Since in Japanese *w* only occurs before *a*, Class II verbs whose stems end in this sound do not show it in all forms of the verb, but only when the suffix begins with *a*.

have considered only informal affirmative forms. Our next step is to cover the formal affirmative which in both verb classes is derived by attaching the auxiliary verb -*mas.u* to the infinitive of the original verb. -*mas.u* occurs only as an ending for other verbs and has no substantive meaning of its own, serving only to raise the level of formality of the verb to which it is attached.

In general -*mas.u* behaves like a Class II verb, but it lacks an infinitive, has dual forms in the provisional, and has a Class I-type ending -*yoo* in the presumptive.

Indicative	-mas.u
Imperative	-mas.e
Presumptive	-mas.yoo
Provisional	-mas.eba / -mas.ureba
Gerund	-masi.te
Past Indicative	-masi.ta
Past Presumptive	-masi.taroo
Conditional	-masi.tara
Alternative	-masi.tari

All of these forms except the presumptive and the past and non-past indicative indicate a higher than normal level of formality or politeness. As a rule the imperative -*mas.e* is only used with honorific verbs such as *nasar.u* 'to do,' and *kudasar.u* 'give to me.' In the past presumptive the infinitive + *masi.taroo* is usually replaced by a combination of the informal past indicative + *des.yoo* (the formal presumptive form of the copula). A similar construction using *des.yoo* is also used in the non-past presumptive category. This differs from the -*mas.yoo* form not in degree of formality, but in the identity of the subject and other modal content. Consequently the -*mas.yoo* form and the informal indicative + *des.yoo* form will be labeled presumptive I and II respectively. The two forms using *des.yoo* are paralleled by informal ones using *dar.oo* the informal presumptive form of the copula.

We are now ready to move to the informal negative category. Here we find that, except for the imperative and presumptive, the "verb" is really an adjective derived by adding the adjectival ending *-ana.i* 'negative' to the stem of the verb. The resulting negative adjective then inflects like any other adjective. It will be noted that our earlier juncture rule works for *-ana.i* too because the initial vowel *-a-* is lost when it is joined to a Class I stem ending in a vowel.

		Class I	Class II
Indicative		ake.nai	kat.anai
Imperative	I	ake.ru na	kat.u na
	II	ake.nasaru na	kati.nasaru na
	III	ake.nai de kudasai	kat.anai de kudasai
Presumptive	*I	ake.mai	kat.umai
	II	ake.nai daroo	kat.anai daroo
Provisional		ake.nakereba	kat.anakereba
Gerund	I	ake.nai de	kat.anai de
	**II	ake.nakute	kat.anakute
Past Indicative		ake.nakatta	kat.anakatta
Past Presumptive		ake.nakattaroo	kat.anakattaroo
		ake.nakatta daroo	kat.anakatta daroo
Conditional		ake.nakattara	kat.anakattara
Alternative		ake.nakattari	kat.anakattari

Here we find three informal imperative constructions corresponding to those mentioned in connection with the informal affirmative imperative. The '*na*' used to form the negative imperative I is a negative command particle.

In the formal negative category we find the *-mas.u* ending again as well as various compounds using the copula.

*In the Class I presumptive I there is optional variation between *ake.mai*, in which *mai* follows the stem directly, and *ake.ru.mai* in which it follows the affirmative non-past indicative as it does with Class II verbs. We shall use the shorter form in our tables.
**While gerund I has the same range of uses as the affirmative gerund, the negative gerund II is more limited. It is not used with auxiliary 'giving' verbs to form polite request or polite command constructions such as negative imperative III.

		Class I	Class II
Indicative		ake.maseñ	kati.maseñ
Imperative		oake nasaimasu na	okati nasaimasu na
Presumptive	I	ake.masumai	kati.masumai
	II	ake.nai desyoo	kat.anai desyoo
Provisional*		ake-maseñ nara(ba)	kati.maseñ nara(ba)
Gerund		ake.maseñ de	kati.maseñ de
Past Indicative		ake.maseñ desita	kati.maseñ desita
Past Presumptive		ake.maseñ desitaroo	kati.maseñ desitaroo
		ake.nakatta desyoo	kat.anakatta desyoo
Conditional		ake.maseñ desitara	kati.maseñ desitara
Alternative		ake.maseñ desitari	kati.maseñ desitari

The semantic difference between the presumptive I and II is the same as that between the two forms of the affirmative formal presumptive. The imperative, gerund, and alternative forms given here occur only in conjunction with honorifics or when using a very formal style.

Up till now we have dealt with derivational endings such as -*mas.u* and -*ana.i* which have a range of inflection only within a given category such as 'formal' or 'informal negative.' *The remaining derivations are different in that they result in new verbs which can themselves take the entire range of inflectional and derivational endings which we have described up to this point.* (See pages 237 and 285 for examples.)

First we will consider the derivation of the passive, potential, causative, and causative passive forms. Since the inflectional endings for these newly derived verbs will be the same as those we have already given for Class I verbs we will show only their informal affirmative indicative (citation) form in the tables which follow.

	(Original) Class I	(Original) Class II
Passive	ake.rareru	kat.areru

*Of the two possible provisional forms of the copula: *nara* and *nar-aba*, the shorter version is used more often in colloquial conversation and is the one we shall use hereinafter in our tables.

		(Original) Class I	(Original) Class II
Potential		ake.rareru	kat.eru
Causative		ake.saseru	kat.aseru
Causative Passive		ake.saserareru	kat.aserareru

Since the newly formed verbs belong to Class I the division between stem and ending of the passive would be *akerare.ru*, *katare.ru*, and so forth. It will be noted that the chief difference between the derivation in original Class I and Class II verbs is that original Class II verbs end up with a separate form for the passive and potential while original Class I verbs use the same derived form for both of these categories. In addition to the causative passive endings shown above (-*saserareru* and -*aserareru*) there are non standard shorter endings -*sasareru* and -*asareru* which have the same meaning. We will not include these in the tables in the main body of the text, but they would be used with any verb which takes the longer forms.

The last two categories are the honorific and humble. Two forms are given for each, the second being that which shows the higher level of deference on the part of the speaker. Here, once again, we are dealing with completely new verbs so we present only their citation forms.

		Class I	Class II
Honorific	I	oake ni naru	okati ni naru
	II	oake nasaru	okati nasaru
Humble	I	oake suru	okati suru
	II	oake itasu	okati itasu

This table shows the typical derivation of honorific and humble forms wherein the infinitive of the original verb becomes a noun by the addition of the prefix *o-* and the inflectional endings are provided by the verbs *nar.u* ('to become'), *nasar.u*, *su.ru*, and *itas.u* (all 'to do'). Of these *nar.u* and *itas.u* are Class II verbs but *su.ru* and *nasar.u* are irregular. The student should consult the appropriate tables in the main body of the text to find out the inflectional forms of these two verbs as well as those of the seven other irregular verbs *ar.u,* *gozar.u, ik.u, irassyar.u, kudasar.u, ku.ru,* and *ossyar.u.*

In the honorific and humble categories a number of common verbs do not follow the typical pattern, but instead use suppletive forms which are not derived from the original verb. For instance, the verbs *nasar.u* and *itas.u* encountered above are, respectively, honorific and humble equivalents of the verb *su.ru.* Normally in such a case there will be only one form each for the honorific and humble categories.

Next we will present tables for the verbs *ake.ru* and *kat.u* showing all the inflectional and derivational categories which we have discussed. The form of these tables is the same as that which will be used throughout the main body of our text. (There is no standard arrangement or list of categories in use for teaching Japanese. The names for the ten basic inflectional categories have been taken from Bloch's study on inflection, but the content and arrangement of the tables in this book represent the author's opinion as to the most important forms of the Japanese verb and the most convenient arrangement for their presentation.) In order to assist the student in learning the distinctions between these verb forms the Japanese tables are followed by a chart containing English translations of each form of *ake.ru.* But before proceeding to these tables, three forms of the verb—the infinitive, the informal indicative, and the informal gerund—demand some additional comment.

The Infinitive

The infinitive is the form of the verb which is used in making compound words. We have already seen how the addition of the prefix *o-* 'deference' changes an infinitive into a noun. There are, in addition, a number of nouns which are added to the end of infinitives to form compound nouns. For instance, *kata* 'method' and *te* 'hand, doer,' when added to the infinitive of *tuka.u* 'to use' give *tukaikata* 'way of using,' and *tukaite* 'one who uses.' Indeed, there are many infinitives which function as nouns without the addition of other elements. For example:

Infinitive/Noun	Meaning	Verb	Meaning
kañgae	'idea'	kañgae.ru	'to think, consider'
warai	'laughter'	wara.u	'to laugh'
yorokobi	'joy'	yorokob.u	'to be happy'
nagusame	'consolation'	nagusame.ru	'to console, comfort'
utagai	'doubt, suspicion'	utaga.u	'to doubt, suspect'

To form an adjective from the infinitive, one simply adds one of a number of adjectival endings. We have already seen this happen when the negative ending *-anai* was added to the infinitive of verbs to form the informal nonpast negative indicative as in *ake.nai*. Other important endings of this type are *-ta.i* 'desiderative,' *-yasu.i* 'easy,' and *-niku.i* 'difficult.' By attaching these endings to *kaki* one gets *kakitai, kakiyasui,* and *kakinikui* which mean respectively 'want to write,' 'easy to write,' and 'difficult to write.'

There are also many verbs which are attached to the infinitives of other verbs to make compound verbs. We have already encountered *-mas.u* which is by far the most common. Three other important ones are *-tagar.u* 'non-first-person desiderative' (which, like *-mas.u,* occurs only as an ending in compound verbs), *-hazimeru* 'to begin,' and *-naosu* 'to repair or fix.' If we add these to *kaki* we get three new verbs: *kakitagaru* 'to wish to write,' *kakihazimeru* 'to begin to write,' and *kakinaosu* 'to rewrite.' Verbs indicating direction are very productive in combination with verbs of motion. For example, when the infinitive of the verb *tob.u* 'to jump, fly' is attached to *agar.u* 'rise,' *ori.ru* 'to descend,' *kos.u* 'to cross over,' and *mawar.u* 'revolve,' one gets the new verbs *tobiagar.u* 'to jump up,' *tobiori.ru* 'to jump down,' *tobikos.u* 'to jump over,' and *tobimawar.u* 'to jump around.'

The Indicative

It is important to remember that all indicative verb forms can function as complete one-word sentences requiring neither subjects nor objects. Thus, regardless of whether they be formal or informal, past or non-past, affirmative or negative,

Akeru.	or	Akemasu.	'(Someone) opens/will open (it).'
Aketa.	or	Akemasita.	'(Someone) opened (it).'
Akenai.	or	Akemaseñ.	'(Someone) does not/will not open (it).'
Akenakatta.	or	Akemaseñ desita.	'(Someone) did not open (it).'

are all sentences.

When we add more information such as subject, object, time, and location, the indicative becomes the last word in a longer sentence as in:

Mado o akeru. or Mado o akemasu.	'(Someone) opens/will open the window.'
Ano hito ga aketa. or Ano hito ga akemasita.	'That person opened (it).'
Kyoo wa akenai. or Kyoo wa akemaseñ.	'(Someone) will not open (it) today.'

The informal indicative plays a very important role in Japanese modification because it is the form which is used to modify nouns. In Japanese the modifier, be it verb, adjective, or noun, always precedes the noun which it modifies. Since the indicative is a sentence or ends a sentence, one is, in effect, modifying nouns with sentences. For example, the sentence *Mado o aketa*. '(Someone) opened the window,' can be used as a modifier in such phrases as:

mado o aketa hito	'the person who opened the window'
mado o aketa toki	'the time when (someone) opened the window'
mado o aketa syooko	'the proof that (someone) opened the window'

mado o aketa riyuu	'the reason why (someone) opened the window'
mado o aketa kekka	'the result of (someone) having opened the window'

The Informal Gerund

When ending a sentence (with or without following particles) the informal gerund indicates an informal request as in:

	Tyotto matte (yo).	'Wait a minute.'
	Soo ossyaranai de.	'Don't say that.'
and	Hayaku kite (yo).	'Come quickly.'

Gerunds have many functions when occurring within a sentence. When a sentence simply lists a number of actions without contrasting them or citing one as the cause of the other, all but the last action are often expressed by gerunds. For example, the two sentences *A-sañ wa zyuusu o nomimasita.* 'Mr. A drank juice.' and *B-sañ wa koohii o nomimasita.* 'Mr. B drank coffee.' can be combined in one sentence as *A-sañ wa zyuusu o noñde, B-sañ was koohii o nomimasita.* 'Mr. A drank juice, and Mr. B drank coffee.' If one wished to give strong contrast to these two actions, one would abandon the gerund in favor of an independent clause ending with the indicative: *A-sañ wa zyuusu o noñda ga, B-sañ wa koohii o nomimasita.* 'Mr. A drank juice, but Mr. B drank coffee.' Similarly, one would use the indicative if a cause-and-effect relationship is to be expressed as in *A-sañ ga koohii o noñda kara, B-sañ mo koohii o nomimasita.* 'Mr. A drank coffee, so Mr. B drank coffee too.'

A sentence in which the subject of all actions is the same, and which uses a gerund for all but the last verb in the sentence, indicates that the actions were performed in chronological order. For instance: *Kao o aratte, gohañ o tabete, gakkoo e ikimasita.* means 'I (you, he, they, etc.) washed my face, ate, and went to school.' But *Kao o aratte, gakkoo e itte, gohañ o tabemasita.* would mean 'I (you, he, they, etc.) washed my face, went to school, and ate.'

The gerund has no tense, mode or aspect of its own, so all such information is expressed by the final verb in the sentence. Therefore, if we change the above sentence to *Kao o aratte, gohañ o tabete, gakkoo e ikimasyoo.* its meaning becomes 'Let's wash our faces, eat, and go to school.'

Gerunds within sentences are also used to express manner as in *Eki made aruite ikimasita.* 'I (he, they, etc.) went to the station on foot.' and *Nani mo iwanai de dete ikimasita.* 'I (he, she, etc.) left without saying anything.'

We have already seen that in the informal imperative III the gerund combines with the imperative of *kudasar.u* to make a polite request as in *Akete kudasai.* 'Please open it.' and *Akenai de kudasai.* 'Please don't open it.' While the gerund may combine with any other verb if the combination makes sense, certain combinations which occur frequently have taken on special fixed meanings. Perhaps the most important of these is the combination of the informal affirmative gerund plus *i.ru* 'to exist.' Generally speaking, when the gerund of a transitive verb is used with *i.ru* the combination shows continuing action as in the English progressive, but when the gerund of an intransitive verb is used, the combination shows the existence of a continuing state. A good example of this contrast is seen in comparing combinations using the gerunds of two verbs which mean 'to open.' *Ake.ru* is transitive and would be used to convey such information as 'I opened the door,' while *ak.u* is intransitive and is used to convey such information as 'The door opened.' The transitive gerund *akete* plus *i.ru* means 'I (or someone else) am opening it.' On the other hand, *aite iru* from *ak.u* means 'It is (in the state of being) open,' *NOT* 'it is opening.'

Other productive gerund-verb combinations are those in which the gerund precedes *sima.u* 'to finish,' *oku* 'to put or place,' and the various verbs for giving and receiving. That with *sima.u* means 'to do something completely, to finish doing something,' or 'to end up by doing something.' That with *ok.u* means 'to do something in advance or with reference to the future,' while those with verbs for giving and receiving mean 'to perform an action for the benefit of another, to have

xxiii

another perform an action for one's own benefit,' or simply 'to benefit from the action of another.' The informal imperative III, which uses the gerund plus the appropriate form of *kudasar.u* 'give to me,' falls into this last group. Verbs of giving and receiving will be discussed at greater length following the main verb tables.

We should also mention the use of the gerund in combination with the particles *mo* and *wa* to express permission and prohibition. In asking for permission one uses the gerund plus *mo* as in *Mite mo ii desu ka.* 'May I look (at it)?' To answer that question in the affirmative one might say *Hai (mite mo) ii desu.* 'Yes, you may (look at it).' To refuse permission one might use the gerund plus *wa* as in *Iie (mite wa) ikemaseñ.* 'No, you must not (look at it).'

We are now ready for our sample verb tables and tables of English equivalents.

TRANSITIVE , *to open*

		AFFIRMATIVE	NEGATIVE
Indicative	INFORMAL	akeru	akenai
	FORMAL	akemasu	akemaseñ
Imperative	INFORMAL I	akero	akeru na
	II	akenasai	akenasaru na
	III	akete kudasai	akenai de kudasai
	FORMAL	oake nasaimase	oake nasaimasu na
Presumptive	INFORMAL I	akeyoo	akemai
	II	akeru daroo	akenai daroo
	FORMAL I	akemasyoo	akemasumai
	II	akeru desyoo	akenai desyoo
Provisional	INFORMAL	akereba	akenakereba
	FORMAL	akemaseba	akemaseñ nara
		akemasureba	
Gerund	INFORMAL I	akete	akenai de
	II		akenakute
	FORMAL	akemasite	akemaseñ de
Past Ind.	INFORMAL	aketa	akenakatta
	FORMAL	akemasita	akemaseñ desita
Past Presump.	INFORMAL	aketaroo	akenakattaroo
		aketa daroo	akenakatta daroo
	FORMAL	akemasitaroo	akemaseñ desitaroo
		aketa desyoo	akenakatta desyoo
Conditional	INFORMAL	aketara	akenakattara
	FORMAL	akemasitara	akemaseñ desitara
Alternative	INFORMAL	aketari	akenakattari
	FORMAL	akemasitari	akemaseñ desitari

INFORMAL AFFIRMATIVE INDICATIVE

Passive	akerareru	*Honorific*	I	oake ni naru
			II	oake nasaru
Potential	akerareru			
		Humble	I	oake suru
Causative	akesaseru		II	oake itasu
Causative Pass.	akesaserareru			

		AFFIRMATIVE	NEGATIVE
Indicative	INFORMAL	katu	katanai
	FORMAL	katimasu	katimaseñ
Imperative	INFORMAL I	kate	katu na
	II	katinasai	katinasaru na
	III	katte kudasai	katanai de kudasai
	FORMAL	okati nasaimase	okati nasaimasu na
Presumptive	INFORMAL I	katoo	katumai
	II	katu daroo	katanai daroo
	FORMAL I	katimasyoo	katimasumai
	II	katu desyoo	katanai desyoo
Provisional	INFORMAL	kateba	katanakereba
	FORMAL	katimaseba	katimaseñ nara
		katimasureba	
Gerund	INFORMAL I	katte	katanai de
	II		katanakute
	FORMAL	katimasite	katimaseñ de
Past Ind.	INFORMAL	katta	katanakatta
	FORMAL	katimasita	katimaseñ desita
Past Presump.	INFORMAL	kattaroo	katanakattaroo
		katta daroo	katanakatta daroo
	FORMAL	katimasitaroo	katimaseñ desitaroo
		katta desyoo	katanakatta desyoo
Conditional	INFORMAL	kattara	katanakattara
	FORMAL	katimasitara	katimaseñ desitara
Alternative	INFORMAL	kattari	katanakattari
	FORMAL	katimasitari	katimaseñ desitari

INFORMAL AFFIRMATIVE INDICATIVE

Passive	katareru	*Honorific*	I	okati ni naru
Potential	kateru		II	okati nasaru
Causative	kataseru	*Humble*	I	
			II	
Causative Pass.	kataserareru			

SAMPLE TABLE OF ENGLISH EQUIVALENTS

In the following table of English equivalents two conventions have been adopted in order to avoid undue redundancy.

1. The same English translation is used to represent both the formal and informal verb forms, with the understanding that the formal will be more polite in tone.
2. Only affirmative translations are given because except where noted the student can easily deduce the meaning of the corresponding negative form.

Needless to say the translations offered here cannot hope to cover all possible cases because meaning is influenced by context. Nevertheless, they should serve to delineate the main semantic boundaries between the various forms.

Infinitive	opening (This form is non-commital as to level of formality, tense, aspect, affirmative or negative. It merely serves as a base for many endings, and sometimes to end a phrase.)
Indicative	I open (it), you open (it), he (she, it) opens (it), we (you, they) open (it)
or:	I (you, he, she, it, we, you, they) will open (it)
Imperative	open (it)! (The Informal Imperative III and the Formal Imperative are closer to 'please open it.')
Presumptive I:	I am going to open (it), we are going to open (it) or: Let's open (it) * (There is no negative form which corresponds to this second meaning of presumptive I.)

*NOTE: In this book and in Japanese dictionaries the informal affirmative indicative is used as the citation form for verbs.

	II:	I (you, he, she, it, we, they) probably open (it) or: I am probably going to open (it), you are probably going to open (it), he (she, it) is probably going to open (it), we (you, they) are probably going to open (it)
Provisional Gerund		if I (you, she, he, it, we, they) open (it) opening (it) (Non-commital as to tense and aspect which are established by the final verb in a clause or sentence.)
Past Indicative		I (you, he, she, it, we, they) opened (it)
	or:	I (you, he, she, it, we, they) have opened (it)
	or:	I (you, he, she, it, we, they) had opened (it) *(Indicates completed action.)*
Past Presumptive		I (you, he, she, it, we, they) probably opened (it)
	or:	I (you, he, she, it, we, they) probably have opened (it)
	or:	I (you, he, she, it, we, they) probably had opened (it)
Conditional		if I (you, he, she, it, we, they) should open (it)
	or:	if I (you, he, she, it, we, they) were to open (it)
	or:	when I (you, he, she, it, we, they) open (it)
	or:	when I (you, he, she, it, we, they) opened (it)
Alternative		opening (it) and—(Non-commital as to tense and aspect. It merely indicates that two or more actions were, are, or will be performed alternately.)

Passive	is opened (by someone or something)
or:	will be opened (by someone or something)
or:	is opened (by someone) with bad result (for someone else)
or:	will be opened (by someone) with bad result (for someone else)
	(This form is sometimes also used as a sort of honorific to show deference for the person who performs the action.)
Potential	can be opened
or:	can open (it)
Causative	I make (someone) open (it), you make (someone) open (it), he (she, it) makes (someone) open (it), we (you, they) make (someone) open (it)
or:	I (you, he, she, it, we, they) will make (someone) open (it)
or:	I allow (someone) to open (it), you allow (someone) to open (it), he (she, it) allows (someone) to open (it), we (you, they) allow (someone) to open (it)
or:	I (you, he, she, it, we, they) will allow (someone) to open (it)
Causative Pass.	I am made to open (it), you are made to open (it), he (she, it) is made to open (it), we (you, they) are made to open (it)
or:	I (you, he, she, it, we, they) will be made to open (it)
Honorific	you open (it), he (she) opens (it), they open (it)
or:	you (he, she, they) will open (it) (all showing deference to the subject of the verb.)

Humble	I (we, or a member of my 'in group'
	open (it)
or:	I (we, or a member of my 'in group'
	will open (it)

(*The speaker shows deference by lowering his own position.*)

Accent Tables

We shall now present tables giving the basic accent patter for verbs. Since the patterns for Class I and Class II verbs a different, four tables will be given, one for an accented ve and one for an unaccented verb in each class. The accent ma indicates a high-pitched mora directly preceding a low-pitch mora. Thus *akéru* indicates *akeru*. The absence of an acce mark indicates a word in which all but the first mora have high pitch as in *osieru*.

Since the accent pattern is the same for all verbs of a giv type in the same class, verb tables in the main part of the bo will only show the accent for the citation form. Since *wakár* is a Class II verb and is marked as accented, it will be cle that the accent of its gerund is *wakátte*, that of its non-pa negative indicative is *wakaránai*, and so on.

It should be kept in mind that the accent shown in the tables is for the verb form in isolation and may change wh the verb becomes part of a larger pause group.

CLASS I ACCENTED VERB
tábe

tabé.ru

TRANSITIVE   *to eat*

			AFFIRMATIVE	NEGATIVE
Indicative	INFORMAL		tabéru	tabénai
	FORMAL		tabemásu	tabemaséñ
Imperative	INFORMAL I		tabéro	tabéru na
		II	tabenasái	tabenasáru na
		III	tábete kudasai	tabénai de kudasai
	FORMAL		mesiagarimáse	mesiagarimásu na
Presumptive	INFORMAL I		tabeyóo	tabemái
		II	tabéru daroo	tabénai daroo
	FORMAL	I	tabemasyóo	tabemasumái
		II	tabéru desyoo	tabénai desyoo
Provisional	INFORMAL		tabéreba	tabénakereba
	FORMAL		tabemáseba	tabemaséñ nara
			tabemasúreba	
Gerund	INFORMAL I		tábete	tabénai de
		II		tabénakute
	FORMAL		tabemásite	tabemaséñ de
Past Ind.	INFORMAL		tábeta	tabénakatta
	FORMAL		tabemásita	tabemaséñ desita
Past Presump.	INFORMAL		tábetaroo	tabénakattaroo
			tábeta daroo	tabénakatta daroo
	FORMAL		tabemásitaroo	tabemaséñ desitaroo
			tábeta desyoo	tabénakatta desyoo
Conditional	INFORMAL		tábetara	tabénakattara
	FORMAL		tabemásitara	tabemaséñ desitara
Alternative	INFORMAL		tábetari	tabénakattari
	FORMAL		tabemásitari	tabemaséñ desitari

INFORMAL AFFIRMATIVE INDICATIVE

Passive	taberaréru	*Honorific*	I	mesiagaru
			II	
Potential	taberaréru	*Humble*	I	itadaku
Causative	tabesaséru		II	
Causative Pass.	tabesaseraréru			

hará.u
harái
to pay TRANSITIVE

		AFFIRMATIVE	NEGATIVE
Indicative	INFORMAL	haráu	harawánai
	FORMAL	haraimásu	haraimáséñ
Imperative	INFORMAL I	haráe	haráu na
	II	harainasái	harainasáru na
	III	harátte kudasai	harawánai de kudasai
	FORMAL	oharai nasaimáse	oharai nasaimásu na
Presumptive	INFORMAL I	haraóo	haraumái
	II	haráu daroo	harawánai daroo
	FORMAL I	haraimasyóo	haraimasumái
	II	haráu desyoo	harawánai desyoo
Provisional	INFORMAL	haráeba	harawánakereba
	FORMAL	haraimáseba	haraimáséñ nara
		haraimasúreba	
Gerund	INFORMAL I	harátte	harawánai de
	II		harawánakute
	FORMAL	haraimásite	haraimáséñ de
Past Ind.	INFORMAL	harátta	harawánakatta
	FORMAL	haraimásita	haraimáséñ desita
Past Presump.	INFORMAL	haráttaroo	harawánakattaroo
		harátta daroo	harawánakatta daroo
	FORMAL	haraimásitaroo	haraimáséñ desitaroo
		harátta desyoo	harawánakatta desyoo
Conditional	INFORMAL	haráttara	harawánakattara
	FORMAL	haraimásitara	haraimáséñ desitara
Alternative	INFORMAL	haráttari	harawánakattari
	FORMAL	haraimásitari	haraimáséñ desitari

INFORMAL AFFIRMATIVE INDICATIVE

Passive	harawaréru	*Honorific*	I	oharai ni náru
			II	oharai nasáru
Potential	haraéru			
		Humble	I	oharai suru
Causative	harawaséru		II	oharai itasu
Causative Pass.	harawaseraréru			

CLASS I UNACCENTED VERB
osie
osie.ru

TRANSITIVE   *to teach, to inform*

			AFFIRMATIVE	NEGATIVE
Indicative	INFORMAL		osieru	osienai
	FORMAL		osiemásu	osiemáséñ
Imperative	INFORMAL	I	osieró	osierú na
		II	osienasái	osienasarú na
		III	osiete kudasái	osienai de kudasái
	FORMAL		oosie nasaimáse	oosie nasaimásu na
Presumptive	INFORMAL	I	*osieyóo	osiemái
		II	osieru daróo	osienai daróo
	FORMAL	I	osiemasyóo	osiemasumái
		II	osieru desyóo	osienai desyóo
Provisional	INFORMAL		osieréba	osienákereba
	FORMAL		osiemáseba	osiemáséñ nara
			osiemasúreba	
Gerund	INFORMAL	I	osiete	osienai de
		II		osienákute
	FORMAL		osiemásite	osiemáséñ de
Past Ind.	INFORMAL		osieta	osienákatta
	FORMAL		osiemásita	osiemáséñ desita
Past Presump.	INFORMAL		*osietaróo	osienákattaroo
			osieta daróo	osienákatta daroo
	FORMAL		osiemásitaroo	osiemáséñ desitaroo
			osieta desyóo	osienákatta desyoo
Conditional	INFORMAL		osietára	osienákattara
	FORMAL		osiemásitara	osiemáséñ desitara
Alternative	INFORMAL		osietári	osienákattari
	FORMAL		osiemásitari	osiemáséñ desitari

INFORMAL AFFIRMATIVE INDICATIVE

Passive	osierareru	*Honorific*	I	oosie ni náru
			II	oosie nasáru
Potential	osierareru			
		Humble	I	oosie suru
Causative	osiesaseru		II	oosie itasu
Causative Pass.	osiesaserareru			

*There are alternate unaccented forms *osieyoo* and *osietaroo*.

ara.u   **arai**
to wash   TRANSITIVE

			AFFIRMATIVE	NEGATIVE
Indicative	INFORMAL		arau	arawanai
	FORMAL		araimasu	araimaséñ
Imperative	INFORMAL I		araé	araú na
		II	arainasái	arainasáru na
		III	aratte kudasái	arawanai de kudasái
	FORMAL		oarai nasaimáse	oarai nasaimásu na
Presumptive	INFORMAL I*		aráo͞o	araumái
		II	arau daróo	arawanai daróo
	FORMAL	I	araimasyóo	araimasumái
		II	arau desyóo	arawanai desyóo
Provisional	INFORMAL		araéba	arawanákereba
	FORMAL		araimáseba	araimaséñ nara
			araimasúreba	
Gerund	INFORMAL I		aratte	arawanai de
		II		arawanákute
	FORMAL		araimásite	araimaséñ de
Past Ind.	INFORMAL		aratta	arawanákatta
	FORMAL		araimásita	araimaséñ desita
Past Presump.	INFORMAL*		arattaróo	arawanákattaroo
			aratta daróo	arawanákatta daroo
	FORMAL		araimásitaroo	araimaséñ desitaroo
			aratta desyóo	arawanákatta desyoo
Conditional	INFORMAL		arattára	arawanákattara
	FORMAL		araimásitara	araimaséñ desitara
Alternative	INFORMAL		arattári	arawanákattari
	FORMAL		araimásitari	araimaséñ desitari

INFORMAL AFFIRMATIVE INDICATIVE				
Passive	arawareru	*Honorific*	I	oarai ni naru
			II	oarai nasaru
Potential	araeru			
		Humble	I	oarai suru
Causative	arawaseru		II	oarai itasu
Causative Pass.	arawaserareru			

*There are alternate unaccented forms *araoo* and *arattaroo*.

Variation in the Accent of 'Unaccented Verbs' Depending on Environment

1. The informal affirmative non-past and past indicative forms of unaccented verbs acquire an accent peak on their final mora when they occur immediately before the particles *ga, ka, kara, keredo, si,* and **yori,* the sentence particles *ka, kai, sa,* and *wa,* the noun-substitute *no,* and some forms of the copula.

Examples: *agarú kara, akerú keredo, hatarakú yori, hazimetá desyoo* (alternates with *hazimeta desyóo*) and *kaetá no.*

2. The informal affirmative gerund of unaccented verbs acquires an accent on its final syllable when it occurs immediately before the particles *mo* and *wa* and the sentence particle *yo.*
Examples: *kiité mo, kesité wa,* and *kimeté yo.*

Loanword + *suru* Verbs

All of the verbs with which we have dealt thus far have been composed of native Japanese elements. Japanese also contains a vast number of verbs which are derived from foreign loanwords (often nouns) by the addition of the native Japanese verb *suru* 'to do.' Thus

siñpai	'worry'	+ suru gives siñpai suru 'to worry'
kekkoñ	'marriage'	+ suru gives kekkoñ suru 'to marry'
and hakkeñ	'discovery'	+ suru gives hakkeñ suru 'to discover'

Up to the mid-nineteenth century the vast majority of such verbs were derived from vocabulary borrowed from Chinese. But from the Meiji period onward an increasing amount of vocabulary has been borrowed from European languages, and from English, French, and German, in particular. These loan-

---

*In the case of *yori,* this alternates with the pattern of unaccented verb plus accented *yóri* as in *hataraku yóri.*

words, which have now reached flood proportions, are assimilated to Japanese in the same manner as the Chinese borrowings. Therefore, one finds in common use today such 'Japanese verbs' as *kopii suru* 'to copy,' *anauñsu suru* 'to announce,' and *saiñ suru* 'to sign.'

If they wish to communicate effectively in Japanese, English-speaking students must keep three points firmly in mind when dealing with Japanese verbs based on borrowings from English.

1) The words must be pronounced as they are by Japanese, not as they are in the original English. Remember, they are Japanese verbs.

2) Their meanings may differ as much from the original English as does their pronunciation.

3) They cannot be coined at random by combining any English word with *suru*. Use ones which you have observed Japanese using, and consult a native speaker if in doubt as to whether a particular combination is in use.

We shall now present one table for verbs of this type derived from Chinese nouns and one for those derived from English nouns. It will be noted that these verbs lack type I honorific and humble forms, that SOME Chinese-derived verbs are prefixed by *go-* rather than *o-* in the formal imperative and honorific forms, and that English-derived verbs are usually not prefixed by either.

			AFFIRMATIVE	NEGATIVE
Indicative	INFORMAL		beñkyoo suru	beñkyoo sinai
	FORMAL		beñkyoo simasu	beñkyoo simaseñ
Imperative	INFORMAL	I	beñkyoo siro	beñkyoo suru na
		II	beñkyoo sinasai	beñkyoo sinasaru na
		III	beñkyoo site kudasai	beñkyoo sinai de kudasai
	FORMAL		gobeñkyoo nasaimase	gobeñkyoo nasaimasu na
Presumptive	INFORMAL	I	beñkyoo siyoo	beñkyoo surumai
		II	beñkyoo suru daroo	beñkyoo sinai daroo
	FORMAL	I	beñkyoo simasyoo	beñkyoo simasumai
		II	beñkyoo suru desyoo	beñkyoo sinai desyoo
Provisional	INFORMAL		beñkyoo sureba	beñkyoo sinakereba
	FORMAL		beñkyoo simaseba	beñkyoo simaseñ nara
			beñkyoo simasureba	
Gerund	INFORMAL	I	beñkyoo site	beñkyoo sinai de
		II		beñkyoo sinakute
	FORMAL		beñkyoo simasite	beñkyoo simaseñ de
Past Ind.	INFORMAL		beñkyoo sita	beñkyoo sinakatta
	FORMAL		beñkyoo simasita	beñkyoo simaseñ desita
Past Presump.	INFORMAL		beñkyoo sitaroo	beñkyoo sinakattaroo
			beñkyoo sita daroo	beñkyoo sinakatta daroo
	FORMAL		beñkyoo simasitaroo	beñkyoo simaseñ desitaroo
			beñkyoo sita desyoo	beñkyoo sinakatta desyoo
Conditional	INFORMAL		beñkyoo sitara	beñkyoo sinakattara
	FORMAL		beñkyoo simasitara	beñkyoo simaseñ desitara
Alternative	INFORMAL		beñkyoo sitari	beñkyoo sinakattari
	FORMAL		beñkyoo simasitari	beñkyoo simaseñ desitari

INFORMAL AFFIRMATIVE INDICATIVE

Passive	beñkyoo sareru	*Honorific*	I	
			II	gobeñkyoo nasaru
Potential	beñkyoo dekiru			
		Humble	I	
Causative	beñkyoo saseru		II	beñkyoo itasu
Causative Pass.	beñkyoo saserareru			

		AFFIRMATIVE	NEGATIVE
Indicative	INFORMAL	kopii suru	kopii sinai
	FORMAL	kopii simasu	kopii simaseñ
Imperative	INFORMAL I	kopii siro	kopii suru na
	II	kopii sinasai	kopii sinasara na
	III	kopii site kudasai	kopii sinai de kudasai
	FORMAL	kopii nasaimase	kopii nasaimasu na
Presumptive	INFORMAL I	kopii siyoo	kopii surumai
	II	kopii suru daroo	kopii sinai daroo
	FORMAL I	kopii simasyoo	kopii simasumai
	II	kopii suru desyoo	kopii sinai desyoo
Provisional	INFORMAL	kopii sureba	kopii sinakereba
	FORMAL	kopii simaseba	kopii simaseñ nara
		kopii simasureba	
Gerund	INFORMAL I	kopii site	kopii sinai de
	II		kopii sinakute
	FORMAL	kopii simasite	kopii simaseñ de
Past Ind.	INFORMAL	kopii sita	kopii sinakatta
	FORMAL	kopii simasita	kopii simaseñ desita
Past Presump.	INFORMAL	kopii sitaroo	kopii sinakattaroo
		kopii sita daroo	kopii sinakatta daroo
	FORMAL	kopii simasitaroo	kopii simaseñ desitaroo
		kopii sita desyoo	kopii sinakatta desyoo
Conditional	INFORMAL	kopii sitara	kopii sinakattara
	FORMAL	kopii simasitara	kopii simaseñ desitara
Alternative	INFORMAL	kopii sitari	kopii sinakattari
	FORMAL	kopii simasitari	kopii simaseñ desitari

INFORMAL AFFIRMATIVE INDICATIVE

Passive	kopii sareru	*Honorific*	I	
			II	kopii nasaru
Potential	kopii dekiru			
		Humble	I	
Causative	kopii saseru		II	kopii itasu
Causative Pass.	kopii saserareru			

ROMANIZATION

The first system of romanization for Japanese was devised by Portuguese missionaries in the sixteenth century, at which time it was used in a number of remarkable books, including a Japanese-Portuguese dictionary which is today used by Japanese scholars as the principal source for data on Japanese pronunciation of that period.

With the reopening of Japan to contact with Europe in the mid-nineteenth century romanizations were developed based on the spelling in various European languages: a French-type romanization, a German-type romanization, and so on. Among them was an English-type romanization which came to be called "Hepburn romanization" because it first appeared in a Japanese-English dictionary published by James Curtis Hepburn, an American medical missionary. It is this system, with some variation, which is commonly used in the U.S. press today.

Within Japan the debate on which romanization system is best has been long, and at times bitter, with competing factions each publishing materials written in their own system. The Japanese government has sought to bring scholars to a consensus on the matter, but even the designation of an official system in 1954 failed to end the debate.

The two main differences between the Hepburn romanization and the one used in this book are their treatment of two identical vowels which occur in juxtaposition and their treatment of certain consonants when they occur before the vowels *i* and *u*. We have already discussed the advantages of *oo* versus *o* in the section on pitch accent, so we will confine our discussion here to the second difference.

Whereas the Hepburn system has: our system has:

sa	shi	su	se	so	sa	si	su	se	so
za	ji	zu	ze	zo	za	zi	zu	ze	zo
ta	chi	tsu	te	to	ta	ti	tu	te	to
ha	hi	fu	he	ho	ha	hi	hu	he	ho

The Hepburn system uses *shi, ji, chi, tsu,* and *fu* because to the ear of a native speaker of English the consonants in the syllables thus represented sound closer to ENGLISH sh, j, ch, ts, and f than they do to ENGLISH s, z, t, and h. Thus it is based upon the perception of speakers of English and on distinctions which are valid in English. Our romanization is based upon the perception of speakers of Japanese and upon distinctions which are valid in Japanese. Analysis of the sound system of Japanese shows that although the pronunciation of JAPANESE *s, z, t,* and *h* is influenced by a following *i* or *u* it is perceived by Japanese as the same sound as when it occurs before other vowels.

Any system of romanization which represents all the sounds of Japanese in a consistent manner can be used in teaching Japanese IF THE ACTUAL JAPANESE PRONUNCIATION REPRESENTED BY THE LETTERS IS CLEARLY AND FULLY EXPLAINED AND DEMONSTRATED.

But the ideal romanization for Japanese is one which is based, not upon the sound systems of French, German, or English, but upon the sound system of Japanese. It is one in which each Japanese phoneme (minimum significant unit of sound) is consistently represented by its own symbol or combination of symbols. This is particularly true in a book like this, in which we are trying to give the clearest possible picture of Japanese inflection and derivation. Our romanization happens to be similar to the official Japanese romanization, but the main reason for our choice is that this romanization represents the Japanese sound system accurately, and hence, represents Japanese inflected forms accurately.

For example, when one uses the Hepburn system the infinitive, indicative, and imperative I of the verb *kat.u* become *kach.i, kats.u,* and *kat.e,* giving the impression that the stem ends in three different consonants. Similarly, these same forms for the verb *kas.u* 'to lend' would be rendered as *kash.i, kas.u,* and *kas.e* giving the false impression that the stem ends in two different consonants. Thus, an attempt to conform to English spelling would result in a distortion of Japanese inflection.

TABLES OF 301 JAPANESE VERBS

We are now ready to enter the main body of the text, which consists of tables of 301 common Japanese verbs showing all of the forms which were presented in our sample tables. The verbs are intransitive unless designated as transitive.

It is likely that students will approach this book looking for two basic types of information. Some will be seeking the inflection and derivation of a Japanese verb whose citation form they already know, while others will be trying to find a Japanese verb which fits a particular meaning in English. To provide for the first case, our verb tables are arranged alphabetically according to the citation form of the verb. Thus students who want to find out a particular form of the verb *taberu* can find it easily on page 243 between *suwaru* and *-tagaru*. For the convenience of students who are seeking a verb with a given meaning in English, an English to Japanese index of all 301 verbs is provided beginning on page 307. Here students can look up 'begin' and find listed the intransitive verb *hazimaru* and the transitive verb *hazimeru* on pages 46 and 47 respectively. Thus, within the narrow limits of 301 verbs, this text also serves as a sort of Japanese-English, English-Japanese dictionary.

		AFFIRMATIVE	NEGATIVE
Indicative	INFORMAL	agaru	agaranai
	FORMAL	agarimasu	agarimaseñ
Imperative	INFORMAL I	agare	agaru na
	II	agarinasai	agarinasaru na
	III	agatte kudasai	agaranai de kudasai
	FORMAL	oagari nasaimase	oagari nasaimasu na
Presumptive	INFORMAL I	agaroo	agarumai
	II	agaru daroo	agaranai daroo
	FORMAL I	agarimasyoo	agarimasumai
	II	agaru desyoo	agaranai desyoo
Provisional	INFORMAL	agareba	agaranakereba
	FORMAL	agarimaseba	agarimaseñ nara
		agarimasureba	
Gerund	INFORMAL I	agatte	agaranai de
	II		agaranakute
	FORMAL	agarimasite	agarimaseñ de
Past Ind.	INFORMAL	agatta	agaranakat
	FORMAL	agarimasita	agarimaseñ desita
Past Presump.	INFORMAL	agattaroo	agaranakattaroo
		agatta daroo	agaranakatta daroo
	FORMAL	agarimasitaroo	agarimaseñ desitaroo
		agatta desyoo	agaranakatta desyoo
Conditional	INFORMAL	agattara	agaranakattara
	FORMAL	agarimasitara	agarimaseñ desitara
Alternative	INFORMAL	agattari	agaranakattari
	FORMAL	agarimasitari	agarimaseñ desitari

INFORMAL AFFIRMATIVE INDICATIVE

Passive	agarareru	*Honorific*	I	oagari ni naru
			II	oagari nasaru
Potential	agareru			
		Humble	I	
Causative	agaraseru		II	
Causative Pass.	agaraserareru			

to give (to second or third person)   TRANSITIVE

			AFFIRMATIVE	NEGATIVE
Indicative	INFORMAL		ageru	agenai
	FORMAL		agemasu	agemaseñ
Imperative	INFORMAL	I	agero	ageru na
		II	agenasai	agenasaru na
		III	agete kudasai	agenai de kudasai
	FORMAL		oage nasaimase	oage nasaimasu na
Presumptive	INFORMAL	I	ageyoo	agemai
		II	ageru daroo	agenai daroo
	FORMAL	I	agemasyoo	agemasumai
		II	ageru desyoo	agenai desyoo
Provisional	INFORMAL		agereba	agenakereba
	FORMAL		agemaseba	agemaseñ nara
			agemasureba	
Gerund	INFORMAL	I	agete	agenai de
		II		agenakute
	FORMAL		agemasite	agemaseñ de
Past Ind.	INFORMAL		ageta	agenakatta
	FORMAL		agemasita	agemaseñ desita
Past Presump.	INFORMAL		agetaroo	agenakattaroo
			ageta daroo	agenakatta daroo
	FORMAL		agemasitaroo	agemaseñ desitaroo
			ageta desyoo	agenakatta desyoo
Conditional	INFORMAL		agetara	agenakattara
	FORMAL		agemasitara	agemaseñ desitara
Alternative	INFORMAL		agetari	agenakattari
	FORMAL		agemasitari	agemaseñ desitari

INFORMAL AFFIRMATIVE INDICATIVE

Passive	agerareru	*Honorific*	I	oage ni naru
			II	oage nasaru
Potential	agerareru			
		Humble	I	sasiageru
Causative	agesaseru		II	
Causative Pass.	agesaserareru			

TRANSITIVE *to open*

		AFFIRMATIVE	NEGATIVE
Indicative	INFORMAL	akeru	akenai
	FORMAL	akemasu	akemaseñ
Imperative	INFORMAL I	akero	akeru na
	II	akenasai	akenasaru na
	III	akete kudasai	akenai de kudasai
	FORMAL	oake nasaimase	oake nasaimasu na
Presumptive	INFORMAL I	akeyoo	akemai
	II	akeru daroo	akenai daroo
	FORMAL I	akemasyoo	akemasumai
	II	akeru desyoo	akenai desyoo
Provisional	INFORMAL	akereba	akenakereba
	FORMAL	akemaseba	akemaseñ nara
		akemasureba	
Gerund	INFORMAL I	akete	akenai de
	II		akenakute
	FORMAL	akemasite	akemaseñ de
Past Ind.	INFORMAL	aketa	akenakatta
	FORMAL	akemasita	akemaseñ desita
Past Presump.	INFORMAL	aketaroo	akenakattaroo
		aketa daroo	akenakatta daroo
	FORMAL	akemasitaroo	akemaseñ desitaroo
		aketa desyoo	akenakatta desyoo
Conditional	INFORMAL	aketara	akenakattara
	FORMAL	akemasitara	akemaseñ desitara
Alternative	INFORMAL	aketari	akenakattari
	FORMAL	akemasitari	akemaseñ desitari

INFORMAL AFFIRMATIVE INDICATIVE

Passive	akerareru	*Honorific*	I	oake ni naru
			II	oake nasaru
Potential	akerareru			
		Humble	I	oake suru
Causative	akesaseru		II	oake itasu
Causative Pass.	akesaserareru			

3

to abandon (an idea), *to resign oneself* (to)   TRANSITIVE

		AFFIRMATIVE	NEGATIVE
Indicative	INFORMAL	akirameru	akiramenai
	FORMAL	akiramemasu	akiramemaseñ
Imperative	INFORMAL I	akiramero	akirameru na
	II	akiramenasai	akiramenasaru na
	III	akiramete kudasai	akiramenai de kudasai
	FORMAL	oakirame nasaimase	oakirame nasaimasu na
Presumptive	INFORMAL I	akirameyoo	akiramemai
	II	akirameru daroo	akiramenai daroo
	FORMAL I	akiramemasyoo	akiramemasumai
	II	akirameru desyoo	akiramenai desyoo
Provisional	INFORMAL	akiramereba	akiramenakereba
	FORMAL	akiramemaseba	akiramemaseñ nara
		akiramemasureba	
Gerund	INFORMAL I	akiramete	akiramenai de
	II		akiramenakute
	FORMAL	akiramemasite	akiramemaseñ de
Past Ind.	INFORMAL	akirameta	akiramenakatta
	FORMAL	akiramemasita	akiramemaseñ desita
Past Presump.	INFORMAL	akirametaroo	akiramenakattaroo
		akirameta daroo	akiramenakatta daroo
	FORMAL	akiramemasitaroo	akiramemaseñ desitaroo
		akirameta desyoo	akiramenakatta desyoo
Conditional	INFORMAL	akirametara	akiramenakattara
	FORMAL	akiramemasitara	akiramemaseñ desitara
Alternative	INFORMAL	akirametari	akiramenakattari
	FORMAL	akiramemasitari	akiramemaseñ desitari

INFORMAL AFFIRMATIVE INDICATIVE

Passive	akiramerareru	*Honorific*	I	oakirame ni naru
			II	oakirame nasaru
Potential	akiramerareru			
		Humble	I	oakirame suru
Causative	akiramesaseru		II	oakirame itasu
Causative Pass.	akiramesaserareru			

4

		AFFIRMATIVE	NEGATIVE
Indicative	INFORMAL	aku	akanai
	FORMAL	akimasu	akimaseñ
Imperative	INFORMAL I		
	II		
	III		
	FORMAL		
Presumptive	INFORMAL I	akoo	akumai
	II	aku daroo	akanai daroo
	FORMAL I	akimasyoo	akimasumai
	II	aku desyoo	akanai desyoo
Provisional	INFORMAL	akeba	akanakereba
	FORMAL	akimaseba	akimaseñ nara
		akimasureba	
Gerund	INFORMAL I	aite	akanai de
	II		akanakute
	FORMAL	akimasite	akimaseñ de
Past Ind.	INFORMAL	aita	akanakatta
	FORMAL	akimasita	akimaseñ desita
Past Presump.	INFORMAL	aitaroo	akanakattaroo
		aita daroo	akanakatta daroo
	FORMAL	akimasitaroo	akimaseñ desitaroo
		aita desyoo	akanakatta desyoo
Conditional	INFORMAL	aitara	akanakattara
	FORMAL	akimasitara	akimaseñ desitara
Alternative	INFORMAL	aitari	akanakattari
	FORMAL	akimasitari	akimaseñ desitari

INFORMAL AFFIRMATIVE INDICATIVE

Passive		*Honorific*	I
			II
Potential			
		Humble	I
Causative			II
Causative Pass.			

		AFFIRMATIVE	NEGATIVE
Indicative	INFORMAL	aññai suru	aññai sinai
	FORMAL	aññai simasu	aññai simaseñ
Imperative	INFORMAL I	aññai siro	aññai suru na
	II	aññai sinasai	aññai sinasaru na
	III	aññai site kudasai	aññai sinai de kudasai
	FORMAL	aññai nasaimase	aññai nasaimasu na
Presumptive	INFORMAL I	aññai siyoo	aññai surumai
	II	aññai suru daroo	aññai sinai daroo
	FORMAL I	aññai simasyoo	aññai simasumai
	II	aññai suru desyoo	aññai sinai desyoo
Provisional	INFORMAL	aññai sureba	aññai sinakereba
	FORMAL	aññai simaseba	aññai simaseñ nara
		aññai simasureba	
Gerund	INFORMAL I	aññai site	aññai sinai de
	II		aññai sinakute
	FORMAL	aññai simasite	aññai simaseñ de
Past Ind.	INFORMAL	aññai sita	aññai sinakatta
	FORMAL	aññai simasita	aññai simaseñ desita
Past Presump.	INFORMAL	aññai sitaroo	aññai sinakattaroo
		aññai sita daroo	aññai sinakatta daroo
	FORMAL	aññai simasitaroo	aññai simaseñ desitaroo
		aññai sita desyoo	aññai sinakatta desyoo
Conditional	INFORMAL	aññai sitara	aññai sinakattara
	FORMAL	aññai simasitara	aññai simaseñ desitara
Alternative	INFORMAL	aññai sitari	aññai sinakattari
	FORMAL	aññai simasitari	aññai simaseñ desitari

INFORMAL AFFIRMATIVE INDICATIVE

Passive	aññai sareru	*Honorific*	I	
			II	aññai nasaru
Potential	aññai dekiru			
		Humble	I	
Causative	aññai saseru		II	aññai itasu
Causative Pass.	aññai saserareru			

		AFFIRMATIVE	NEGATIVE
Indicative	INFORMAL	añsiñ suru	añsiñ sinai
	FORMAL	añsiñ simasu	añsiñ simaseñ
Imperative	INFORMAL I	añsiñ siro	añsiñ suru na
	II	añsiñ sinasai	añsiñ sinasaru na
	III	añsiñ site kudasai	añsiñ sinai de kudasai
	FORMAL	añsiñ nasaimase	añsiñ nasaimasu na
Presumptive	INFORMAL I	añsiñ siyoo	añsiñ surumai
	II	añsiñ suru daroo	añsiñ sinai daroo
	FORMAL I	añsiñ simasyoo	añsiñ simasumai
	II	añsiñ suru desyoo	añsiñ sinai desyoo
Provisional	INFORMAL	añsiñ sureba	añsiñ sinakereba
	FORMAL	añsiñ simaseba	añsiñ simaseñ nara
		añsiñ simasureba	
Gerund	INFORMAL I	añsiñ site	añsiñ sinai de
	II		añsiñ sinakute
	FORMAL	añsiñ simasite	añsiñ simaseñ de
Past Ind.	INFORMAL	añsiñ sita	añsiñ sinakatta
	FORMAL	añsiñ simasita	añsiñ simaseñ desita
Past Presump.	INFORMAL	añsiñ sitaroo	añsiñ sinakattaroo
		añsiñ sita daroo	añsiñ sinakatta daroo
	FORMAL	añsiñ simasitaroo	añsiñ simaseñ desitaroo
		añsiñ sita desyoo	añsiñ sinakatta desyoo
Conditional	INFORMAL	añsiñ sitara	añsiñ sinakattara
	FORMAL	añsiñ simasitara	añsiñ simaseñ desitara
Alternative	INFORMAL	añsiñ sitari	añsiñ sinakattari
	FORMAL	añsiñ simasitari	añsiñ simaseñ desitari

INFORMAL AFFIRMATIVE INDICATIVE

Passive	añsiñ sareru	*Honorific*	I	
			II	añsiñ nasaru
Potential	añsiñ dekiru			
		Humble	I	
Causative	añsiñ saseru		II	añsiñ itasu
Causative Pass.	añsiñ saserareru			

			AFFIRMATIVE	NEGATIVE
Indicative	INFORMAL		arau	arawanai
	FORMAL		araimasu	araimaseñ
Imperative	INFORMAL	I	arae	arau na
		II	arainasai	arainasaru na
		III	aratte kudasai	arawanai de kudasai
	FORMAL		oarai nasaimase	oarai nasaimasu na
Presumptive	INFORMAL	I	araoo	araumai
		II	arau daroo	arawanai daroo
	FORMAL	I	araimasyoo	araimasumai
		II	arau desyoo	arawanai desyoo
Provisional	INFORMAL		araeba	arawanakereba
	FORMAL		araimaseba	araimaseñ nara
			araimasureba	
Gerund	INFORMAL	I	aratte	arawanai de
		II		arawanakute
	FORMAL		araimasite	araimaseñ de
Past Ind.	INFORMAL		aratta	arawanakatta
	FORMAL		araimasita	araimaseñ desita
Past Presump.	INFORMAL		arattaroo	arawanakattaroo
			aratta daroo	arawanakatta daroo
	FORMAL		araimasitaroo	araimaseñ desitaroo
			aratta desyoo	arawanakatta desyoo
Conditional	INFORMAL		arattara	arawanakattara
	FORMAL		araimasitara	araimaseñ desitara
Alternative	INFORMAL		arattari	arawanakattari
	FORMAL		araimasitari	araimaseñ desitari

INFORMAL AFFIRMATIVE INDICATIVE

Passive	arawareru	*Honorific* I	oarai ni naru
		II	oarai nasaru
Potential	araeru		
		Humble I	oarai suru
Causative	arawaseru	II	oarai itasu
Causative Pass.	arawaserareru		

		AFFIRMATIVE	NEGATIVE
Indicative	**INFORMAL**	arawareru	arawarenai
	FORMAL	arawaremasu	arawaremaseñ
Imperative	**INFORMAL I**	arawarero	arawareru na
	II	arawarenasai	arawarenasaru na
	III	arawarete kudasai	arawarenai de kudasai
	FORMAL		
Presumptive	**INFORMAL I**	arawareyoo	arawaremai
	II	arawareru daroo	arawarenai daroo
	FORMAL I	arawaremasyoo	arawaremasumai
	II	arawareru desyoo	arawarenai desyoo
Provisional	**INFORMAL**	arawarereba	arawarenakereba
	FORMAL	arawaremaseba	arawaremaseñ nara
		arawaremasureba	
Gerund	**INFORMAL I**	arawarete	arawarenai de
	II		arawarenakute
	FORMAL	arawaremasite	arawaremaseñ de
Past Ind.	**INFORMAL**	arawareta	arawarenakatta
	FORMAL	arawaremasita	arawaremaseñ desita
Past Presump.	**INFORMAL**	arawaretaroo	arawarenakattaroo
		arawareta daroo	arawarenakatta daroo
	FORMAL	arawaremasitaroo	arawaremaseñ desitaroo
		arawareta desyoo	arawarenakatta desyoo
Conditional	**INFORMAL**	arawaretara	arawarenakattara
	FORMAL	arawaremasitara	arawaremaseñ desitara
Alternative	**INFORMAL**	arawaretari	arawarenakattari
	FORMAL	arawaremasitari	arawaremaseñ desitari

INFORMAL AFFIRMATIVE INDICATIVE

Passive		*Honorific*	**I**
			II
Potential	arawarerareru		
		Humble	**I**
Causative	arawaresaseru		**II**
Causative Pass.	arawaresaserareru		

9

		AFFIRMATIVE	NEGATIVE
Indicative	INFORMAL	arawasu	arawasanai
	FORMAL	arawasimasu	arawasimaseñ
Imperative	INFORMAL I	arawase	arawasu na
	II	arawasinasai	arawasinasaru na
	III	arawasite kudasai	arawasanai de kudasai
	FORMAL	oarawasi nasaimase	oarawasi nasaimasu na
Presumptive	INFORMAL I	arawasoo	arawasumai
	II	arawasu daroo	arawasanai daroo
	FORMAL I	arawasimasyoo	arawasimasumai
	II	arawasu desyoo	arawasanai desyoo
Provisional	INFORMAL	arawaseba	arawasanakereba
	FORMAL	arawasimaseba	arawasimaseñ nara
		arawasimasureba	
Gerund	INFORMAL I	arawasite	arawasanai de
	II		arawasanakute
	FORMAL	arawasimasite	arawasimaseñ de
Past Ind.	INFORMAL	arawasita	arawasanakatta
	FORMAL	arawasimasita	arawasimaseñ desita
Past Presump.	INFORMAL	arawasitaroo	arawasanakattaroo
		arawasita daroo	arawasanakatta daroo
	FORMAL	arawasimasitaroo	arawasimaseñ desitaroo
		arawasita desyoo	arawasanakatta desyoo
Conditional	INFORMAL	arawasitara	arawasanakattara
	FORMAL	arawasimasitara	arawasimaseñ desitara
Alternative	INFORMAL	arawasitari	arawasanakattari
	FORMAL	arawasimasitari	arawasimaseñ desitari

INFORMAL AFFIRMATIVE INDICATIVE

Passive	arawasareru	*Honorific*	I	oarawasi ni naru
			II	oarawasi nasaru
Potential	arawaseru			
		Humble	I	
Causative	arawasaseru		II	
Causative Pass.	arawasaserareru			

		AFFIRMATIVE	NEGATIVE
Indicative	INFORMAL	aru	nai
	FORMAL	arimasu	arimaseñ
Imperative	INFORMAL I		
	II		
	III		
	FORMAL		
Presumptive	INFORMAL I	aroo	arumai
	II	aru daroo	nai daroo
	FORMAL I	arimasyoo	arimasumai
	II	aru desyoo	nai desyoo
Provisional	INFORMAL	areba	nakereba
	FORMAL	arimaseba	arimaseñ nara
		arimasureba	
Gerund	INFORMAL I	atte	
	II		nakute
	FORMAL	arimasite	arimaseñ de
Past Ind.	INFORMAL	atta	nakatta
	FORMAL	arimasita	arimaseñ desita
Past Presump.	INFORMAL	attaroo	nakattaroo
		atta daroo	nakatta daroo
	FORMAL	arimasitaroo	arimaseñ desitaroo
		atta desyoo	nakatta desyoo
Conditional	INFORMAL	attara	nakattara
	FORMAL	arimasitara	arimaseñ desitara
Alternative	INFORMAL	attari	nakattari
	FORMAL	arimasitari	arimaseñ desitari

INFORMAL AFFIRMATIVE INDICATIVE

Passive	*Polite**	gozaru
Potential		
Causative		
Causative Pass.		

*This is neither honorific nor humble (because the subject is inanimate), but rather neutral polite.

			AFFIRMATIVE	NEGATIVE
Indicative	INFORMAL		aruku	arukanai
	FORMAL		arukimasu	arukimaseñ
Imperative	INFORMAL	I	aruke	aruku na
		II	arukinasai	arukinasaru na
		III	aruite kudasai	arukanai de kudasai
	FORMAL		oaruki nasaimase	oaruki nasaimasu na
Presumptive	INFORMAL	I	arukoo	arukumai
		II	aruku daroo	arukanai daroo
	FORMAL	I	arukimasyoo	arukimasumai
		II	aruku desyoo	arukanai desyoo
Provisional	INFORMAL		arukeba	arukanakereba
	FORMAL		arukimaseba	arukimaseñ nara
			arukimasureba	
Gerund	INFORMAL	I	aruite	arukanai de
		II		arukanakute
	FORMAL		arukimasite	arukimaseñ de
Past Ind.	INFORMAL		aruita	arukanakatta
	FORMAL		arukimasita	arukimaseñ desita
Past Presump.	INFORMAL		aruitaroo	arukanattaroo
			aruita daroo	arukanakatta daroo
	FORMAL		arukimasitaroo	arukimaseñ desitaroo
			aruita desyoo	arukanakatta desyoo
Conditional	INFORMAL		aruitara	arukanakattara
	FORMAL		arukimasitara	arukimaseñ desitara
Alternative	INFORMAL		aruitari	arukanakattari
	FORMAL		arukimasitari	arukimaseñ desitari

INFORMAL AFFIRMATIVE INDICATIVE

Passive	arukareru	*Honorific*	I oaruki ni naru
			II oaruki nasaru
Potential	arukeru		
		Humble	I
Causative	arukaseru		II
Causative Pass.	arukaserareru		

12

		AFFIRMATIVE	NEGATIVE
Indicative	INFORMAL	asobu	asobanai
	FORMAL	asobimasu	asobimaseñ
Imperative	INFORMAL I	asobe	asobu na
	II	asobinasai	asobinasaru na
	III	asoñde kudasai	asobanai de kudasai
	FORMAL	oasobi nasaimase	oasobi nasimasu na
Presumptive	INFORMAL I	asoboo	asobumai
	II	asobu daroo	asobanai daroo
	FORMAL I	asobimasyoo	asobimasumai
	II	asobu desyoo	asobanai desyoo
Provisional	INFORMAL	asobeba	asobanakereba
	FORMAL	asobimaseba	asobimaseñ nara
		asobimasureba	
Gerund	INFORMAL I	asoñde	asobanai de
	II		asobanakute
	FORMAL	asobimasite	asobimaseñ de
Past Ind.	INFORMAL	asoñda	asobanakatta
	FORMAL	asobimasita	asobimaseñ desita
Past Presump.	INFORMAL	asoñdaroo	asobanakattaroo
		asoñda daroo	asobanakatta daroo
	FORMAL	asobimasitaroo	asobimaseñ desitaroo
		asoñda desyoo	asobanakatta desyoo
Conditional	INFORMAL	asoñdara	asobanakattara
	FORMAL	asobimasitara	asobimaseñ desitara
Alternative	INFORMAL	asoñdari	asobanakattari
	FORMAL	asobimasitari	asobimaseñ desitari

INFORMAL AFFIRMATIVE INDICATIVE

Passive	asobareru	*Honorific*	I	oasobi ni naru
			II	oasobi nasaru
Potential	asoberu			
		Humble	I	
Causative	asobaseru		II	
Causative Pass.	asobaserareru			

		AFFIRMATIVE	NEGATIVE
Indicative	INFORMAL	atatameru	atatamenai
	FORMAL	atatamemasu	atatamemaseñ
Imperative	INFORMAL I	atatamero	atatameru na
	II	atatamenasai	atatamenasaru na
	III	atatamete kudasai	atatamenai de kudasai
	FORMAL	oatatame nasaimase	oatatame nasaimasu na
Presumptive	INFORMAL I	atatameyoo	atatamemai
	II	atatameru daroo	atatamenai daroo
	FORMAL I	atatamemasyoo	atatamemasumai
	II	atatameru desyoo	atatamenai desyoo
Provisional	INFORMAL	atatamereba	atatamenakereba
	FORMAL	atatamemaseba	atatamemaseñ nara
		atatamemasureba	
Gerund	INFORMAL I	atatamete	atatamenai de
	II		atatamenakute
	FORMAL	atatamemasite	atatamemaseñ de
Past Ind.	INFORMAL	atatameta	atatamenakatta
	FORMAL	atatamemasita	atatamemaseñ desita
Past Presump.	INFORMAL	atatametaroo	atatamenakattaroo
		atatameta daroo	atatamenakatta daroo
	FORMAL	atatamemasitaroo	atatamemaseñ desitaroo
		atatameta desyoo	atatamenakatta desyoo
Conditional	INFORMAL	atatametara	atatamenakattara
	FORMAL	atatamemasitara	atatamemaseñ desitara
Alternative	INFORMAL	atatametari	atatamenakattari
	FORMAL	atatamemasitari	atatamemaseñ desitari

INFORMAL AFFIRMATIVE INDICATIVE

Passive	atatamerareru	*Honorific*	I	oatatame ni naru
			II	oatatame nasaru
Potential	atatamerareru			
		Humble	I	oatatame suru
Causative	atatamesaseru		II	oatatame itasu
Causative Pass.	atatamesaserareru			

to gather, to assemble

		AFFIRMATIVE	NEGATIVE
Indicative	INFORMAL	atumaru	atumaranai
	FORMAL	atumarimasu	atumarimaseñ
Imperative	INFORMAL I	atumare	atumaru na
	II	atumarinasai	atumarinasaru na
	III	atumatte kudasai	atumaranai de kudasai
	FORMAL	oatumari nasaimase	oatumari nasaimasu na
Presumptive	INFORMAL I	atumaroo	atumarumai
	II	atumaru daroo	atumaranai daroo
	FORMAL I	atumarimasyoo	atumarimasumai
	II	atumaru desyoo	atumaranai desyoo
Provisional	INFORMAL	atumareba	atumaranakereba
	FORMAL	atumarimaseba	atumarimaseñ nara
		atumarimasureba	
Gerund	INFORMAL I	atumatte	atumaranai de
	II		atumaranakute
	FORMAL	atumarimasite	atumarimaseñ de
Past Ind.	INFORMAL	atumatta	atumaranakatta
	FORMAL	atumarimasita	atumarimaseñ desita
Past Presump.	INFORMAL	atumattaroo	atumaranakattaroo
		atumatta daroo	atumaranakatta daroo
	FORMAL	atumarimasitaroo	atumarimaseñ desitaroo
		atumatta desyoo	atumaranakatta desyoo
Conditional	INFORMAL	atumattara	atumaranakattara
	FORMAL	atumarimasitara	atumarimaseñ desitara
Alternative	INFORMAL	atumattari	atumaranakattari
	FORMAL	atumarimasitari	atumarimasen desitari

INFORMAL AFFIRMATIVE INDICATIVE

Passive	atumarareru	*Honorific*	I	oatumari ni naru
			II	oatumari nasaru
Potential	atumareru			
		Humble	I	oatumari suru
Causative	atumaraseru		II	oatumari itasu
Causative Pass.	atumaraserareru			

		AFFIRMATIVE	NEGATIVE
Indicative	INFORMAL	atumeru	atumenai
	FORMAL	atumemasu	atumemaseñ
Imperative	INFORMAL I	atumero	atumeru na
	II	atumenasai	atumenasaru na
	III	atumete kudasai	atumenai de kudasai
	FORMAL	oatume nasaimase	oatume nasaimasu na
Presumptive	INFORMAL I	atumeyoo	atumemai
	II	atumeru daroo	atumenai daroo
	FORMAL I	atumemasyoo	atumemasumai
	II	atumeru desyoo	atumenai desyoo
Provisional	INFORMAL	atumereba	atumenakereba
	FORMAL	atumemaseba	atumemaseñ nara
		atumemasureba	
Gerund	INFORMAL I	atumete	atumenai de
	II		atumenakute
	FORMAL	atumemasite	atumemaseñ de
Past Ind.	INFORMAL	atumeta	atumenakatta
	FORMAL	atumemasita	atumemaseñ desita
Past Presump.	INFORMAL	atumetaroo	atumenakattaroo
		atumeta daroo	atumenakatta daroo
	FORMAL	atumemesitaroo	atumemaseñ desitaroo
		atumeta desyoo	atumenakatta desyoo
Conditional	INFORMAL	atumetara	atumenakattara
	FORMAL	atumemasitara	atumemaseñ desitara
Alternative	INFORMAL	atumetari	atumenakattari
	FORMAL	atumemasitari	atumemaseñ desitari

INFORMAL AFFIRMATIVE INDICATIVE

Passive	atumerareru	*Honorific*	I	oatume ni nar
			II	oatume nasaru
Potential	atumerareru			
		Humble	I	oatume suru
Causative	atumesaseru		II	oatume itasu
Causative Pass.	atumesaserareru			

		AFFIRMATIVE	NEGATIVE
Indicative	**INFORMAL**	au	awanai
	FORMAL	aimasu	aimaseñ
Imperative	**INFORMAL I**	ae	au na
	II	ainasai	ainasaru na
	III	atte kudasai	awanai de kudasai
	FORMAL	oai nasaimase	oai nasaimasu na
Presumptive	**INFORMAL I**	aoo	aumai
	II	au daroo	awanai daroo
	FORMAL I	aimasyoo	aimasumai
	II	au desyoo	awanai desyoo
Provisional	**INFORMAL**	aeba	awanakereba
	FORMAL	aimaseba	aimaseñ nara
		aimasureba	
Gerund	**INFORMAL I**	atte	awanai de
	II		awanakute
	FORMAL	aimasite	aimaseñ de
Past Ind.	**INFORMAL**	atta	awanakatta
	FORMAL	aimasita	aimaseñ desita
Past Presump.	**INFORMAL**	attaroo	awanakattaroo
		atta daroo	awanakatta daroo
	FORMAL	aimasitaroo	aimaseñ desitaroo
		atta desyoo	awanakatta desyoo
Conditional	**INFORMAL**	attara	awanakattara
	FORMAL	aimasitara	aimaseñ desitara
Alternative	**INFORMAL**	attari	awanakattari
	FORMAL	aimasitari	aimaseñ desitari

INFORMAL AFFIRMATIVE INDICATIVE

Passive	awareru	*Honorific*	**I**	oai ni naru
			II	oai nasaru
Potential	aeru			
		Humble	**I**	ome ni kakaru
Causative	awaseru		**II**	
Causative Pass.	awaserareru			

17

		AFFIRMATIVE	NEGATIVE
Indicative	INFORMAL	ayamaru	ayamaranai
	FORMAL	ayamarimasu	ayamarimaseñ
Imperative	INFORMAL I	ayamare	ayamaru na
	II	ayamarinasai	ayamarinasaru na
	III	ayamatte kudasai	ayamaranai de kudasai
	FORMAL	oayamari nasaimase	oayamari nasaimasu na
Presumptive	INFORMAL I	ayamaroo	ayamarumai
	II	ayamaru daroo	ayamaranai daroo
	FORMAL I	ayamarimasyoo	ayamarimasumai
	II	ayamaru desyoo	ayamaranai desyoo
Provisional	INFORMAL	ayamareba	ayamaranakereba
	FORMAL	ayamarimaseba	ayamarimaseñ nara
		ayamarimasureba	
Gerund	INFORMAL I	ayamatte	ayamaranai de
	II		ayamaranakute
	FORMAL	ayamarimasite	ayamarimaseñ de
Past Ind.	INFORMAL	ayamatta	ayamaranakatta
	FORMAL	ayamarimasita	ayamarimaseñ desita
Past Presump.	INFORMAL	ayamattaroo	ayamaranakattaroo
		ayamatta daroo	ayamaranakatta daroo
	FORMAL	ayamarimasitaroo	ayamarimaseñ desitaroo
		ayamatta desyoo	ayamaranakatta desyoo
Conditional	INFORMAL	ayamattara	ayamaranakattara
	FORMAL	ayamarimasitara	ayamarimaseñ desitara
Alternative	INFORMAL	ayamattari	ayamaranakattari
	FORMAL	ayamarimasitari	ayamarimaseñ desitari

INFORMAL AFFIRMATIVE INDICATIVE

Passive	ayamarareru	*Honorific*	I	oayamari ni naru
Potential	ayamareru		II	oayamari nasaru
Causative	ayamaraseru	*Humble*	I	oayamari suru
			II	oayamari itasu
Causative Pass.	ayamaraserareru			

		AFFIRMATIVE	NEGATIVE
Indicative	INFORMAL	ayaturu	ayaturanai
	FORMAL	ayaturimasu	ayaturimaseñ
Imperative	INFORMAL I	ayature	ayaturu na
	II	ayaturinasai	ayaturinasaru na
	III	ayatutte kudasai	ayaturanai de kudasai
	FORMAL	oayaturi nasaimase	oayaturi nasaimasu na
Presumptive	INFORMAL I	ayaturoo	ayaturumai
	II	ayaturu daroo	ayaturanai daroo
	FORMAL I	ayaturimasyoo	ayaturimasumai
	II	ayaturu desyoo	ayaturanai desyoo
Provisional	INFORMAL	ayatureba	ayaturanakereba
	FORMAL	ayaturimaseba	ayaturimaseñ nara
		ayaturimasureba	
Gerund	INFORMAL I	ayatutte	ayaturanai de
	II		ayaturanakute
	FORMAL	ayaturimasite	ayaturimaseñ de
Past Ind.	INFORMAL	ayatutta	ayaturanakatta
	FORMAL	ayaturimasita	ayaturimaseñ desita
Past Presump.	INFORMAL	ayatuttaroo	ayaturanakattaroo
		ayatutta daroo	ayaturanakatta daroo
	FORMAL	ayaturimasitaroo	ayaturimaseñ desitaroo
		ayatutta desyoo	ayaturanakatta desyoo
Conditional	INFORMAL	ayatuttara	ayaturanakattara
	FORMAL	ayaturimasitara	ayaturimaseñ desitara
Alternative	INFORMAL	ayatuttari	ayaturanakattari
	FORMAL	ayaturimasitari	ayaturimaseñ desitari

INFORMAL AFFIRMATIVE INDICATIVE

Passive	ayaturareru	*Honorific*	I	oayaturi ni naru
			II	oayaturi nasaru
Potential	ayatureru			
		Humble	I	oayaturi suru
Causative	ayaturaseru		II	oayaturi itasu
Causative Pass.	ayaturaserareru			

			AFFIRMATIVE	NEGATIVE
Indicative	INFORMAL		azukaru	azukaranai
	FORMAL		azukarimasu	azukarimaseñ
Imperative	INFORMAL	I	azukare	azukaru na
		II	azukarinasai	azukarinasaru na
		III	azukatte kudasai	azukaranai de kudasai
	FORMAL		oazukari nasaimase	oazukari nasaimasu na
Presumptive	INFORMAL	I	azukaroo	azukarumai
		II	azukaru daroo	azukaranai daroo
	FORMAL	I	azukarimasyoo	azukarimasumai
		II	azukaru desyoo	azukaranai desyoo
Provisional	INFORMAL		azukareba	azukaranakereba
	FORMAL		azukarimaseba	azukarimaseñ nara
			azukarimasureba	
Gerund	INFORMAL	I	azukatte	azukaranai de
		II		azukaranakute
	FORMAL		azukarimasite	azukarimaseñ de
Past Ind.	INFORMAL		azukatta	azukaranakatta
	FORMAL		azukarimasita	azukarimaseñ desita
Past Presump.	INFORMAL		azukattaroo	azukaranakattaroo
			azukatta daroo	azukaranakatta daroo
	FORMAL		azukarimasitaroo	azukarimaseñ desitaroo
			azukatta desyoo	azukaranakatta desyoo
Conditional	INFORMAL		azukattara	azukaranakattara
	FORMAL		azukarimasitara	azukarimaseñ desitara
Alternative	INFORMAL		azukattari	azukaranakattari
	FORMAL		azukarimasitari	azukarimaseñ desitari

INFORMAL AFFIRMATIVE INDICATIVE

Passive	azukarareru	*Honorific*	I	oazukari ni n
			II	oazukari nasa
Potential	azukareru			
		Humble	I	oazukari suru
Causative	azukaraseru		II	oazukari itasu
Causative Pass.	azukaraserareru			

azuke

TRANSITIVE *to put in someone's charge*

		AFFIRMATIVE	NEGATIVE
Indicative	INFORMAL	azukeru	azukenai
	FORMAL	azukemasu	azukemaseñ
Imperative	INFORMAL I	azukero	azukeru na
	II	azukenasai	azukenasaru na
	III	azukete kudasai	azukenai de kudasai
	FORMAL	oazuke nasaimase	oazuke nasaimasu na
Presumptive	INFORMAL I	azukeyoo	azukemai
	II	azukeru daroo	azukenai daroo
	FORMAL I	azukemasyoo	azukemasumai
	II	azukeru desyoo	azukenai desyoo
Provisional	INFORMAL	azukereba	azukenakereba
	FORMAL	azukemaseba	azukemaseñ nara
		azukemasureba	
Gerund	INFORMAL I	azukete	azukenai de
	II		azukenakute
	FORMAL	azukemasite	azukemaseñ de
Past Ind.	INFORMAL	azuketa	azukenakatta
	FORMAL	azukemasita	azukemaseñ desita
Past Presump.	INFORMAL	azuketaroo	azukenakattaroo
		azuketa daroo	azukenakatta daroo
	FORMAL	azukemasitaroo	azukemaseñ desitaroo
		azuketa desyoo	azukenakatta desyoo
Conditional	INFORMAL	azuketara	azukenakattara
	FORMAL	azukemasitara	azukemaseñ desitara
Alternative	INFORMAL	azuketari	azukenakattari
	FORMAL	azukemasitari	azukemaseñ desitari

INFORMAL AFFIRMATIVE INDICATIVE

Passive	azukerareru	*Honorific*	I	oazuke ni naru
			II	oazuke nasaru
Potential	azukerareru			
		Humble	I	oazuke suru
Causative	azukesaseru		II	oazuke itasu
Causative Pass.	azukesaserareru			

21

		AFFIRMATIVE	NEGATIVE
Indicative	INFORMAL	beñkyoo suru	beñkyoo sinai
	FORMAL	beñkyoo simasu	beñkyoo simaseñ
Imperative	INFORMAL I	beñkyoo siro	beñkyoo suru na
	II	beñkyoo sinasai	beñkyoo sinasaru na
	III	beñkyoo site kudasai	beñkyoo sinai de kudasai
	FORMAL	gobeñkyoo nasaimase	gobeñkyoo nasaimasu na
Presumptive	INFORMAL I	beñkyoo siyoo	beñkyoo surumai
	II	beñkyoo suru daroo	beñkyoo sinai daroo
	FORMAL I	beñkyoo simasyoo	beñkyoo simasumai
	II	beñkyoo suru desyoo	beñkyoo sinai desyoo
Provisional	INFORMAL	beñkyoo sureba	beñkyoo sinakereba
	FORMAL	beñkyoo simaseba	beñkyoo simaseñ nara
		beñkyoo simasureba	
Gerund	INFORMAL I	beñkyoo site	beñkyoo sinai de
	II		beñkyoo sinakute
	FORMAL	beñkyoo simasite	beñkyoo simaseñ de
Past Ind.	INFORMAL	beñkyoo sita	beñkyoo sinakatta
	FORMAL	beñkyoo simasita	beñkyoo simaseñ desita
Past Presump.	INFORMAL	beñkyoo sitaroo	beñkyoo sinakattaroo
		beñkyoo sita daroo	beñkyoo sinakatta daroo
	FORMAL	beñkyoo simasitaroo	beñkyoo simaseñ desitaroo
		beñkyoo sita desyoo	beñkyoo sinakatta desyoo
Conditional	INFORMAL	beñkyoo sitara	beñkyoo sinakattara
	FORMAL	beñkyoo simasitara	beñkyoo simaseñ desitara
Alternative	INFORMAL	beñkyoo sitari	beñkyoo sinakattari
	FORMAL	beñkyoo simasitari	beñkyoo simaseñ desitari

INFORMAL AFFIRMATIVE INDICATIVE

Passive	beñkyoo sareru	*Honorific*	I	
			II	gobeñkyoo nasaru
Potential	beñkyoo dekiru			
		Humble	I	
Causative	beñkyoo saseru		II	beñkyoo itasu
Causative Pass.	beñkyoo saserareru			

TRANSITIVE   *to represent* (a group etc.)

			AFFIRMATIVE	NEGATIVE
Indicative	**INFORMAL**		daihyoo suru	daihyoo sinai
	FORMAL		daihyoo simasu	daihyoo simaseñ
Imperative	**INFORMAL**	**I**	daihyoo siro	daihyoo suru na
		II	daihyoo sinasai	daihyoo sinasaru na
		III	daihyoo site kudasai	daihyoo sinai de kudasai
	FORMAL		daihyoo nasaimase	daihyoo nasaimasu na
Presumptive	**INFORMAL**	**I**	daihyoo siyoo	daihyoo surumai
		II	daihyoo suru daroo	daihyoo sinai daroo
	FORMAL	**I**	daihyoo simasyoo	daihyoo simasumai
		II	daihyoo suru desyoo	daihyoo sinai desyoo
Provisional	**INFORMAL**		daihyoo sureba	daihyoo sinakereba
	FORMAL		daihyoo simaseba	daihyoo simaseñ nara
			daihyoo simasureba	
Gerund	**INFORMAL**	**I**	daihyoo site	daihyoo sinai de
		II		daihyoo sinakute
	FORMAL		daihyoo simasite	daihyoo simaseñ de
Past Ind.	**INFORMAL**		daihyoo sita	daihyoo sinakatta
	FORMAL		daihyoo simasita	daihyoo simaseñ desita
Past Presump.	**INFORMAL**		daihyoo sitaroo	daihyoo sinakattaroo
			daihyoo sita daroo	daihyoo sinakatta daroo
	FORMAL		daihyoo simasitaroo	daihyoo simaseñ desitaroo
			daihyoo sita desyoo	daihyoo sinakatta desyoo
Conditional	**INFORMAL**		daihyoo sitara	daihyoo sinakattara
	FORMAL		daihyoo simasitara	daihyoo simaseñ desitara
Alternative	**INFORMAL**		daihyoo sitari	daihyoo sinakattari
	FORMAL		daihyoo simasitari	daihyoo simaseñ desitari

INFORMAL AFFIRMATIVE INDICATIVE

Passive	daihyoo sareru	*Honorific*	**I**	
			II	daihyoo nasaru
Potential	daihyoo dekiru			
		Humble	**I**	
Causative	daihyoo saseru		**II**	daihyoo itasu
Causative Pass.	daihyoo saserareru			

to embrace   TRANSITIVE

		AFFIRMATIVE	NEGATIVE
Indicative	INFORMAL	daku	dakanai
	FORMAL	dakimasu	dakimaseñ
Imperative	INFORMAL I	dake	daku na
	II	dakinasai	dakinasaru na
	III	daite kudasai	dakanai de kudasai
	FORMAL	odaki nasaimase	odaki nasaimasu na
Presumptive	INFORMAL I	dakoo	dakumai
	II	daku daroo	dakanai daroo
	FORMAL I	dakimasyoo	dakimasumai
	II	daku desyoo	dakanai desyoo
Provisional	INFORMAL	dakeba	dakanakereba
	FORMAL	dakimaseba	dakimaseñ nara
		dakimasureba	
Gerund	INFORMAL I	daite	dakanai de
	II		dakanakute
	FORMAL	dakimasite	dakimaseñ de
Past Ind.	INFORMAL	daita	dakanakatta
	FORMAL	dakimasita	dakimaseñ desita
Past Presump.	INFORMAL	daitaroo	dakanakattaroo
		daita daroo	dakanakatta daroo
	FORMAL	dakimasitaroo	dakimaseñ desitaroo
		daita desyoo	dakanakatta desyoo
Conditional	INFORMAL	daitara	dakanakattara
	FORMAL	dakimasitara	dakimaseñ desitara
Alternative	INFORMAL	daitari	dakanakattari
	FORMAL	dakimasitari	dakimaseñ desitari

INFORMAL AFFIRMATIVE INDICATIVE

Passive	dakareru	*Honorific*	I	odaki ni naru
			II	odaki nasaru
Potential	dakeru			
		Humble	I	odaki suru
Causative	dakaseru		II	odaki itasu
Causative Pass.	dakaserareru			

		AFFIRMATIVE	NEGATIVE
Indicative	INFORMAL	damaru	damaranai
	FORMAL	damarimasu	damarimaseñ
Imperative	INFORMAL I	damare	damaru na
	II	damarinasai	damarinasaru na
	III	damatte kudasai	damaranai de kudasai
	FORMAL	odamari nasaimase	odamari nasaimasu na
Presumptive	INFORMAL I	damaroo	damarumai
	II	damaru daroo	damaranai daroo
	FORMAL I	damarimasyoo	damarimasumai
	II	damaru desyoo	damaranai desyoo
Provisional	INFORMAL	damareba	damaranakereba
	FORMAL	damarimaseba	damarimaseñ nara
		damarimasureba	
Gerund	INFORMAL I	damatte	damaranai de
	II		damaranakute
	FORMAL	damarimasite	damarimaseñ de
Past Ind.	INFORMAL	damatta	damaranakatta
	FORMAL	damarimasita	damarimaseñ desita
Past Presump.	INFORMAL	damattaroo	damaranakattaroo
		damatta daroo	damaranakatta daroo
	FORMAL	damarimasitaroo	damarimaseñ desitaroo
		damatta desyoo	damaranakatta desyoo
Conditional	INFORMAL	damattara	damaranakattara
	FORMAL	damarimasitara	damarimaseñ desitara
Alternative	INFORMAL	damattari	damaranakattari
	FORMAL	damarimasitari	damarimaseñ desitari

INFORMAL AFFIRMATIVE INDICATIVE

Passive	damarareru	*Honorific*	I	odamari ni naru
			II	odamari nasaru
Potential	damareru			
		Humble	I	
Causative	damaraseru		II	
Causative Pass.	damaraserareru			

to trick   **TRANSITIVE**

		AFFIRMATIVE	NEGATIVE
Indicative	INFORMAL	damasu	damasanai
	FORMAL	damasimasu	damasimaseñ
Imperative	INFORMAL I	damase	damasu na
	II	damasinasai	damasinasaru na
	III	damasite kudasai	damasanai de kudasai
	FORMAL	odamasi nasaimase	odamasi nasaimasu na
Presumptive	INFORMAL I	damasoo	damasumai
	II	damasu daroo	damasanai daroo
	FORMAL I	damasimasyoo	damasimasumai
	II	damasu desyoo	damasanai desyoo
Provisional	INFORMAL	damaseba	damasanakereba
	FORMAL	damasimaseba	damasimaseñ nara
		damasimasureba	
Gerund	INFORMAL I	damasite	damasanai de
	II		damasanakute
	FORMAL	damasimasite	damasimaseñ de
Past Ind.	INFORMAL	damasita	damasanakatta
	FORMAL	damasimasita	damasimaseñ desita
Past Presump.	INFORMAL	damasitaroo	damasanakattaroo
		damasita daroo	damasanakatta daroo
	FORMAL	damasimasitaroo	damasimaseñ desitaroo
		damasita desyoo	damasanakatta desyoo
Conditional	INFORMAL	damasitara	damasanakattara
	FORMAL	damasimasitara	damasimaseñ desitara
Alternative	INFORMAL	damasitari	damasanakattari
	FORMAL	damasimasitari	damasimaseñ desitari

INFORMAL AFFIRMATIVE INDICATIVE

Passive	damasareru	*Honorific* I	odamasi ni naru
		II	odamasi nasaru
Potential	damaseru		
		Humble I	
Causative	damasaseru	II	
Causative Pass.	damasaserareru		

dasi

dás.u
TRANSITIVE *to extract*

		AFFIRMATIVE	NEGATIVE
Indicative	**INFORMAL**	dasu	dasanai
	FORMAL	dasimasu	dasimaseñ
Imperative	**INFORMAL I**	dase	dasu na
	II	dasinasai	dasinasaru na
	III	dasite kudasai	dasanai de kudasai
	FORMAL	odasi nasaimase	odasi nasaimasu na
Presumptive	**INFORMAL I**	dasoo	dasumai
	II	dasu daroo	dasanai daroo
	FORMAL I	dasimasyoo	dasimasumai
	II	dasu desyoo	dasanai desyoo
Provisional	**INFORMAL**	daseba	dasanakereba
	FORMAL	dasimaseba	dasimaseñ nara
		dasimasureba	
Gerund	**INFORMAL I**	dasite	dasanai de
	II		dasanakute
	FORMAL	dasimasite	dasimaseñ de
Past Ind.	**INFORMAL**	dasita	dasanakatta
	FORMAL	dasimasita	dasimaseñ desita
Past Presump.	**INFORMAL**	dasitaroo	dasanakattaroo
		dasita daroo	dasanakatta daroo
	FORMAL	dasimasitaroo	dasimaseñ desitaroo
		dasita desyoo	dasanakatta desyoo
Conditional	**INFORMAL**	dasitara	dasanakattara
	FORMAL	dasimasitara	dasimaseñ desitara
Alternative	**INFORMAL**	dasitari	dasanakattari
	FORMAL	dasimasitari	dasimaseñ desitari

INFORMAL AFFIRMATIVE INDICATIVE

Passive	dasareru	*Honorific*	**I**	odasi ni naru
			II	odasi nasaru
Potential	daseru			
		Humble	**I**	odasi suru
Causative	dasaseru		**II**	odasi itasu
Causative Pass.	dasaserareru			

		AFFIRMATIVE	NEGATIVE
Indicative	INFORMAL	dekiru	dekinai
	FORMAL	dekimasu	dekimaseñ
Imperative	INFORMAL I	dekiro	dekiru na
	II	dekinasai	dekinasaru na
	III		
	FORMAL		
Presumptive	INFORMAL I	dekiyoo	dekimai
	II	dekiru daroo	dekinai daroo
	FORMAL I	dekimasyoo	dekimasumai
	II	dekiru desyoo	dekinai desyoo
Provisional	INFORMAL	dekireba	dekinakereba
	FORMAL	dekimaseba	dekimaseñ nara
		dekimasureba	
Gerund	INFORMAL I	dekite	dekinai de
	II		dekinakute
	FORMAL	dekimasite	dekimaseñ de
Past Ind.	INFORMAL	dekita	dekinakatta
	FORMAL	dekimasita	dekimaseñ desita
Past Presump.	INFORMAL	dekitaroo	dekinakattaroo
		dekita daroo	dekinakatta daroo
	FORMAL	dekimasitaroo	dekimaseñ desitaroo
		dekita desyoo	dekinakatta desyoo
Conditional	INFORMAL	dekitara	dekinakattara
	FORMAL	dekimasitara	dekimaseñ desitara
Alternative	INFORMAL	dekitari	dekinakattari
	FORMAL	dekimasitari	dekimaseñ desitari

INFORMAL AFFIRMATIVE INDICATIVE

Passive		*Honorific*	I	odeki ni naru
			II	odeki nasaru
Potential				
		Humble	I	
Causative			II	
Causative Pass.				

		AFFIRMATIVE	NEGATIVE
Indicative	INFORMAL	deru	denai
	FORMAL	demasu	demaseñ
Imperative	INFORMAL I	dero	deru na
	II	denasai	denasaru na
	III	dete kudasai	denai de kudasai
	FORMAL	ode nasaimase	ode nasaimasu na
Presumptive	INFORMAL I	deyoo	demai
	II	deru daroo	denai daroo
	FORMAL I	demasyoo	demasumai
	II	deru desyoo	denai desyoo
Provisional	INFORMAL	dereba	denakereba
	FORMAL	demaseba	demaseñ nara
		demasureba	
Gerund	INFORMAL I	dete	denai de
	II		denakute
	FORMAL	demasite	demaseñ de
Past Ind.	INFORMAL	deta	denakatta
	FORMAL	demasita	demaseñ desita
Past Presump.	INFORMAL	detaroo	denakattaroo
		deta daroo	denakatta daroo
	FORMAL	demasitaroo	demaseñ desitaroo
		deta desyoo	denakatta desyoo
Conditional	INFORMAL	detara	denakattara
	FORMAL	demasitara	demaseñ desitara
Alternative	INFORMAL	detari	denakattari
	FORMAL	demasitari	demaseñ desitari

INFORMAL AFFIRMATIVE INDICATIVE

Passive	derareru	Honorific	I	ode ni naru
			II	ode nasaru
Potential	derareru			
		Humble	I	
Causative	desaseru		II	
Causative Pass.	desaserareru			

to restrain oneself in deference to others   TRANSITIVE

		AFFIRMATIVE	NEGATIVE
Indicative	**INFORMAL**	eñryo suru	eñryo sinai
	FORMAL	eñryo simasu	eñryo simaseñ
Imperative	**INFORMAL I**	eñryo siro	eñryo suru na
	II	eñryo sinasai	eñryo sinasaru na
	III	eñryo site kudasai	eñryo sinai de kudasai
	FORMAL	goeñryo nasaimase	goeñryo nasaimasu na
Presumptive	**INFORMAL I**	eñryo siyoo	eñryo surumai
	II	eñryo suru daroo	eñryo sinai daroo
	FORMAL I	eñryo simasyoo	eñryo simasumai
	II	eñryo suru desyoo	eñryo sinai desyoo
Provisional	**INFORMAL**	eñryo sureba	eñryo sinakereba
	FORMAL	eñryo simaseba	eñryo simaseñ nara
		eñryo simasureba	
Gerund	**INFORMAL I**	eñryo site	eñryo sinai de
	II		eñryo sinakute
	FORMAL	eñryo simasite	eñryo simaseñ de
Past Ind.	**INFORMAL**	eñryo sita	eñryo sinakatta
	FORMAL	eñryo simasita	eñryo simaseñ desita
Past Presump.	**INFORMAL**	eñryo sitaroo	eñryo sinakattaroo
		eñryo sita daroo	eñryo sinakatta daroo
	FORMAL	eñryo simasitaroo	eñryo simaseñ desitaroo
		eñryo sita desyoo	eñryo sinakatta desyoo
Conditional	**INFORMAL**	eñryo sitara	eñryo sinakattara
	FORMAL	eñryo simasitara	eñryo simaseñ desitara
Alternative	**INFORMAL**	eñryo sitari	eñryo sinakattari
	FORMAL	eñryo simasitari	eñryo simaseñ desitari

INFORMAL AFFIRMATIVE INDICATIVE

Passive	eñryo sareru	*Honorific*	**I**	
			II	goeñryo nasaru
Potential	eñryo dekiru			
		Humble	**I**	goeñryo suru
Causative	eñryo saseru		**II**	goeñryo itasu
Causative Pass.	eñryo saserareru			

30

		AFFIRMATIVE	NEGATIVE
Indicative	**INFORMAL**	erabu	erabanai
	FORMAL	erabimasu	erabimaseñ
Imperative	**INFORMAL I**	erabe	erabu na
	II	erabinasai	erabinasaru na
	III	erañde kudasai	erabanai de kudasai
	FORMAL	oerabi nasaimase	oerabi nasaimasu na
Presumptive	**INFORMAL I**	eraboo	erabumai -
	II	erabu daroo	erabanai daroo
	FORMAL I	erabimasyoo	erabimasumai
	II	erabu desyoo	erabanai desyoo
Provisional	**INFORMAL**	erabeba	erabanakereba
	FORMAL	erabimaseba	erabimaseñ nara
		erabimasureba	
Gerund	**INFORMAL I**	erañde	erabanai de
	II		erabanakute
	FORMAL	erabimasite	erabimaseñ de
Past Ind.	**INFORMAL**	erañda	erabanakatta
	FORMAL	erabimasita	erabimaseñ desita
Past Presump.	**INFORMAL**	erañdaroo	erabanakattaroo
		erañda daroo	erabanakatta daroo
	FORMAL	erabimasitaroo	erabimaseñ desitaroo
		erañda desyoo	erabanakatta desyoo
Conditional	**INFORMAL**	erañdara	erabanakattara
	FORMAL	erabimasitara	erabimaseñ desitara
Alternative	**INFORMAL**	erañdari	erabanakattari
	FORMAL	erabimasitari	erabimaseñ desitari

INFORMAL AFFIRMATIVE INDICATIVE

Passive	erabareru	*Honorific*	**I**	oerabi ni naru
			II	oerabi nasaru
Potential	eraberu			
		Humble	**I**	oerabi suru
Causative	erabaseru		**II**	oerabi itasu
Causative Pass.	erabaserareru			

		AFFIRMATIVE	NEGATIVE
Indicative	**INFORMAL**	eru	enai
	FORMAL	emasu	emaseñ
Imperative	**INFORMAL I**	ero	eru na
	II	enasai	enasaru na
	III	ete kudasai	enai de kudasai
	FORMAL		
Presumptive	**INFORMAL I**	eyoo	emai
	II	eru daroo	enai daroo
	FORMAL I	emasyoo	emasumai
	II	eru desyoo	enai desyoo
Provisional	**INFORMAL**	ereba	enakereba
	FORMAL	emaseba	emaseñ nara
		emasureba	
Gerund	**INFORMAL I**	ete	enai de
	II		enakute
	FORMAL	emasite	emaseñ de
Past Ind.	**INFORMAL**	eta	enakatta
	FORMAL	emasita	emaseñ desita
Past Presump.	**INFORMAL**	etaroo	enakattaroo
		eta daroo	enakatta daroo
	FORMAL	emasitaroo	emaseñ desitaroo
		eta desyoo	enakatta desyoo
Conditional	**INFORMAL**	etara	enakattara
	FORMAL	emasitara	emaseñ desitara
Alternative	**INFORMAL**	etari	enakattari
	FORMAL	emasitari	emaseñ desitari

INFORMAL AFFIRMATIVE INDICATIVE

Passive	erareru	*Honorific*	**I**
			II
Potential	erareru		
		Humble	**I**
Causative	esaseru		**II**
Causative Pass.	esaserareru		

		AFFIRMATIVE	NEGATIVE
Indicative	INFORMAL	gakkari suru	gakkari sinai
	FORMAL	gakkari simasu	gakkari simaseñ
Imperative	INFORMAL I	gakkari siro	gakkari suru na
	II	gakkari sinasai	gakkari sinasaru na
	III	gakkari site kudasai	gakkari sinai de kudasai
	FORMAL	gakkari nasaimase	gakkari nasaimasu na
Presumptive	INFORMAL I	gakkari siyoo	gakkari surumai
	II	gakkari suru daroo	gakkari sinai daroo
	FORMAL I	gakkari simasyoo	gakkari simasumai
	II	gakkari suru desyoo	gakkari sinai desyoo
Provisional	INFORMAL	gakkari sureba	gakkari sinakereba
	FORMAL	gakkari simaseba	gakkari simaseñ nara
		gakkari simasureba	
Gerund	INFORMAL I	gakkari site	gakkari sinai de
	II		gakkari sinakute
	FORMAL	gakkari simasite	gakkari simaseñ de
Past Ind.	INFORMAL	gakkari sita	gakkari sinakatta
	FORMAL	gakkari simasita	gakkari simaseñ desita
Past Presump.	INFORMAL	gakkari sitaroo	gakkari sinakattaroo
		gakkari sita daroo	gakkari sinakatta daroo
	FORMAL	gakkari simasitaroo	gakkari simaseñ desitaroo
		gakkari sita desyoo	gakkari sinakatta desyoo
Conditional	INFORMAL	gakkari sitara	gakkari sinakattara
	FORMAL	gakkari simasitara	gakkari simaseñ desitara
Alternative	INFORMAL	gakkari sitari	gakkari sinakattari
	FORMAL	gakkari simasitari	gakkari simaseñ desitari

INFORMAL AFFIRMATIVE INDICATIVE

Passive	gakkari sareru	*Honorific*	I	
			II	gakkari nasaru
Potential	gakkari dekiru			
		Humble	I	
Causative	gakkari saseru		II	gakkari itasu
Causative Pass.	gakkari saserareru			

		AFFIRMATIVE	NEGATIVE
Indicative	INFORMAL	gañbaru	gañbaranai
	FORMAL	gañbarimasu	gañbarimaseñ
Imperative	INFORMAL I	gañbare	gañbaru na
	II	gañbarinasai	gañbarinasaru na
	III	gañbatte kudasai	gañbaranai de kudasai
	FORMAL	ogañbari nasaimase	ogañbari nasaimasu na
Presumptive	INFORMAL I	gañbaroo	gañbarumai
	II	gañbaru daroo	gañbaranai daroo
	FORMAL I	gañbarimasyoo	gañbarimasumai
	II	gañbaru desyoo	gañbaranai desyoo
Provisional	INFORMAL	gañbareba	gañbaranakereba
	FORMAL	gañbarimaseba	gañbarimaseñ nara
		gañbarimasureba	
Gerund	INFORMAL I	gañbatte	gañbaranai de
	II		gañbaranakute
	FORMAL	gañbarimasite	gañbarimaseñ de
Past Ind.	INFORMAL	gañbatta	gañbaranakatta
	FORMAL	gañbarimasita	gañbarimaseñ desita
Past Presump.	INFORMAL	gañbattaroo	gañbaranakattaroo
		gañbatta daroo	gañbaranakatta daroo
	FORMAL	gañbarimasitaroo	gañbarimaseñ desitaroo
		gañbatta desyoo	gañbaranakatta desyoo
Conditional	INFORMAL	gañbattara	gañbaranakattara
	FORMAL	gañbarimasitara	gañbarimaseñ desitara
Alternative	INFORMAL	gañbattari	gañbaranakattari
	FORMAL	gañbarimasitari	gañbarimaseñ desitari

INFORMAL AFFIRMATIVE INDICATIVE

Passive	gañbarareru	*Honorific*	I	ogañbari ni naru
			II	ogañbari nasaru
Potential	gañbareru			
		Humble	I	
Causative	gañbaraseru		II	
Causative Pass.	gañbaraserareru			

		AFFIRMATIVE	**NEGATIVE**
Indicative	INFORMAL	gozaru	
	FORMAL	gozaimasu	gozaimaseñ
Imperative	INFORMAL I		
	II		
	III		
	FORMAL		
Presumptive	INFORMAL I	gozaroo	gozarumai
	II		
	FORMAL I	gozaimasyoo	gozaimasumai
	II		
Provisional	INFORMAL		
	FORMAL	gozaimaseba	gozaimaseñ nara
		gozaimasureba	
Gerund	INFORMAL I		
	II		
	FORMAL	gozaimasite	gozaimaseñ de
Past Ind.	INFORMAL		
	FORMAL	gozaimasita	gozaimaseñ desita
Past Presump.	INFORMAL		
	FORMAL	gozaimasitaroo	gozaimaseñ desitaroo
Conditional	INFORMAL		
	FORMAL	gozaimasitara	gozaimaseñ desitara
Alternative	INFORMAL		
	FORMAL	gozaimasitari	gozaimaseñ desitari

INFORMAL AFFIRMATIVE INDICATIVE

Passive		*Honorific*	I
			II
Potential			
		Humble	I
Causative			II

Causative Pass.

*The forms *gozaru, gozaroo,* and *gozarumai* are rarely used in standard conversation, being replaced by their formal equivalents.

35

			AFFIRMATIVE	NEGATIVE
Indicative	INFORMAL		hairu	hairanai
	FORMAL		hairimasu	hairimaseñ
Imperative	INFORMAL	I	haire	hairu na
		II	hairinasai	hairinasaru na
		III	haitte kudasai	hairanai de kudasai
	FORMAL		ohairi nasaimase	ohairi nasaimasu na
Presumptive	INFORMAL	I	hairoo	hairumai
		II	hairu daroo	hairanai daroo
	FORMAL	I	hairimasyoo	hairimasumai
		II	hairu desyoo	hairanai desyoo
Provisional	INFORMAL		haireba	hairanakereba
	FORMAL		hairimaseba	hairimaseñ nara
			hairimasureba	
Gerund	INFORMAL	I	haitte	hairanai de
		II		hairanakute
	FORMAL		hairimasite	hairimaseñ de
Past Ind.	INFORMAL		haitta	hairanakatta
	FORMAL		hairimasita	hairimaseñ desita
Past Presump.	INFORMAL		haittaroo	hairanakattaroo
			haitta daroo	hairanakatta daroo
	FORMAL		hairimasitaroo	hairimaseñ desitaroo
			haitta desyoo	hairanakatta desyoo
Conditional	INFORMAL		haittara	hairanakattara
	FORMAL		hairimasitara	hairimaseñ desitara
Alternative	INFORMAL		haittari	hairanakattari
	FORMAL		hairimasitari	hairimasen desitari

INFORMAL AFFIRMATIVE INDICATIVE

Passive	hairareru	*Honorific*	I	ohairi ni naru
			II	ohairi nasaru
Potential	haireru			
		Humble	I	
Causative	hairaseru		II	
Causative Pass.	hairaserareru			

TRANSITIVE　*to measure*

		AFFIRMATIVE	NEGATIVE
Indicative	INFORMAL	hakaru	hakaranai
	FORMAL	hakarimasu	hakarimaseñ
Imperative	INFORMAL I	hakare	hakaru na
	II	hakarinasai	hakarinasaru na
	III	hakatte kudasai	hakaranai de kudasai
	FORMAL	ohakari nasaimase	ohakari nasaimasu na
Presumptive	INFORMAL I	hakaroo	hakarumai
	II	hakaru daroo	hakaranai daroo
	FORMAL I	hakarimasyoo	hakarimasumai
	II	hakaru desyoo	hakaranai desyoo
Provisional	INFORMAL	hakareba	hakaranakereba
	FORMAL	hakarimaseba	hakarimaseñ nara
		hakarimasureba	
Gerund	INFORMAL I	hakatte	hakaranai de
	II		hakaranakute
	FORMAL	hakarimasite	hakarimaseñ de
Past Ind.	INFORMAL	hakatta	hakaranakatta
	FORMAL	hakarimasita	hakarimaseñ desita
Past Presump.	INFORMAL	hakattaroo	hakaranakattaroo
		hakatta daroo	hakaranakatta daroo
	FORMAL	hakarimasitaroo	hakarimaseñ desitaroo
		hakatta desyoo	hakaranakatta desyoo
Conditional	INFORMAL	hakattara	hakaranakattara
	FORMAL	hakarimasitara	hakarimaseñ desitara
Alternative	INFORMAL	hakattari	hakaranakattari
	FORMAL	hakarimasitari	hakarimaseñ desitari

INFORMAL AFFIRMATIVE INDICATIVE

Passive	hakarareru	*Honorific*	I	ohakari ni naru
			II	ohakari nasaru
Potential	hakareru			
		Humble	I	ohakari suru
Causative	hakaraseru		II	ohakari itasu
Causative Pass.	hakaraserareru			

		AFFIRMATIVE	NEGATIVE
Indicative	INFORMAL	hakkeñ suru	hakkeñ sinai
	FORMAL	hakkeñ simasu	hakkeñ simaseñ
Imperative	INFORMAL I	hakkeñ siro	hakkeñ suru na
	II	hakkeñ sinasai	hakkeñ sinasaru na
	III	hakkeñ site kudasai	hakkeñ sinai de kudasai
	FORMAL	gohakkeñ nasaimase	gohakkeñ nasaimasu na
Presumptive	INFORMAL I	hakkeñ siyoo	hakkeñ surumai
	II	hakkeñ suru daroo	hakkeñ sinai daroo
	FORMAL I	hakkeñ simasyoo	hakkeñ simasumai
	II	hakkeñ suru desyoo	hakkeñ sinai desyoo
Provisional	INFORMAL	hakkeñ sureba	hakkeñ sinakereba
	FORMAL	hakkeñ simaseba	hakkeñ simaseñ nara
		hakkeñ simasureba	
Gerund	INFORMAL I	hakkeñ site	hakkeñ sinai de
	II		hakkeñ sinakute
	FORMAL	hakkeñ simasite	hakkeñ simaseñ de
Past Ind.	INFORMAL	hakkeñ sita	hakkeñ sinakatta
	FORMAL	hakkeñ simasita	hakkeñ simaseñ desita
Past Presump.	INFORMAL	hakkeñ sitaroo	hakkeñ sinakattaroo
		hakkeñ sita daroo	hakkeñ sinakatta daroo
	FORMAL	hakkeñ simasitaroo	hakkeñ simaseñ desitaroo
		hakkeñ sita desyoo	hakkeñ sinakatta desyoo
Conditional	INFORMAL	hakkeñ sitara	hakkeñ sinakattara
	FORMAL	hakkeñ simasitara	hakkeñ simaseñ desitara
Alternative	INFORMAL	hakkeñ sitari	hakkeñ sinakattari
	FORMAL	hakkeñ simasitari	hakkeñ simaseñ desitari

INFORMAL AFFIRMATIVE INDICATIVE

Passive	hakkeñ sareru	*Honorific*	I	
			II	hakkeñ nasaru
Potential	hakkeñ dekiru			
		Humble	I	
Causative	hakkeñ saseru		II	hakkeñ itasu
Causative Pass.	hakkeñ saserareru			

TRANSITIVE   *to put on or wear on the feet or legs* (as with shoes, trousers, etc.)

		AFFIRMATIVE	NEGATIVE
Indicative	INFORMAL	haku	hakanai
	FORMAL	hakimasu	hakimaseñ
Imperative	INFORMAL I	hake	haku na
	II	hakinasai	hakinasaru na
	III	haite kudasai	hakanai de kudasai
	FORMAL	ohaki nasaimase	ohaki nasimasu na
Presumptive	INFORMAL I	hakoo	hakumaı
	II	haku daroo	hakanai daroo
	FORMAL I	hakimasyoo	hakimasumai
	II	haku desyoo	hakanai desyoo
Provisional	INFORMAL	hakeba	hakanakereba
	FORMAL	hakimaseba	hakimaseñ nara
		hakimasureba	
Gerund	INFORMAL I	haite	hakanai de
	II		hakanakute
	FORMAL	hakimasite	hakimaseñ de
Past Ind.	INFORMAL	haita	hakanakatta
	FORMAL	hakimasita	hakimaseñ desita
Past Presump.	INFORMAL	haitaroo	hakanakattaroo
		haita daroo	hakanakatta daroo
	FORMAL	hakimasitaroo	hakimaseñ desitaroo
		haita desyoo	hakanakatta desyoo
Conditional	INFORMAL	haitara	hakanakattara
	FORMAL	hakimasitara	hakimaseñ desitara
Alternative	INFORMAL	haitari	hakanakattari
	FORMAL	hakimasitari	hakimaseñ desitari

INFORMAL AFFIRMATIVE INDICATIVE

Passive	hakareru	*Honorific*	I	ohaki ni naru
			II	ohaki nasaru
Potential	hakeru			
		Humble	I	
Causative	hakaseru		II	
Causative Pass.	hakaserareru			

		AFFIRMATIVE	**NEGATIVE**
Indicative	INFORMAL	hanareru	hanarenai
	FORMAL	hanaremasu	hanaremseñ
Imperative	INFORMAL I	hanarero	hanareru na
	II	hanarenasai	hanarenasaru na
	III	hanarete kudasai	hanarenai de kudasai
	FORMAL	ohanare nasaimase	ohanare nasaimasu na
Presumptive	INFORMAL I	hanareyoo	hanaremai
	II	hanareru daroo	hanarenai daroo
	FORMAL I	hanaremasyoo	hanaremasumai
	II	hanareru desyoo	hanarenai desyoo
Provisional	INFORMAL	hanarereba	hanarenakereba
	FORMAL	hanaremaseba	hanaremseñ nara
		hanaremasureba	
Gerund	INFORMAL I	hanarete	hanarenai de
	II		hanarenakute
	FORMAL	hanaremasite	hanaremseñ de
Past Ind.	INFORMAL	hanareta	hanarenakatta
	FORMAL	hanaremasita	hanaremseñ desita
Past Presump.	INFORMAL	hanaretaroo	hanarenakattaroo
		hanareta daroo	hanarenakatta daroo
	FORMAL	hanaremasitaroo	hanaremseñ desitaroo
		hanareta desyoo	hanarenakatta desyoo
Conditional	INFORMAL	hanaretara	hanarenakattara
	FORMAL	hanaremasitara	hanaremseñ desitara
Alternative	INFORMAL	hanaretari	hanarenakattari
	FORMAL	hanaremasitari	hanaremañ desitari

INFORMAL AFFIRMATIVE INDICATIVE

Passive	hanarerareru	*Honorific*	I	ohanare ni naru
Potential	hanarerareru		II	ohanare nasaru
Causative	hanaresaseru	*Humble*	I	ohanare suru
			II	ohanare itasu
Causative Pass.	hanaresaserareru			

		AFFIRMATIVE	NEGATIVE
Indicative	INFORMAL	hanasu	hanasanai
	FORMAL	hanasimasu	hanasimaseñ
Imperative	INFORMAL I	hanase	hanasu na
	II	hanasinasai	hanasinasaru na
	III	hanasite kudasai	hanasanai de kudasai
	FORMAL	ohanasi nasaimase	ohanasi nasaimasu na
Presumptive	INFORMAL I	hanasoo	hanasumai
	II	hanasu daroo	hanasanai daroo
	FORMAL I	hanasimasyoo	hanasimasumai
	II	hanasu desyoo	hanasanai desyoo
Provisional	INFORMAL	hanaseba	hanasanakereba
	FORMAL	hanasimaseba	hanasimaseñ nara
		hanasimasureba	
Gerund	INFORMAL I	hanasite	hanasanai de
	II		hanasanakute
	FORMAL	hanasimasite	hanasimaseñ de
Past Ind.	INFORMAL	hanasita	hanasanakatta
	FORMAL	hanasimasita	hanasimaseñ desita
Past Presump.	INFORMAL	hanasitaroo	hanasanakattaroo
		hanasita daroo	hanasanakatta daroo
	FORMAL	hanasimasitaroo	hanasimaseñ desitaroo
		hanasita desyoo	hanasanakatta desyoo
Conditional	INFORMAL	hanasitara	hanasanakattara
	FORMAL	hanasimasitara	hanasimaseñ desitara
Alternative	INFORMAL	hanasitari	hanasanakattari
	FORMAL	hanasimasitari	hanasimaseñ desitari

INFORMAL AFFIRMATIVE INDICATIVE

Passive	hanasareru	*Honorific*	I	ohanasi ni naru
			II	ohanasi nasaru
Potential	hanaseru			
		Humble	I	ohanasi suru
Causative	hanasaseru		II	ohanasi itasu
Causative Pass.	hanasaserareru			

		AFFIRMATIVE	NEGATIVE
Indicative	INFORMAL	hañtai suru	hañtai sinai
	FORMAL	hañtai simasu	hañtai simaseñ
Imperative	INFORMAL I	hañtai siro	hañtai suru na
	II	hañtai sinasai	hañtai sinasaru na
	III	hañtai site kudasai	hañtai sinai de kudasai
	FORMAL		
Presumptive	INFORMAL I	hañtai siyoo	hañtai surumai
	II	hañtai suru daroo	hañtai sinai daroo
	FORMAL I	hañtai simasyoo	hañtai simasumai
	II	hañtai suru desyoo	hañtai sinai desyoo
Provisional	INFORMAL	hañtai sureba	hañtai sinakereba
	FORMAL	hañtai simaseba	hañtai simaseñ nara
		hañtai simasureba	
Gerund	INFORMAL I	hañtai site	hañtai sinai de
	II		hañtai sinakute
	FORMAL	hañtai simasite	hañtai simaseñ de
Past Ind.	INFORMAL	hañtai sita	hañtai sinakatta
	FORMAL	hañtai simasita	hañtai simaseñ desita
Past Presump.	INFORMAL	hañtai sitaroo	hañtai sinakattaroo
		hañtai sita daroo	hañtai sinakatta daroo
	FORMAL	hañtai simasitaroo	hañtai simaseñ desitaroo
		hañtai sita desyoo	hañtai sinakatta desyoo
Conditional	INFORMAL	hañtai sitara	hañtai sinakattara
	FORMAL	hañtai simasitara	hañtai simaseñ desitara
Alternative	INFORMAL	hañtai sitari	hañtai sinakattari
	FORMAL	hañtai simasitari	hañtai simaseñ desitari

INFORMAL AFFIRMATIVE INDICATIVE

Passive	hañtai sareru	*Honorific*	I	
			II	hañtai nasaru
Potential	hañtai dekiru			
		Humble	I	
Causative	hañtai saseru		II	hañtai itasu
Causative Pass.	hañtai saserareru			

		AFFIRMATIVE	NEGATIVE
Indicative	INFORMAL	harau	harawanai
	FORMAL	haraimasu	haraimaseñ
Imperative	INFORMAL I	harae	harau na
	II	harainasai	harainasaru na
	III	haratte kudasai	harawanai de kudasai
	FORMAL	oharai nasaimase	oharai nasaimasu na
Presumptive	INFORMAL I	haraoo	haraumai
	II	harau daroo	harawanai daroo
	FORMAL I	haraimasyoo	haraimasumai
	II	harau desyoo	harawanai desyoo
Provisional	INFORMAL	haraeba	harawanakereba
	FORMAL	haraimaseba	haraimaseñ nara
		haraimasureba	
Gerund	INFORMAL I	haratte	harawanai de
	II		harawanakute
	FORMAL	haraimasite	haraimaseñ de
Past Ind.	INFORMAL	haratta	harawanakatta
	FORMAL	haraimasita	haraimaseñ desita
Past Presump.	INFORMAL	harattaroo	harawanakattaroo
		haratta daroo	harawanakatta daroo
	FORMAL	haraimasitaroo	haraimaseñ desitaroo
		haratta desyoo	harawanakatta desyoo
Conditional	INFORMAL	harattara	harawanakattara
	FORMAL	haraimasitara	haraimaseñ desitara
Alternative	INFORMAL	harattari	harawanakattari
	FORMAL	haraimasitari	haraimaseñ desitari

INFORMAL AFFIRMATIVE INDICATIVE

Passive	harawareru	*Honorific*	I	oharai ni naru
			II	oharai nasaru
Potential	haraeru			
		Humble	I	oharai suru
Causative	harawaseru		II	oharai itasu
Causative Pass.	harawaserareru			

		AFFIRMATIVE	NEGATIVE
Indicative	INFORMAL	hataraku	hatarakanai
	FORMAL	hatarakimasu	hatarakimaseñ
Imperative	INFORMAL I	hatarake	hataraku na
	II	hatarakinasai	hatarakinasaru na
	III	hataraite kudasai	hatarakanai de kudasai
	FORMAL	ohataraki nasaimase	ohataraki nasaimasu na
Presumptive	INFORMAL I	hatarakoo	hatarakumai
	II	hataraku daroo	hatarakanai daroo
	FORMAL I	hatarakimasyoo	hatarakimasumai
	II	hataraku desyoo	hatarakanai desyoo
Provisional	INFORMAL	hatarakeba	hatarakanakereba
	FORMAL	hatarakimaseba	hatarakimaseñ nara
		hatarakimasureba	
Gerund	INFORMAL I	hataraite	hatarakanai de
	II		hatarakanakute
	FORMAL	hatarakimasite	hatarakimaseñ de
Past Ind.	INFORMAL	hataraita	hatarakanakatta
	FORMAL	hatarakimasita	hatarakimaseñ desita
Past Presump.	INFORMAL	hataraitaroo	hatarakanakattaroo
		hataraita daroo	hatarakanakatta daroo
	FORMAL	hatarakimasitaroo	hatarakimaseñ desitaroo
		hataraita desyoo	hatarakanakatta desyoo
Conditional	INFORMAL	hataraitara	hatarakanakattara
	FORMAL	hatarakimasitara	hatarakimaseñ desitara
Alternative	INFORMAL	hataraitari	hatarakanakattari
	FORMAL	hatarakimasitari	hatarakimaseñ desitari

INFORMAL AFFIRMATIVE INDICATIVE

Passive		*Honorific*	I	ohataraki ni naru
			II	ohataraki nasaru
Potential	hatarakeru			
		Humble	I	
Causative	hatarakaseru		II	
Causative Pass.	hatarakaserareru			

		AFFIRMATIVE	NEGATIVE
Indicative	INFORMAL	hatumei suru	hatumei sinai
	FORMAL	hatumei simasu	hatumei simaseñ
Imperative	INFORMAL I	hatumei siro	hatumei suru na
	II	hatumei sinasai	hatumei sinasaru na
	III	hatumei site kudasai	hatumei sinai de kudasai
	FORMAL		
Presumptive	INFORMAL I	hatumei siyoo	hatumei surumai
	II	hatumei suru daroo	hatumei sinai daroo
	FORMAL I	hatumei simasyoo	hatumei simasumai
	II	hatumei suru desyoo	hatumei sinai desyoo
Provisional	INFORMAL	hatumei sureba	hatumei sinakereba
	FORMAL	hatumei simaseba	hatumei simaseñ nara
		hatumei simasureba	
Gerund	INFORMAL I	hatumei site	hatumei sinai de
	II		hatumei sinakute
	FORMAL	hatumei simasite	hatumei simaseñ de
Past Ind.	INFORMAL	hatumei sita	hatumei sinakatta
	FORMAL	hatumei simasita	hatumei simaseñ desita
Past Presump.	INFORMAL	hatumei sitaroo	hatumei sinakattaroo
		hatumei sita daroo	hatumei sinakatta daroo
	FORMAL	hatumei simasitaroo	hatumei simaseñ desitaroo
		hatumei sita desyoo	hatumei sinakatta desyoo
Conditional	INFORMAL	hatumei sitara	hatumei sinakattara
	FORMAL	hatumei simasitara	hatumei simaseñ desitara
Alternative	INFORMAL	hatumei sitari	hatumei sinakattari
	FORMAL	hatumei simasitari	hatumei simaseñ desitari

INFORMAL AFFIRMATIVE INDICATIVE

Passive	hatumei sareru	*Honorific*	I	
			II	hatumei nasaru
Potential	hatumei dekiru			
		Humble	I	
Causative	hatumei saseru		II	hatumei itasu
Causative Pass.	hatumei saserareru			

		AFFIRMATIVE	NEGATIVE
Indicative	INFORMAL	hazimaru	hazimaranai
	FORMAL	hazimarimasu	hazimarimaseñ
Imperative	INFORMAL I	hazimare	hazimaru na
	II		
	III		
	FORMAL		
Presumptive	INFORMAL I	hazimaroo	hazimarumai
	II	hazimaru daroo	hazimaranai daroo
	FORMAL I	hazimarimasyoo	hazimarumasumai
	II	hazimaru desyoo	hazimaranai desyoo
Provisional	INFORMAL	hazimareba	hazimaranakereba
	FORMAL	hazimarimaseba	hazimarimaseñ nara
		hazimarimasureba	
Gerund	INFORMAL I	hazimatte	hazimaranai de
	II		hazimaranakute
	FORMAL	hazimarimasite	hazimarimaseñ de
Past Ind.	INFORMAL	hazimatta	hazimaranakatta
	FORMAL	hazimarimasita	hazimarimaseñ desita
Past Presump.	INFORMAL	hazimattaroo	hazimaranakattaroo
		hazimatta daroo	hazimaranakatta daroo
	FORMAL	hazimarimasitaroo	hazimarimaseñ desitaroo
		hazimatta desyoo	hazimaranakatta desyoo
Conditional	INFORMAL	hazimattara	hazimaranakattara
	FORMAL	hazimarimasitara	hazimarimaseñ desitara
Alternative	INFORMAL	hazimattari	hazimaranakattari
	FORMAL	hazimarimasitari	hazimarimaseñ desitari

INFORMAL AFFIRMATIVE INDICATIVE

Passive		*Honorific*	I
			II
Potential			
		Humble	I
Causative	hazimaraseru		II

Causative Pass.

TRANSITIVE　*to begin*

		AFFIRMATIVE	NEGATIVE
Indicative	INFORMAL	hazimeru	hazimenai
	FORMAL	hazimemasu	hazimemaseñ
Imperative	INFORMAL I	hazimero	hazimeru na
	II	hazimenasai	hazimenasaru na
	III	hazimete kudasai	hazimenai de kudasai
	FORMAL	ohazime nasaimase	ohazime nasaimasu na
Presumptive	INFORMAL I	hazimeyoo	hazimemai
	II	hazimeru daroo	hazimenai daroo
	FORMAL I	hazimemasyoo	hazimemasumai
	II	hazimeru desyoo	hazimenai desyoo
Provisional	INFORMAL	hazimereba	hazimenakereba
	FORMAL	hazimemaseba	hazimemaseñ nara
		hazimemasureba	
Gerund	INFORMAL I	hazimete	hazimenai de
	II		hazimenakute
	FORMAL	hazimemasite	hazimemaseñ de
Past Ind.	INFORMAL	hazimeta	hazimenakatta
	FORMAL	hazimemasita	hazimemaseñ desita
Past Presump.	INFORMAL	hazimetaroo	hazimenakattaroo
		hazimeta daroo	hazimenakatta daroo
	FORMAL	hazimemasitaroo	hazimemaseñ desitaroo
		hazimeta desyoo	hazimenakatta desyoo
Conditional	INFORMAL	hazimetara	hazimenakattara
	FORMAL	hazimemasitara	hazimemaseñ desitara
Alternative	INFORMAL	hazimetari	hazimenakattari
	FORMAL	hazimemasitari	hazimemaseñ desitari

INFORMAL AFFIRMATIVE INDICATIVE

Passive	hazimerareru	*Honorific*	I	ohazime ni naru
			II	ohazime nasaru
Potential	hazimerareru			
		Humble	I	
Causative	hazimesaseru		II	
Causative Pass.	hazimesaserareru			

			AFFIRMATIVE	NEGATIVE
Indicative	INFORMAL		hikaru	hikaranai
	FORMAL		hikarimasu	hikarimaseñ
Imperative	INFORMAL	I	hikare	hikaru na
		II	hikarinasai	hikarinasaru na
		III	hikatte kudasai	hikaranai de kudasai
	FORMAL		ohikari nasaimase	ohikari nasaimasu na
Presumptive	INFORMAL	I	hikaroo	hikarumai
		II	hikaru daroo	hikaranai daroo
	FORMAL	I	hikarimasyoo	hikarimasumai
		II	hikaru desyoo	hikaranai desyoo
Provisional	INFORMAL		hikareba	hikaranakereba
	FORMAL		hikarimaseba	hikarimaseñ nara
			hikarimasureba	
Gerund	INFORMAL	I	hikatte	hikaranai de
		II		hikaranakute
	FORMAL		hikarimasite	hikarimaseñ de
Past Ind.	INFORMAL		hikatta	hikaranakatta
	FORMAL		hikarimasita	hikarimaseñ desita
Past Presump.	INFORMAL		hikattaroo	hikaranakattaroo
			hikatta daroo	hikaranakatta daroo
	FORMAL		hikarimasitaroo	hikarimaseñ desitaroo
			hikatta desyoo	hikaranakatta desyoo
Conditional	INFORMAL		hikattara	hikaranakattara
	FORMAL		hikarimasitara	hikarimaseñ desitara
Alternative	INFORMAL		hikattari	hikaranakattari
	FORMAL		hikarimasitari	hikarimaseñ desitari

INFORMAL AFFIRMATIVE INDICATIVE

Passive	hikarareru	*Honorific*	I ohikari ni naru
			II ohikari nasaru
Potential	hikareru		
		Humble	I
Causative	hikaraseru		II
Causative Pass.	hikaraserareru		

TRANSITIVE　　*to pull*

		AFFIRMATIVE	NEGATIVE
Indicative	INFORMAL	hiku	hikanai
	FORMAL	hikimasu	hikimaseñ
Imperative	INFORMAL I	hike	hiku na
	II	hikinasai	hikinasaru na
	III	hiite kudasai	hikanai de kudasai
	FORMAL	ohiki nasaimase	ohiki nasaimasu na
Presumptive	INFORMAL I	hikoo	hikumai
	II	hiku daroo	hikanai daroo
	FORMAL I	hikimasyoo	hikimasumai
	II	hiku desyoo	hikanai desyoo
Provisional	INFORMAL	hikeba	hikanakereba
	FORMAL	hikimaseba	hikimaseñ nara
		hikimasureba	
Gerund	INFORMAL I	hiite	hikanai de
	II		hikanakute
	FORMAL	hikimasite	hikimaseñ de
Past Ind.	INFORMAL	hiita	hikanakatta
	FORMAL	hikimasita	hikimaseñ desita
Past Presump.	INFORMAL	hiitaroo	hikanakattaroo
		hiita daroo	hikanakatta daroo
	FORMAL	hikimasitaroo	hikimaseñ desitaroo
		hiita desyoo	hikanakatta desyoo
Conditional	INFORMAL	hittara	hikanakattara
	FORMAL	hikimasitara	hikimaseñ desitara
Alternative	INFORMAL	hiitari	hikanakattari
	FORMAL	hikimasitari	hikimaseñ desitari

INFORMAL AFFIRMATIVE INDICATIVE

Passive	hikareru	*Honorific*	I	ohiki ni naru
			II	ohiki nasaru
Potential	hikeru			
		Humble	I	ohiki suru
Causative	hikaseru		II	ohiki itasu
Causative Pass.	hikaserareru			

to pick up (from ground etc.) *to find* (by accident)   TRANSITIVE

			AFFIRMATIVE	NEGATIVE
Indicative	INFORMAL		hirou	hirowanai
	FORMAL		hiroimasu	hiroimaseñ
Imperative	INFORMAL	I	hiroe	hirou na
		II	hiroinasai	hiroinasaru na
		III	hirotte kudasai	hirowanai de kudasai
	FORMAL		ohiroi nasaimase	ohiroi nasaimasu na
Presumptive	INFORMAL	I	hirooo	hiroumai
		II	hirou daroo	hirowanai daroo
	FORMAL	I	hiroimasyoo	hiroimasumai
		II	hirou desyoo	hirowanai desyoo
Provisional	INFORMAL		hiroeba	hirowanakereba
	FORMAL		hiroimaseba	hiroimaseñ nara
			hiroimasureba	
Gerund	INFORMAL	I	hirotte	hirowanai de
		II		hirowanakute
	FORMAL		hiroimasite	hiroimaseñ de
Past Ind.	INFORMAL		hirotta	hirowanakatta
	FORMAL		hiroimasita	hiroimaseñ desita
Past Presump.	INFORMAL		hirottaroo	hirowanakattaroo
			hirotta daroo	hirowanakatta daroo
	FORMAL		hiroimasitaroo	hiroimaseñ desitaroo
			hirotta desyoo	hirowanakatta desyoo
Conditional	INFORMAL		hirottara	hirowanakattara
	FORMAL		hiroimasitara	hiroimaseñ desitarà
Alternative	INFORMAL		hirottari	hirowanakattari
	FORMAL		hiroimasitari	hiroimaseñ desitari

INFORMAL AFFIRMATIVE INDICATIVE

Passive	hirowareru	*Honorific*	I	ohiroi ni naru
			II	ohiroi nasaru
Potential	hiroeru			
		Humble	I	ohiroi suru
Causative	hirowaseru		II	ohiroi itasu
Causative Pass.	hirowaserareru			

		AFFIRMATIVE	NEGATIVE
Indicative	INFORMAL	homeru	homenai
	FORMAL	homemasu	homemaseñ
Imperative	INFORMAL I	homero	homeru na
	II	homenasai	homenasaru na
	III	homete kudasai	homenai de kudasai
	FORMAL	ohome nasaimase	ohome nasaimasu na
Presumptive	INFORMAL I	homeyoo	homemai
	II	homeru daroo	homenai daroo
	FORMAL I	homemasyoo	homemasumai
	II	homeru desyoo	homenai desyoo
Provisional	INFORMAL	homereba	homenakereba
	FORMAL	homemaseba	homemaseñ nara
		homemasureba	
Gerund	INFORMAL I	homete	homenai de
	II		homenakute
	FORMAL	homemasite	homemaseñ de
Past Ind.	INFORMAL	hometa	homenakatta
	FORMAL	homemasita	homemaseñ desita
Past Presump.	INFORMAL	hometaroo	homenakattaroo
		hometa daroo	homenakatta daroo
	FORMAL	homemasitaroo	homemaseñ desitaroo
		hometa desyoo	homenakatta desyoo
Conditional	INFORMAL	hometara	homenakattara
	FORMAL	homemasitara	homemaseñ desitara
Alternative	INFORMAL	hometari	homenakattari
	FORMAL	homemasitari	homemaseñ desitari

INFORMAL AFFIRMATIVE INDICATIVE

Passive	homerareru	*Honorific*	I	ohome ni naru
			II	ohome nasaru
Potential	homerareru			
		Humble	I	ohome suru
Causative	homesaseru		II	ohome itasu
Causative Pass.	homesaserareru			

		AFFIRMATIVE	NEGATIVE
Indicative	INFORMAL	hosigaru	hosigaranai
	FORMAL	hosigarimasu	hosigarimaseñ
Imperative	INFORMAL I	hosigare	hosigaru na
	II	hosigarinasai	hosigarinasaru na
	III	hosigatte kudasai	hosigaranai de kudasai
	FORMAL	ohosigari nasaimase	ohosigari nasaimasu na
Presumptive	INFORMAL I	hosigaroo	hosigarumai
	II	hosigaru daroo	hosigaranai daroo
	FORMAL I	hosigarimasyoo	hosigarimasumai
	II	hosigaru desyoo	hosigaranai desyoo
Provisional	INFORMAL	hosigareba	hosigaranakereba
	FORMAL	hosigarimaseba	hosigarimaseñ nara
		hosigarimasureba	
Gerund	INFORMAL I	hosigatte	hosigaranai de
	II		hosigaranakute
	FORMAL	hosigarimasite	hosigarimaseñ de
Past Ind.	INFORMAL	hosigatta	hosigaranakatta
	FORMAL	hosigarimasita	hosigarimaseñ desita
Past Presump.	INFORMAL	hosigattaroo	hosigaranakattaroo
		hosigatta daroo	hosigaranakatta daroo
	FORMAL	hosigarimasitaroo	hosigarimaseñ desitaroo
		hosigatta desyoo	hosigaranakatta desyoo
Conditional	INFORMAL	hosigattara	hosigaranakattara
	FORMAL	hosigarimasitara	hosigarimaseñ desitara
Alternative	INFORMAL	hosigattari	hosigaranakattari
	FORMAL	hosigarimasitari	hosigarimaseñ desitari

INFORMAL AFFIRMATIVE INDICATIVE

Passive	hosigarareru	*Honorific*	I	ohosigari ni naru
			II	ohosigari nasaru
Potential	hosigareru			
		Humble	I	
Causative	hosigaraseru		II	
Causative Pass.	hosigaraserareru			

TRANSITIVE   *to dry, to air*

		AFFIRMATIVE	NEGATIVE
Indicative	INFORMAL	hosu	hosanai
	FORMAL	hosimasu	hosimaseñ
Imperative	INFORMAL I	hose	hosu na
	II	hosinasai	hosinasaru na
	III	hosite kudasai	hosanai de kudasai
	FORMAL	ohosi nasaimase	ohosi nasaimasu na
Presumptive	INFORMAL I	hosoo	hosumai
	II	hosu daroo	hosanai daroo
	FORMAL I	hosimasyoo	hosimasumai
	II	hosu desyoo	hosanai desyoo
Provisional	INFORMAL	hoseba	hosanakereba
	FORMAL	hosimaseba	hosimaseñ nara
		hosimasureba	
Gerund	INFORMAL I	hosite	hosanai de
	II		hosanakute
	FORMAL	hosimasite	hosimaseñ de
Past Ind.	INFORMAL	hosita	hosanakatta
	FORMAL	hosimasita	hosimaseñ desita
Past Presump.	INFORMAL	hositaroo	hosanakattaroo
		hosita daroo	hosanakatta daroo
	FORMAL	hosimasitaroo	hosimaseñ desitaroo
		hosita desyoo	hosanakatta desyoo
Conditional	INFORMAL	hositara	hosanakattara
	FORMAL	hosimasitara	hosimaseñ desitara
Alternative	INFORMAL	hositari	hosanakattari
	FORMAL	hosimasitari	hosimaseñ desitari

INFORMAL AFFIRMATIVE INDICATIVE

Passive	hosareru	*Honorific*	I	ohosi ni naru
			II	ohosi nasaru
Potential	hoseru			
		Humble	I	ohosi suru
Causative	hosaseru		II	ohosi itasu
Causative Pass.	hosaserareru			

		AFFIRMATIVE	NEGATIVE
Indicative	INFORMAL	hueru	huenai
	FORMAL	huemasu	huemaseñ
Imperative	INFORMAL I	huero	hueru na
	II	huenasai	huenasaru na
	III	huete kudasai	huenai de kudasai
	FORMAL	ohue nasaimase	ohue nasaimasu na
Presumptive	INFORMAL I	hueyoo	huemai
	II	hueru daroo	huenai daroo
	FORMAL I	huemasyoo	huemasumai
	II	hueru desyoo	huenai desyoo
Provisional	INFORMAL	huereba	huenakereba
	FORMAL	huemaseba	huemaseñ nara
		huemasureba	
Gerund	INFORMAL I	huete	huenai de
	II		huenakute
	FORMAL	huemasite	huemaseñ de
Past Ind.	INFORMAL	hueta	huenakatta
	FORMAL	huemasita	huemaseñ desita
Past Presump.	INFORMAL	huetaroo	huenakattaroo
		hueta daroo	huenakatta daroo
	FORMAL	huemasitaroo	huemaseñ desitaroo
		hueta desyoo	huenakatta desyoo
Conditional	INFORMAL	huetara	huenakattara
	FORMAL	huemasitara	huemaseñ desitara
Alternative	INFORMAL	huetari	huenakattari
	FORMAL	huemasitari	huemaseñ desitari

INFORMAL AFFIRMATIVE INDICATIVE

Passive	huerareru	*Honorific*	I	ohue ni naru
			II	ohue nasaru
Potential	huerareru			
		Humble	I	
Causative	huesaseru		II	
Causative Pass.	huesaserareru			

TRANSITIVE   *to blow*

			AFFIRMATIVE	NEGATIVE
Indicative	INFORMAL		huku	hukanai
	FORMAL		hukimasu	hukimaseñ
Imperative	INFORMAL	I	huke	huku na
		II	hukinasai	hukinasaru na
		III	huite kudasai	hukanai de kudasai
	FORMAL		ohuki nasaimase	ohuki nasaimasu na
Presumptive	INFORMAL	I	hukoo	hukumai
		II	huku daroo	hukanai daroo
	FORMAL	I	hukimasyoo	hukimasumai
		II	huku desyoo	hukanai desyoo
Provisional	INFORMAL		hukeba	hukanakereba
	FORMAL		hukimaseba	hukimaseñ nara
			hukimasureba	
Gerund	INFORMAL	I	huite	hukanai de
		II		hukanakute
	FORMAL		hukimasite	hukimaseñ de
Past Ind.	INFORMAL		huita	hukanakatta
	FORMAL		hukimasita	hukimaseñ desita
Past Presump.	INFORMAL		huitaroo	hukanakattaroo
			huita daroo	hukanakatta daroo
	FORMAL		hukimasitaroo	hukimaseñ desitaroo
			huita desyoo	hukanakatta desyoo
Conditional	INFORMAL		huitara	hukanakattara
	FORMAL		hukimasitara	hukimaseñ desitara
Alternative	INFORMAL		huitari	hukanakattari
	FORMAL		hukimasitari	hukimaseñ desitari

INFORMAL AFFIRMATIVE INDICATIVE

Passive	hukareru	*Honorific*	I	ohuki ni naru
			II	ohuki nasaru
Potential	hukeru			
		Humble	I	ohuki suru
Causative	hukaseru		II	ohuki itasu
Causative Pass.	hukaserareru			

			AFFIRMATIVE	NEGATIVE
Indicative	INFORMAL		huku	hukanai
	FORMAL		hukimasu	hukimaseñ
Imperative	INFORMAL	I	huke	huku na
		II	hukinasai	hukinasaru na
		III	huite kudasai	hukanai de kudasai
	FORMAL		ohuki nasaimase	ohuki nasaimasu na
Presumptive	INFORMAL	I	hukoo	hukumai
		II	huku daroo	hukanai daroo
	FORMAL	I	hukimasyoo	hukimasumai
		II	huku desyoo	hukanai desyoo
Provisional	INFORMAL		hukeba	hukanakereba
	FORMAL		hukimaseba	hukimaseñ nara
			hukimasureba	
Gerund	INFORMAL	I	huite	hukanai de
		II		hukanakute
	FORMAL		hukimasite	hukimaseñ de
Past Ind.	INFORMAL		huita	hukanakatta
	FORMAL		hukimasita	hukimaseñ desita
Past Presump.	INFORMAL		huitaroo	hukanakattaroo
			huita daroo	hukanakatta daroo
	FORMAL		hukimasitaroo	hukimaseñ desitaroo
			huita desyoo	hukanakatta desyoo
Conditional	INFORMAL		huitara	hukanakattara
	FORMAL		hukimasitara	hukimaseñ desitara
Alternative	INFORMAL		huitari	hukanakattari
	FORMAL		hukimasitari	hukimaseñ desitari

INFORMAL AFFIRMATIVE INDICATIVE

Passive	hukareru	*Honorific*	I	ohuki ni naru
			II	ohuki nasaru
Potential	hukeru			
		Humble	I	ohuki suru
Causative	hukaseru		II	ohuki itasu
Causative Pass.	hukaserareru			

		AFFIRMATIVE	NEGATIVE
Indicative	**INFORMAL**	hukumeru	hukumenai
	FORMAL	hukumemasu	hukumemaseñ
Imperative	**INFORMAL I**	hukumero	hukumeru na
	II	hukumenasai	hukumenasaru na
	III	hukumete kudasai	hukumenai de kudasai
	FORMAL	ohukume nasaimase	ohukume nasaimasu na
Presumptive	**INFORMAL I**	hukumeyoo	hukumemai
	II	hukumeru daroo	hukumenai daroo
	FORMAL I	hukumemasyoo	hukumemasumai
	II	hukumeru desyoo	hukumenai desyoo
Provisional	**INFORMAL**	hukumereba	hukumenakereba
	FORMAL	hukumemaseba	hukumemaseñ nara
		hukumemasureba	
Gerund	**INFORMAL I**	hukumete	hukumenai de
	II		hukumenakute
	FORMAL	hukumemasite	hukumemaseñ de
Past Ind.	**INFORMAL**	hukumeta	hukumenakatta
	FORMAL	hukumemasita	hukumemaseñ desita
Past Presump.	**INFORMAL**	hukumetaroo	hukumenakattaroo
		hukumeta daroo	hukumenakatta daroo
	FORMAL	hukumemasitaroo	hukumemaseñ desitaroo
		hukumeta desyoo	hukumenakatta desyoo
Conditional	**INFORMAL**	hukumetara	hukumenakattara
	FORMAL	hukumemasitara	hukumemaseñ desitara
Alternative	**INFORMAL**	hukumetari	hukumenakattari
	FORMAL	hukumemasitari	hukumemaseñ desitari

INFORMAL AFFIRMATIVE INDICATIVE

Passive	hukumerareru	*Honorific*	**I**	ohukume ni naru
			II	ohukume nasaru
Potential	hukumerareru			
		Humble	**I**	ohukume suru
Causative	hukumesaseru		**II**	ohukume itasu
Causative Pass.	hukumesaserareru			

		AFFIRMATIVE	NEGATIVE
Indicative	INFORMAL	huru	huranai
	FORMAL	hurimasu	hurimaseñ
Imperative	INFORMAL I	hure	huru na
	II	hurinasai	hurinasaru na
	III	hutte kudasai	huranai de kudasai
	FORMAL		
Presumptive	INFORMAL I	huroo	hurumai
	II	huru daroo	huranai daroo
	FORMAL I	hurimasyoo	hurimasumai
	II	huru desyoo	huranai desyoo
Provisional	INFORMAL	hureba	huranakereba
	FORMAL	hurimaseba	hurimaseñ nara
		hurimasureba	
Gerund	INFORMAL I	hutte	huranai de
	II		huranakute
	FORMAL	hurimasite	hurimaseñ de
Past Ind.	INFORMAL	hutta	huranakatta
	FORMAL	hurimasita	hurimaseñ desita
Past Presump.	INFORMAL	huttaroo	huranakattaroo
		hutta daroo	huranakatta daroo
	FORMAL	hurimasitaroo	hurimaseñ desitaroo
		hutta desyoo	huranakatta desyoo
Conditional	INFORMAL	huttara	huranakattara
	FORMAL	hurimasitara	hurimaseñ desitara
Alternative	INFORMAL	huttari	huranakattari
	FORMAL	hurimasitari	hurimaseñ desitari

INFORMAL AFFIRMATIVE INDICATIVE

Passive	hurareru	*Honorific*	I
			II
Potential	hureru		
		Humble	I
Causative	huraseru		II
Causative Pass.	huraserareru		

		AFFIRMATIVE	NEGATIVE
Indicative	INFORMAL	hurueru	huruenai
	FORMAL	huruemasu	huruemaseñ
Imperative	INFORMAL I	huruero	hurueru na
	II	huruenasai	huruenasaru na
	III	huruete kudasai	huruenai de kudasai
	FORMAL	ohurue nasaimase	ohurue nasaimasu na
Presumptive	INFORMAL I	hurueyoo	huruemai
	II	hurueru daroo	huruenai daroo
	FORMAL I	huruemasyoo	huruemasumai
	II	hurueru desyoo	huruenai desyoo
Provisional	INFORMAL	huruereba	huruenakereba
	FORMAL	huruemaseba	huruemaseñ nara
		huruemasureba	
Gerund	INFORMAL I	huruete	huruenai de
	II		huruenakute
	FORMAL	huruemasite	huruemaseñ de
Past Ind.	INFORMAL	hurueta	huruenakatta
	FORMAL	buruemasita	huruemaseñ desita
Past Presump.	INFORMAL	huruetaroo	huruenakattaroo
		hurueta daroo	huruenakatta daroo
	FORMAL	huruemasitaroo	huruemaseñ desitaroo
		huruete desyoo	huruenakatta desyoo
Conditional	INFORMAL	huruetara	huruenakattara
	FORMAL	huruemasitara	huruemaseñ desitara
Alternative	INFORMAL	huruetari	huruenakattari
	FORMAL	huruemasitari	huruemaseñ desitari

INFORMAL AFFIRMATIVE INDICATIVE

Passive	huruerareru	*Honorific*	I	ohurue ni naru
			II	ohurue nasaru
Potential	huruerareru			
		Humble	I	
Causative	huruesaseru		II	
Causative Pass.	huruesaserareru			

		AFFIRMATIVE	NEGATIVE
Indicative	INFORMAL	husegu	huseganai
	FORMAL	husegimasu	husegimaseñ
Imperative	INFORMAL I	husege	husegu na
	II	huseginasai	huseginasaru na
	III	huseide kudasai	huseganai de kudasai
	FORMAL	ohusegi nasaimase	ohusegi nasaimasu na
Presumptive	INFORMAL I	husegoo	husegumai
	II	husegu daroo	huseganai daroo
	FORMAL I	husegimasyoo	husegimasumai
	II	husegu desyoo	huseganai desyoo
Provisional	INFORMAL	husegeba	huseganakereba
	FORMAL	husegimaseba	husegimaseñ nara
		husegimasureba	
Gerund	INFORMAL I	huseide	huseganai de
	II		huseganakute
	FORMAL	husegimasite	husegimaseñ de
Past Ind.	INFORMAL	huseida	huseganakatta
	FORMAL	husegimasita	husegimaseñ desita
Past Presump.	INFORMAL	huseidaroo	huseganakattaroo
		huseida daroo	huseganakatta daroo
	FORMAL	husegimasitaroo	husegimaseñ desitaroo
		huseida desyoo	huseganakatta desyoo
Conditional	INFORMAL	huseidara	huseganakattara
	FORMAL	husegimasitara	husegimaseñ desitara
Alternative	INFORMAL	huseidari	huseganakattari
	FORMAL	husegimasitari	husegimaseñ desitari

INFORMAL AFFIRMATIVE INDICATIVE

Passive	husegareru	*Honorific*	I	ohusegi ni naru
			II	ohusegi nasaru
Potential	husegeru			
		Humble	I	ohusegi suru
Causative	husegaseru		II	ohusegi itasu
Causative Pass.	husegaserareru			

		AFFIRMATIVE	NEGATIVE
Indicative	**INFORMAL**	hutoru	hutoranai
	FORMAL	hutorimasu	hutorimaseñ
Imperative	**INFORMAL I**	hutore	hutoru na
	II	hutorinasai	hutorinasaru na
	III	hutotte kudasai	hutoranai de kudasai
	FORMAL	ohutori nasaimase	ohutori nasaimasu na
Presumptive	**INFORMAL I**	hutoroo	hutorumai
	II	hutoru daroo	hutoranai daroo
	FORMAL I	hutorimasyoo	hutorimasumai
	II	hutoru desyoo	hutoranai desyoo
Provisional	**INFORMAL**	hutoreba	hutoranakereba
	FORMAL	hutorimaseba	hutorimaseñ nara
		hutorimasureba	
Gerund	**INFORMAL I**	hutotte	hutoranai de
	II		hutoranakute
	FORMAL	hutorimasite	hutorimaseñ de
Past Ind.	**INFORMAL**	hutotta	hutoranakatta
	FORMAL	hutorimasita	hutorimaseñ desita
Past Presump.	**INFORMAL**	hutottaroo	hutoranakattaroo
		hutotta daroo	hutoranakatta daroo
	FORMAL	hutorimasitaroo	hutorimaseñ desitaroo
		hutotta desyoo	hutoranakatta desyoo
Conditional	**INFORMAL**	hutottara	hutoranakattara
	FORMAL	hutorimasitara	hutorimaseñ desitara
Alternative	**INFORMAL**	hutottari	hutoranakattari
	FORMAL	hutorimasitari	hutorimaseñ desitari

INFORMAL AFFIRMATIVE INDICATIVE

Passive	hutorareru	*Honorific*	**I**	ohutori ni naru
			II	ohutori nasaru
Potential	hutoreru			
		Humble	**I**	
Causative	hutoraseru		**II**	
Causative Pass.	hutoraserareru			

huyás.u   **huyasi**
to increase (something)   TRANSITIVE

		AFFIRMATIVE	NEGATIVE
Indicative	INFORMAL	huyasu	huyasanai
	FORMAL	huyasimasu	huyasimaseñ
Imperative	INFORMAL I	huyase	huyasu na
	II	huyasinasai	huyasinasaru na
	III	huyasite kudasai	huyasanai de kudasai
	FORMAL	ohuyasi nasaimase	ohuyasi nasaimasu na
Presumptive	INFORMAL I	huyasoo	huyasumai
	II	huyasu daroo	huyasanai daroo
	FORMAL I	huyasimasyoo	huyasimasumai
	II	huyasu desyoo	huyasanai desyoo
Provisional	INFORMAL	huyaseba	huyasanakereba
	FORMAL	huyasimaseba	huyasimaseñ nara
		huyasimasureba	
Gerund	INFORMAL I	huyasite	huyasanai de
	II		huyasanakute
	FORMAL	huyasimasite	huyasimaseñ de
Past Ind.	INFORMAL	huyasita	huyasanakatta
	FORMAL	huyasimasita	huyasimaseñ desita
Past Presump.	INFORMAL	huyasitaroo	huyasanakattaroo
		huyasita daroo	huyasanakatta daroo
	FORMAL	huyasimasitaroo	huyasimaseñ desitaroo
		huyasita desyoo	huyasanakatta desyoo
Conditional	INFORMAL	huyasitara	huyasanakattara
	FORMAL	huyasimasitara	huyasimaseñ desitara
Alternative	INFORMAL	huyasitari	huyasanakattari
	FORMAL	huyasimasitari	huyasimaseñ desitari

INFORMAL AFFIRMATIVE INDICATIVE

Passive	huyasareru	*Honorific* I	ohuyasi ni naru
		II	ohuyasi nasaru
Potential	huyaseru		
		Humble I	ohuyasi suru
Causative	huyasaseru	II	ohuyasi itasu
Causative Pass.	huyasaserareru		

62

		AFFIRMATIVE	NEGATIVE
Indicative	INFORMAL	huzakeru	huzakenai
	FORMAL	huzakemasu	huzakemaseñ
Imperative	INFORMAL I	huzakero	huzakeru na
	II	huzakenasai	huzakenasaru na
	III	huzakete kudasai	huzakenai de kudasai
	FORMAL	ohuzake nasaimase	ohuzake nasaimasu na
Presumptive	INFORMAL I	huzakeyoo	huzakemai
	II	huzakeru daroo	huzakenai daroo
	FORMAL I	huzakemasyoo	huzakemasumai
	II	huzakeru desyoo	huzakenai desyoo
Provisional	INFORMAL	huzakereba	huzakenakereba
	FORMAL	huzakemaseba	huzakemaseñ nara
		huzakemasureba	
Gerund	INFORMAL I	huzakete	huzakenai de
	II		huzakenakute
	FORMAL	huzakemasite	huzakemaseñ de
Past Ind.	INFORMAL	huzaketa	huzakenakatta
	FORMAL	huzakemasita	huzakemaseñ desita
Past Presump.	INFORMAL	huzaketaroo	huzakenakattaroo
		huzaketa daroo	huzakenakatta daroo
	FORMAL	huzakemasitaroo	huzakemaseñ desitaroo
		huzaketa desyoo	huzakenakatta desyoo
Conditional	INFORMAL	huzaketara	huzakenakattara
	FORMAL	huzakemasitara	huzakemaseñ desitara
Alternative	INFORMAL	huzaketari	huzakenakattari
	FORMAL	huzakemasitari	huzakemaseñ desitari

INFORMAL AFFIRMATIVE INDICATIVE

Passive	huzakerareru	*Honorific*	I	ohuzake ni naru
			II	ohuzake nasaru
Potential	huzakerareru			
		Humble	I	ohuzake suru
Causative	huzakesaseru		II	ohuzake itasu
Causative Pass.	huzakesaserareru			

		AFFIRMATIVE	NEGATIVE
Indicative	INFORMAL	ibaru	ibaranai
	FORMAL	ibarimasu	ibarimaseñ
Imperative	INFORMAL I	ibare	ibaru na
	II	ibarinasai	ibarinasaru na
	III	ibatte kudasai	ibaranai de kudasai
	FORMAL	oibari nasaimase	oibari nasaimasu na
Presumptive	INFORMAL I	ibaroo	ibarumai
	II	ibaru daroo	ibaranai daroo
	FORMAL I	ibarimasyoo	ibarimasumai
	II	ibaru desyoo	ibaranai desyoo
Provisional	INFORMAL	ibareba	ibaranakereba
	FORMAL	ibarimaseba	ibarimaseñ nara
		ibarimasureba	
Gerund	INFORMAL I	ibatte	ibaranai de
	II		ibaranakute
	FORMAL	ibarimasite	ibarimaseñ de
Past Ind.	INFORMAL	ibatta	ibaranakatta
	FORMAL	ibarimasita	ibarimaseñ desita
Past Presump.	INFORMAL	ibattaroo	ibaranakattaroo
		ibatta daroo	ibaranakatta daroo
	FORMAL	ibarimasitaroo	ibarimaseñ desitaroo
		ibatta desyoo	ibaranakatta desyoo
Conditional	INFORMAL	ibattara	ibaranakattara
	FORMAL	ibarimasitara	ibarimaseñ desitara
Alternative	INFORMAL	ibattari	ibaranakattari
	FORMAL	ibarimasitari	ibarimaseñ desitari

INFORMAL AFFIRMATIVE INDICATIVE

Passive	ibarareru	*Honorific*	I	oibari ni naru
			II	oibari nasaru
Potential	ibareru			
		Humble	I	
Causative	ibaraseru		II	
Causative Pass.	ibaraserareru			

TRANSITIVE   *to rephrase, to correct oneself*

		AFFIRMATIVE	NEGATIVE
Indicative	INFORMAL	iinaosu	iinaosanai
	FORMAL	iinaosimasu	iinaosimaseñ
Imperative	INFORMAL I	iinaose	iinaosu na
	II	iinaosinasai	iinaosinasaru na
	III	iinaosite kudasai	iinosanai de kudasai
	FORMAL	oiinaosi nasaimase	oiinaosi nasaimasu na
Presumptive	INFORMAL I	iinaosoo	iinaosumai
	II	iinaosu daroo	iinaosanai daroo
	FORMAL I	iinaosimasyoo	iinaosimasumai
	II	iinaosu desyoo	iinaosanai desyoo
Provisional	INFORMAL	iinaoseba	iinaosanakereba
	FORMAL	iinaosimaseba	iinaosimaseñ nara
		iinaosimasureba	
Gerund	INFORMAL I	iinaosite	iinaosanai de
	II		iinaosanakute
	FORMAL	iinaosimasite	iinaosimaseñ de
Past Ind.	INFORMAL	iinaosita	iinaosanakatta
	FORMAL	iinaosimasita	iinaosimaseñ desita
Past Presump.	INFORMAL	iinaositaroo	iinaosanakattaroo
		iinaosita daroo	iinaosanakatta daroo
	FORMAL	iinaosimasitaroo	iinaosimaseñ desitaroo
		iinaosita desyoo	iinaosanakatta desyoo
Conditional	INFORMAL	iinaositara	iinaosanakattara
	FORMAL	iinaosimasitara	iinasimaseñ desitara
Alternative	INFORMAL	iinaositari	iinaosanakattari
	FORMAL	iinaosimasitari	iinaosimaseñ desitari

INFORMAL AFFIRMATIVE INDICATIVE

Passive	iinaosareru	*Honorific*	I	oiinaosi ni naru
			II	oiinaosi nasaru
Potential	iinaoseru			
		Humble	I	
Causative	iinaosaseru		II	
Causative Pass.	iinaosaserareru			

		AFFIRMATIVE	NEGATIVE
Indicative	INFORMAL	iisugiru	iisuginai
	FORMAL	iisugimasu	iisugimaseñ
Imperative	INFORMAL I	iisugiro	iisugiru na
	II	iisuginasai	iisuginasaru na
	III	iisugite kudasai	iisuginai de kudasai
	FORMAL	oiisugi nasaimase	oiisugi nasaimasu na
Presumptive	INFORMAL I	iisugiyoo	iisugimai
	II	iisugiru daroo	iisuginai daroo
	FORMAL I	iisugimasyoo	iisugimasumai
	II	iisugiru desyoo	iisuginai desyoo
Provisional	INFORMAL	iisugireba	iisuginakereba
	FORMAL	iisugimaseba	iisugimaseñ nara
		iisugimasureba	
Gerund	INFORMAL I	iisugite	iisuginai de
	II		iisuginakute
	FORMAL	iisugimasite	iisugimaseñ de
Past Ind.	INFORMAL	iisugita	iisuginakatta
	FORMAL	iisugimasita	iisugimaseñ desita
Past Presump.	INFORMAL	iisugitaroo	iisuginakattaroo
		iisugita daroo	iisuginakatta daroo
	FORMAL	iisugimasitaroo	iisugimaseñ desitaroo
		iisugita desyoo	iisuginakatta desyoo
Conditional	INFORMAL	iisugitara	iisuginakattara
	FORMAL	iisugimasitara	iisugimaseñ desitara
Alternative	INFORMAL	iisugitari	iisuginakattari
	FORMAL	iisugimasitari	iisugimaseñ desitari

INFORMAL AFFIRMATIVE INDICATIVE

Passive	iisugirareru		*Honorific*	I	oiisugi ni naru
				II	oiisugi nasaru
Potential	iisugirareru				
			Humble	I	
Causative	iisugisaseru			II	
Causative Pass.	iisugisaserareru				

to be alive

		AFFIRMATIVE	NEGATIVE
Indicative	INFORMAL	ikiru	ikinai
	FORMAL	ikimasu	ikimaseñ
Imperative	INFORMAL I	ikiro	ikiru na
	II	ikinasai	ikinasaru na
	III	ikite kudasai	ikinai de kudasai
	FORMAL	oiki nasaimase	oiki nasaimasu na
Presumptive	INFORMAL I	ikiyoo	ikimai
	II	ikiru daroo	ikinai daroo
	FORMAL I	ikimasyoo	ikimasumai
	II	ikiru desyoo	ikinai desyoo
Provisional	INFORMAL	ikireba	ikinakereba
	FORMAL	ikimaseba	ikimaseñ nara
		ikimasureba	
Gerund	INFORMAL I	ikite	ikinai de
	II		ikinakute
	FORMAL	ikimasite	ikimaseñ de
Past Ind.	INFORMAL	ikita	ikinakatta
	FORMAL	ikimasita	ikimaseñ desita
Past Presump.	INFORMAL	ikitaroo	ikinakattaroo
		ikita daroo	ikinakatta daroo
	FORMAL	ikimasitaroo	ikimaseñ desitaroo
		ikita desyoo	ikinakatta desyoo
Conditional	INFORMAL	ikitara	ikinakattara
	FORMAL	ikimasitara	ikimaseñ desitara
Alternative	INFORMAL	ikitari	ikinakattari
	FORMAL	ikimasitari	ikimaseñ desitari

INFORMAL AFFIRMATIVE INDICATIVE

Passive	ikirareru	*Honorific*	I	oiki ni naru
			II	oiki nasaru
Potential	ikirareru			
		Humble	I	
Causative	ikisaseru		II	
Causative Pass.	ikisaserareru			

		AFFIRMATIVE	NEGATIVE
Indicative	INFORMAL	iku	ikanai
	FORMAL	ikimasu	ikimaseñ
Imperative	INFORMAL I	ike	iku na
	II	ikinasai	ikinasaru na
	III	itte kudasai	ikanai de kudasai
	FORMAL	oide nasaimase	oide nasaimasu na
Presumptive	INFORMAL I	ikoo	ikumai
	II	iku daroo	ikanai daroo
	FORMAL I	ikimasyoo	ikimasumai
	II	iku desyoo	ikanai desyoo
Provisional	INFORMAL	ikeba	ikanakereba
	FORMAL	ikimaseba	ikimaseñ nara
		ikimasureba	
Gerund	INFORMAL I	itte	ikanai de
	II		ikanakute
	FORMAL	ikimasite	ikimaseñ de
Past Ind.	INFORMAL	itta	ikanakatta
	FORMAL	ikimasita	ikimaseñ desita
Past Presump.	INFORMAL	ittaroo	ikanakattaroo
		itta daroo	ikanakatta daroo
	FORMAL	ikimasitaroo	ikimaseñ desitaroo
		itta desyoo	ikanakatta desyoo
Conditional	INFORMAL	ittara	ikanakattara
	FORMAL	ikimasitara	ikimaseñ desitara
Alternative	INFORMAL	ittari	ikanakattari
	FORMAL	ikimasitari	ikimaseñ desitari

INFORMAL AFFIRMATIVE INDICATIVE

Passive	ikareru		*Honorific*	irassyaru	oide ni naru (I)
Potential	ikareru	ikeru			oide nasaru (II)
			Humble	mairu	
Causative	ikaseru				
Causative Pass.	ikaserareru				

TRANSITIVE   *to pray, to wish for*

		AFFIRMATIVE	NEGATIVE
Indicative	INFORMAL	inoru	inoranai
	FORMAL	inorimasu	inorimaseñ
Imperative	INFORMAL I	inore	inoru na
	II	inorinasai	inorinasaru na
	III	inotte kudasai	inoranai de kudasai
	FORMAL	oinori nasaimase	oinori nasaimasu na
Presumptive	INFORMAL I	inoroo	inorumai
	II	inoru daroo	inoranai daroo
	FORMAL I	inorimasyoo	inorimasumai
	II	inoru desyoo	inoranai desyoo
Provisional	INFORMAL	inoreba	inoranakereba
	FORMAL	inorimaseba	inorimaseñ nara
		inorimasureba	
Gerund	INFORMAL I	inotte	inoranai de
	II		inoranakute
	FORMAL	inorimasite	inorimaseñ de
Past Ind.	INFORMAL	inotta	inoranakatta
	FORMAL	inorimasita	inorimaseñ desita
Past Presump.	INFORMAL	inottaroo	inoranakattaroo
		inotta daroo	inoranakatta daroo
	FORMAL	inorimasitaroo	inorimaseñ desitaroo
		inotta desyoo	inoranakatta desyoo
Conditional	INFORMAL	inottara	inoranakattara
	FORMAL	inorimasitara	inorimaseñ desitara
Alternative	INFORMAL	inottari	inoranakattari
	FORMAL	inorimasitari	inorimaseñ desitari

INFORMAL AFFIRMATIVE INDICATIVE

Passive	inorareru	*Honorific*	I	oinori ni naru
			II	oinori nasaru
Potential	inoreru			
		Humble	I	oinori suru
Causative	inoraseru		II	oinori itasu
Causative Pass.	inoraserareru			

			AFFIRMATIVE	NEGATIVE
Indicative	INFORMAL		irassyaru	irassyaranai
	FORMAL		irassyaimasu	irassyaimaseñ
Imperative	INFORMAL	I	irassyai	irassyaru na
		II		
		III	irassyatte kudasai	irassyaranai de kudasai
	FORMAL		irassyaimase	irassyaimasu na
Presumptive	INFORMAL	I	irassyaroo	irassyarumai
		II	irassyaru daroo	irassyaranai daroo
	FORMAL	I	irassyaimasyoo	irassyaimasumai
		II	irassyaru desyoo	irassyaranai desyoo
Provisional	INFORMAL		irassyareba	irassyaranakereba
	FORMAL		irassyaimaseba	irassyaimaseñ nara
			irassyaimasureba	
Gerund	INFORMAL	I	irassyatte*	irassyaranai de
		II		irassyaranakute
	FORMAL		irassyaimasite	irassyaimaseñ de
Past Ind.	INFORMAL		irassyatta*	irassyaranakatta
	FORMAL		irassyaimasita	irassyaimaseñ desita
Past Presump.	INFORMAL		irassyattaroo*	irassyaranakattaroo
			irassyatta daroo	irassyaranakatta daroo
	FORMAL		irassyaimasitaroo	irassyaimaseñ desitaroo
			irassyatta desyoo	irassyaranakatta desyoo
Conditional	INFORMAL		irassyattara*	irassyaranakattara
	FORMAL		irassyaimasitara	irassyaimaseñ desitara
Alternative	INFORMAL		irassyattari*	irassyaranakattari
	FORMAL		irassyaimasitari	irassyaimaseñ desitari

INFORMAL AFFIRMATIVE INDICATIVE			
Passive		*Honorific*	I
			II
Potential			
		Humble	I
Causative			II

Causative Pass.

*Shorter forms: *irasite, irasita, irasitaroo, irasitara,* and *irasitari* also occur in the same environments as the longer forms given above.

		AFFIRMATIVE	NEGATIVE
Indicative	INFORMAL	ireru	irenai
	FORMAL	iremasu	iremaseñ
Imperative	INFORMAL I	irero	ireru na
	II	irenasai	irenasaru na
	III	irete kudasai	irenai de kudasai
	FORMAL	oire nasaimase	oire nasaimasu na
Presumptive	INFORMAL I	ireyoo	iremai
	II	ireru daroo	irenai daroo
	FORMAL I	iremasyoo	iremasumai
	II	ireru desyoo	irenai desyoo
Provisional	INFORMAL	irereba	irenakereba
	FORMAL	iremaseba	iremaseñ nara
		iremasureba	
Gerund	INFORMAL I	irete	irenai de
	II		irenakute
	FORMAL	iremasite	iremaseñ de
Past Ind.	INFORMAL	ireta	irenakatta
	FORMAL	iremasita	iremaseñ desita
Past Presump.	INFORMAL	iretaroo	irenakattaroo
		ireta daroo	irenakatta daroo
	FORMAL	iremasitaroo	iremaseñ desitaroo
		ireta desyoo	irenakatta desyoo
Conditional	INFORMAL	iretara	irenakattara
	FORMAL	iremasitara	iremaseñ desitara
Alternative	INFORMAL	iretari	irenakattari
	FORMAL	iremasitari	iremaseñ desitari

INFORMAL AFFIRMATIVE INDICATIVE

Passive	irerareru	*Honorific*	I	oire ni naru
			II	oire nasaru
Potential	irerareru			
		Humble	I	oire suru
Causative	iresaseru		II	oire itasu
Causative Pass.	iresaserareru			

		AFFIRMATIVE	NEGATIVE
Indicative	INFORMAL	iru	inai
	FORMAL	imasu	imaseñ
Imperative	INFORMAL I	iro	iru na
	II	inasai	inasaru na
	III	ite kudasai	inai de kudasai
	FORMAL	oide nasaimase	oide nasaimasu na
Presumptive	INFORMAL I	iyoo	imai
	II	iru daroo	inai daroo
	FORMAL I	imasyoo	imasumai
	II	iru desyoo	inai desyoo
Provisional	INFORMAL	ireba	inakereba
	FORMAL	imaseba	imaseñ nara
		imasureba	
Gerund	INFORMAL I	ite	inai de
	II		inakute
	FORMAL	imasite	imaseñ de
Past Ind.	INFORMAL	ita	inakatta
	FORMAL	imasita	imaseñ desita
Past Presump.	INFORMAL	itaroo	inakattaroo
		ita daroo	inakatta daroo
	FORMAL	imasitaroo	imaseñ desitaroo
		ita desyoo	inakatta desyoo
Conditional	INFORMAL	itara	inakattara
	FORMAL	imasitara	imaseñ desitara
Alternative	INFORMAL	itari	inakattari
	FORMAL	imasitari	imaseñ desitari

INFORMAL AFFIRMATIVE INDICATIVE

Passive	irareru	*Honorific*	irassyaru	oide ni naru
Potential	irareru			
Causative	isaseru	*Humble*	oru	
Causative Pass.	isaserareru			

		AFFIRMATIVE	**NEGATIVE**
Indicative	INFORMAL	iru	iranai
	FORMAL	irimasu	irimaseñ
Imperative	INFORMAL I		
	II		
	III		
	FORMAL		
Presumptive	INFORMAL I	iroo	irumai
	II	iru daroo	iranai daroo
	FORMAL I	irimasyoo	irimasumai
	II	iru desyoo	iranai desyoo
Provisional	INFORMAL	ireba	iranakereba
	FORMAL	irimaseba	irimaseñ nara
		irimasureba	
Gerund	INFORMAL I	itte	iranai de
	II		iranakute
	FORMAL	irimasite	irimaseñ de
Past Ind.	INFORMAL	itta	iranakatta
	FORMAL	irimasita	irimaseñ desita
Past Presump.	INFORMAL	ittaroo	iranakattaroo
		itta daroo	iranakatta daroo
	FORMAL	irimasitaroo	irimaseñ desitaroo
		itta desyoo	iranakatta desyoo
Conditional	INFORMAL	ittara	iranakattara
	FORMAL	irimasitara	irimaseñ desitara
Alternative	INFORMAL	ittari	iranakattari
	FORMAL	irimasitari	irimaseñ desitari

INFORMAL AFFIRMATIVE INDICATIVE

Passive		*Honorific*	I
			II
Potential			
		Humble	I
Causative			II

Causative Pass.

		AFFIRMATIVE	NEGATIVE
Indicative	**INFORMAL**	isogu	isoganai
	FORMAL	isogimasu	isogimaseñ
Imperative	**INFORMAL I**	isoge	isogu na
	II	isoginasai	isoginasaru na
	III	isoide kudasai	isoganai de kudasai
	FORMAL	oisogi nasaimase	oisogi nasaimasu na
Presumptive	**INFORMAL I**	isogoo	isogumai
	II	isogu daroo	isoganai daroo
	FORMAL I	isogimasyoo	isogimasumai
	II	isogu desyoo	isoganai desyoo
Provisional	**INFORMAL**	isogeba	isoganakereba
	FORMAL	isogimaseba	isogimaseñ nara
		isogimasureba	
Gerund	**INFORMAL I**	isoide	isoganai de
	II		isoganakute
	FORMAL	isogimasite	isogimaseñ de
Past Ind.	**INFORMAL**	isoida	isoganakatta
	FORMAL	isogimasita	isogimaseñ desita
Past Presump.	**INFORMAL**	isoidaroo	isoganakattaroo
		isoida daroo	isoganakatta daroo
	FORMAL	isogimasitaroo	isogimaseñ desitaroo
		isoida desyoo	isoganakatta desyoo
Conditional	**INFORMAL**	isoidara	isoganakattara
	FORMAL	isogimasitara	isogimaseñ desitara
Alternative	**INFORMAL**	isoidari	isoganakattari
	FORMAL	isogimasitari	isogimaseñ desitari

INFORMAL AFFIRMATIVE INDICATIVE

Passive	isogareru	*Honorific*	**I**	oisogi ni naru
			II	oisogi nasaru
Potential	isogeru			
		Humble	**I**	
Causative	isogaseru		**II**	
Causative Pass.	isogaserareru			

TRANSITIVE   *to receive, to take food or drink* (humble)

		AFFIRMATIVE	NEGATIVE
Indicative	INFORMAL	itadaku	itadakanai
	FORMAL	itadakimasu	itadakimaseñ
Imperative	INFORMAL I		
	II		
	III		
	FORMAL		
Presumptive	INFORMAL I	itadakoo	itadakumai
	II	itadaku daroo	itadakanai daroo
	FORMAL I	itadakimasyoo	itadakimasumai
	II	itadaku desyoo	itadakanai desyoo
Provisional	INFORMAL	itadakeba	itadakanakereba
	FORMAL	itadakimaseba	itadakimaseñ nara
		itadakimasureba	
Gerund	INFORMAL I	itadaite	itadakanai de
	II		itadakanakute
	FORMAL	itadakimasite	itadakimaseñ de
Past Ind.	INFORMAL	itadaita	itadakanakatta
	FORMAL	itadakimasita	itadakimaseñ desita
Past Presump.	INFORMAL	itadaitaroo	itadakanakattaroo
		itadaita daroo	itadakanakatta daroo
	FORMAL	itadakimasitaroo	itadakimaseñ desitaroo
		itadaita desyoo	itadakanakatta desyoo
Conditional	INFORMAL	itadaitara	itadakanakattara
	FORMAL	itadakimasitara	itadakimaseñ desitara
Alternative	INFORMAL	jtadaitari	itadakanakattari
	FORMAL	itadakimasitari	itadakimaseñ desitari

INFORMAL AFFIRMATIVE INDICATIVE

Passive		*Honorific* I	
		II	
Potential	itadakeru		
		Humble I	
Causative	itadakaseru	II	
Causative Pass.	itadakaserareru		

		AFFIRMATIVE	NEGATIVE
Indicative	INFORMAL	itamu	itamanai
	FORMAL	itamimasu	itamimaseñ
Imperative	INFORMAL I		
	II		
	III		
	FORMAL		
Presumptive	INFORMAL I	itamoo	itamumai
	II	itamu daroo	itamanai daroo
	FORMAL I	itamimasyoo	itamimasumai
	II	itamu desyoo	itamanai desyoo
Provisional	INFORMAL	itameba	itamanakereba
	FORMAL	itamimaseba	itamimaseñ nara
		itamimasureba	
Gerund	INFORMAL I	itañde	itamanai de
	II		itamanakute
	FORMAL	itamimasite	itamimaseñ de
Past Ind.	INFORMAL	itañda	itamanakatta
	FORMAL	itamimasita	itamimaseñ desita
Past Presump.	INFORMAL	itañdaroo	itamanakattaroo
		itañda daroo	itamanakatta daroo
	FORMAL	itamimasitaroo	itamimaseñ desitaroo
		itañda desyoo	itamanakatta desyoo
Conditional	INFORMAL	itañdara	itamanakattara
	FORMAL	itamimasitara	itamimaseñ desitara
Alternative	INFORMAL	itañdari	itamanakattari
	FORMAL	itamimasitari	itamimaseñ desitari

INFORMAL AFFIRMATIVE INDICATIVE

Passive	itamareru		*Honorific*	I	oitami ni naru
				II	oitami nasaru
Potential	itameru				
			Humble	I	
Causative	itamaseru			II	
Causative Pass.	itamaserareru				

TRANSITIVE   *to do* (humble)

		AFFIRMATIVE	NEGATIVE
Indicative	INFORMAL	itasu	itasanai
	FORMAL	itasimasu	itasimaseñ
Imperative	INFORMAL I	itase	itasu na
	II		
	III		
	FORMAL		
Presumptive	INFORMAL I	itasoo	itasumai
	II	itasu daroo	itasanai daroo
	FORMAL I	itasimasyoo	itasimasumai
	II	itasu desyoo	itasanai desyoo
Provisional	INFORMAL	itaseba	itasanakereba
	FORMAL	itasimaseba	itasimaseñ nara
		itasimasureba	
Gerund	INFORMAL I	itasite	itasanai de
	II		itasanakute
	FORMAL	itasimasite	itasimaseñ de
Past Ind.	INFORMAL	itasita	itasanakatta
	FORMAL	itasimasita	itasimaseñ desita
Past Presump.	INFORMAL	itasitaroo	itasanakattaroo
		itasita daroo	itasanakatta daroo
	FORMAL	itasimasitaroo	itasimaseñ desitaroo
		itasita desyoo	itasanakatta desyoo
Conditional	INFORMAL	itasitara	itasanakattara
	FORMAL	itasimasitara	itasimaseñ desitara
Alternative	INFORMAL	itasitari	itasanakattari
	FORMAL	itasimasitari	itasimaseñ desitari

INFORMAL AFFIRMATIVE INDICATIVE

Passive		*Honorific*	I	
			II	
Potential				
		Humble	I	
Causative			II	

Causative Pass.

			AFFIRMATIVE	NEGATIVE
Indicative	INFORMAL		iu	iwanai
	FORMAL		iimasu	iimaseñ
Imperative	INFORMAL	I	ie	iu na
		II	iinasai	iinasaru na
		III	itte kudasai	iwanai de kudasai
	FORMAL		ossyaimase	ossyaimasu na
Presumptive	INFORMAL	I	ioo	iumai
		II	iu daroo	iwanai daroo
	FORMAL	I	iimasyoo	iimasumai
		II	iu desyoo	iwanai desyoo
Provisional	INFORMAL		ieba	iwanakereba
	FORMAL		iimaseba	iimaseñ nara
			iimasureba	
Gerund	INFORMAL	I	itte	iwanai de
		II		iwanakute
	FORMAL		iimasite	iimaseñ de
Past Ind.	INFORMAL		itta	iwanakatta
	FORMAL		iimasita	iimaseñ desita
Past Presump.	INFORMAL		ittaroo	iwanakattaroo
			itta daroo	iwanakatta daroo
	FORMAL		iimasitaroo	iimaseñ desitaroo
			itta desyoo	iwanakatta desyoo
Conditional	INFORMAL		ittara	iwanakattara
	FORMAL		iimasitara	iimaseñ desitara
Alternative	INFORMAL		ittari	iwanakattari
	FORMAL		iimasitari	iimaseñ desitari

INFORMAL AFFIRMATIVE INDICATIVE			
Passive	iwareru	*Honorific*	ossyaru
Potential	ieru		
Causative	iwaseru	*Humble*	moosu
Causative Pass.	iwaserareru		

TRANSITIVE *to dislike, to hate*

		AFFIRMATIVE	NEGATIVE
Indicative	INFORMAL	iyagaru	iyagaranai
	FORMAL	iyagarimasu	iyagarimaseñ
Imperative	INFORMAL I	iyagare	iyagaru na
	II	iyagarinasai	iyagarinasaru na
	III	iyagatte kudasai	iyagaranai de kudasai
	FORMAL	oiyagari nasaimase	oiyagari nasaimasu na
Presumptive	INFORMAL I	iyagaroo	iyagarumai
	II	iyagaru daroo	iyagaranai daroo
	FORMAL I	iyagarimasyoo	iyagarimasumai
	II	iyagaru desyoo	iyagaranai desyoo
Provisional	INFORMAL	iyagareba	iyagaranakereba
	FORMAL	iyagarimaseba	iyagarimaseñ nara
		iyagarimasureba	
Gerund	INFORMAL I	iyagatte	iyagaranai de
	II		iyagaranakute
	FORMAL	iyagarimasite	iyagarimaseñ de
Past Ind.	INFORMAL	iyagatta	iyagaranakatta
	FORMAL	iyagarimasita	iyagarimaseñ desita
Past Presump.	INFORMAL	iyagattaroo	iyagaranakattaroo
		iyagatta daroo	iyagaranakatta daroo
	FORMAL	iyagarimasitaroo	iyagarimaseñ desitaroo
		iyagatta desyoo	iyagaranakatta desyoo
Conditional	INFORMAL	iyagattara	iyagaranakattara
	FORMAL	iyagarimasitara	iyagarimaseñ desitara
Alternative	INFORMAL	iyagattari	iyagaranakattari
	FORMAL	iyagarimasitari	iyagarimaseñ desitari

INFORMAL AFFIRMATIVE INDICATIVE

Passive	iyagarareru	*Honorific*	I	oiyagari ni naru
Potential			II	oiyagari nasaru
		Humble	I	
Causative	iyagaraseru		II	
Causative Pass.	iyagaraserareru			

			AFFIRMATIVE	NEGATIVE
Indicative	INFORMAL		iyasimu	iyasimanai
	FORMAL		iyasimimasu	iyasimimaseñ
Imperative	INFORMAL	I	iyasime	iyasimu na
		II	iyasiminasai	iyasiminasaru na
		III	iyasiñde kudasai	iyasimanai de kudasai
	FORMAL		oiyasimi nasaimase	oiyasimi nasaimasu na
Presumptive	INFORMAL	I	iyasimoo	iyasimumai
		II	iyasimu daroo	iyasimanai daroo
	FORMAL	I	iyasimimasyoo	iyasimimasumai
		II	iyasimu desyoo	iyasimanai desyoo
Provisional	INFORMAL		iyasimeba	iyasimanakereba
	FORMAL		iyasimimaseba	iyasimimaseñ nara
			iyasimimasureba	
Gerund	INFORMAL	I	iyasiñde	iyasimanai de
		II		iyasimanakute
	FORMAL		iyasimimasite	iyasimimaseñ de
Past Ind.	INFORMAL		iyasiñda	iyasimanakatta
	FORMAL		iyasimimasita	iyasimimaseñ desita
Past Presump.	INFORMAL		iyasiñdaroo	iyasimanakattaroo
			iyasiñda daroo	iyasimanakatta daroo
	FORMAL		iyasimimasitaroo	iyasimimaseñ desitaroo
			iyasiñda desyoo	iyasimanakatta desyoo
Conditional	INFORMAL		iyasiñdara	iyasimanakattara
	FORMAL		iyasimimasitara	iyasimimaseñ desitara
Alternative	INFORMAL		iyasiñdari	iyasimanakattari
	FORMAL		iyasimimasitari	iyasimimaseñ desitari

INFORMAL AFFIRMATIVE INDICATIVE

Passive	iyasimareru	*Honorific*	I	oiyasimi ni naru
			II	oiyasimi nasaru
Potential	iyasimeru			
		Humble	I	oiyasimi suru
Causative	iyasimaseru		II	oiyasimi itasu
Causative Pass.	iyasimaserareru			

TRANSITIVE   *to bully, to torment*

			AFFIRMATIVE	NEGATIVE
Indicative	**INFORMAL**		izimeru	izimenai
	FORMAL		izimemasu	izimemaseñ
Imperative	**INFORMAL**	**I**	izimero	izimeru na
		II	izimenasai	izimenasaru na
		III	izimete kudasai	izimenai de kudasai
	FORMAL		oizime nasaimase	oizime nasaimasu na
Presumptive	**INFORMAL**	**I**	izimeyoo	izimemai
		II	izimeru daroo	izimenai daroo
	FORMAL	**I**	izimemasyoo	izimemasumai
		II	izimeru desyoo	izimenai desyoo
Provisional	**INFORMAL**		izimereba	izimenakereba
	FORMAL		izimemaseba	izimemaseñ nara
			izimemasureba	
Gerund	**INFORMAL**	**I**	izimete	izimenai de
		II		izimenakute
	FORMAL		izimemasite	izimemaseñ de
Past Ind.	**INFORMAL**		izimeta	izimenakatta
	FORMAL		izimemasita	izimemaseñ desita
Past Presump.	**INFORMAL**		izimetaroo	izimenakattaroo
			izimeta daroo	izimenakatta daroo
	FORMAL		izimemasitaroo	izimemaseñ desitaroo
			izimeta desyoo	izimenakatta desyoo
Conditional	**INFORMAL**		izimetara	izimenakattara
	FORMAL		izimemasitara	izimemaseñ desitara
Alternative	**INFORMAL**		izimetari	izimenakattari
	FORMAL		izimemasitari	izimemaseñ desitari

INFORMAL AFFIRMATIVE INDICATIVE

Passive	izimerareru	*Honorific*	**I**	oizime ni naru
			II	oizime nasaru
Potential	izimerareru			
		Humble	**I**	oizime suru
Causative	izimesaseru		**II**	oizime itasu
Causative Pass.	izimesaserareru			

		AFFIRMATIVE	NEGATIVE
Indicative	INFORMAL	kaeru	kaenai
	FORMAL	kaemasu	kaemaseñ
Imperative	INFORMAL I	kaero	kaeru na
	II	kaenasai	kaenasaru na
	III	kaete kudasai	kaenai de kudasai
	FORMAL	okae nasaimase	okae nasaimasu na
Presumptive	INFORMAL I	kaeyoo	kaemai
	II	kaeru daroo	kaenai daroo
	FORMAL I	kaemasyoo	kaemasumai
	II	kaeru desyoo	kaenai desyoo
Provisional	INFORMAL	kaereba	kaenakereba
	FORMAL	kaemaseba	kaemaseñ nara
		kaemasureba	
Gerund	INFORMAL I	kaete	kaenai de
	II		kaenakute
	FORMAL	kaemasite	kaemaseñ de
Past Ind.	INFORMAL	kaeta	kaenakatta
	FORMAL	kaemasita	kaemaseñ desita
Past Presump.	INFORMAL	kaetaroo	kaenakattaroo
		kaeta daroo	kaenakatta daroo
	FORMAL	kaemasitaroo	kaemaseñ desitaroo
		kaeta desyoo	kaenakatta desyoo
Conditional	INFORMAL	kaetara	kaenakattara
	FORMAL	kaemasitara	kaemaseñ desitara
Alternative	INFORMAL	kaetari	kaenakattari
	FORMAL	kaemasitari	kaemaseñ desitari

INFORMAL AFFIRMATIVE INDICATIVE

Passive	kaerareru	*Honorific*	I	okae ni naru
			II	okae nasaru
Potential	kaerareru			
		Humble	I	okae suru
Causative	kaesaseru		II	okae itasu
Causative Pass.	kaesaserareru			

		AFFIRMATIVE	NEGATIVE
Indicative	INFORMAL	kaeru	kaeranai
	FORMAL	kaerimasu	kaerimaseñ
Imperative	INFORMAL I	kaere	kaeru na
	II	kaerinasai	kaerinasaru na
	III	kaette kudasai	kaeranai de kudasai
	FORMAL	okaeri nasaimase	okaeri nasaimasu na
Presumptive	INFORMAL I	kaeroo	kaerumai
	II	kaeru daroo	kaeranai daroo
	FORMAL I	kaerimasyoo	kaerimasumai
	II	kaeru desyoo	kaeranai desyoo
Provisional	INFORMAL	kaereba	kaeranakereba
	FORMAL	kaerimaseba	kaerimaseñ nara
		kaerimasureba	
Gerund	INFORMAL I	kaette	kaeranai de
	II		kaeranakute
	FORMAL	kaerimasite	kaerimaseñ de
Past Ind.	INFORMAL	kaetta	kaeranakatta
	FORMAL	kaerimasita	kaerimaseñ desita
Past Presump.	INFORMAL	kaettaroo	kaeranakattaroo
		kaetta daroo	kaeranakatta daroo
	FORMAL	kaerimasitaroo	kaerimaseñ desitaroo
		kaetta desyoo	kaeranakatta desyoo
Conditional	INFORMAL	kaettara	kaeranakattara
	FORMAL	kaerimasitara	kaerimaseñ desitara
Alternative	INFORMAL	kaettari	kaeranakattari
	FORMAL	kaerimasitari	kaerimaseñ desitari

INFORMAL AFFIRMATIVE INDICATIVE

Passive	kaerareru	*Honorific*	I	okaeri ni naru
			II	okaeri nasaru
Potential	kaereru			
		Humble	I	
Causative	kaeraseru		II	
Causative Pass.	kaeraserareru			

83

		AFFIRMATIVE	NEGATIVE
Indicative	INFORMAL	kaesu	kaesanai
	FORMAL	kaesimasu	kaesimaseñ
Imperative	INFORMAL I	kaese	kaesu na
	II	kaesinasai	kaesinasaru na
	III	kaesite kudasai	kaesanai de kudasai
	FORMAL	okaesi nasaimase	okaesi nasaimasu na
Presumptive	INFORMAL I	kaesoo	kaesumai
	II	kaesu daroo	kaesanai daroo
	FORMAL I	kaesimasyoo	kaesimasumai
	II	kaesu desyoo	kaesanai desyoo
Provisional	INFORMAL	kaeseba	kaesanakereba
	FORMAL	kaesimaseba	kaesimaseñ nara
		kaesimasureba	
Gerund	INFORMAL I	kaesite	kaesanai de
	II		kaesanakute
	FORMAL	kaesimasite	kaesimaseñ de
Past Ind.	INFORMAL	kaesita	kaesanakatta
	FORMAL	kaesimasita	kaesimaseñ desita
Past Presump.	INFORMAL	kaesitaroo	kaesanakattaroo
		kaesita daroo	kaesanakatta daroo
	FORMAL	kaesimasitaroo	kaesimaseñ desitaroo
		kaesita desyoo	kaesanakatta desyoo
Conditional	INFORMAL	kaesitara	kaesanakattara
	FORMAL	kaesimasitara	kaesimaseñ desitara
Alternative	INFORMAL	kaesitari	kaesanakattari
	FORMAL	kaesimasitari	kaesimaseñ desitari

INFORMAL AFFIRMATIVE INDICATIVE

Passive	kaesareru	*Honorific*	I	okaesi ni naru
			II	okaesi nasaru
Potential	kaeseru			
		Humble	I	okaesi suru
Causative	kaesaseru		II	okaesi itasu
Causative Pass.	kaesaserareru			

kakari
kakár.u

to begin, to be hanging (from), *to require* (time, money etc.)

		AFFIRMATIVE	NEGATIVE
Indicative	**INFORMAL**	kakaru	kakaranai
	FORMAL	kakarimasu	kakarimaseñ
Imperative	**INFORMAL I**	kakare	kakaru na
	II	kakarinasai	kakarinasaru na
	III	kakatte kudasai	kakaranai de kudasai
	FORMAL	okakari nasaimase	okakari nasaimasu na
Presumptive	**INFORMAL I**	kakaroo	kakarumai
	II	kakaru daroo	kakaranai daroo
	FORMAL I	kakarimasyoo	kakarimasumai
	II	kakaru desyoo	kakaranai desyoo
Provisional	**INFORMAL**	kakareba	kakaranakereba
	FORMAL	kakarimaseba	kakarimaseñ nara
		kakarimasureba	
Gerund	**INFORMAL I**	kakatte	kakaranai de
	II		kakaranakute
	FORMAL	kakarimasite	kakarimaseñ de
Past Ind.	**INFORMAL**	kakatta	kakaranakatta
	FORMAL	kakarimasita	kakarimaseñ desita
Past Presump.	**INFORMAL**	kakattaroo	kakaranakattaroo
		kakatta daroo	kakaranakatta daroo
	FORMAL	kakarimasitaroo	kakarimaseñ desitaroo
		kakatta desyoo	kakaranakatta desyoo
Conditional	**INFORMAL**	kakattara	kakaranakattara
	FORMAL	kakarimasitara	kakarimaseñ desitara
Alternative	**INFORMAL**	kakattari	kakaranakattari
	FORMAL	kakarimasitari	kakarimaseñ desitari

INFORMAL AFFIRMATIVE INDICATIVE

Passive	kakarareru	*Honorific*	**I**	okakari ni naru
			II	okakari nasaru
Potential	kakareru			
		Humble	**I**	okakari suru
Causative	kakaraseru		**II**	okakari itasu
Causative Pass.	kakaraserareru			

		AFFIRMATIVE	NEGATIVE
Indicative	INFORMAL	kakeru	kakenai
	FORMAL	kakemasu	kakemaseñ
Imperative	INFORMAL I	kakero	kakeru na
	II	kakenasai	kakenasaru na
	III	kakete kudasai	kakenai de kudasai
	FORMAL	okake nasaimase	okake nasaimasu na
Presumptive	INFORMAL I	kakeyoo	kakemai
	II	kakeru daroo	kakenai daroo
	FORMAL I	kakemasyoo	kakemasumai
	II	kakeru desyoo	kakenai desyoo
Provisional	INFORMAL	kakereba	kakenakereba
	FORMAL	kakemaseba	kakemaseñ nara
		kakemasureba	
Gerund	INFORMAL I	kakete	kakenai de
	II		kakenakute
	FORMAL	kakemasite	kakemaseñ de
Past Ind.	INFORMAL	kaketa	kakenakatta
	FORMAL	kakemasita	kakemaseñ desita
Past Presump.	INFORMAL	kaketaroo	kakenakattaroo
		kaketa daroo	kakenakatta daroo
	FORMAL	kakemasitaroo	kakemaseñ desitaroo
		kaketa desyoo	kakenakatta desyoo
Conditional	INFORMAL	kaketara	kakenakattara
	FORMAL	kakemasitara	kakemaseñ desitara
Alternative	INFORMAL	kaketari	kakenakattari
	FORMAL	kakemasitari	kakemaseñ desitari

INFORMAL AFFIRMATIVE INDICATIVE

Passive	kakerareru	*Honorific*	I	okake ni naru
			II	okake nasaru
Potential	kakerareru			
		Humble	I	okake suru
Causative	kakesaseru		II	okake itasu
Causative Pass.	kakesaserareru			

kaki

kák.u
TRANSITIVE *to write*

		AFFIRMATIVE	NEGATIVE
Indicative	INFORMAL	kaku	kakanai
	FORMAL	kakimasu	kakimaseñ
Imperative	INFORMAL I	kake	kaku na
	II	kakinasai	kakinasaru na
	III	kaite kudasai	kakanai de kudasai
	FORMAL	okaki nasaimase	okaki nasaimasu na
Presumptive	INFORMAL I	kakoo	kakumai
	II	kaku daroo	kakanai daroo
	FORMAL I	kakimasyoo	kakimasumai
	II	kaku desyoo	kakanai desyoo
Provisional	INFORMAL	kakeba	kakanakereba
	FORMAL	kakimaseba	kakimaseñ nara
		kakimasureba	
Gerund	INFORMAL I	kaite	kakanai de
	II		kakanakute
	FORMAL	kakimasite	kakimaseñ de
Past Ind.	INFORMAL	kaita	kakanakatta
	FORMAL	kakimasita	kakimaseñ desita
Past Presump.	INFORMAL	kaitaroo	kakanakattaroo
		kaita daroo	kakanakatta daroo
	FORMAL	kakimasitaroo	kakimaseñ desitaroo
		kaita desyoo	kakanakatta desyoo
Conditional	INFORMAL	kaitara	kakanakattara
	FORMAL	kakimasitara	kakimaseñ desitara
Alternative	INFORMAL	kaitari	kakanakattari
	FORMAL	kakimasitari	kakimaseñ desitari

INFORMAL AFFIRMATIVE INDICATIVE

Passive	kakareru	*Honorific*	I	okaki ni naru
			II	okaki nasaru
Potential	kakeru			
		Humble	I	okaki suru
Causative	kakaseru		II	okaki itasu
Causative Pass.	kakaserareru			

		AFFIRMATIVE	NEGATIVE
Indicative	INFORMAL	kakureru	kakurenai
	FORMAL	kakuremasu	kakuremaseñ
Imperative	INFORMAL I	kakurero	kakureru na
	II	kakurenasai	kakurenasaru na
	III	kakurete kudasai	kakurenai de kudasai
	FORMAL	okakure nasaimase	okakure nasaimasu na
Presumptive	INFORMAL I	kakureyoo	kakuremai
	II	kakureru daroo	kakurenai daroo
	FORMAL I	kakuremasyoo	kakuremasumai
	II	kakureru desyoo	kakurenai desyoo
Provisional	INFORMAL	kakurereba	kakurenakereba
	FORMAL	kakuremaseba	kakuremaseñ nara
		kakuremasureba	
Gerund	INFORMAL I	kakurete	kakurenai de
	II		kakurenakute
	FORMAL	kakuremasite	kakuremaseñ de
Past Ind.	INFORMAL	kakureta	kakurenakatta
	FORMAL	kakuremasita	kakuremaseñ desita
Past Presump.	INFORMAL	kakuretaroo	kakurenakattaroo
		kakureta daroo	kakurenakatta daroo
	FORMAL	kakuremasitaroo	kakuremaseñ desitaroo
		kakureta desyoo	kakurenakatta desyoo
Conditional	INFORMAL	kakuretara	kakurenakattara
	FORMAL	kakuremasitara	kakuremaseñ desitara
Alternative	INFORMAL	kakuretari	kakurenakattari
	FORMAL	kakuremasitari	kakuremaseñ desitari

INFORMAL AFFIRMATIVE INDICATIVE

Passive	kakurerareru	*Honorific*	I	okakure ni naru
			II	okakure nasaru
Potential	kakurerareru			
		Humble	I	
Causative	kakuresaseru		II	
Causative Pass.	kakuresaserareru			

TRANSITIVE *to hide* (something)

		AFFIRMATIVE	NEGATIVE
Indicative	**INFORMAL**	kakusu	kakusanai
	FORMAL	kakusimasu	kakusimaseñ
Imperative	**INFORMAL I**	kakuse	kakusu na
	II	kakusinasai	kakusinasaru na
	III	kakusite kudasai	kakusanai de kudasai
	FORMAL	okakusi nasaimase	okakusi nasaimasu na
Presumptive	**INFORMAL I**	kakusoo	kakusumai
	II	kakusu daroo	kakusanai daroo
	FORMAL I	kakusimasyoo	kakusimasumai
	II	kakusu desyoo	kakusanai desyoo
Provisional	**INFORMAL**	kakuseba	kakusanakereba
	FORMAL	kakusimaseba	kakusimaseñ nara
		kakusimasureba	
Gerund	**INFORMAL I**	kakusite	kakusanai de
	II		kakusanakute
	FORMAL	kakusimasite	kakusimaseñ de
Past Ind.	**INFORMAL**	kakusita	kakusanakatta
	FORMAL	kakusimasita	kakusimaseñ desita
Past Presump.	**INFORMAL**	kakusitaroo	kakusanakattaroo
		kakusita daroo	kakusanakatta daroo
	FORMAL	kakusimasitaroo	kakusimaseñ desitaroo
		kakusita desyoo	kakusanakatta desyoo
Conditional	**INFORMAL**	kakusitara	kakusanakattara
	FORMAL	kakusimasitara	kakusimaseñ desitara
Alternative	**INFORMAL**	kakusitari	kakusanakattari
	FORMAL	kakusimasitari	kakusimaseñ desitari

INFORMAL AFFIRMATIVE INDICATIVE

Passive	kakusareru	*Honorific*	**I**	okakusi ni naru
			II	okakusi nasaru
Potential	kakuseru			
		Humble	**I**	okakusi suru
Causative	kakusaseru		**II**	okakusi itasu
Causative Pass.	kakusaserareru			

		AFFIRMATIVE	NEGATIVE
Indicative	INFORMAL	kamau	kamawanai
	FORMAL	kamaimasu	kamaimaseñ
Imperative	INFORMAL I	kamae	kamau na
	II	kamainasai	kamainasaru na
	III	kamatte kudasai	kamawanai de kudasai
	FORMAL	okamai nasaimase	okamai nasaimasu na
Presumptive	INFORMAL I	kamaoo	kamaumai
	II	kamau daroo	kamawanai daroo
	FORMAL I	kamaimasyoo	kamaimasumai
	II	kamau desyoo	kamawanai desyoo
Provisional	INFORMAL	kamaeba	kamawanakereba
	FORMAL	kamaimaseba	kamaimaseñ nara
		kamaimasureba	
Gerund	INFORMAL I	kamatte	kamawanai de
	II		kamawanakute
	FORMAL	kamaimasite	kamaimaseñ de
Past Ind.	INFORMAL	kamatta	kamawanakatta
	FORMAL	kamaimasita	kamaimaseñ desita
Past Presump.	INFORMAL	kamattaroo	kamawanakattaroo
		kamatta daroo	kamawanakatta daroo
	FORMAL	kamaimasitaroo	kamaimaseñ desitaroo
		kamatta desyoo	kamawanakatta desyoo
Conditional	INFORMAL	kamattara	kamawanakattara
	FORMAL	kamaimasitara	kamaimaseñ desitara
Alternative	INFORMAL	kamattari	kamawanakattari
	FORMAL	kamaimasitari	kamaimaseñ desitari

INFORMAL AFFIRMATIVE INDICATIVE

Passive		*Honorific*	I	okamai ni naru
			II	okamai nasaru
Potential	kamaeru			
		Humble	I	okamai suru
Causative	kamawaseru		II	okamai itasu
Causative Pass.	kamawaserareru			

		AFFIRMATIVE	NEGATIVE
Indicative	INFORMAL	kamu	kamanai
	FORMAL	kamimasu	kamimaseñ
Imperative	INFORMAL I	kame	kamu na
	II	kaminasai	kaminasaru na
	III	kañde kudasai	kamanai de kudasai
	FORMAL	okami nasaimase	okami nasaimasu na
Presumptive	INFORMAL I	kamoo	kamumai
	II	kamu daroo	kamanai daroo
	FORMAL I	kamimasyoo	kamimasumai
	II	kamu desyoo	kamanai desyoo
Provisional	INFORMAL	kameba	kamanakereba
	FORMAL	kamimaseba	kamimaseñ nara
		kamimasureba	
Gerund	INFORMAL I	kañde	kamanai de
	II		kamanakute
	FORMAL	kamimasite	kamimaseñ de
Past Ind.	INFORMAL	kañda	kamanakatta
	FORMAL	kamimasita	kamimaseñ desita
Past Presump.	INFORMAL	kañdaroo	kamanakattaroo
		kañda daroo	kamanakatta daroo
	FORMAL	kamimasitaroo	kamimaseñ desitaroo
		kañda desyoo	kamanakatta desyoo
Conditional	INFORMAL	kañdara	kamanakattara
	FORMAL	kamimasitara	kamimaseñ desitara
Alternative	INFORMAL	kañdari	kamanakattari
	FORMAL	kamimasitari	kamimaseñ desitari

INFORMAL AFFIRMATIVE INDICATIVE

Passive	kamareru	*Honorific*	I	okami ni naru
			II	okami nasaru
Potential	kameru			
		Humble	I	okami suru
Causative	kamaseru		II	okami itasu
Causative Pass.	kamaserareru			

to be sad, to grieve   TRANSITIVE

		AFFIRMATIVE	NEGATIVE
Indicative	INFORMAL	kanasimu	kanasimanai
	FORMAL	kanasimimasu	kanasimimaseñ
Imperative	INFORMAL I	kanasime	kanasimu na
	II	kanasiminasai	kanasiminasaru na
	III	kanasiñde kudasai	kanasimanai de kudasai
	FORMAL	okanasimi nasaimase	okanasimi nasaimasu na
Presumptive	INFORMAL I	kanasimoo	kanasimumai
	II	kanasimu daroo	kanasimanai daroo
	FORMAL I	kanasimimasyoo	kanasimimasumai
	II	kanasimu desyoo	kanasimanai desyoo
Provisional	INFORMAL	kanasimeba	kanasimanakereba
	FORMAL	kanasimimaseba	kanasimimaseñ nara
		kanasimimasureba	
Gerund	INFORMAL I	kanasiñde	kanasimanai de
	II		kanasimanakute
	FORMAL	kanasimimasite	kanasimimaseñ de
Past Ind.	INFORMAL	kanasiñda	kanasimanakatta
	FORMAL	kanasimimasita	kanasimimaseñ desita
Past Presump.	INFORMAL	kanasiñdaroo	kanasimanakattaroo
		kanasiñda daroo	kanasimanakatta daroo
	FORMAL	kanasimimasitaroo	kanasimimaseñ desitaroo
		kanasiñda desyoo	kanasimanakatta desyoo
Conditional	INFORMAL	kanasiñdara	kanasimanakattara
	FORMAL	kanasimimasitara	kanasimimaseñ desitara
Alternative	INFORMAL	kanasiñdari	kanasimanakattari
	FORMAL	kanasimimasitari	kanasimimaseñ desitari

INFORMAL AFFIRMATIVE INDICATIVE

Passive	kanasimareru	*Honorific*	I	okanasimi ni naru
			II	okanasimi nasaru
Potential	kanasimeru			
		Humble	I	
Causative	kanasimaseru		II	
Causative Pass.	kanasimaserareru			

TRANSITIVE　*to consider, to ponder*

		AFFIRMATIVE	NEGATIVE
Indicative	INFORMAL	kañgaeru	kañgaenai
	FORMAL	kañgaemasu	kañgaemaseñ
Imperative	INFORMAL I	kañgaero	kañgaeru na
	II	kañgaenasai	kañgaenasaru na
	III	kañgaete kudasai	kañgaenai de kudasai
	FORMAL	okañgae nasaimase	okañgae nasaimasu na
Presumptive	INFORMAL I	kañgaeyoo	kañgaemai
	II	kañgaeru daroo	kañgaenai daroo
	FORMAL I	kañgaemasyoo	kañgaemasumai
	II	kañgaeru desyoo	kañgaenai desyoo
Provisional	INFORMAL	kañgaereba	kañgaenakereba
	FORMAL	kañgaemaseba	kañgaemaseñ nara
		kañgaemasureba	
Gerund	INFORMAL I	kañgaete	kañgaenai de
	II		kañgaenakute
	FORMAL	kañgaemasite	kañgaemaseñ de
Past Ind.	INFORMAL	kañgaeta	kañgaenakatta
	FORMAL	kañgaemasita	kañgaemaseñ desita
Past Presump.	INFORMAL	kañgaetaroo	kañgaenakattaroo
		kañgaeta daroo	kañgaenakatta daroo
	FORMAL	kañgaemasitaroo	kañgaemaseñ desitaroo
		kañgaeta desyoo	kañgaenakatta desyoo
Conditional	INFORMAL	kañgaetara	kañgaenakattara
	FORMAL	kañgaemasitara	kañgaemaseñ desitara
Alternative	INFORMAL	kañgaetari	kañgaenakattari
	FORMAL	kañgaemasitari	kañgaemaseñ desitari

INFORMAL AFFIRMATIVE INDICATIVE

Passive	kañgaerareru	*Honorific* I	okañgae ni naru
		II	okañgae nasaru
Potential	kañgaerareru		
		Humble I	
Causative	kañgaesaseru	II	
Causative Pass.	kañgaesaserareru		

		AFFIRMATIVE	**NEGATIVE**
Indicative	**INFORMAL**	kañziru	kañzinai
	FORMAL	kañzimasu	kañzimaseñ
Imperative	**INFORMAL I**	kañziro	kañziru na
	II	kañzinasai	kañzinasaru na
	III	kañzite kudasai	kañzinai de kudasai
	FORMAL	okañzi nasaimase	okañzi nasaimasu na
Presumptive	**INFORMAL I**	kañziyoo	kañzimai
	II	kañziru daroo	kañzinai daroo
	FORMAL I	kañzimasyoo	kañzimasumai
	II	kañziru desyoo	kañzinai desyoo
Provisional	**INFORMAL**	kañzireba	kañzinakereba
	FORMAL	kañzimaseba	kañzimaseñ nara
		kañzimasureba	
Gerund	**INFORMAL I**	kañzite	kañzinai de
	II		kañzinakute
	FORMAL	kañzimasite	kañzimaseñ de
Past Ind.	**INFORMAL**	kañzita	kañzinakatta
	FORMAL	kañzimasita	kañzimaseñ desita
Past Presump.	**INFORMAL**	kañzitaroo	kañzinakattaroo
		kañzita daroo	kañzinakatta daroo
	FORMAL	kañzimasitaroo	kañzimaseñ desitaroo
		kañzita desyoo	kañzinakatta desyoo
Conditional	**INFORMAL**	kañzitara	kañzinakattara
	FORMAL	kañzimasitara	kañzimaseñ desitara
Alternative	**INFORMAL**	kañzitari	kañzinakattari
	FORMAL	kañzimasitari	kañzimaseñ desitari

INFORMAL AFFIRMATIVE INDICATIVE

Passive	kañzirareru	*Honorific*	**I**	okañzi ni naru
			II	okañzi nasaru
Potential	kañzirareru			
		Humble	**I**	
Causative	kañzisaseru		**II**	
Causative Pass.	kañzisaserareru			

TRANSITIVE   *to tease, to play jokes on*

		AFFIRMATIVE	NEGATIVE
Indicative	INFORMAL	karakau	karakawanai
	FORMAL	karakaimasu	karakaimaseñ
Imperative	INFORMAL I	karakae	karakau na
	II	karakainasai	karakainasaru na
	III	karakatte kudasai	karakawanai de kudasai
	FORMAL	okarakai nasaimase	okarakai nasaimasu na
Presumptive	INFORMAL I	karakaoo	karakaumai
	II	karakau daroo	karakawanai daroo
	FORMAL I	karakaimasyoo	karakaimasumai
	II	karakau desyoo	karakawanai desyoo
Provisional	INFORMAL	karakaeba	karakawanakereba
	FORMAL	karakaimaseba	karakaimaseñ nara
		karakaimasureba	
Gerund	INFORMAL I	karakatte	karakawanai de
	II		karakawanakute
	FORMAL	karakaimasite	karakaimaseñ de
Past Ind.	INFORMAL	karakatta	karakawanakatta
	FORMAL	karakaimasita	karakaimaseñ desita
Past Presump.	INFORMAL	karakattaroo	karakawanakattaroo
		karakatta daroo	karakawanakatta daroo
	FORMAL	karakaimasitaroo	karakaimaseñ desitaroo
		karakatta desyoo	karakawanakatta desyoo
Conditional	INFORMAL	karakattara	karakawanakattara
	FORMAL	karakaimasitara	karakaimaseñ desitara
Alternative	INFORMAL	karakattari	karakawanakattari
	FORMAL	karakaimasitari	karakaimaseñ desitari

INFORMAL AFFIRMATIVE INDICATIVE

Passive	karakawareru	*Honorific*	I	okarakai ni naru
			II	okarakai nasaru
Potential	karakaeru			
		Humble	I	okarakai suru
Causative	karakawaseru		II	okarakai itasu
Causative Pass.	karakawaserareru			

			AFFIRMATIVE	NEGATIVE
Indicative	INFORMAL		kariru	karinai
	FORMAL		karimasu	karimaseñ
Imperative	INFORMAL	I	kariro	kariru na
		II	karinasai	karinasaru na
		III	karite kudasai	karinai de kudasai
	FORMAL		okari nasaimase	okari nasaimasu na
Presumptive	INFORMAL	I	kariyoo	karimai
		II	kariru daroo	karinai daroo
	FORMAL	I	karimasyoo	karimasumai
		II	kariru desyoo	karinai desyoo
Provisional	INFORMAL		karireba	karinakereba
	FORMAL		karimaseba	karimaseñ nara
			karimasureba	
Gerund	INFORMAL	I	karite	karinai de
		II		karinakute
	FORMAL		karimasite	karimaseñ de
Past Ind.	INFORMAL		karita	karinakatta
	FORMAL		karimasita	karimaseñ desita
Past Presump.	INFORMAL		karitaroo	karinakattaroo
			karita daroo	karinakatta daroo
	FORMAL		karimasitaroo	karimaseñ desitaroo
			karita desyoo	karinakatta desyoo
Conditional	INFORMAL		karitara	karinakattara
	FORMAL		karimasitara	karimaseñ desitara
Alternative	INFORMAL		karitari	karinakattari
	FORMAL		karimasitari	karimaseñ desitari

INFORMAL AFFIRMATIVE INDICATIVE

Passive	karirareru	*Honorific*	I	okari ni naru
			II	okari nasaru
Potential	karirareru			
		Humble	I	okari suru
Causative	karisaseru		II	okari itasu
Causative Pass.	karisaserareru			

		AFFIRMATIVE	NEGATIVE
Indicative	INFORMAL	kasaneru	kasanenai
	FORMAL	kasanemasu	kasanemaseñ
Imperative	INFORMAL I	kasanero	kasaneru na
	II	kasanenasai	kasanenasaru na
	III	kasanete kudasai	kasanenai de kudasai
	FORMAL	okasane nasaimase	okasane nasaimasu na
Presumptive	INFORMAL I	kasaneyoo	kasanemai
	II	kasaneru daroo	kasanenai daroo
	FORMAL I	kasanemasyoo	kasanemasumai
	II	kasaneru desyoo	kasanenai desyoo
Provisional	INFORMAL	kasanereba	kasanenakereba
	FORMAL	kasanemaseba	kasanemaseñ nara
		kasanemasureba	
Gerund	INFORMAL I	kasanete	kasanenai de
	II		kasanenakute
	FORMAL	kasanemasite	kasanemaseñ de
Past Ind.	INFORMAL	kasaneta	kasanenakatta
	FORMAL	kasanemasita	kasanemaseñ desita
Past Presump.	INFORMAL	kasanetaroo	kasanenakattaroo
		kasaneta daroo	kasanenakatta daroo
	FORMAL	kasanemasitaroo	kasanemaseñ desitaroo
		kasaneta desyoo	kasanenakatta desyoo
Conditional	INFORMAL	kasanetara	kasanenakattara
	FORMAL	kasanemasitara	kasanemaseñ desitara
Alternative	INFORMAL	kasanetari	kasanenakattari
	FORMAL	kasanemasitari	kasanemaseñ desitari

INFORMAL AFFIRMATIVE INDICATIVE

Passive	kasanerareru	*Honorific*	I	okasane ni naru
			II	okasane nasaru
Potential	kasanerareru			
		Humble	I	okasane suru
Causative	kasanesaseru		II	okasane itasu
Causative Pass.	kasanesaserareru			

kaség.u   **kasegi**
to earn one's living   TRANSITIVE

		AFFIRMATIVE	NEGATIVE
Indicative	INFORMAL	kasegu	kaseganai
	FORMAL	kasegimasu	kasegimaseñ
Imperative	INFORMAL I	kasege	kasegu na
	II	kaseginasai	kaseginasaru na
	III	kaseide kudasai	kaseganai de kudasai
	FORMAL	okasegi nasaimase	okasegi nasaimasu na
Presumptive	INFORMAL I	kasegoo	kasegumai
	II	kasegu daroo	kaseganai daroo
	FORMAL I	kasegimasyoo	kasegimasumai
	II	kasegu desyoo	kaseganai desyoo
Provisional	INFORMAL	kasegeba	kaseganakereba
	FORMAL	kasegimaseba	kasegimaseñ nara
		kasegimasureba	
Gerund	INFORMAL I	kaseide	kaseganai de
	II		kaseganakute
	FORMAL	kasegimasite	kasegimaseñ de
Past Ind.	INFORMAL	kaseida	kaseganakatta
	FORMAL	kasegimasita	kasegimaseñ desita
Past Presump.	INFORMAL	kaseidaroo	kaseganakattaroo
		kaseida daroo	kaseganakatta daroo
	FORMAL	kasegimasitaroo	kasegimaseñ desitaroo
		kaseida desyoo	kaseganakatta desyoo
Conditional	INFORMAL	kaseidara	kaseganakattara
	FORMAL	kasegimasitara	kasegimaseñ desitara
Alternative	INFORMAL	kaseidari	kaseganakattari
	FORMAL	kasegimasitari	kasegimaseñ desitari

INFORMAL AFFIRMATIVE INDICATIVE

Passive	kasegareru	*Honorific*	I	okasegi ni naru
			II	okasegi nasaru
Potential	kasegeru			
		Humble	I	okasegi suru
Causative	kasegaseru		II	okasegi itasu
Causative Pass.	kasegaserareru			

TRANSITIVE   *to lend, to rent* (to)

		AFFIRMATIVE	NEGATIVE
Indicative	INFORMAL	kasu	kasanai
	FORMAL	kasimasu	kasimaseñ
Imperative	INFORMAL I	kase	kasu na
	II	kasinasai	kasinasaru na
	III	kasite kudasai	kasanai de kudasai
	FORMAL	okasi nasaimase	okasi nasaimasu na
Presumptive	INFORMAL I	kasoo	kasumai
	II	kasu daroo	kasanai daroo
	FORMAL I	kasimasyoo	kasimasumai
	II	kasu desyoo	kasanai desyoo
Provisional	INFORMAL	kaseba	kasanakereba
	FORMAL	kasimaseba	kasimaseñ nara
		kasimasureba	
Gerund	INFORMAL I	kasite	kasanai de
	II		kasanakute
	FORMAL	kasimasite	kasimaseñ de
Past Ind.	INFORMAL	kasita	kasanakatta
	FORMAL	kasimasita	kasimaseñ desita
Past Presump.	INFORMAL	kasitaroo	kasanakattaroo
		kasita daroo	kasanakatta daroo
	FORMAL	kasimasitaroo	kasimaseñ desitaroo
		kasita desyoo	kasanakatta desyoo
Conditional	INFORMAL	kasitara	kasanakattara
	FORMAL	kasimasitara	kasimaseñ desitara
Alternative	INFORMAL	kasitari	kasanakattari
	FORMAL	kasimasitari	kasimaseñ desitari

INFORMAL AFFIRMATIVE INDICATIVE

Passive	kasareru	*Honorific*	I	okasi ni naru
			II	okasi nasaru
Potential	kaseru			
		Humble	I	okasi suru
Causative	kasaseru		II	okasi itasu
Causative Pass.	kasaserareru			

		AFFIRMATIVE	NEGATIVE
Indicative	INFORMAL	katazukeru	katazukenai
	FORMAL	katazukemasu	katazukemaseñ
Imperative	INFORMAL I	katazukero	katazukeru na
	II	katazukenasai	katazukenasaru na
	III	katazukete kudasai	katazukenai de kudasai
	FORMAL	okatazuke nasaimase	okatazuke nasaimasu na
Presumptive	INFORMAL I	katazukeyoo	katazukemai
	II	katazukeru daroo	katazukenai daroo
	FORMAL I	katazukemasyoo	katazukemasumai
	II	katazukeru desyoo	katazukenai desyoo
Provisional	INFORMAL	katazukereba	katazukenakereba
	FORMAL	katazukemaseba	katazukemaseñ nara
		katazukemasureba	
Gerund	INFORMAL I	katazukete	katazukenai de
	II		katazukenakute
	FORMAL	katazukemasite	katazukemaseñ de
Past Ind.	INFORMAL	katazuketa	katazukenakatta
	FORMAL	katazukemasita	katazukemaseñ desita
Past Presump.	INFORMAL	katazuketaroo	katazukenakattaroo
		katazuketa daroo	katazukenakatta daroo
	FORMAL	katazukemasitaroo	katazukemaseñ desitaroo
		katazuketa desyoo	katazukenakatta desyoo
Conditional	INFORMAL	katazuketara	katazukenakattara
	FORMAL	katazukemasitara	katazukemaseñ desitara
Alternative	INFORMAL	katazuketari	katazukenakattari
	FORMAL	katazukemasitari	katazukemaseñ desitari

INFORMAL AFFIRMATIVE INDICATIVE

Passive	katazukerareru	*Honorific*	I	okatazuke ni naru
			II	okatazuke nasaru
Potential	katazukerareru			
		Humble	I	okatazuke suru
Causative	katazukesaseru		II	okatazuke itasu
Causative Pass.	katazukesaserareru			

		AFFIRMATIVE	NEGATIVE
Indicative	INFORMAL	katu	katanai
	FORMAL	katimasu	katimaseñ
Imperative	INFORMAL I	kate	katu na
	II	katinasai	katinasaru na
	III	katte kudasai	katanai de kudasai
	FORMAL	okati nasaimase	okati nasaimasu na
Presumptive	INFORMAL I	katoo	katumai
	II	katu daroo	katanai daroo
	FORMAL I	katimasyoo	katimasumai
	II	katu desyoo	katanai desyoo
Provisional	INFORMAL	kateba	katanakereba
	FORMAL	katimaseba	katimaseñ nara
		katimasureba	
Gerund	INFORMAL I	katte	katanai de
	II		katanakute
	FORMAL	katimasite	katimaseñ de
Past Ind.	INFORMAL	katta	katanakatta
	FORMAL	katimasita	katimaseñ desita
Past Presump.	INFORMAL	kattaroo	katanakattaroo
		katta daroo	katanakatta daroo
	FORMAL	katimasitaroo	katimaseñ desitaroo
		katta desyoo	katanakatta desyoo
Conditional	INFORMAL	kattara	katanakattara
	FORMAL	katimasitara	katimaseñ desitara
Alternative	INFORMAL	kattari	katanakattari
	FORMAL	katimasitari	katimaseñ desitari

INFORMAL AFFIRMATIVE INDICATIVE

Passive	katareru	*Honorific*	I	okati ni naru
			II	okati nasaru
Potential	kateru			
		Humble	I	
Causative	kataseru		II	
Causative Pass.	kataserareru			

101

			AFFIRMATIVE	NEGATIVE
Indicative	INFORMAL		kau	kawanai
	FORMAL		kaimasu	kaimaseñ
Imperative	INFORMAL	I	kae	kau na
		II	kainasai	kainasaru na
		III	katte kudasai	kawanai de kudasai
	FORMAL		okai nasaimase	okai nasaimasu na
Presumptive	INFORMAL	I	kaoo	kaumai
		II	kau daroo	kawanai daroo
	FORMAL	I	kaimasyoo	kaimasumai
		II	kau desyoo	kawanai desyoo
Provisional	INFORMAL		kaeba	kawanakereba
	FORMAL		kaimaseba	kaimaseñ nara
			kaimasureba	
Gerund	INFORMAL	I	katte	kawanai de
		II		kawanakute
	FORMAL		kaimasite	kaimaseñ de
Past Ind.	INFORMAL		katta	kawanakatta
	FORMAL		kaimasita	kaimaseñ desita
Past Presump.	INFORMAL		kattaroo	kawanakattaroo
			katta daroo	kawanakatta daroo
	FORMAL		kaimasitaroo	kaimaseñ desitaroo
			katta desyoo	kawanakatta desyoo
Conditional	INFORMAL		kattara	kawanakattara
	FORMAL		kaimasitara	kaimaseñ desitara
Alternative	INFORMAL		kattari	kawanakattari
	FORMAL		kaimasitari	kaimaseñ desitari

INFORMAL AFFIRMATIVE INDICATIVE

Passive	kawareru	*Honorific*	I	okai ni naru
			II	okai nasaru
Potential	kaeru			
		Humble	I	okai suru
Causative	kawaseru		II	okai itasu
Causative Pass.	kawaserareru			

TRANSITIVE　*to love or treat with affection* (someone or something weaker than oneself)

		AFFIRMATIVE	NEGATIVE
Indicative	INFORMAL	kawaigaru	kawaigaranai
	FORMAL	kawaigarimasu	kawaigarimaseñ
Imperative	INFORMAL I	kawaigare	kawaigaru na
	II	kawaigarinasai	kawaigarinasaru na
	III	kawaigatte kudasai	kawaigaranai de kudasai
	FORMAL	okawaigari nasaimase	okawaigari nasaimasu na
Presumptive	INFORMAL I	kawaigaroo	kawaigarumai
	II	kawaigaru daroo	kawaigaranai daroo
	FORMAL I	kawaigarimasyoo	kawaigarimasumai
	II	kawaigaru desyoo	kawaigaranai desyoo
Provisional	INFORMAL	kawaigareba	kawaigaranakereba
	FORMAL	kawaigarimaseba	kawaigarimaseñ nara
		kawaigarimasureba	
Gerund	INFORMAL I	kawaigatte	kawaigaranai de
	II		kawaigaranakute
	FORMAL	kawaigarimasite	kawaigarimaseñ de
Past Ind.	INFORMAL	kawaigatta	kawaigaranakatta
	FORMAL	kawaigarimasita	kawaigarimaseñ desita
Past Presump.	INFORMAL	kawaigattaroo	kawaigaranakattaroo
		kawaigatta daroo	kawaigaranakatta daroo
	FORMAL	kawaigarimasitaroo	kawaigarimaseñ desitaroo
		kawaigatta desyoo	kawaigaranakatta desyoo
Conditional	INFORMAL	kawaigattara	kawaigaranakattara
	FORMAL	kawaigarimasitara	kawaigarimaseñ desitara
Alternative	INFORMAL	kawaigattari	kawaigaranakattari
	FORMAL	kawaigarimasitari	kawaigarimaseñ desitari

INFORMAL AFFIRMATIVE INDICATIVE

Passive .	kawaigarareru	*Honorific*	I	okawaigari ni naru
			II	okawaigari nasaru
Potential	kawaigareru			
		Humble	I	
Causative	kawaigaraseru		II	
Causative Pass.	kawaigaraserareru			

		AFFIRMATIVE	NEGATIVE
Indicative	**INFORMAL**	kawakasu	kawakasanai
	FORMAL	kawakasimasu	kawakasimaseñ
Imperative	**INFORMAL I**	kawakase	kawakasu na
	II	kawakasinasai	kawakasinasaru na
	III	kawakasite kudasai	kawakasanai de kudasai
	FORMAL	okawakasi nasaimase	okawakasi nasaimasu na
Presumptive	**INFORMAL I**	kawakasoo	kawakasumai
	II	kawakasu daroo	kawakasanai daroo
	FORMAL I	kawakasimasyoo	kawakasimasumai
	II	kawakasu desyoo	kawakasanai desyoo
Provisional	**INFORMAL**	kawakaseba	kawakasanakereba
	FORMAL	kawakasimaseba	kawakasimaseñ nara
		kawakasimasureba	
Gerund	**INFORMAL I**	kawakasite	kawakasanai de
	II		kawakasanakute
	FORMAL	kawakasimasite	kawakasimaseñ de
Past Ind.	**INFORMAL**	kawakasita	kawakasanakatta
	FORMAL	kawakasimasita	kawakasimaseñ desita
Past Presump.	**INFORMAL**	kawakasitaroo	kawakasanakattaroo
		kawakasita daroo	kawakasanakatta daroo
	FORMAL	kawakasimasitaroo	kawakasimaseñ desitaroo
		kawakasita desyoo	kawakasanakatta desyoo
Conditional	**INFORMAL**	kawakasitara	kawakasanakattara
	FORMAL	kawakasimasitara	kawakasimaseñ desitara
Alternative	**INFORMAL**	kawakasitari	kawakasanakattari
	FORMAL	kawakasimasitari	kawakasimaseñ desitari

INFORMAL AFFIRMATIVE INDICATIVE

Passive	kawakasareru	*Honorific*	**I**	okawakasi ni naru
			II	okawakasi nasaru
Potential	kawakaseru			
		Humble	**I**	okawakasi suru
Causative	kawakasaseru		**II**	okawakasi itasu
Causative Pass.	kawakasaserareru			

		AFFIRMATIVE	**NEGATIVE**
Indicative	**INFORMAL**	kawaku	kawakanai
	FORMAL	kawakimasu	kawakimaseñ
Imperative	**INFORMAL I**	kawake	kawaku na
	II		
	III		
	FORMAL		
Presumptive	**INFORMAL I**	kawakoo	kawakumai
	II	kawaku daroo	kawakanai daroo
	FORMAL I	kawakimasyoo	kawakumai
	II	kawaku desyoo	kawakanai desyoo
Provisional	**INFORMAL**	kawakeba	kawakanakereba
	FORMAL	kawakimaseba	kawakimaseñ nara
		kawakimasureba	
Gerund	**INFORMAL I**	kawaite	kawakanai de
	II		kawakanakute
	FORMAL	kawakimasite	kawakimaseñ de
Past Ind.	**INFORMAL**	kawaita	kawakanakatta
	FORMAL	kawakimasita	kawakimaseñ desita
Past Presump.	**INFORMAL**	kawaitaroo	kawakanakattaroo
		kawaita daroo	kawakanakatta daroo
	FORMAL	kawakimasitaroo	kawakimaseñ desitaroo
		kawaita desyoo	kawakanakatta desyoo
Conditional	**INFORMAL**	kawaitara	kawakanakattara
	FORMAL	kawakimasitara	kawakimaseñ desitara
Alternative	**INFORMAL**	kawaitari	kawakanakattari
	FORMAL	kawakimasitari	kawakimaseñ desitari

INFORMAL AFFIRMATIVE INDICATIVE

Passive		*Honorific*	**I**
			II
Potential			
		Humble	**I**
Causative			**II**
Causative Pass.			

		AFFIRMATIVE	NEGATIVE
Indicative	INFORMAL	kawaru	kawaranai
	FORMAL	kawarimasu	kawarimaseñ
Imperative	INFORMAL I	kaware	kawaru na
	II	kawarinasai	kawarinasaru na
	III	kawatte kudasai	kawaranai de kudasai
	FORMAL	okawari nasaimase	okawari nasaimasu na
Presumptive	INFORMAL I	kawaroo	kawarumai
	II	kawaru daroo	kawaranai daroo
	FORMAL I	kawarimasyoo	kawarimasumai
	II	kawaru desyoo	kawaranai desyoo
Provisional	INFORMAL	kawareba	kawaranakereba
	FORMAL	kawarimaseba	kawarimaseñ nara
		kawarimasureba	
Gerund	INFORMAL I	kawatte	kawaranai de
	II		kawaranakute
	FORMAL	kawarimasite	kawarimaseñ de
Past Ind.	INFORMAL	kawatta	kawaranakatta
	FORMAL	kawarimasita	kawarimaseñ desita
Past Presump.	INFORMAL	kawattaroo	kawaranakattaroo
		kawatta daroo	kawaranakatta daroo
	FORMAL	kawarimasitaroo	kawarimaseñ desitaroo
		kawatta desyoo	kawaranakatta desyoo
Conditional	INFORMAL	kawattara	kawaranakattara
	FORMAL	kawarimasitara	kawarimaseñ desitara
Alternative	INFORMAL	kawattari	kawaranakattari
	FORMAL	kawarimasitari	kawarimaseñ desitari

INFORMAL AFFIRMATIVE INDICATIVE

Passive	kawarareru	*Honorific*	I	okawari ni naru
			II	okawari nasaru
Potential	kawareru			
		Humble	I	
Causative	kawaraseru		II	
Causative Pass.	kawaraserareru			

		AFFIRMATIVE	NEGATIVE
Indicative	INFORMAL	kayou	kayowanai
	FORMAL	kayoimasu	kayoimaseñ
Imperative	INFORMAL I	kayoe	kayou na
	II	kayoinasai	kayoinasaru na
	III	kayotte kudasai	kayowanai de kudasai
	FORMAL	okayoi nasaimase	okayoi nasaimasu na
Presumptive	INFORMAL I	kayooo	kayoumai
	II	kayou daroo	kayowanai daroo
	FORMAL I	kayoimasyoo	kayoimasumai
	II	kayou desyoo	kayowanai desyoo
Provisional	INFORMAL	kayoeba	kayowanakereba
	FORMAL	kayoimaseba	kayoimaseñ nara
		kayoimasureba	
Gerund	INFORMAL I	kayotte	kayowanai de
	II		kayowanakute
	FORMAL	kayoimasite	kayoimaseñ de
Past Ind.	INFORMAL	kayotta	kayowanakatta
	FORMAL	kayoimasita	kayoimaseñ desita
Past Presump.	INFORMAL	kayottaroo	kayowanakattaroo
		kayotta daroo	kayowanakatta daroo
	FORMAL	kayoimasitaroo	kayoimaseñ desitaroo
		kayotta desyoo	kayowanakatta desyoo
Conditional	INFORMAL	kayottara	kayowanakattara
	FORMAL	kayoimasitara	kayoimaseñ desitara
Alternative	INFORMAL	kayottari	kayowanakattari
	FORMAL	kayoimasitari	kayoimaseñ desitari

INFORMAL AFFIRMATIVE INDICATIVE

Passive	kayowareru	*Honorific*	I	okayoi ni naru
			II	okayoi nasaru
Potential	kayoeru			
		Humble	I	
Causative	kayowaseru		II	
Causative Pass.	kayowaserareru			

kazar.u

to ornament, to decorate   TRANSITIVE

kazari

			AFFIRMATIVE	**NEGATIVE**
Indicative	INFORMAL		kazaru	kazaranai
	FORMAL		kazarimasu	kazarimaseñ
Imperative	INFORMAL I		kazare	kazaru na
		II	kazarinasai	kazarinasaru na
		III	kazatte kudasai	kazaranai de kudasai
	FORMAL		okazari nasaimase	okazari nasaimasu na
Presumptive	INFORMAL I		kazaroo	kazarumai
		II	kazaru daroo	kazaranai daroo
	FORMAL I		kazarimasyoo	kazarimasumai
		II	kazaru desyoo	kazaranai desyoo
Provisional	INFORMAL		kazareba	kazaranakereba
	FORMAL		kazarimaseba	kazarimaseñ nara
			kazarimasureba	
Gerund	INFORMAL I		kazatte	kazaranai de
		II		kazaranakute
	FORMAL		kazarimasite	kazarimaseñ de
Past Ind.	INFORMAL		kazatta	kazaranakatta
	FORMAL		kazarimasita	kazarimaseñ desita
Past Presump.	INFORMAL		kazattaroo	kazaranakattaroo
			kazatta daroo	kazaranakatta daroo
	FORMAL		kazarimasitaroo	kazarimaseñ desitaroo
			kazatta desyoo	kazaranakatta desyoo
Conditional	INFORMAL		kazattara	kazaranakattara
	FORMAL		kazarimasitara	kazarimaseñ desitara
Alternative	INFORMAL		kazattari	kazaranakattari
	FORMAL		kazarimasitari	kazarimaseñ desitari

INFORMAL AFFIRMATIVE INDICATIVE

Passive	kazarareru	*Honorific*	I	okazari ni naru
			II	okazari nasaru
Potential	kazareru			
		Humble	I	okazari suru
Causative	kazaraseru		II	okazari itasu
Causative Pass.	kazaraserareru			

TRANSITIVE   *to count*

		AFFIRMATIVE	NEGATIVE
Indicative	INFORMAL	kazoeru	kazoenai
	FORMAL	kazoemasu	kazoemaseñ
Imperative	INFORMAL I	kazoero	kazoeru na
	II	kazoenasai	kazoenasaru na
	III	kazoete kudasai	kazoenai de kudasai
	FORMAL	okazoe nasaimase	okazoe nasaimasu na
Presumptive	INFORMAL I	kazoeyoo	kazoemai
	II	kazoeru daroo	kazoenai daroo
	FORMAL I	kazoemasyoo	kazoemasumai
	II	kazoeru desyoo	kazoenai desyoo
Provisional	INFORMAL	kazoereba	kazoenakereba
	FORMAL	kazoemaseba	kazoemaseñ nara
		kazoemasureba	
Gerund	INFORMAL I	kazoete	kazoenai de
	II		kazoenakute
	FORMAL	kazoemasite	kazoemaseñ de
Past Ind.	INFORMAL	kazoeta	kazoenakatta
	FORMAL	kazoemasita	kazoemaseñ desita
Past Presump.	INFORMAL	kazoetaroo	kazoenakattaroo
		kazoeta daroo	kazoenakatta daroo
	FORMAL	kazoemasitaroo	kazoemaseñ desitaroo
		kazoeta desyoo	kazoenakatta desyoo
Conditional	INFORMAL	kazoetara	kazoenakattara
	FORMAL	kazoemasitara	kazoemaseñ desitara
Alternative	INFORMAL	kazoetari	kazoenakattari
	FORMAL	kazoemasitari	kazoemaseñ desitari

INFORMAL AFFIRMATIVE INDICATIVE

Passive	kazoerareru	*Honorific*	I	okazoe ni naru
			II	okazoe nasaru
Potential	kazoerareru			
		Humble	I	okazoe suru
Causative	kazoesaseru		II	okazoe itasu
Causative Pass.	kazoesaserareru			

to stain, to defile, to disgrace   TRANSITIVE

		AFFIRMATIVE	NEGATIVE
Indicative	INFORMAL	kegasu	kegasanai
	FORMAL	kegasimasu	kegasimaseñ
Imperative	INFORMAL I	kegase	kegasu na
	II	kegasinasai	kegasinasaru na
	III	kegasite kudasai	kegasanai de kudasai
	FORMAL	okegasi nasaimase	okegasi nasaimasu na
Presumptive	INFORMAL I	kegasoo	kegasumai
	II	kegasu daroo	kegasanai daroo
	FORMAL I	kegasimasyoo	kegasimasumai
	II	kegasu desyoo	kegasanai desyoo
Provisional	INFORMAL	kegaseba	kegasanakereba
	FORMAL	kegasimaseba	kegasimaseñ nara
		kegasimasureba	
Gerund	INFORMAL I	kegasite	kegasanai de
	II		kegasanakute
	FORMAL	kegasimasite	kegasimaseñ de
Past Ind.	INFORMAL	kegasita	kegasanakatta
	FORMAL	kegasimasita	kegasimaseñ desita
Past Presump.	INFORMAL	kegasitaroo	kegasanakattaroo
		kegasita daroo	kegasanakatta daroo
	FORMAL	kegasimasitaroo	kegasimaseñ desitaroo
		kegasita desyoo	kegasanakatta desyoo
Conditional	INFORMAL	kegasitara	kegasanakattara
	FORMAL	kegasimasitara	kegasimaseñ desitara
Alternative	INFORMAL	kegasitari	kegasanakattari
	FORMAL	kegasimasitari	kegasimaseñ desitari

INFORMAL AFFIRMATIVE INDICATIVE

Passive	kegasareru	*Honorific*	I	okegasi ni naru
			II	okegasi nasaru
Potential	kegaseru			
		Humble	I	
Causative	kegasaseru		II	
Causative Pass.	kegasaserareru			

TRANSITIVE   *to erase, to extinguish*

		AFFIRMATIVE	NEGATIVE
Indicative	INFORMAL	kesu	kesanai
	FORMAL	kesimasu	kesimaseñ
Imperative	INFORMAL I	kese	kesu na
	II	kesinasai	kesinasaru na
	III	kesite kudasai	kesanai de kudasai
	FORMAL	okesi nasaimase	okesi nasaimasu na
Presumptive	INFORMAL I	kesoo	kesumai
	II	kesu daroo	kesanai daroo
	FORMAL I	kesimasyoo	kesimasumai
	II	kesu desyoo	kesanai desyoo
Provisional	INFORMAL	keseba	kesanakereba
	FORMAL	kesimaseba	kesimaseñ nara
		kesimasureba	
Gerund	INFORMAL I	kesite	kesanai de
	II		kesanakute
	FORMAL	kesimasite	kesimaseñ de
Past Ind.	INFORMAL	kesita	kesanakatta
	FORMAL	kesimasita	kesimaseñ desita
Past Presump.	INFORMAL	kesitaroo	kesanakattaroo
		kesita daroo	kesanakatta daroo
	FORMAL	kesimasitaroo	kesimaseñ desitaroo
		kesita desyoo	kesanakatta desyoo
Conditional	INFORMAL	kesitara	kesanakattara
	FORMAL	kesimasitara	kesimaseñ desitara
Alternative	INFORMAL	kesitari	kesanakattari
	FORMAL	kesimasitari	kesimaseñ desitari

INFORMAL AFFIRMATIVE INDICATIVE

Passive	kesareru	*Honorific*	I	okesi ni naru
			II	okesi nasaru
Potential	keseru			
		Humble	I	okesi suru
Causative	kesaseru		II	okesi itasu
Causative Pass.	kesaserareru			

		AFFIRMATIVE	NEGATIVE
Indicative	**INFORMAL**	kieru	kienai
	FORMAL	kiemasu	kiemaseñ
Imperative	**INFORMAL I**	kiero	kieru na
	II		
	III		
	FORMAL		
Presumptive	**INFORMAL I**	kieyoo	kiemai
	II	kieru daroo	kienai daroo
	FORMAL I	kiemasyoo	kiemasumai
	II	kieru desyoo	kienai desyoo
Provisional	**INFORMAL**	kiereba	kienakereba
	FORMAL	kiemaseba	kiemaseñ nara
		kiemasureba	
Gerund	**INFORMAL I**	kiete	kienai de
	II		kienakute
	FORMAL	kiemasite	kiemaseñ de
Past Ind.	**INFORMAL**	kieta	kienakatta
	FORMAL	kiemasita	kiemaseñ desita
Past Presump.	**INFORMAL**	kietaroo	kienakattaroo
		kieta daroo	kienakatta daroo
	FORMAL	kiemasitaroo	kiemaseñ desitaroo
		kieta desyoo	kienakatta desyoo
Conditional	**INFORMAL**	kietara	kienakattara
	FORMAL	kiemasitara	kiemaseñ desitara
Alternative	**INFORMAL**	kietari	kienakattari
	FORMAL	kiemasitari	kiemaseñ desitari

INFORMAL AFFIRMATIVE INDICATIVE

Passive	kierareru	*Honorific*	**I**
			II
Potential	kierareru		
		Humble	**I**
Causative	kiesaseru		**II**
Causative Pass.	kiesaserareru		

		AFFIRMATIVE	NEGATIVE
Indicative	**INFORMAL**	kikaeru	kikaenai
	FORMAL	kikaemasu	kikaemseñ
Imperative	**INFORMAL I**	kikaero	kikaeru na
	II	kikaenasai	kikaenasaru na
	III	kikaete kudasai	kikaenai de kudasai
	FORMAL	okikae nasaimase	okikae nasaimasu na
Presumptive	**INFORMAL I**	kikaeyoo	kikaemai
	II	kikaeru daroo	kikaenai daroo
	FORMAL I	kikaemasyoo	kikaemasumai
	II	kikaeru desyoo	kikaenai desyoo
Provisional	**INFORMAL**	kikaereba	kikaenakereba
	FORMAL	kikaemaseba	kikaemseñ nara
		kikaemasureba	
Gerund	**INFORMAL I**	kikaete	kikaenai de
	II		kikaenakute
	FORMAL	kikaemasite	kikaemañ de
Past Ind.	**INFORMAL**	kikaeta	kikaenakatta
	FORMAL	kikaemasita	kikaemañ desita
Past Presump.	**INFORMAL**	kikaetaroo	kikaenakattaroo
		kikaeta daroo	kikaenakatta daroo
	FORMAL	kikaemasitaroo	kikaemañ desitaroo
		kikaeta desyoo	kikaenakatta desyoo
Conditional	**INFORMAL**	kikaetara	kikaenakattara
	FORMAL	kikaemasitara	kikaemañ desitara
Alternative	**INFORMAL**	kikaetari	kikaenakattari
	FORMAL	kikaemasitari	kikaemañ desitari

INFORMAL AFFIRMATIVE INDICATIVE

Passive	kikaerareru	*Honorific*	**I**	okikae ni naru
			II	okikae nasaru
Potential	kikaerareru			
		Humble	**I**	
Causative	kikaesaseru		**II**	
Causative Pass.	kikaesaserareru			

		AFFIRMATIVE	NEGATIVE
Indicative	INFORMAL	kikoeru	kikoenai
	FORMAL	kikoemasu	kikoemaseñ
Imperative	INFORMAL I		
	II		
	III		
	FORMAL		
Presumptive	INFORMAL I	kikoeyoo	kikoemai
	II	kikoeru daroo	kikoenai daroo
	FORMAL I	kikoemasyoo	kikoemasumai
	II	kikoeru desyoo	kikoenai desyoo
Provisional	INFORMAL	kikoereba	kikoenakereba
	FORMAL	kikoemaseba	kikoemaseñ nara
		kikoemasureba	
Gerund	INFORMAL I	kikoete	kikoenai de
	II		kikoenakute
	FORMAL	kikoemasite	kikoemaseñ de
Past Ind.	INFORMAL	kikoeta	kikoenakatta
	FORMAL	kikoemasita	kikoemaseñ desita
Past Presump.	INFORMAL	kikoetaroo	kikoenakattaroo
		kikoeta daroo	kikoenakatta daroo
	FORMAL	kikoemasitaroo	kikoemaseñ desitaroo
		kikoeta desyoo	kikoenakatta desyoo
Conditional	INFORMAL	kikoetara	kikoenakattara
	FORMAL	kikoemasitara	kikoemaseñ desitara
Alternative	INFORMAL	kikoetari	kikoenakattari
	FORMAL	kikoemasitari	kikoemaseñ desitari

INFORMAL AFFIRMATIVE INDICATIVE

Passive		*Honorific*	I
			II
Potential			
		Humble	I
Causative			II

Causative Pass.

		TRANSITIVE	*to ask, to listen, to hear*
		AFFIRMATIVE	**NEGATIVE**
Indicative	INFORMAL	kiku	kikanai
	FORMAL	kikimasu	kikimaseñ
Imperative	INFORMAL I	kike	kiku na
	II	kikinasai	kikinasaru na
	III	kiite kudasai	kikanai de kudasai
	FORMAL	okiki nasaimase	okiki nasaimasu na
Presumptive	INFORMAL I	kikoo	kikumai
	II	kiku daroo	kikanai daroo
	FORMAL I	kikimasyoo	kikimasumai
	II	kiku desyoo	kikanai desyoo
Provisional	INFORMAL	kikeba	kikanakereba
	FORMAL	kikimaseba	kikimaseñ nara
		kikimasureba	
Gerund	INFORMAL I	kiite	kikanai de
	II		kikanakute
	FORMAL	kikimasite	kikimaseñ de
Past Ind.	INFORMAL	kiita	kikanakatta
	FORMAL	kikimasita	kikimaseñ desita
Past Presump.	INFORMAL	kiitaroo	kikanakattaroo
		kiita daroo	kikanakatta daroo
	FORMAL	kikimasitaroo	kikimaseñ desitaroo
		kiita desyoo	kikanakatta desyoo
Conditional	INFORMAL	kiitara	kikanakattara
	FORMAL	kikimasitara	kikimaseñ desitara
Alternative	INFORMAL	kiitari	kikanakattari
	FORMAL	kikimasitari	kikimaseñ desitari

INFORMAL AFFIRMATIVE INDICATIVE

Passive	kikareru	*Honorific*	I	okiki ni naru	
			II	okiki nasaru	
Potential	kikeru*				
		*Humble** **		ukagau	uketamawaru
Causative	kikaseru				
Causative Pass.	kikaserareru				

*Only in the sense of 'can ask or listen,' 'to be audible' is a separate verb *kikoeru.*
**Ukagau* means 'to ask,' while *uketamawaru* means 'to hear or listen.'

		AFFIRMATIVE	NEGATIVE
Indicative	INFORMAL	kimaru	kimaranai
	FORMAL	kimarimasu	kimarimaseñ
Imperative	INFORMAL I		
	II		
	III		
	FORMAL		
Presumptive	INFORMAL I	kimaroo	kimarumai
	II	kimaru daroo	kimaranai daroo
	FORMAL I	kimarimasyoo	kimarimasumai
	II	kimaru desyoo	kimaranai desyoo
Provisional	INFORMAL	kimareba	kimaranakereba
	FORMAL	kimarimaseba	kimarimaseñ nara
		kimarimasureba	
Gerund	INFORMAL I	kimatte	kimaranai de
	II		kimaranakute
	FORMAL	kimarimasite	kimarimaseñ de
Past Ind.	INFORMAL	kimatta	kimaranakatta
	FORMAL	kimarimasita	kimarimaseñ desita
Past Presump.	INFORMAL	kimattaroo	kimaranakattaroo
		kimatta daroo	kimaranakatta daroo
	FORMAL	kimarimasitaroo	kimarimaseñ desitaroo
		kimatta desyoo	kimaranakatta desyoo
Conditional	INFORMAL	kimattara	kimaranakattara
	FORMAL	kimarimasitara	kimarimaseñ desitara
Alternative	INFORMAL	kimattari	kimaranakattari
	FORMAL	kimarimasitari	kimarimaseñ desitari

INFORMAL AFFIRMATIVE INDICATIVE

Passive	kimarareru	*Honorific*	I
			II
Potential	kimareru		
		Humble	I
Causative	kimaraseru		II
Causative Pass.	kimaraserareru		

		AFFIRMATIVE	NEGATIVE
Indicative	INFORMAL	kimeru	kimenai
	FORMAL	kimemasu	kimemaseñ
Imperative	INFORMAL I	kimero	kimeru na
	II	kimenasai	kimenasaru na
	III	kimete kudasai	kimenai de kudasai
	FORMAL	okime nasaimase	okime nasaimasu na
Presumptive	INFORMAL I	kimeyoo	kimemai
	II	kimeru daroo	kimenai daroo
	FORMAL I	kimemasyoo	kimemasumai
	II	kimeru desyoo	kimenai desyoo
Provisional	INFORMAL	kimereba	kimenakereba
	FORMAL	kimemaseba	kimemaseñ nara
		kimemasureba	
Gerund	INFORMAL I	kimete	kimenai de
	II		kimenakute
	FORMAL	kimemasite	kimemaseñ de
Past Ind.	INFORMAL	kimeta	kimenakatta
	FORMAL	kimemasita	kimemaseñ desita
Past Presump.	INFORMAL	kimetaroo	kimenakattaroo
		kimeta daroo	kimenakatta daroo
	FORMAL	kimemasitaroo	kimemaseñ desitaroo
		kimeta desyoo	kimenakatta desyoo
Conditional	INFORMAL	kimetara	kimenakattara
	FORMAL	kimemasitara	kimemaseñ desitara
Alternative	INFORMAL	kimetari	kimenakattari
	FORMAL	kimemasitari	kimemaseñ desitari

INFORMAL AFFIRMATIVE INDICATIVE

Passive	kimerareru	*Honorific*	I	okime ni naru
			II	okime nasaru
Potential	kimerareru			
		Humble	I	okime suru
Causative	kimesaseru		II	okime itasu
Causative Pass.	kimesaserareru			

		AFFIRMATIVE	NEGATIVE
Indicative	INFORMAL	kiñziru	kiñzinai
	FORMAL	kiñzimasu	kiñzimaseñ
Imperative	INFORMAL I	kiñziro	kiñziru na
	II	kiñzinasai	kiñzinasaru na
	III	kiñzite kudasai	kiñzinai de kudasai
	FORMAL	okiñzi nasaimase	okiñzi nasaimasu na
Presumptive	INFORMAL I	kiñziyoo	kiñzimai
	II	kiñziru daroo	kiñzinai daroo
	FORMAL I	kiñzimasyoo	kiñzimasumai
	II	kiñziru desyoo	kiñzinai desyoo
Provisional	INFORMAL	kiñzireba	kiñzinakereba
	FORMAL	kiñzimaseba	kiñzimaseñ nara
		kiñzimasureba	
Gerund	INFORMAL I	kiñzite	kiñzinai de
	II		kiñzinakute
	FORMAL	kiñzimasite	kiñzimaseñ de
Past Ind.	INFORMAL	kiñzita	kiñzinakatta
	FORMAL	kiñzimasita	kiñzimaseñ desita
Past Presump.	INFORMAL	kiñzitaroo	kiñzinakattaroo
		kiñzita daroo	kiñzinakatta daroo
	FORMAL	kiñzimasitaroo	kiñzimaseñ desitaroo
		kiñzita desyoo	kiñzinakatta desyoo
Conditional	INFORMAL	kiñzitara	kiñzinakattara
	FORMAL	kiñzimasitara	kiñzimaseñ desitara
Alternative	INFORMAL	kiñzitari	kiñzinakattari
	FORMAL	kiñzimasitari	kiñzimaseñ desitari

INFORMAL AFFIRMATIVE INDICATIVE

Passive	kiñzirareru	*Honorific*	I	okiñzi ni naru
			II	okiñzi nasaru
Potential	kiñzirareru			
		Humble	I	okiñzi suru
Causative	kiñzisaseru		II	okiñzi itasu
Causative Pass.	kiñzisaserareru			

		AFFIRMATIVE	NEGATIVE
Indicative	INFORMAL	kiru	kiranai
	FORMAL	kirimasu	kirimaseñ
Imperative	INFORMAL I	kire	kiru na
	II	kirinasai	kirinasaru na
	III	kitte kudasai	kiranai de kudasai
	FORMAL	okiri nasaimase	okiri nasaimasu na
Presumptive	INFORMAL I	kiroo	kirumai
	II	kiru daroo	kiranai daroo
	FORMAL I	kirimasyoo	kirimasumai
	II	kiru desyoo	kiranai desyoo
Provisional	INFORMAL	kireba	kiranakereba
	FORMAL	kirimaseba	kirimaseñ nara
		kirimasureba	
Gerund	INFORMAL I	kitte	kiranai de
	II		kiranakute
	FORMAL	kirimasite	kirimaseñ de
Past Ind.	INFORMAL	kitta	kiranakatta
	FORMAL	kirimasita	kirimaseñ desita
Past Presump.	INFORMAL	kittaroo	kiranakattaroo
		kitta daroo	kiranakatta daroo
	FORMAL	kirimasitaroo	kirimaseñ desitaroo
		kitta desyoo	kiranakatta desyoo
Conditional	INFORMAL	kittara	kiranakattara
	FORMAL	kirimasitara	kirimaseñ desitara
Alternative	INFORMAL	kittari	kiranakattari
	FORMAL	kirimasitari	kirimaseñ desitari

INFORMAL AFFIRMATIVE INDICATIVE

Passive	kirareru		*Honorific*	I	okiri ni naru
				II	okiri nasaru
Potential	kireru				
			Humble	I	okiri suru
Causative	kiraseru			II	okiri itasu
Causative Pass.	kiraserareru				

		AFFIRMATIVE	NEGATIVE
Indicative	INFORMAL	kiru	kinai
	FORMAL	kimasu	kimaseñ
Imperative	INFORMAL I	kiro	kiru na
	II	kinasai	kinasaru na
	III	kite kudasai	kinai de kudasai
	FORMAL	omesi nasaimase	omesi nasaimasu na
Presumptive	INFORMAL I	kiyoo	kimai
	II	kiru daroo	kinai daroo
	FORMAL I	kimasyoo	kimasumai
	II	kiru desyoo	kinai desyoo
Provisional	INFORMAL	kireba	kinakereba
	FORMAL	kimaseba	kimaseñ nara
		kimasureba	
Gerund	INFORMAL I	kite	kinai de
	II		kinakute
	FORMAL	kimasite	kimaseñ de
Past Ind.	INFORMAL	kita	kinakatta
	FORMAL	kimasita	kimaseñ desita
Past Presump.	INFORMAL	kitaroo	kinakattaroo
		kita daroo	kinakatta daroo
	FORMAL	kimasitaroo	kimaseñ desitaroo
		kita desyoo	kinakatta desyoo
Conditional	INFORMAL	kitara	kinakattara
	FORMAL	kimasitara	kimaseñ desitara
Alternative	INFORMAL	kitari	kinakattari
	FORMAL	kimasitari	kimaseñ desitari

INFORMAL AFFIRMATIVE INDICATIVE

Passive	kirareru	*Honorific*	I	omesi ni naru
			II	omesi nasaru
Potential	kirareru			
		Humble	I	
Causative	kisaseru		II	
Causative Pass.	kisaserareru			

		AFFIRMATIVE	NEGATIVE
Indicative	INFORMAL	koboreru	koborenai
	FORMAL	koboremasu	koboremaseñ
Imperative	INFORMAL I	koborero	koboreru na
	II		
	III		
	FORMAL		
Presumptive	INFORMAL I	koboreyoo	koboremai
	II	koboreru daroo	koborenai daroo
	FORMAL I	koboremasyoo	koboremasumai
	II	koboreru desyoo	koborenai desyoo
Provisional	INFORMAL	koborereba	koborenakereba
	FORMAL	koboremaseba	koboremaseñ nara
		koboremasureba	
Gerund	INFORMAL I	koborete	koborenai de
	II		koborenakute
	FORMAL	koboremasite	koboremaseñ de
Past Ind.	INFORMAL	koboreta	koborenakatta
	FORMAL	koboremasita	koboremaseñ desita
Past Presump.	INFORMAL	koboretaroo	koborenakattaroo
		koboreta daroo	koborenakatta daroo
	FORMAL	koboremasitaroo	koboremaseñ desitaroo
		koboreta desyoo	koborenakatta desyoo
Conditional	INFORMAL	koboretara	koborenakattara
	FORMAL	koboremasitara	koboremaseñ desitara
Alternative	INFORMAL	koboretari	koborenakattari
	FORMAL	koboremasitari	koboremaseñ desitari

INFORMAL AFFIRMATIVE INDICATIVE

Passive	koborerareru	*Honorific*	I
			II
Potential	koborerareru		
		Humble	I
Causative	koboresaseru		II

Causative Pass.

			AFFIRMATIVE	NEGATIVE
Indicative	INFORMAL		kobosu	kobosanai
	FORMAL		kobosimasu	kobosimaseñ
Imperative	INFORMAL	I	kobose	kobosu na
		II	kobosinasai	kobosinasaru na
		III	kobosite kudasai	kobosanai de kudasai
	FORMAL		okobosi nasaimase	okobosi nasaimasu na
Presumptive	INFORMAL	I	kobosoo	kobosumai
		II	kobosu daroo	kobosanai daroo
	FORMAL	I	kobosimasyoo	kobosimasumai
		II	kobosu desyoo	kobosanai desyoo
Provisional	INFORMAL		koboseba	kobosanakereba
	FORMAL		kobosimaseba	kobosimaseñ nara
			kobosimasureba	
Gerund	INFORMAL	I	kobosite	kobosanai de
		II		kobosanakute
	FORMAL		kobosimasite	kobosimaseñ de
Past Ind.	INFORMAL		kobosita	kobosanakatta
	FORMAL		kobosimasita	kobosimaseñ desita
Past Presump.	INFORMAL		kobositaroo	kobosanakattaroo
			kobosita daroo	kobosanakatta daroo
	FORMAL		kobosimasitaroo	kobosimaseñ desitaroo
			kobosita desyoo	kobosanakatta desyoo
Conditional	INFORMAL		kobositara	kobosanakattara
	FORMAL		kobosimasitara	kobosimaseñ desitara
Alternative	INFORMAL		kobositari	kobosanakattari
	FORMAL		kobosimasitari	kobosimaseñ desitari

INFORMAL AFFIRMATIVE INDICATIVE

Passive	kobosareru	*Honorific*	I	okobosi ni naru
			II	okobosi nasaru
Potential	koboseru			
		Humble	I	okobosi suru
Causative	kobosaseru		II	okobosi itasu
Causative Pass.	kobosaserareru			

TRANSITIVE   *to cross over, to exceed*

		AFFIRMATIVE	**NEGATIVE**
Indicative	**INFORMAL**	koeru	koenai
	FORMAL	koemasu	koemaseñ
Imperative	**INFORMAL I**	koero	koeru na
	II	koenasai	koenasaru na
	III	koete kudasai	koenai de kudasai
	FORMAL	okoe nasaimase	okoe nasaimasu na
Presumptive	**INFORMAL I**	koeyoo	koemai
	II	koeru daroo	koenai daroo
	FORMAL I	koemasyoo	koemasumai
	II	koeru desyoo	koenai desyoo
Provisional	**INFORMAL**	koereba	koenakereba
	FORMAL	koemaseba	koemaseñ nara
		koemasureba	
Gerund	**INFORMAL I**	koete	koenai de
	II		koenakute
	FORMAL	koemasite	koemaseñ de
Past Ind.	**INFORMAL**	koeta	koenakatta
	FORMAL	koemasita	koemaseñ desita
Past Presump.	**INFORMAL**	koetaroo	koenakattaroo
		koeta daroo	koenakatta daroo
	FORMAL	koemasitaroo	koemaseñ desitaroo
		koeta desyoo	koenakatta desyoo
Conditional	**INFORMAL**	koetara	koenakattara
	FORMAL	koemasitara	koemaseñ desitara
Alternative	**INFORMAL**	koetari	koenakattari
	FORMAL	koemasitari	koemaseñ desitari

INFORMAL AFFIRMATIVE INDICATIVE

Passive	koerareru	*Honorific*	**I**	okoe ni naru
			II	okoe nasaru
Potential	koerareru			
		Humble	**I**	okoe suru
Causative	koesaseru		**II**	okoe itasu
Causative Pass.	koesaserareru			

		AFFIRMATIVE	NEGATIVE
Indicative	INFORMAL	komaru	komaranai
	FORMAL	komarimasu	komarimaseñ
Imperative	INFORMAL I	komare	komaru na
	II		
	III		
	FORMAL		
Presumptive	INFORMAL I	komaroo	komarumai
	II	komaru daroo	komaranai daroo
	FORMAL I	komarimasyoo	komarimasumai
	II	komaru desyoo	komaranai desyoo
Provisional	INFORMAL	komareba	komaranakereba
	FORMAL	komarimaseba	komarimaseñ nara
		komarimasureba	
Gerund	INFORMAL I	komatte	komaranai de
	II		komaranakute
	FORMAL	komarimasite	komarimaseñ de
Past Ind.	INFORMAL	komatta	komaranakatta
	FORMAL	komarimasita	komarimaseñ desita
Past Presump.	INFORMAL	komattaroo	komaranakattaroo
		komatta daroo	komaranakatta daroo
	FORMAL	komarimasitaroo	komarimaseñ desitaroo
		komatta desyoo	komaranakatta desyoo
Conditional	INFORMAL	komattara	komaranakattara
	FORMAL	komarimasitara	komarimaseñ desitara
Alternative	INFORMAL	komattari	komaranakattari
	FORMAL	komarimasitari	komarimaseñ desitari

INFORMAL AFFIRMATIVE INDICATIVE

Passive	komarareru	*Honorific*	I	okomari ni naru
			II	okomari nasaru
Potential				
		Humble	I	
Causative	komaraseru		II	
Causative Pass.	komaraserareru			

		AFFIRMATIVE	NEGATIVE
Indicative	INFORMAL	komu	komanai
	FORMAL	komimasu	komimaseñ
Imperative	INFORMAL I		
	II		
	III		
	FORMAL		
Presumptive	INFORMAL I	komoo	komumai
	II	komu daroo	komanai daroo
	FORMAL I	komimasyoo	komimasumai
	II	komu desyoo	komanai desyoo
Provisional	INFORMAL	komeba	komanakereba
	FORMAL	komimaseba	komimaseñ nara
		komimasureba	
Gerund	INFORMAL I	koñde	komanai de
	II		komanakute
	FORMAL	komimasite	komimaseñ de
Past Ind.	INFORMAL	koñda	komanakatta
	FORMAL	komimasita	komimaseñ desita
Past Presump.	INFORMAL	koñdaroo	komanakattaroo
		koñda daroo	komanakatta daroo
	FORMAL	komimasitaroo	komimaseñ desitaroo
		koñda desyoo	komanakatta desyoo
Conditional	INFORMAL	koñdara	komanakattara
	FORMAL	komimasitara	komimaseñ desitara
Alternative	INFORMAL	koñdari	komanakattari
	FORMAL	komimasitari	komimaseñ desitari

INFORMAL AFFIRMATIVE INDICATIVE

Passive		*Honorific*	I
			II
Potential			
		Humble	I
Causative			II

Causative Pass.

		AFFIRMATIVE	NEGATIVE
Indicative	INFORMAL	konomu	konomanai
	FORMAL	konomimasu	konomimaseñ
Imperative	INFORMAL I	konome	konomu na
	II	konominasai	konominasaru na
	III	konoñde kudasai	konomanai de kudasai
	FORMAL	okonomi nasaimase	okonomi nasaimasu na
Presumptive	INFORMAL I	konomoo	konomumai
	II	konomu daroo	konomanai daroo
	FORMAL I	konomimasyoo	konomimasumai
	II	konomu desyoo	konomanai desyoo
Provisional	INFORMAL	konomeba	konomanakereba
	FORMAL	konomimaseba	konomimaseñ nara
		konomimasureba	
Gerund	INFORMAL I	konoñde	konomanai de
	II		konomanakute
	FORMAL	konomimasite	konomimaseñ de
Past Ind.	INFORMAL	konoñda	konomanakatta
	FORMAL	konomimasita	konomimaseñ desita
Past Presump.	INFORMAL	konoñdaroo	konomanakattaroo
		konoñda daroo	konomanakatta daroo
	FORMAL	konomimasitaroo	konomimaseñ desitaroo
		konoñda desyoo	konomanakatta desyoo
Conditional	INFORMAL	konoñdara	konomanakattara
	FORMAL	konomimasitara	konomimaseñ desitara
Alternative	INFORMAL	konoñdari	konomanakattari
	FORMAL	konomimasitari	konomimaseñ desitari

INFORMAL AFFIRMATIVE INDICATIVE

Passive	konomareru	*Honorific*	I	okonomi ni naru
			II	okonomi nasaru
Potential	konomeru			
		Humble	I	
Causative	konomaseru		II	
Causative Pass.	konomaserareru			

		AFFIRMATIVE	NEGATIVE
Indicative	INFORMAL	kooru	kooranai
	FORMAL	koorimasu	koorimaseñ
Imperative	INFORMAL I	koore	kooru na
	II		
	III		
	FORMAL		
Presumptive	INFORMAL I	kooroo	koorumai
	II	kooru daroo	kooranai daroo
	FORMAL I	koorimasyoo	koorimasumai
	II	kooru desyoo	kooranai desyoo
Provisional	INFORMAL	kooreba	kooranakereba
	FORMAL	koorimaseba	koorimaseñ nara
		koorimasureba	
Gerund	INFORMAL I	kootte	kooranai de
	II		kooranakute
	FORMAL	koorimasite	koorimaseñ de
Past Ind.	INFORMAL	kootta	kooranakatta
	FORMAL	koorimasita	koorimaseñ desita
Past Presump.	INFORMAL	koottaroo	kooranakattaroo
		kootta daroo	kooranakatta daroo
	FORMAL	koorimasitaroo	koorimaseñ desitaroo
		kootta desyoo	kooranakatta desyoo
Conditional	INFORMAL	koottara	kooranakattara
	FORMAL	koorimasitara	koorimaseñ desitara
Alternative	INFORMAL	koottari	kooranakattari
	FORMAL	koorimasitari	koorimaseñ desitari

INFORMAL AFFIRMATIVE INDICATIVE

Passive	koorareru	*Honorific*	I	
			II	
Potential	kooreru			
		Humble	I	
Causative	kooraseru		II	
Causative Pass.	kooraserareru			

			AFFIRMATIVE	NEGATIVE
Indicative	INFORMAL		koraeru	koraenai
	FORMAL		koraemasu	koraemaseñ
Imperative	INFORMAL	I	koraero	koraeru na
		II	koraenasai	koraenasaru na
		III	koraete kudasai	koraenai de kudasai
	FORMAL		okorae nasaimase	okorae nasaimasu na
Presumptive	INFORMAL	I	koraeyoo	koraemai
		II	koraeru daroo	koraenai daroo
	FORMAL	I	koraemasyoo	koraemasumai
		II	koraeru desyoo	koraenai desyoo
Provisional	INFORMAL		koraereba	koraenakereba
	FORMAL		koraemaseba	koraemaseñ nara
			koraemasureba	
Gerund	INFORMAL	I	koraete	koraenai de
		II		koraenakute
	FORMAL		koraemasite	koraemaseñ de
Past Ind.	INFORMAL		koraeta	koraenakatta
	FORMAL		koraemasita	koraemaseñ desita
Past Presump.	INFORMAL		koraetaroo	koraenakattaroo
			koraeta daroo	koraenakatta daroo
	FORMAL		koraemasitaroo	koraemaseñ desitaroo
			koraeta desyoo	koraenakatta desyoo
Conditional	INFORMAL		koraetara	koraenakattara
	FORMAL		koraemasitara	koraemaseñ desitara
Alternative	INFORMAL		koraetari	koraenakattari
	FORMAL		koraemasitari	koraemaseñ desitari

INFORMAL AFFIRMATIVE INDICATIVE

Passive	koraerareru	*Honorific*	I	okorae ni naru
			II	okorae nasaru
Potential	koraerareru			
		Humble	I	okorae suru
Causative	koraesaseru		II	okorae itasu
Causative Pass.	koraesaserareru			

		AFFIRMATIVE	NEGATIVE
Indicative	**INFORMAL**	korasimeru	korasimenai
	FORMAL	korasimemasu	korasimemaseñ
Imperative	**INFORMAL I**	korasimero	korasimeru na
	II	korasimenasai	korasimenasaru na
	III	korasimete kudasai	korasimenai de kudasai
	FORMAL	okorasime nasaimase	okorasime nasaimasu na
Presumptive	**INFORMAL I**	korasimeyoo	korasimemai
	II	korasimeru daroo	korasimenai daroo
	FORMAL I	korasimemasyoo	korasimemasumai
	II	korasimeru desyoo	korasimenai desyoo
Provisional	**INFORMAL**	korasimereba	korasimenakereba
	FORMAL	korasimemaseba	korasimemaseñ nara
		korasimemasureba	
Gerund	**INFORMAL I**	korasimete	korasimenai de
	II		korasimenakute
	FORMAL	korasimemasite	korasimemaseñ de
Past Ind.	**INFORMAL**	korasimeta	korasimenakatta
	FORMAL	korasimemasita	korasimemaseñ desita
Past Presump.	**INFORMAL**	korasimetaroo	korasimenakattaroo
		korasimeta daroo	korasimenakatta daroo
	FORMAL	korasimemasitaroo	korasimemaseñ desitaroo
		korasimeta desyoo	korasimenakatta desyoo
Conditional	**INFORMAL**	korasimetara	korasimenakattara
	FORMAL	korasimemasitara	korasimemaseñ desitara
Alternative	**INFORMAL**	korasimetari	korasimenakattari
	FORMAL	korasimemasitari	korasimemaseñ desitari

INFORMAL AFFIRMATIVE INDICATIVE

Passive	korasimerareru	*Honorific*	**I**	okorasime ni naru
			II	okorasime nasaru
Potential	korasimerareru			
		Humble	**I**	okorasime suru
Causative	korasimesaseru		**II**	okorasime itasu
Causative Pass.	korasimesaserareru			

		AFFIRMATIVE	NEGATIVE
Indicative	INFORMAL	korobu	korobanai
	FORMAL	korobimasu	korobimaseñ
Imperative	INFORMAL I	korobe	korobu na
	II	korobinasai	korobinasaru na
	III	koroñde kudasai	korobanai de kudasai
	FORMAL	okorobi nasaimase	okorobi nasaimasu na
Presumptive	INFORMAL I	koroboo	korobumai
	II	korobu daroo	korobanai daroo
	FORMAL I	korobimasyoo	korobimasumai
	II	korobu desyoo	korobanai desyoo
Provisional	INFORMAL	korobeba	korobanakereba
	FORMAL	korobimaseba	korobimaseñ nara
		korobimasureba	
Gerund	INFORMAL I	koroñde	korobanai de
	II		korobanakute
	FORMAL	korobimasite	korobimaseñ de
Past Ind.	INFORMAL	koroñda	korobanakatta
	FORMAL	korobimasita	korobimaseñ desita
Past Presump.	INFORMAL	koroñdaroo	korobanakattaroo
		koroñda daroo	korobanakatta daroo
	FORMAL	korobimasitaroo	korobimaseñ desitaroo
		koroñda desyoo	korobanakatta desyoo
Conditional	INFORMAL	koroñdara	korobanakattara
	FORMAL	korobimasitara	korobimaseñ desitara
Alternative	INFORMAL	koroñdari	korobanakattari
	FORMAL	korobimasitari	korobimaseñ desitari

INFORMAL AFFIRMATIVE INDICATIVE

Passive	korobareru	*Honorific*	I	okorobi ni naru
			II	okorobi nasaru
Potential	koroberu	*Humble*	I	
Causative	korobaseru		II	
Causative Pass.	korobaserareru			

TRANSITIVE   *to kill*

		AFFIRMATIVE	NEGATIVE
Indicative	INFORMAL	korosu	korosanai
	FORMAL	korosimasu	korosimaseñ
Imperative	INFORMAL I	korose	korosu na
	II	korosinasai	korosinasaru na
	III	korosite kudasai	korosanai de kudasai
	FORMAL	okorosi nasaimase	okorosi nasaimasu na
Presumptive	INFORMAL I	korosoo	korosumai
	II	korosu daroo	korosanai daroo
	FORMAL I	korosimasyoo	korosimasumai
	II	korosu desyoo	korosanai desyoo
Provisional	INFORMAL	koroseba	korosanakereba
	FORMAL	korosimaseba	korosimaseñ nara
		korosimasureba	
Gerund	INFORMAL I	korosite	korosanai de
	II		korosanakute
	FORMAL	korosimasite	korosimaseñ de
Past Ind.	INFORMAL	korosita	korosanakatta
	FORMAL	korosimasita	korosimaseñ desita
Past Presump.	INFORMAL	korositaroo	korosanakattaroo
		korosita daroo	korosanakatta daroo
	FORMAL	korosimasitaroo	korosimaseñ desitaroo
		korosita desyoo	korosanakatta desyoo
Conditional	INFORMAL	korositara	korosanakattara
	FORMAL	korosimasitara	korosimaseñ desitara
Alternative	INFORMAL	korositari	korosanakattari
	FORMAL	korosimasitari	korosimaseñ desitari

INFORMAL AFFIRMATIVE INDICATIVE

Passive	korosareru	*Honorific*	I	okorosi ni naru
			II	okorosi nasaru
Potential	koroseru			
		Humble	I	okorosi suru
Causative	korosaseru		II	okorosi itasu
Causative Pass.	korosaserareru			

			AFFIRMATIVE	NEGATIVE
Indicative	**INFORMAL**		kosikakeru	kosikakenai
	FORMAL		kosikakemasu	kosikakemaseñ
Imperative	**INFORMAL**	**I**	kosikakero	kosikakeru na
		II	kosikakenasai	kosikakenasaru na
		III	kosikakete kudasai	kosikakenai de kudasai
	FORMAL		okosikake nasaimase	okosikake nasaimasu na
Presumptive	**INFORMAL**	**I**	kosikakeyoo	kosikakemai
		II	kosikakeru daroo	kosikakenai daroo
	FORMAL	**I**	kosikakemasyoo	kosikakemasumai
		II	kosikakeru desyoo	kosikakenai desyoo
Provisional	**INFORMAL**		kosikakereba	kosikakenakereba
	FORMAL		kosikakemaseba	kosikakemaseñ nara
			kosikakemasureba	
Gerund	**INFORMAL**	**I**	kosikakete	kosikakenai de
		II		kosikakenakute
	FORMAL		kosikakemasite	kosikakemaseñ de
Past Ind.	**INFORMAL**		kosikaketa	kosikakenakatta
	FORMAL		kosikakemasita	kosikakemaseñ desita
Past Presump.	**INFORMAL**		kosikaketaroo	kosikakenakattaroo
			kosikaketa daroo	kosikakenakatta daroo
	FORMAL		kosikakemasitaroo	kosikakemaseñ desitaroo
			kosikaketa desyoo	kosikakenakatta desyoo
Conditional	**INFORMAL**		kosikaketara	kosikakenakattara
	FORMAL		kosikakemasitara	kosikakemaseñ desitara
Alternative	**INFORMAL**		kosikaketari	kosikakenakattari
	FORMAL		kosikakemasitari	kosikakemaseñ desitari

INFORMAL AFFIRMATIVE INDICATIVE

Passive	kosikakerareru	*Honorific*	**I**	okosikake ni naru
			II	okosikake nasaru
Potential	kosikakerareru			
		Humble	**I**	
Causative	kosikakesaseru		**II**	
Causative Pass.	kosikakesaserareru			

		AFFIRMATIVE	NEGATIVE
Indicative	**INFORMAL**	kotaeru	kotaenai
	FORMAL	kotaemasu	kotaemaseñ
Imperative	**INFORMAL I**	kotaero	kotaeru na
	II	kotaenasai	kotaenasaru na
	III	kotaete kudasai	kotaenai de kudasai
	FORMAL	okotae nasaimase	okotae nasaimasu na
Presumptive	**INFORMAL I**	kotaeyoo	kotaemai
	II	kotaeru daroo	kotaenai daroo
	FORMAL I	kotaemasyoo	kotaemasumai
	II	kotaeru desyoo	kotaenai desyoo
Provisional	**INFORMAL**	kotaereba	kotaenakereba
	FORMAL	kotaemaseba	kotaemaseñ nara
		kotaemasureba	
Gerund	**INFORMAL I**	kotaete	kotaenai de
	II		kotaenakute
	FORMAL	kotaemasite	kotaemaseñ de
Past Ind.	**INFORMAL**	kotaeta	kotaenakatta
	FORMAL	kotaemasita	kotaemaseñ desita
Past Presump.	**INFORMAL**	kotaetaroo	kotaenakattaroo
		kotaeta daroo	kotaenakatta daroo
	FORMAL	kotaemasitaroo	kotaemaseñ desitaroo
		kotaeta desyoo	kotaenakatta desyoo
Conditional	**INFORMAL**	kotaetara	kotaenakattara
	FORMAL	kotaemasitara	kotaemaseñ desitara
Alternative	**INFORMAL**	kotaetari	kotaenakattari
	FORMAL	kotaemasitari	kotaemaseñ desitari

INFORMAL AFFIRMATIVE INDICATIVE

Passive	kotaerareru	*Honorific*	**I**	okotae ni naru
			II	okotae nasaru
Potential	kotaerareru			
		Humble	**I**	okotae suru
Causative	kotaesaseru		**II**	okotae itasu
Causative Pass.	kotaesaserareru			

		AFFIRMATIVE	NEGATIVE
Indicative	INFORMAL	kotonaru	kotonaranai
	FORMAL	kotonarimasu	kotonarimaseñ
Imperative	INFORMAL I	kotonare	kotonaru na
	II		
	III	kotonatte kudasai	kotonaranai de kudasai
	FORMAL		
Presumptive	INFORMAL I	kotonaroo	kotonarumai
	II	kotonaru daroo	kotonaranai daroo
	FORMAL I	kotonarimasyoo	kotonarimasumai
	II	kotonaru desyoo	kotonaranai desyoo
Provisional	INFORMAL	kotonareba	kotonaranakereba
	FORMAL	kotonarimaseba	kotonarimaseñ nara
		kotonarimasureba	
Gerund	INFORMAL I	kotonatte	kotonaranai de
	II		kotonaranakute
	FORMAL	kotonarimasite	kotonarimaseñ de
Past Ind.	INFORMAL	kotonatta	kotonaranakatta
	FORMAL	kotonarimasita	kotonarimaseñ desita
Past Presump.	INFORMAL	kotonattaroo	kotonaranakattaroo
		kotonatta daroo	kotonaranakatta daroo
	FORMAL	kotonarimasitaroo	kotonarimaseñ desitaroo
		kotonatta desyoo	kotonaranakatta desyoo
Conditional	INFORMAL	kotonattara	kotonaranakattara
	FORMAL	kotonarimasitara	kotonarimaseñ desitara
Alternative	INFORMAL	kotonattari	kotonaranakattari
	FORMAL	kotonarimasitari	kotonarimaseñ desitari

INFORMAL AFFIRMATIVE INDICATIVE

Passive		*Honorific*	I
			II
Potential			
		Humble	I
Causative	kotonaraseru		II
Causative Pass.	kotonaraserareru		

TRANSITIVE *to refuse*

		AFFIRMATIVE	NEGATIVE
Indicative	INFORMAL	kotowaru	kotowaranai
	FORMAL	kotowarimasu	kotowarimaseñ
Imperative	INFORMAL I	kotoware	kotowaru na
	II	kotowarinasai	kotowarinasaru na
	III	kotowatte kudasai	kotowaranai de kudasai
	FORMAL	okotowari nasaimase	okotowari nasaimasu na
Presumptive	INFORMAL I	kotowaroo	kotowarumai
	II	kotowaru daroo	kotowaranai daroo
	FORMAL I	kotowarimasyoo	kotowarimasumai
	II	kotowaru desyoo	kotowaranai desyoo
Provisional	INFORMAL	kotowareba	kotowaranakereba
	FORMAL	kotowarimaseba	kotowarimaseñ nara
		kotowarimasureba	
Gerund	INFORMAL I	kotowatte	kotowaranai de
	II		kotowaranakute
	FORMAL	kotowarimasite	kotowarimaseñ de
Past Ind.	INFORMAL	kotowatta	kotowaranakatta
	FORMAL	kotowarimasita	kotowarimaseñ desita
Past Presump.	INFORMAL	kotowattaroo	kotowaranakattaroo
		kotowatta daroo	kotowaranakatta daroo
	FORMAL	kotowarimasitaroo	kotowarimaseñ desitaroo
		kotowatta desyoo	kotowaranakatta desyoo
Conditional	INFORMAL	kotowattara	kotowaranakattara
	FORMAL	kotowarimasitara	kotowaranakatta desitara
Alternative	INFORMAL	kotowattari	kotowaranakattari
	FORMAL	kotowarimasitari	kotowarimaseñ desitari

INFORMAL AFFIRMATIVE INDICATIVE

Passive	kotowarareru	*Honorific*	I	okotowari ni naru
			II	okotowari nasaru
Potential	kotowareru			
		Humble	I	okotowari suru
Causative	kotowaraseru		II	okotowari itasu
Causative Pass.	kotowaraserareru			

135

		AFFIRMATIVE	NEGATIVE
Indicative	INFORMAL	kowagaru	kowagaranai
	FORMAL	kowagarimasu	kowagarimaseñ
Imperative	INFORMAL I	kowagare	kowagaru na
	II	kowagarinasai	kowagarinasaru na
	III	kowagatte kudasai	kowagaranai de kudasai
	FORMAL	okowagari nasaimase	okowagari nasaimasu na
Presumptive	INFORMAL I	kowagaroo	kowagarumai
	II	kowagaru daroo	kowagaranai daroo
	FORMAL I	kowagarimasyoo	kowagarimasumai
	II	kowagaru desyoo	kowagaranai desyoo
Provisional	INFORMAL	kowagareba	kowagaranakereba
	FORMAL	kowagarimaseba	kowagarimaseñ nara
		kowagarimasureba	
Gerund	INFORMAL I	kowagatte	kowagaranai de
	II		kowagaranakute
	FORMAL	kowagarimasite	kowagarimaseñ de
Past Ind.	INFORMAL	kowagatta	kowagaranakatta
	FORMAL	kowagarimasita	kowagarimaseñ desita
Past Presump.	INFORMAL	kowagattaroo	kowagaranakattaroo
		kowagatta daroo	kowagaranakatta daroo
	FORMAL	kowagarimasitaroo	kowagarimaseñ desitaroo
		kowagatta desyoo	kowagaranakatta desyoo
Conditional	INFORMAL	kowagattara	kowagaranakattara
	FORMAL	kowagarimasitara	kowagarimaseñ desitara
Alternative	INFORMAL	kowagattari	kowagaranakattari
	FORMAL	kowagarimasitari	kowagarimaseñ desitari

INFORMAL AFFIRMATIVE INDICATIVE

Passive	kowagarareru	*Honorific*	I	okowagari ni naru
			II	okowagari nasaru
Potential				
		Humble	I	
Causative	kowagaraseru		II	
Causative Pass.	kowagaraserareru			

		AFFIRMATIVE	NEGATIVE
Indicative	INFORMAL	kowareru	kowarenai
	FORMAL	kowaremasu	kowaremaseñ
Imperative	INFORMAL I	kowarero	kowareru na
	II		
	III		
	FORMAL		
Presumptive	INFORMAL I	kowareyoo	kowaremai
	II	kowareru daroo	kowarenai daroo
	FORMAL I	kowaremasyoo	kowaremasumai
	II	kowareru desyoo	kowarenai desyoo
Provisional	INFORMAL	kowarereba	kowarenakereba
	FORMAL	kowaremaseba	kowaremaseñ nara
Gerund	INFORMAL I	kowarete	kowarenai de
	II		kowarenakute
	FORMAL	kowaremasite	kowaremaseñ de
Past Ind.	INFORMAL	kowareta	kowarenakatta
	FORMAL	kowaremasita	kowaremaseñ desita
Past Presump.	INFORMAL	kowaretaroo	kowarenakattaroo
		kowareta daroo	kowarenakatta daroo
	FORMAL	kowaremasitaroo	kowaremaseñ desitaroo
		kowareta desyoo	kowarenakatta desyoo
Conditional	INFORMAL	kowaretara	kowarenakattara
	FORMAL	kowaremasitara	kowaremaseñ desitara
Alternative	INFORMAL	kowaretari	kowarenakattari
	FORMAL	kowaremasitari	kowaremaseñ desitari

INFORMAL AFFIRMATIVE INDICATIVE

Passive			*Honorific*	I
				II
Potential	kowarerareru			
			Humble	I
Causative	*			II
Causative Pass.	*			

See *kowas.u*, the transitive verb for 'to break.'

		AFFIRMATIVE	NEGATIVE
Indicative	INFORMAL	kowasu	kowasanai
	FORMAL	kowasimasu	kowasimaseñ
Imperative	INFORMAL I	kowase	kowasu na
	II	kowasinasai	kowasinasaru na
	III	kowasite kudasai	kowasanai de kudasai
	FORMAL	okowasi nasaimase	okowasi nasaimasu na
Presumptive	INFORMAL I	kowasoo	kowasumai
	II	kowasu daroo	kowasanai daroo
	FORMAL I	kowasimasyoo	kowasimasumai
	II	kowasu desyoo	kowasanai desyoo
Provisional	INFORMAL	kowaseba	kowasanakereba
	FORMAL	kowasimaseba	kowasimaseñ nara
		kowasimasureba	
Gerund	INFORMAL I	kowasite	kowasanai de
	II		kowasanakute
	FORMAL	kowasimasite	kowasimaseñ de
Past Ind.	INFORMAL	kowasita	kowasanakatta
	FORMAL	kowasimasita	kowasimaseñ desita
Past Presump.	INFORMAL	kowasitaroo	kowasanakattaroo
		kowasita daroo	kowasanakatta daroo
	FORMAL	kowasimasitaroo	kowasimaseñ desitaroo
		kowasita desyoo	kowasanakatta desyoo
Conditional	INFORMAL	kowasitara	kowasanakattara
	FORMAL	kowasimasitara	kowasimaseñ desitara
Alternative	INFORMAL	kowasitari	kowasanakattari
	FORMAL	kowasimasitari	kowasimaseñ desitari

INFORMAL AFFIRMATIVE INDICATIVE

Passive	kowasareru	*Honorific*	I okowasi ni na
			II okowasi nasai
Potential	kowaseru		
		Humble	I okowasi suru
Causative	kowasaseru		II okowasi itasu
Causative Pass.	kowasaserareru		

TRANSITIVE   *to give* (to me)*

		AFFIRMATIVE	NEGATIVE
Indicative	INFORMAL	kudasaru	kudasaranai
	FORMAL	kudasaimasu	kudasaimaseñ
Imperative	INFORMAL I	kudasai	kudasaru na
	II		
	III		
	FORMAL	kudasaimase	kudasaimasu na
Presumptive	INFORMAL I	kudasaroo	kudasarumai
	II	kudasaru daroo	kudasaranai daroo
	FORMAL I	kudasaimasyoo	kudasaimasumai
	II	kudasaru desyoo	kudasaranai desyoo
Provisional	INFORMAL	kudasareba	kudasaranakereba
	FORMAL	kudasaimaseba	kudasaimaseñ nara
		kudasaimasureba	
Gerund	INFORMAL I	kudasatte	kudasaranai de
	II		kudasaranakute
	FORMAL	kudasaimasite	kudasaimaseñ de
Past Ind.	INFORMAL	kudasatta	kudasaranakatta
	FORMAL	kudasaimasita	kudasaimaseñ desita
Past Presump.	INFORMAL	kudasattaroo	kudasaranakattaroo
		kudasatta daroo	kudasaranakatta daroo
	FORMAL	kudasaimasitaroo	kudasaimaseñ desitaroo
		kudasatta desyoo	kudasaranakatta desyoo
Conditional	INFORMAL	kudasattara	kudasaranakattara
	FORMAL	kudasaimasitara	kudasaimaseñ desitara
Alternative	INFORMAL	kudasattari	kudasaranakattari
	FORMAL	kudasaimasitari	kudasaimaseñ desitari

INFORMAL AFFIRMATIVE INDICATIVE

Passive		*Honorific*	I
			II
Potential			
		Humble	I
Causative			II
Causative Pass.			

*Or to a member of my "in group."

		AFFIRMATIVE	NEGATIVE
Indicative	INFORMAL	kumoru	kumoranai
	FORMAL	kumorimasu	kumorimaseñ
Imperative	INFORMAL I	kumore	kumoru na
	II		
	III		
	FORMAL		
Presumptive	INFORMAL I	kumoroo	kumorumai
	II	kumoru daroo	kumoranai daroo
	FORMAL I	kumorimasyoo	kumorimasumai
	II	kumoru desyoo	kumoranai desyoo
Provisional	INFORMAL	kumoreba	kumoranakereba
	FORMAL	kumorimaseba	kumorimaseñ nara
		kumorimasureba	
Gerund	INFORMAL I	kumotte	kumoranai de
	II		kumoranakute
	FORMAL	kumorimasite	kumorimaseñ de
Past Ind.	INFORMAL	kumotta	kumoranakatta
	FORMAL	kumorimasita	kumorimaseñ desita
Past Presump.	INFORMAL	kumottaroo	kumoranakattaroo
		kumotta daroo	kumoranakatta daroo
	FORMAL	kumorimasitaroo	kumorimaseñ desitaroo
		kumotta desyoo	kumoranakatta desyoo
Conditional	INFORMAL	kumottara	kumoranakattara
	FORMAL	kumorimasitara	kumorimaseñ desitara
Alternative	INFORMAL	kumottari	kumoranakattari
	FORMAL	kumorimasitari	kumorimaseñ desitari

INFORMAL AFFIRMATIVE INDICATIVE

Passive	kumorareru	*Honorific*	I
			II
Potential			
		Humble	I
Causative	kumoraseru		II
Causative Pass.	kumoraserareru		

			AFFIRMATIVE	NEGATIVE
Indicative	INFORMAL		kuraberu	kurabenai
	FORMAL		kurabemasu	kurabemaseñ
Imperative	INFORMAL I		kurabero	kuraberu na
	II		kurabenasai	kurabenasaru na
	III		kurabete kudasai	kurabenai de kudasai
	FORMAL		okurabe nasaimase	okurabe nasaimasu na
Presumptive	INFORMAL I		kurabeyoo	kurabemai
	II		kuraberu daroo	kurabenai daroo
	FORMAL I		kurabemasyoo	kurabemasumai
	II		kuraberu desyoo	kurabenai desyoo
Provisional	INFORMAL		kurabereba	kurabenakereba
	FORMAL		kurabemaseba	kurabemaseñ nara
			kurabemasureba	
Gerund	INFORMAL I		kurabete	kurabenai de
	II			kurabenakute
	FORMAL		kurabemasite	kurabemaseñ de
Past Ind.	INFORMAL		kurabeta	kurabenakatta
	FORMAL		kurabemasita	kurabemaseñ desita
Past Presump.	INFORMAL		kurabetaroo	kurabenakattaroo
			kurabeta daroo	kurabenakatta daroo
	FORMAL		kurabemasitaroo	kurabemaseñ desitaroo
			kurabeta desyoo	kurabenakatta desyoo
Conditional	INFORMAL		kurabetara	kurabenakattara
	FORMAL		kurabemasitara	kurabemaseñ desitara
Alternative	INFORMAL		kurabetari	kurabenakattari
	FORMAL		kurabemasitari	kurabemaseñ desitari

INFORMAL AFFIRMATIVE INDICATIVE

Passive	kuraberareru	*Honorific*	I	okurabe ni naru
			II	okurabe nasaru
Potential	kuraberareru			
		Humble	I	okurabe suru
Causative	kurabesaseru		II	okurabe itasu
Causative Pass.	kurabesaserareru			

141

		AFFIRMATIVE	NEGATIVE
Indicative	INFORMAL	kurasu	kurasanai
	FORMAL	kurasimasu	kurasimaseñ
Imperative	INFORMAL I	kurase	kurasu na
	II	kurasinasai	kurasinasaru na
	III	kurasite kudasai	kurasanai de kudasai
	FORMAL	okurasi nasaimase	okurasi nasaimasu na
Presumptive	INFORMAL I	kurasoo	kurasumai
	II	kurasu daroo	kurasanai daroo
	FORMAL I	kurasimasyoo	kurasimasumai
	II	kurasu desyoo	kurasanai desyoo
Provisional	INFORMAL	kuraseba	kurasanakereba
	FORMAL	kurasimaseba	kurasimaseñ nara
		kurasimasureba	
Gerund	INFORMAL I	kurasite	kurasanai de
	II		kurasanakute
	FORMAL	kurasimasite	kurasimaseñ de
Past Ind.	INFORMAL	kurasita	kurasanakatta
	FORMAL	kurasimasita	kurasimaseñ desita
Past Presump.	INFORMAL	kurasitaroo	kurasanakattaroo
		kurasita daroo	kurasanakatta daroo
	FORMAL	kurasimasitaroo	kurasimaseñ desitaroo
		kurasita desyoo	kurasanakatta desyoo
Conditional	INFORMAL	kurasitara	kurasanakattara
	FORMAL	kurasimasitara	kurasimaseñ desitara
Alternative	INFORMAL	kurasitari	kurasanakattari
	FORMAL	kurasimasitari	kurasimaseñ desitari

INFORMAL AFFIRMATIVE INDICATIVE

Passive	kurasareru	*Honorific*	I	okurasi ni naru
			II	okurasi nasaru
Potential	kuraseru			
		Humble	I	
Causative	kurasaseru		II	
Causative Pass.	kurasaserareru			

TRANSITIVE   *to give* (the giver is someone other than the speaker)

		AFFIRMATIVE	NEGATIVE
Indicative	**INFORMAL**	kureru	kurenai
	FORMAL	kuremasu	kuremaseñ
Imperative	**INFORMAL I**	kure	kureru na
	II	kurenasai	kurenasaru na
	III		
	FORMAL		
Presumptive	**INFORMAL I**	kureyoo	kuremai
	II	kureru daroo	kurenai daroo
	FORMAL I	kuremasyoo	kuremasumai
	II	kureru desyoo	kurenai desyoo
Provisional	**INFORMAL**	kurereba	kurenakereba
	FORMAL	kuremaseba	kuremaseñ nara
		kuremasureba	
Gerund	**INFORMAL I**	kurete	kurenai de
	II		kurenakute
	FORMAL	kuremasite	kuremaseñ de
Past Ind.	**INFORMAL**	kureta	kurenakatta
	FORMAL	kuremasita	kuremaseñ desita
Past Presump.	**INFORMAL**	kuretaroo	kurenakattaroo
		kureta daroo	kurenakatta daroo
	FORMAL	kuremasitaroo	kuremaseñ desitaroo
		kureta desyoo	kurenakatta desyoo
Conditional	**INFORMAL**	kuretara	kurenakattara
	FORMAL	kuremasitara	kuremaseñ desitara
Alternative	**INFORMAL**	kuretari	kurenakattari
	FORMAL	kuremasitari	kuremaseñ desitari

INFORMAL AFFIRMATIVE INDICATIVE

Passive	kurerareru	*Honorific*	**I**
			II
Potential	kurerareru	*Humble*	**I**
Causative	kuresaseru		**II**
Causative Pass.	kuresaserareru		

to repeat (an action)   TRANSITIVE

			AFFIRMATIVE	NEGATIVE
Indicative	INFORMAL		kurikaesu	kurikaesanai
	FORMAL		kurikaesimasu	kurikaesimaseñ
Imperative	INFORMAL	I	kurikaese	kurikaesu na
		II	kurikaesinasai	kurikaesinasaru na
		III	kurikaesite kudasai	kurikaesanai de kudasai
	FORMAL		okurikaesi nasaimase	okurikaesi nasaimasu na
Presumptive	INFORMAL	I	kurikaesoo	kurikaesumai
		II	kurikaesu daroo	kurikaesanai daroo
	FORMAL	I	kurikaesimasyoo	kurikaesimasumai
		II	kurikaesu desyoo	kurikaesanai desyoo
Provisional	INFORMAL		kurikaeseba	kurikaesanakereba
	FORMAL		kurikaesimaseba	kurikaesimaseñ nara
			kurikaesimasureba	
Gerund	INFORMAL	I	kurikaesite	kurikaesanai de
		II		kurikaesanakute
	FORMAL		kurikaesimasite	kurikaesimaseñ de
Past Ind.	INFORMAL		kurikaesita	kurikaesanakatta
	FORMAL		kurikaesimasita	kurikaesimaseñ desita
Past Presump.	INFORMAL		kurikaesitaroo	kurikaesanakattaroo
			kurikaesita daroo	kurikaesanakatta daroo
	FORMAL		kurikaesimasitaroo	kurikaesimaseñ desitaroo
			kurikaesita desyoo	kurikaesanakatta desyoo
Conditional	INFORMAL		kurikaesitara	kurikaesanakattara
	FORMAL		kurikaesimasitara	kurikaesimaseñ desitara
Alternative	INFORMAL		kurikaesitari	kurikaesanakattari
	FORMAL		kurikaesimasitari	kurikaesimaseñ desitari

INFORMAL AFFIRMATIVE INDICATIVE

Passive	kurikaesareru	*Honorific*	I	okurikaesi ni naru
			II	okurikaesi nasaru
Potential	kurikaeseru			
		Humble	I	
Causative	kurikaesaseru		II	
Causative Pass.	kurikaesaserareru			

		AFFIRMATIVE	NEGATIVE
Indicative	INFORMAL	kuru	konai
	FORMAL	kimasu	kimaseñ
Imperative	INFORMAL I	koi	kuru na
	II	kinasai	kinasaru na
	III	kite kudasai	konai de kudasai
	FORMAL	oide nasaimase	oide nasaimasu na
Presumptive	INFORMAL I	koyoo	kurumai
	II	kuru daroo	konai daroo
	FORMAL I	kimasyoo	kimasumai
	II	kuru desyoo	konai desyoo
Provisional	INFORMAL	kureba	konakereba
	FORMAL	kimaseba	kimaseñ nara
		kimasureba	
Gerund	INFORMAL I	kite	konai de
	II		konakute
	FORMAL	kimasite	kimaseñ de
Past Ind.	INFORMAL	kita	konakatta
	FORMAL	kimasita	kimaseñ desita
Past Presump.	INFORMAL	kitaroo	konakattaroo
		kita daroo	konakatta daroo
	FORMAL	kimasitaroo	kimaseñ desitaroo
		kita desyoo	konakatta desyoo
Conditional	INFORMAL	kitara	konakattara
	FORMAL	kimasitara	kimaseñ desitara
Alternative	INFORMAL	kitari	konakattari
	FORMAL	kimasitari	kimaseñ desitari

INFORMAL AFFIRMATIVE INDICATIVE

Passive	korareru	*Honorific*	irassyaru	oide ni naru (I)
Potential	korareru			oide nasaru (II)
		Humble	nairu	
Causative	kosaseru			
Causative Pass.	kosaserareru			

		AFFIRMATIVE	NEGATIVE
Indicative	**INFORMAL**	kurusimeru	kurusimenai
	FORMAL	kurusimemasu	kurusimemaseñ
Imperative	**INFORMAL I**	kurusimero	kurusimeru na
	II	kurusimenasai	kurusimenasaru na
	III	kurusimete kudasai	kurusimenai de kudasai
	FORMAL	okurusime nasaimase	okurusime nasaimasu na
Presumptive	**INFORMAL I**	kurusimeyoo	kurusimemai
	II	kurusimeru daroo	kurusimenai daroo
	FORMAL I	kurusimemasyoo	kurusimemasumai
	II	kurusimeru desyoo	kurusimenai desyoo
Provisional	**INFORMAL**	kurusimereba	kurusimenakereba
	FORMAL	kurusimemaseba	kurusimemaseñ nara
		kurusimemasureba	
Gerund	**INFORMAL I**	kurusimete	kurusimenai de
	II		kurusimenakute
	FORMAL	kurusimemasite	kurusimemaseñ de
Past Ind.	**INFORMAL**	kurusimeta	kurusimenakatta
	FORMAL	kurusimemasita	kurusimemaseñ desita
Past Presump.	**INFORMAL**	kurusimetaroo	kurusimenakattaroo
		kurusimeta daroo	kurusimenakatta daroo
	FORMAL	kurusimemasitaroo	kurusimemaseñ desitaroo
		kurusimeta desyoo	kurusimenakatta desyoo
Conditional	**INFORMAL**	kurusimetara	kurusimenakattara
	FORMAL	kurusimemasitara	kurusimemaseñ desitara
Alternative	**INFORMAL**	kurusimetari	kurusimenakattari
	FORMAL	kurusimemasitari	kurusimemaseñ desitari

INFORMAL AFFIRMATIVE INDICATIVE

Passive	kurusimerareru	*Honorific*	**I**	okurusime ni naru
			II	okurusime nasaru
Potential	kurusimerareru			
		Humble	**I**	okurusime suru
Causative	kurusimesaseru		**II**	okurusime itasu
Causative Pass.	kurusimesaserareru			

		AFFIRMATIVE	NEGATIVE
Indicative	INFORMAL	kurusimu	kurusimanai
	FORMAL	kurusimimasu	kurusimimaseñ
Imperative	INFORMAL I	kurusime	kurusimu na
	II	kurusiminasai	kurusiminasaru na
	III	kurusiñde kudasai	kurusimanai de kudasai
	FORMAL	okurusimi nasaimase	okurusimi nasaimasu na
Presumptive	INFORMAL I	kurusimoo	kurusimumai
	II	kurusimu daroo	kurusimanai daroo
	FORMAL I	kurusimimasyoo	kurusimasumai
	II	kurusimu desyoo	kurusimanai desyoo
Provisional	INFORMAL	kurusimeba	kurusimanakereba
	FORMAL	kurusimimaseba	kurusimimaseñ nara
		kurusimimasureba	
Gerund	INFORMAL I	kurusiñde	kurusimanai de
	II		kurusimanakute
	FORMAL	kurusimimasite	kurusimimaseñ de
Past Ind.	INFORMAL	kurusiñda	kurusimanakatta
	FORMAL	kurusimimasita	kurusimimaseñ desita
Past Presump.	INFORMAL	kurusiñdaroo	kurusimanakattaroo
		kurusiñda daroo	kurusimanakatta daroo
	FORMAL	kurusimimasitaroo	kurusimimaseñ desitaroo
		kurusiñda desyoo	kurusimanakatta desyoo
Conditional	INFORMAL	kurusiñdara	kurusimanakattara
	FORMAL	kurusimimasitara	kurusimimaseñ desitara
Alternative	INFORMAL	kurusiñdari	kurusimanakattari
	FORMAL	kurusimimasitari	kurusimimaseñ desitari

INFORMAL AFFIRMATIVE INDICATIVE

Passive	kurusimareru	*Honorific*	I	okurusimi ni naru
			II	okurusimi nasaru
Potential	kurusimeru			
		Humble	I	
Causative	kurusimaseru		II	
Causative Pass.	kurusimaserareru			

		AFFIRMATIVE	NEGATIVE
Indicative	INFORMAL	kuruu	kuruwanai
	FORMAL	kuruimasu	kuruimaseñ
Imperative	INFORMAL I	kurue	kuruu na
	II	kuruinasai	kuruinasaru na
	III	kurutte kudasai	kuruwanai de kudasai
	FORMAL	okurui nasaimase	okurui nasaimasu na
Presumptive	INFORMAL I	kuruoo	kuruumai
	II	kuruu daroo	kuruwanai daroo
	FORMAL I	kuruimasyoo	kuruimasumai
	II	kuruu desyoo	kuruwanai desyoo
Provisional	INFORMAL	kurueba	kuruwanakereba
	FORMAL	kuruimaseba	kuruimaseñ nara
		kuruimasureba	
Gerund	INFORMAL I	kurutte	kuruwanai de
	II		kuruwanakute
	FORMAL	kuruimasite	kuruimaseñ de
Past Ind.	INFORMAL	kurutta	kuruwanakatta
	FORMAL	kuruimasita	kuruimaseñ desita
Past Presump.	INFORMAL	kuruttaroo	kuruwanakattaroo
		kurutta daroo	kuruwanakatta daroo
	FORMAL	kuruimasitaroo	kuruimaseñ desitaroo
		kurutta desyoo	kuruwanakatta desyoo
Conditional	INFORMAL	kuruttara	kuruwanakattara
	FORMAL	kuruimasitara	kuruimaseñ desitara
Alternative	INFORMAL	kuruttari	kuruwanakattari
	FORMAL	kuruimasitari	kuruimaseñ desitari

INFORMAL AFFIRMATIVE INDICATIVE

Passive	kuruwareru	*Honorific*	I	okurui ni naru
Potential	kurueru		II	okurui nasaru
Causative	kuruwaseru	*Humble*	I	
			II	
Causative Pass.	kuruwaserareru			

		AFFIRMATIVE	NEGATIVE
Indicative	INFORMAL	kusaru	kusaranai
	FORMAL	kusarimasu	kusarimaseñ
Imperative	INFORMAL I	kusare	kusaru na
	II	kusarinasai	kusarinasaru na
	III	kusatte kudasai	kusaranai de kudasai
	FORMAL	okusari nasaimase	okusari nasaimasu na
Presumptive	INFORMAL I	kusaroo	kusarumai
	II	kusaru daroo	kusaranai daroo
	FORMAL I	kusarimasyoo	kusarimasumai
	II	kusaru desyoo	kusaranai desyoo
Provisional	INFORMAL	kusareba	kusaranakereba
	FORMAL	kusarimaseba	kusarimaseñ nara
		kusarimasureba	
Gerund	INFORMAL I	kusatte	kusaranai de
	II		kusaranakute
	FORMAL	kusarimasite	kusarimaseñ de
Past Ind.	INFORMAL	kusatta	kusaranakatta
	FORMAL	kusarimasita	kusarimaseñ desita
Past Presump.	INFORMAL	kusattaroo	kusaranakattaroo
		kusatta daroo	kusaranakatta daroo
	FORMAL	kusarimasitaroo	kusarimaseñ desitaroo
		kusatta desyoo	kusaranakatta desyoo
Conditional	INFORMAL	kusattara	kusaranakattara
	FORMAL	kusarimasitara	kusarimaseñ desitara
Alternative	INFORMAL	kusattari	kusaranakattari
	FORMAL	kusarimasitari	kusarimaseñ desitari

INFORMAL AFFIRMATIVE INDICATIVE

Passive	kusarareru	*Honorific*	I
			II
Potential	kusareru		
		Humble	I
Causative	kusaraseru		II
Causative Pass.	kusaraserareru		

		AFFIRMATIVE	NEGATIVE
Indicative	INFORMAL	kuzureru	kuzurenai
	FORMAL	kuzuremasu	kuzuremaseñ
Imperative	INFORMAL I	kuzurero	kuzureru na
	II		
	III		
	FORMAL		
Presumptive	INFORMAL I	kuzureyoo	kuzuremai
	II	kuzureru daroo	kuzurenai daroo
	FORMAL I	kuzuremasyoo	kuzuremasumai
	II	kuzureru desyoo	kuzurenai desyoo
Provisional	INFORMAL	kuzurereba	kuzurenakereba
	FORMAL	kuzuremaseba	kuzuremaseñ nara
		kuzuremasureba	
Gerund	INFORMAL I	kuzurete	kuzurenai de
	II		kuzurenakute
	FORMAL	kuzuremasite	kuzuremaseñ de
Past Ind.	INFORMAL	kuzureta	kuzurenakatta
	FORMAL	kuzuremasita	kuzuremaseñ desita
Past Presump.	INFORMAL	kuzuretaroo	kuzurenakattaroo
		kuzureta daroo	kuzurenakatta daroo
	FORMAL	kuzuremasitaroo	kuzuremaseñ desitaroo
		kuzureta desyoo	kuzurenakatta desyoo
Conditional	INFORMAL	kuzuretara	kuzurenakattara
	FORMAL	kuzuremasitara	kuzuremaseñ desitara
Alternative	INFORMAL	kuzuretari	kuzurenakattari
	FORMAL	kuzuremasitari	kuzuremaseñ desitari

INFORMAL AFFIRMATIVE INDICATIVE

Passive	kuzurerareru	*Honorific*	I	okuzure ni naru
Potential			II	okuzure nasaru
Causative	kuzuresaseru	*Humble*	I	
Causative Pass.	kuzuresaserareru		II	

TRANSITIVE   *to destroy, to break down*

		AFFIRMATIVE	NEGATIVE
Indicative	INFORMAL	kuzusu	kuzusanai
	FORMAL	kuzusimasu	kuzusimaseñ
Imperative	INFORMAL I	kuzuse	kuzusu na
	II	kuzusinasai	kuzusinasaru na
	III	kuzusite kudasai	kuzusanai de kudasai
	FORMAL	okuzusi nasaimase	okuzusi nasaimasu na
Presumptive	INFORMAL I	kuzusoo	kuzusumai
	II	kuzusu daroo	kuzusanai daroo
	FORMAL I	kuzusimasyoo	kuzusimasumai
	II	kuzusu desyoo	kuzusanai desyoo
Provisional	INFORMAL	kuzuseba	kuzusanakereba
	FORMAL	kuzusimaseba	kuzusimaseñ nara
		kuzusimasureba	
Gerund	INFORMAL I	kuzusite	kuzusanai de
	II		kuzusanakute
	FORMAL	kuzusimasite	kuzusimaseñ de
Past Ind.	INFORMAL	kuzusita	kuzusanakatta
	FORMAL	kuzusimasita	kuzusimaseñ desita
Past Presump.	INFORMAL	kuzusitaroo	kuzusanakattaroo
		kuzusita daroo	kuzusanakatta daroo
	FORMAL	kuzusimasitaroo	kuzusimaseñ desitaroo
		kuzusita desyoo	kuzusanakatta desyoo
Conditional	INFORMAL	kuzusitara	kuzusanakatta
	FORMAL	kuzusimasitara	kuzusimaseñ desitara
Alternative	INFORMAL	kuzusitari	kuzusanakattari
	FORMAL	kuzusimasitari	kuzusimaseñ desitari

INFORMAL AFFIRMATIVE INDICATIVE

Passive	kuzusareru	*Honorific*	I	okuzusi ni naru
			II	okuzusi nasaru
Potential	kuzuseru			
		Humble	I	okuzusi suru
Causative	kuzusaseru		II	okuzusi itasu
Causative Pass.	kuzusaserareru			

to turn a corner (transitive) *to bend* (intransitive)

		AFFIRMATIVE	NEGATIVE
Indicative	INFORMAL	magaru	magaranai
	FORMAL	magarimasu	magarimaseñ
Imperative	INFORMAL I	magare	magaru na
	II	magarinasai	magarinasaru na
	III	magatte kudasai	magaranai de kudasai
	FORMAL	omagari nasaimase	omagari nasaimasu na
Presumptive	INFORMAL I	magaroo	magarumai
	II	magaru daroo	magaranai daroo
	FORMAL I	magarimasyoo	magarimasumai
	II	magaru desyoo	magaranai desyoo
Provisional	INFORMAL	magareba	magaranakereba
	FORMAL	magarimaseba	magarimaseñ nara
		magarimasureba	
Gerund	INFORMAL I	magatte	magaranai de
	II		magaranakute
	FORMAL	magarimasite	magarimaseñ de
Past Ind.	INFORMAL	magatta	magaranakatta
	FORMAL	magarimasita	magarimaseñ desita
Past Presump.	INFORMAL	magattaroo	magaranakattaroo
		magatta daroo	magaranakatta daroo
	FORMAL	magarimasitaroo	magarimaseñ desitaroo
		magatta desyoo	magaranakatta desyoo
Conditional	INFORMAL	magattara	magaranakattara
	FORMAL	magarimasitara	magarimaseñ desitara
Alternative	INFORMAL	magattari	magaranakattari
	FORMAL	magarimasitari	magarimaseñ desitari

INFORMAL AFFIRMATIVE INDICATIVE

Passive		*Honorific*	I	omagari ni naru
			II	omagari nasaru
Potential	magareru			
		Humble	I	
Causative	magaraseru		II	
Causative Pass.	magaraserareru			

		AFFIRMATIVE	NEGATIVE
Indicative	INFORMAL	mageru	magenai
	FORMAL	magemasu	magemaseñ
Imperative	INFORMAL I	magero	mageru na
	II	magenasai	magenasaru na
	III	magete kudasai	magenai de kudasai
	FORMAL	omage nasaimase	omage nasaimasu na
Presumptive	INFORMAL I	mageyoo	magemai
	II	mageru daroo	magenai daroo
	FORMAL I	magemasyoo	magemasumai
	II	mageru desyoo	magenai desyoo
Provisional	INFORMAL	magereba	magenakereba
	FORMAL	magemaseba	magemaseñ nara
		magemasureba	
Gerund	INFORMAL I	magete	magenai de
	II		magenakute
	FORMAL	magemasite	magemaseñ de
Past Ind.	INFORMAL	mageta	magenakatta
	FORMAL	magemasita	magemaseñ desita
Past Presump.	INFORMAL	magetaroo	magenakattaroo
		mageta daroo	magenakatta daroo
	FORMAL	magemasitaroo	magemaseñ desitaroo
		mageta desyoo	magenakatta desyoo
Conditional	INFORMAL	magetara	magenakattara
	FORMAL	magemasitara	magemaseñ desitara
Alternative	INFORMAL	magetari	magenakattari
	FORMAL	magemasitari	magemaseñ desitari

INFORMAL AFFIRMATIVE INDICATIVE

Passive	magerareru	*Honorific*	I	omage ni naru
			II	omage nasaru
Potential	magerareru			
		Humble	I	omage suru
Causative	magesaseru		II	omage itasu
Causative Pass.	magesaserareru			

		AFFIRMATIVE	NEGATIVE
Indicative	INFORMAL	mairu	mairanai
	FORMAL	mairimasu	mairimaseñ
Imperative	INFORMAL I	maire	mairu na
	II		
	III		
	FORMAL		
Presumptive	INFORMAL I	mairoo	mairumai
	II	mairu daroo	mairanai daroo
	FORMAL I	mairimasyoo	mairimasumai
	II	mairu desyoo	mairanai desyoo
Provisional	INFORMAL	maireba	mairanakereba
	FORMAL	mairimaseba	mairimaseñ nara
		mairimasureba	
Gerund	INFORMAL I	maitte	mairanai de
	II		mairanakute
	FORMAL	mairimasite	mairimaseñ de
Past Ind.	INFORMAL	maitta	mairanakatta
	FORMAL	mairimasita	mairimaseñ desita
Past Presump.	INFORMAL	maittaroo	mairanakattaroo
		maitta daroo	mairanakatta daroo
	FORMAL	mairimasitaroo	mairimaseñ desitaroo
		maitta desyoo	mairanakatta desyoo
Conditional	INFORMAL	maittara	mairanakattara
	FORMAL	mairimasitara	mairimaseñ desitara
Alternative	INFORMAL	maittari	mairanakattari
	FORMAL	mairimasitari	mairimaseñ desitari

INFORMAL AFFIRMATIVE INDICATIVE

Passive		*Honorific*	I
			II
Potential			
		Humble	I
Causative	mairaseru		II
Causative Pass.	mairaserareru		

TRANSITIVE   *to leave (a matter) to someone, to leave things to others*

		AFFIRMATIVE	NEGATIVE
Indicative	INFORMAL	makaseru	makasenai
	FORMAL	makasemasu	makasemaseñ
Imperative	INFORMAL I	makasero	makaseru na
	II	makasenasai	makasenasaru na
	III	makasete kudasai	makasenai de kudasai
	FORMAL	omakase nasaimase	omakase nasaimasu na
Presumptive	INFORMAL I	makaseyoo	makasemai
	II	makaseru daroo	makasenai daroo
	FORMAL I	makasemasyoo	makasemasumai
	II	makaseru desyoo	makasenai desyoo
Provisional	INFORMAL	makasereba	makasenakereba
	FORMAL	makasemaseba	makasemaseñ nara
		makasemasureba	
Gerund	INFORMAL I	makasete	makasenai de
	II		makasenakute
	FORMAL	makasemasite	makasemaseñ de
Past Ind.	INFORMAL	makaseta	makasenakatta
	FORMAL	makasemasita	makasemaseñ desita
Past Presump.	INFORMAL	makasetaroo	makasenakattaroo
		makaseta daroo	makasenakatta daroo
	FORMAL	makasemasitaroo	makasemaseñ desitaroo
		makaseta desyoo	makasenakatta desyoo
Conditional	INFORMAL	makasetara	makasenakattara
	FORMAL	makasemasitara	makasemaseñ desitara
Alternative	INFORMAL	makasetari	makasenakattari
	FORMAL	makasemasitari	makasemaseñ desitari

INFORMAL AFFIRMATIVE INDICATIVE

Passive	makaserareru	*Honorific*	I	omakase ni naru
			II	omakase nasaru
Potential	makaserareru			
		Humble	I	omakase suru
Causative	makasesaseru		II	omakase itasu
Causative Pass.	makasesaserareru			

		AFFIRMATIVE	NEGATIVE
Indicative	INFORMAL	makasu	makasanai
	FORMAL	makasimasu	makasimaseñ
Imperative	INFORMAL I	makase	makasu na
	II	makasinasai	makasinasaru na
	III	makasite kudasai	makasanai de kudasai
	FORMAL	omakasi nasaimase	omakasi nasaimasu na
Presumptive	INFORMAL I	makasoo	makasumai
	II	makasu daroo	makasanai daroo
	FORMAL I	makasimasyoo	makasimasumai
	II	makasu desyoo	makasanai desyoo
Provisional	INFORMAL	makaseba	makasanakereba
	FORMAL	makasimaseba	makasimaseñ nara
		makasimasureba	
Gerund	INFORMAL I	makasite	makasanai de
	II		makasanakute
	FORMAL	makasimasite	makasimaseñ de
Past Ind.	INFORMAL	makasita	makasanakatta
	FORMAL	makasimasita	makasimaseñ desita
Past Presump.	INFORMAL	makasitaroo	makasanakattaroo
		makasita daroo	makasanakatta daroo
	FORMAL	makasimasitaroo	makasimaseñ desitaroo
		makasita desyoo	makasanakatta desyoo
Conditional	INFORMAL	makasitara	makasanakattara
	FORMAL	makasimasitara	makasimaseñ desitara
Alternative	INFORMAL	makasitari	makasanakattari
	FORMAL	makasimasitari	makasimaseñ desitari

INFORMAL AFFIRMATIVE INDICATIVE

Passive	makasareru	*Honorific*	I	omakasi ni naru
			II	omakasi nasaru
Potential	makaseru			
		Humble	I	omakasi suru
Causative			II	omakasi itasu
Causative Pass.				

		AFFIRMATIVE	NEGATIVE
Indicative	INFORMAL	makeru	makenai
	FORMAL	makemasu	makemaseñ
Imperative	INFORMAL I	makero	makeru na
	II	makenasai	makenasaru na
	III	makete kudasai	makenai de kudasai
	FORMAL	omake nasaimase	omake nasaimasu na
Presumptive	INFORMAL I	makeyoo	makemai
	II	makeru daroo	makenai daroo
	FORMAL I	makemasyoo	makemasumai
	II	makeru desyoo	makenai desyoo
Provisional	INFORMAL	makereba	makenakereba
	FORMAL	makemaseba	makemaseñ nara
		makemasureba	
Gerund	INFORMAL I	makete	makenai de
	II		makenakute
	FORMAL	makemasite	makemaseñ de
Past Ind.	INFORMAL	maketa	makenakatta
	FORMAL	makemasita	makemaseñ desita
Past Presump.	INFORMAL	maketaroo	makenakattaroo
		maketa daroo	makenakatta daroo
	FORMAL	makemasitaroo	makemaseñ desitaroo
		maketa desyoo	makenakatta desyoo
Conditional	INFORMAL	maketara	makenakattara
	FORMAL	makemasitara	makemaseñ desitara
Alternative	INFORMAL	maketari	makenakattari
	FORMAL	makemasitari	makemaseñ desitari

INFORMAL AFFIRMATIVE INDICATIVE

Passive	makerareru	*Honorific*	I	omake ni naru
Potential	makerareru		II	omake nasaru
Causative	makesaseru	*Humble*	I	omake suru
			II	omake itasu
Causative Pass.	makesaserareru			

		AFFIRMATIVE	NEGATIVE
Indicative	INFORMAL	mamoru	mamoranai
	FORMAL	mamorimasu	mamorimaseñ
Imperative	INFORMAL I	mamore	mamoru na
	II	mamorinasai	mamorinasaru na
	III	mamotte kudasai	mamoranai de kudasai
	FORMAL	omamori nasaimase	omamori nasaimasu na
Presumptive	INFORMAL I	mamoroo	mamorumai
	II	mamoru daroo	mamoranai daroo
	FORMAL I	mamorimasyoo	mamorimasumai
	II	mamoru desyoo	mamoranai desyoo
Provisional	INFORMAL	mamoreba	mamoranakereba
	FORMAL	mamorimaseba	mamorimaseñ nara
		mamorimasureba	
Gerund	INFORMAL I	mamotte	mamoranai de
	II		mamoranakute
	FORMAL	mamorimasite	mamorimaseñ de
Past Ind.	INFORMAL	mamotta	mamoranakatta
	FORMAL	mamorimasita	mamorimaseñ desita
Past Presump.	INFORMAL	mamottaroo	mamoranakattaroo
		mamotta daroo	mamoranakatta daroo
	FORMAL	mamorimasitaroo	mamorimaseñ desitaroo
		mamotta desyoo	mamoranakatta desyoo
Conditional	INFORMAL	mamottara	mamoranakattara
	FORMAL	mamorimasitara	mamorimaseñ desitara
Alternative	INFORMAL	mamottari	mamoranakattari
	FORMAL	mamorimasitari	mamorimaseñ desitari

INFORMAL AFFIRMATIVE INDICATIVE

Passive	mamorareru	*Honorific*	I	omamori ni naru
			II	omamori nasaru
Potential	mamoreru			
		Humble	I	omamori suru
Causative	mamoraseru		II	omamori itasu
Causative Pass.	mamoraserareru			

TRANSITIVE   *to learn, to study*

		AFFIRMATIVE	NEGATIVE
Indicative	INFORMAL	manabu	manabanai
	FORMAL	manabimasu	manabimaseñ
Imperative	INFORMAL I	manabe	manabu na
	II	manabinasai	manabinasaru na
	III	manañde kudasai	manabanai de kudasai
	FORMAL	omanabi nasaimase	omanabi nasaimasu na
Presumptive	INFORMAL I	manaboo	manabumai
	II	manabu daroo	manabanai daroo
	FORMAL I	manabimasyoo	manabimasumai
	II	manabu desyoo	manabanai desyoo
Provisional	INFORMAL	manabeba	manabanakereba
	FORMAL	manabimaseba	manabimaseñ nara
		manabimasureba	
Gerund	INFORMAL I	manañde	manabanai de
	II		manabanakute
	FORMAL	manabimasle	manabimaseñ de
Past Ind.	INFORMAL	manañda	manabanakatta
	FORMAL	manabimasita	manabimaseñ desita
Past Presump.	INFORMAL	manañdaroo	manabanakattaroo
		manañda daroo	manabanakatta daroo
	FORMAL	manabimasitaroo	manabimaseñ desitaroo
		manañda desyoo	manabanakatta desyoo
Conditional	INFORMAL	manañdara	manabanakattara
	FORMAL	manabimasitara	manabimaseñ desitara
Alternative	INFORMAL	manañdari	manabanakattari
	FORMAL	manabimasitari	manabimaseñ desitari

INFORMAL AFFIRMATIVE INDICATIVE

Passive	manabareru	*Honorific*	I	omanabi ni naru
			II	omanabi nasaru
Potential	manaberu			
		Humble	I	omanabi suru
Causative	manabaseru		II	omanabi itasu
Causative Pass.	manabaserareru			

		AFFIRMATIVE	NEGATIVE
Indicative	INFORMAL	maneku	manekanai
	FORMAL	manekimasu	manekimaseñ
Imperative	INFORMAL I	maneke	maneku na
	II	manekinasai	manekinasaru na
	III	maneite kudasai	manekanai de kudasai
	FORMAL	omaneki nasaimase	omaneki nasaimasu na
Presumptive	INFORMAL I	manekoo	manekumai
	II	maneku daroo	manekanai daroo
	FORMAL I	manekimasyoo	manekimasumai
	II	maneku desyoo	manekanai desyoo
Provisional	INFORMAL	manekeba	manekanakereba
	FORMAL	manekimaseba	manekimaseñ nara
		manekimasureba	
Gerund	INFORMAL I	maneite	manekanai de
	II		manekanakute
	FORMAL	manekimasite	manekimaseñ de
Past Ind.	INFORMAL	maneita	manekanakatta
	FORMAL	manekimasita	manekimaseñ desita
Past Presump.	INFORMAL	maneitaroo	manekanakattaroo
		maneita daroo	manekanakatta daroo
	FORMAL	manekimasitaroo	manekimaseñ desitaroo
		maneita desyoo	manekanakatta desyoo
Conditional	INFORMAL	maneitara	manekanakattara
	FORMAL	manekimasitara	manekimaseñ desitara
Alternative	INFORMAL	maneitari	manekanakattari
	FORMAL	manekimasitari	manekimaseñ desitari

INFORMAL AFFIRMATIVE INDICATIVE

Passive	manekareru	*Honorific*	I	omaneki ni naru
Potential	manekeru		II	omaneki nasaru
Causative	manekaseru	*Humble*	I	omaneki suru
			II	omaneki itasu
Causative Pass.	manekaserareru			

TRANSITIVE   *to make a mistake, to mistake one thing for another*

		AFFIRMATIVE	**NEGATIVE**
Indicative	INFORMAL	matigaeru	matigaenai
	FORMAL	matigaemasu	matigaemaseñ
Imperative	INFORMAL I	matigaero	matigaeru na
	II	matigaenasai	matigaenasaru na
	III	matigaete kudasai	matigaenai de kudasai
	FORMAL	omatigae nasaimase	omatigae nasaimasu na
Presumptive	INFORMAL I	matigaeyoo	matigaemai
	II	matigaeru daroo	matigaemai daroo
	FORMAL I	matigaemasyoo	matigaemasumai
	II	matigaeru desyoo	matigaenai desyoo
Provisional	INFORMAL	matigaereba	matigaenakereba
	FORMAL	matigaemaseba	matigaemaseñ nara
		matigaemasureba	
Gerund	INFORMAL I	matigaete	matigaenai de
	II		matigaenakute
	FORMAL	matigaemasite	matigaemaseñ de
Past Ind.	INFORMAL	matigaeta	matigaenakatta
	FORMAL	matigaemasita	matigaemaseñ desita
Past Presump.	INFORMAL	matigaetaroo	matigaenakattaroo
		matigaeta daroo	matigaenakatta daroo
	FORMAL	matigaemasitaroo	matigaemaseñ desitaroo
		matigaeta desyoo	matigaenakatta desyoo
Conditional	INFORMAL	matigaetara	matigaenakattara
	FORMAL	matigaemasitara	matigaemaseñ desitara
Alternative	INFORMAL	matigaetari	matigaenakattari
	FORMAL	matigaemasitari	matigaemaseñ desitari

INFORMAL AFFIRMATIVE INDICATIVE

Passive	matigaerareru	*Honorific*	I	omatigae ni naru
			II	omatigae nasaru
Potential	matigaerareru			
		Humble	I	
Causative	matigaesaseru		II	
Causative Pass.	matigaesaserareru			

		AFFIRMATIVE	NEGATIVE
Indicative	INFORMAL	matigau	matigawanai
	FORMAL	matigaimasu	matigaimaseñ
Imperative	INFORMAL I		
	II		
	III		
	FORMAL		
Presumptive	INFORMAL I	matigaoo	matigaumai
	II	matigau daroo	matigawanai daroo
	FORMAL I	matigaimasyoo	matigaimasumai
	II	matigau desyoo	matigawanai desyoo
Provisional	INFORMAL	matigaeba	matigawanakereba
	FORMAL	matigaimaseba	matigaimaseñ nara
		matigaimasureba	
Gerund	INFORMAL I	matigatte	matigawanai de
	II		matigawanakute
	FORMAL	matigaimasite	matigaimaseñ de
Past Ind.	INFORMAL	matigatta	matigawanakatta
	FORMAL	matigaimasita	matigaimaseñ desita
Past Presump.	INFORMAL	matigattaroo	matigawanakattaroo
		matigatta daroo	matigawanakatta daroo
	FORMAL	matigaimasitaroo	matigaimaseñ desitaroo
		matigatta desyoo	matigawanakatta desyoo
Conditional	INFORMAL	matigattara	matigawanakattara
	FORMAL	matigaimasitara	matigaimaseñ desitara
Alternative	INFORMAL	matigattari	matigawanakattari
	FORMAL	matigaimasitari	matigaimaseñ desitari

INFORMAL AFFIRMATIVE INDICATIVE

Passive	matigawareru	*Honorific*	I
			II
Potential	matigaeru		
		Humble	I
Causative	matigawaseru		II
Causative Pass.	matigawaserareru		

TRANSITIVE   *to settle* (a dispute), *to arrange* (a matter), *to complete*

		AFFIRMATIVE	NEGATIVE
Indicative	INFORMAL	matomeru	matomenai
	FORMAL	matomemasu	matomemaseñ
Imperative	INFORMAL I	matomero	matomeru na
	II	matomenasai	matomenasaru na
	III	matomete kudasai	matomenai de kudasai
	FORMAL	omatome nasaimase	omatome nasaimasu na
Presumptive	INFORMAL I	matomeyoo	matomemai
	II	matomeru daroo	matomenai daroo
	FORMAL I	matomemasyoo	matomemasumai
	II	matomeru desyoo	matomenai desyoo
Provisional	INFORMAL	matomereba	matomenakereba
	FORMAL	matomemaseba	matomemaseñ nara
		matomemasureba	
Gerund	INFORMAL I	matomete	matomenai de
	II		matomenakute
	FORMAL	matomemasite	matomemaseñ de
Past Ind.	INFORMAL	matometa	matomenakatta
	FORMAL	matomemasita	matomemaseñ desita
Past Presump.	INFORMAL	matometaroo	matomenakattaroo
		matometa daroo	matomenakatta daroo
	FORMAL	matomemasitaroo	matomemaseñ desitaroo
		matometa desyoo	matomenakatta desyoo
Conditional	INFORMAL	matometara	matomenakattara
	FORMAL	matomemasitara	matomemaseñ desitara
Alternative	INFORMAL	matometari	matomenakattari
	FORMAL	matomemasitari	matomemaseñ desitari

INFORMAL AFFIRMATIVE INDICATIVE

Passive	matomerareru	*Honorific*	I	omatome ni naru
			II	omatome nasaru
Potential	matomerareru			
		Humble	I	omatome suru
Causative	matomesaseru		II	omatome itasu
Causative Pass.	matomesaserareru			

		AFFIRMATIVE	NEGATIVE
Indicative	INFORMAL	matu	matanai
	FORMAL	matimasu	matimaseñ
Imperative	INFORMAL I	mate	matu na
	II	matinasai	matinasaru na
	III	matte kudasai	matanai de kudasai
	FORMAL	omati nasaimase	omati nasaimasu na
Presumptive	INFORMAL I	matoo	matumai
	II	matu daroo	matanai daroo
	FORMAL I	matimasyoo	matimasumai
	II	matu desyoo	matanai desyoo
Provisional	INFORMAL	mateba	matanakereba
	FORMAL	matimaseba	matimaseñ nara
		matimasureba	
Gerund	INFORMAL I	matte	matanai de
	II		matanakute
	FORMAL	matimasite	matimaseñ de
Past Ind.	INFORMAL	matta	matanakatta
	FORMAL	matimasita	matimaseñ desita
Past Presump.	INFORMAL	mattaroo	matanakattaroo
		matta daroo	matanakatta daroo
	FORMAL	matimasitaroo	matimaseñ desitaroo
		matta desyoo	matanakatta desyoo
Conditional	INFORMAL	mattara	matanakattara
	FORMAL	matimasitara	matimaseñ desitara
Alternative	INFORMAL	mattari	matanakattari
	FORMAL	matimasitari	matimaseñ desitari

INFORMAL AFFIRMATIVE INDICATIVE

Passive	matareru	*Honorific*	I	omati ni naru
			II	omati nasaru
Potential	materu			
		Humble	I	omati suru
Causative	mataseru		II	omati itasu
Causative Pass.	mataserareru			

TRANSITIVE   *to mix*

		AFFIRMATIVE	NEGATIVE
Indicative	INFORMAL	mazeru	mazenai
	FORMAL	mazemasu	mazemaseñ
Imperative	INFORMAL I	mazero	mazeru na
	II	mazenasai	mazenasaru na
	III	mazete kudasai	mazenai de kudasai
	FORMAL	omaze nasaimase	omaze nasaimasu na
Presumptive	INFORMAL I	mazeyoo	mazemai
	II	mazeru daroo	mazenai daroo
	FORMAL I	mazemasyoo	mazemasumai
	II	mazeru desyoo	mazenai desyoo
Provisional	INFORMAL	mazereba	mazenakereba
	FORMAL	mazemaseba	mazemaseñ nara
		mazemasureba	
Gerund	INFORMAL I	mazete	mazenai de
	II		mazenakute
	FORMAL	mazemasite	mazemaseñ de
Past Ind.	INFORMAL	mazeta	mazenakatta
	FORMAL	mazemasita	mazemaseñ desita
Past Presump.	INFORMAL	mazetaroo	mazenakattaroo
		mazeta daroo	mazenakatta daroo
	FORMAL	mazemasitaroo	mazemaseñ desitaroo
		mazeta desyoo	mazenakatta desyoo
Conditional	INFORMAL	mazetara	mazenakattara
	FORMAL	mazemasitara	mazemaseñ desitara
Alternative	INFORMAL	mazetari	mazenakattari
	FORMAL	mazemasitari	mazemaseñ desitari

INFORMAL AFFIRMATIVE INDICATIVE

Passive	mazerareru	*Honorific*	I	omaze ni naru
			II	omaze nasaru
Potential	mazerareru			
		Humble	I	omaze suru
Causative	mazesaseru		II	omaze itasu
Causative Pass.	mazesaserareru			

		AFFIRMATIVE	NEGATIVE
Indicative	INFORMAL	mesiagaru	mesiagaranai
	FORMAL	mesiagarimasu	mesiagarimaseñ
Imperative	INFORMAL I	mesiagare	
	II		mesiagarinasaru na
	III	mesiagatte kudasai	mesiagaranai de kudasai
	FORMAL	omesiagari nasaimase	omesiagari nasaimasu na
Presumptive	INFORMAL I	mesiagaroo	mesiagarumai
	II	mesiagaru daroo	mesiagaranai daroo
	FORMAL I	mesiagarimasyoo	mesiagarimasumai
	II	mesiagaru desyoo	mesiagaranai desyoo
Provisional	INFORMAL	mesiagareba	mesiagaranakereba
	FORMAL	mesiagarimaseba	mesiagarimaseñ nara
		mesiagarimasureba	
Gerund	INFORMAL I	mesiagatte	mesiagaranai de
	II		mesiagaranakute
	FORMAL	mesiagarimasite	mesiagarimaseñ de
Past Ind.	INFORMAL	mesiagatta	mesiagaranakatta
	FORMAL	mesiagarimasita	mesiagarimaseñ desita
Past Presump.	INFORMAL	mesiagattaroo	mesiagaranakattaroo
		mesiagatta daroo	mesiagaranakatta daroo
	FORMAL	mesiagarimasitaroo	mesiagarimaseñ desitaroo
		mesiagatta desyoo	mesiagaranakatta desyoo
Conditional	INFORMAL	mesiagattara	mesiagaranakattara
	FORMAL	mesiagarimasitara	mesiagarimaseñ desitara
Alternative	INFORMAL	mesiagattari	mesiagaranakattari
	FORMAL	mesiagarimasitari	mesiagarimaseñ desitari

INFORMAL AFFIRMATIVE INDICATIVE

Passive	mesiagarareru	*Honorific*	I	omesiagari ni naru
			II	omesiagari nasaru
Potential	mesiagareru			
		Humble	I	
Causative			II	
Causative Pass.	mesiagaraserareru			

to be visible, to be able to see, honorific for to visit

		AFFIRMATIVE	NEGATIVE
Indicative	INFORMAL	mieru	mienai
	FORMAL	miemasu	miemaseñ
Imperative	INFORMAL I		
	II		
	III		
	FORMAL		
Presumptive	INFORMAL I	mieyoo	miemai
	II	mieru daroo	mienai daroo
	FORMAL I	miemasyoo	miemasumai
	II	mieru desyoo	mienai desyoo
Provisional	INFORMAL	miereba	mienakereba
	FORMAL	miemaseba	miemaseñ nara
		miemasureba	
Gerund	INFORMAL I	miete	mienai de
	II		mienakute
	FORMAL	micmasite	miemaseñ de
Past Ind.	INFORMAL	mieta	mienakatta
	FORMAL	miemasita	miemaseñ desita
Past Presump.	INFORMAL	mietaroo	mienakattaroo
		mieta daroo	mienakatta daroo
	FORMAL	miemasitaroo	miemaseñ desitaroo
		mieta desyoo	mienakatta desyoo
Conditional	INFORMAL	mietara	mienakattara
	FORMAL	miemasitara	miemaseñ desitara
Alternative	INFORMAL	mietari	mienakattari
	FORMAL	miemasitari	miemaseñ desitari

INFORMAL AFFIRMATIVE INDICATIVE

Passive		*Honorific*	I	omie ni naru
			II	omie nasaru
Potential				
		Humble	I	
Causative			II	
Causative Pass.				

		AFFIRMATIVE	NEGATIVE
Indicative	INFORMAL	migaku	migakanai
	FORMAL	migakimasu	migakimaseñ
Imperative	INFORMAL I	migake	migaku na
	II	migakinasai	migakinasaru na
	III	migaite kudasai	migakanai de kudasai
	FORMAL	omigaki nasaimase	omigaki nasaimasu na
Presumptive	INFORMAL I	migakoo	migakumai
	II	migaku daroo	migakanai daroo
	FORMAL I	migakimasyoo	migakimasumai
	II	migaku desyoo	migakanai desyoo
Provisional	INFORMAL	migakeba	migakanakereba
	FORMAL	migakimaseba	migakimaseñ nara
		migakimasureba	
Gerund	INFORMAL I	migaite	migakanai de
	II		migakanakute
	FORMAL	migakimasite	migakimaseñ de
Past Ind.	INFORMAL	migaita	migakanakatta
	FORMAL	migakimasita	migakimaseñ desita
Past Presump.	INFORMAL	migaitaroo	migakanakattaroo
		migaita daroo	migakanakatta daroo
	FORMAL	migakimasitaroo	migakimaseñ desitaroo
		migaita desyoo	migakanakatta desyoo
Conditional	INFORMAL	migaitara	migakanakattara
	FORMAL	migakimasitara	migakimaseñ desitara
Alternative	INFORMAL	migaitari	migakanakattari
	FORMAL	migakimasitari	migakimaseñ desitari

INFORMAL AFFIRMATIVE INDICATIVE

Passive	migakareru	*Honorific*	I	omigaki ni naru
			II	omigaki nasaru
Potential	migakeru			
		Humble	I	omigaki suru
Causative	migakaseru		II	omigaki itasu
Causative Pass.	migakaserareru			

TRANSITIVE   *to stand guard, to keep a lookout*

		AFFIRMATIVE	NEGATIVE
Indicative	INFORMAL	miharu	miharanai
	FORMAL	miharimasu	miharimaseñ
Imperative	INFORMAL I	mihare	miharu na
	II	miharinasai	miharinasaru na
	III	mihatte kudasai	miharanai de kudasai
	FORMAL	omihari nasaimase	omihari nasaimasu na
Presumptive	INFORMAL I	miharoo	miharumai
	II	miharu daroo	miharanai daroo
	FORMAL I	miharimasyoo	miharimasumai
	II	miharu desyoo	miharanai desyoo
Provisional	INFORMAL	mihareba	miharanakereba
	FORMAL	miharimaseba	miharimaseñ nara
		miharimasureba	
Gerund	INFORMAL I	mihatte	miharanai de
	II		miharanakute
	FORMAL	miharimasite	miharimaseñ de
Past Ind.	INFORMAL	mihatta	miharanakatta
	FORMAL	miharimasita	miharimaseñ desita
Past Presump.	INFORMAL	mihattaroo	miharanakattaroo
		mihatta daroo	miharanakatta daroo
	FORMAL	miharimasitaroo	miharimaseñ desitaroo
		mihatta desyoo	miharanakatta desyoo
Conditional	INFORMAL	mihattara	miharanakattara
	FORMAL	miharimasitara	miharimaseñ desitara
Alternative	INFORMAL	mihattari	miharanakattari
	FORMAL	miharimasitari	miharimaseñ desitari

INFORMAL AFFIRMATIVE INDICATIVE

Passive	miharareru	*Honorific*	I	omihari ni naru
			II	omihari nasaru
Potential	mihareru			
		Humble	I	omihari suru
Causative	miharaseru		II	omihari itasu
Causative Pass.	miharaserareru			

		AFFIRMATIVE	NEGATIVE
Indicative	INFORMAL	minogasu	minogasanai
	FORMAL	minogasimasu	minogasimaseñ
Imperative	INFORMAL I	minogase	minogasu na
	II	minogasinasai	minogasinasaru na
	III	minogasite kudasai	minogasanai de kudasai
	FORMAL	ominogasi nasaimase	ominogasi nasaimasu na
Presumptive	INFORMAL I	minogasoo	minogasumai
	II	minogasu daroo	minogasanai daroo
	FORMAL I	minogasimasyoo	minogasumai
	II	minogasu desyoo	minogasanai desyoo
Provisional	INFORMAL	minogaseba	minogasanakereba
	FORMAL	minogasimaseba	minogasimaseñ nara
		minogasimasureba	
Gerund	INFORMAL I	minogasite	minogasanai de
	II		minogasanakute
	FORMAL	minogasimasite	minogasimaseñ de
Past Ind.	INFORMAL	minogasita	minogasanakatta
	FORMAL	minogasimasita	minogasimaseñ desita
Past Presump.	INFORMAL	minogasitaroo	minogasanakattaroo
		minogasita daroo	minogasanakatta daroo
	FORMAL	minogasimasitaroo	minogasimaseñ desitaroo
		minogasita desyoo	minogasanakatta desyoo
Conditional	INFORMAL	minogasitara	minogasanakattara
	FORMAL	minogasimasitara	minogasimaseñ desitara
Alternative	INFORMAL	minogasitari	minogasanakattari
	FORMAL	minogasimasitari	minogasimaseñ desitari

INFORMAL AFFIRMATIVE INDICATIVE

Passive	minogasareru	*Honorific*	I	ominogasi ni na
Potential	minogaseru		II	ominogasi nasai
Causative	minogasaseru	*Humble*	I	ominogasi suru
			II	ominogasi itasu
Causative Pass.	minogasaserareru			

TRANSITIVE   *to look* (at) *to see*

		AFFIRMATIVE	NEGATIVE
Indicative	INFORMAL	miru	minai
	FORMAL	mimasu	mimaseñ
Imperative	INFORMAL I	miro	miru na
	II	minasai	minasaru na
	III	mite kudasai	minai de kudasai
	FORMAL	gorañ nasaimase	gorañ nasaimasu na
Presumptive	INFORMAL I	miyoo	mimai
	II	miru daroo	minai daroo
	FORMAL I	mimasyoo	mimasumai
	II	miru desyoo	minai desyoo
Provisional	INFORMAL	mireba	minakereba
	FORMAL	mimaseba	mimaseñ nara
		mimasureba	
Gerund	INFORMAL I	mite	minai de
	II		minakute
	FORMAL	mimasite	mimaseñ de
Past Ind.	INFORMAL	mita	minakatta
	FORMAL	mimasita	mimaseñ desita
Past Presump.	INFORMAL	mitaroo	minakattaroo
		mita daroo	minakatta daroo
	FORMAL	mimasitaroo	mimaseñ desitaroo
		mita desyoo	minakatta desyoo
Conditional	INFORMAL	mitara	minakattara
	FORMAL	mimasitara	mimaseñ desitara
Alternative	INFORMAL	mitari	minakattari
	FORMAL	mimasitari	mimaseñ desitari

INFORMAL AFFIRMATIVE INDICATIVE

Passive	mirareru		*Honorific*	I gorañ ni naru
				II gorañ nasaru
Potential	mirareru*			
			Humble	I haikeñ suru
Causative	misaseru			II haikeñ itasu
Causative Pass.	misaserareru			

*This form means 'can be seen' in the sense that it exists at the time one wants to look at it. 'To be visible' is a separate verb *mieru*.

		AFFIRMATIVE	NEGATIVE
Indicative	INFORMAL	miseru	misenai
	FORMAL	misemasu	misemaseñ
Imperative	INFORMAL I	misero	miseru na
	II	misenasai	misenasaru na
	III	misete kudasai	misenai de kudasai
	FORMAL	omise nasaimase	omise nasaimasu na
Presumptive	INFORMAL I	miseyoo	misemai
	II	miseru daroo	misenai daroo
	FORMAL I	misemasyoo	misemasumai
	II	miseru desyoo	misenai desyoo
Provisional	INFORMAL	misereba	misenakereba
	FORMAL	misemaseba	misemaseñ nara
		misemasureba	
Gerund	INFORMAL I	misete	misenai de
	II		misenakute
	FORMAL	misemasite	misemaseñ de
Past Ind.	INFORMAL	miseta	misenakatta
	FORMAL	misemasita	misemaseñ desita
Past Presump.	INFORMAL	misetaroo	misenakattaroo
		miseta daroo	misenakatta daroo
	FORMAL	misemasitaroo	misemaseñ desitaroo
		miseta desyoo	misenakatta desyoo
Conditional	INFORMAL	misetara	misenakattara
	FORMAL	misemasitara	misemaseñ desitara
Alternative	INFORMAL	misetari	misenakattari
	FORMAL	misemasitari	misemaseñ desitari

INFORMAL AFFIRMATIVE INDICATIVE

Passive	miserareru	*Honorific*	I	omise ni naru
			II	omise nasaru
Potential	miserareru			
		Humble		gorañ ni ireru
Causative	misesaseru			
Causative Pass.	misesaserareru			

TRANSITIVE   *to admit*

		AFFIRMATIVE	NEGATIVE
Indicative	**INFORMAL**	mitomeru	mitomenai
	FORMAL	mitomemasu	mitomemaseñ
Imperative	**INFORMAL I**	mitomero	mitomeru na
	II	mitomenasai	mitomenasaru na
	III	mitomete kudasai	mitomenai de kudasai
	FORMAL	omitome nasaimase	omitome nasaimasu na
Presumptive	**INFORMAL I**	mitomeyoo	mitomemai
	II	mitomeru daroo	mitomenai daroo
	FORMAL I	mitomemasyoo	mitomemasumai
	II	mitomeru desyoo	mitomenai desyoo
Provisional	**INFORMAL**	mitomereba	mitomenakereba
	FORMAL	mitomemaseba	mitomemaseñ nara
		mitomemasureba	
Gerund	**INFORMAL I**	mitomete	mitomenai de
	II		mitomenakute
	FORMAL	mitomemasite	mitomemaseñ de
Past Ind.	**INFORMAL**	mitometa	mitomenakatta
	FORMAL	mitomemasita	mitomemaseñ desita
Past Presump.	**INFORMAL**	mitometaroo	mitomenakattaroo
		mitometa daroo	mitomenakatta daroo
	FORMAL	mitomemasitaroo	mitomemaseñ desitaroo
		mitometa desyoo	mitomenakatta desyoo
Conditional	**INFORMAL**	mitometara	mitomenakattara
	FORMAL	mitomemasitara	mitomemaseñ desitara
Alternative	**INFORMAL**	mitometari	mitomenakattari
	FORMAL	mitomemasitari	mitomemaseñ desitari

INFORMAL AFFIRMATIVE INDICATIVE

Passive	mitomerareru	*Honorific*	**I**	omitome ni naru
			II	omitome nasaru
Potential	mitomerareru			
		Humble	**I**	
Causative	mitomesaseru		**II**	
Causative Pass.	mitomesaserareru			

		AFFIRMATIVE	NEGATIVE
Indicative	INFORMAL	mitukaru	mitukaranai
	FORMAL	mitukarimasu	mitukarimaseñ
Imperative	INFORMAL I		
	II		
	III		
	FORMAL		
Presumptive	INFORMAL I	mitukaroo	mitukarumai
	II	mitukaru daroo	mitukaranai daroo
	FORMAL I	mitukarimasyoo	mitukarimasumai
	II	mitukaru desyoo	mitukaranai desyoo
Provisional	INFORMAL	mitukareba	mitukaranakereba
	FORMAL	mitukarimaseba	mitukarimaseñ nara
		mitukarimasureba	
Gerund	INFORMAL I	mitukatte	mitukaranai de
	II		mitukaranakute
	FORMAL	mitukarimasite	mitukarimaseñ de
Past Ind.	INFORMAL	mitukatta	mitukaranakatta
	FORMAL	mitukarimasita	mitukarimaseñ desita
Past Presump.	INFORMAL	mitukattaroo	mitukaranakattaroo
		mitukatta daroo	mitukaranakatta daroo
	FORMAL	mitukarimasitaroo	mitukarimaseñ desitaroo
		mitukatta desyoo	mitukaranakatta desyoo
Conditional	INFORMAL	mitukattara	mitukaranakattara
	FORMAL	mitukarimasitara	mitukarimaseñ desitara
Alternative	INFORMAL	mitukattari	mitukaranakattari
	FORMAL	mitukarimasitari	mitukarimaseñ desitari

INFORMAL AFFIRMATIVE INDICATIVE

Passive	*Honorific*	I
		II
Potential		
	Humble	I
Causative		II
Causative Pass.		

174

		AFFIRMATIVE	NEGATIVE
Indicative	INFORMAL	mitukeru	mitukenai
	FORMAL	mitukemasu	mitukemaseñ
Imperative	INFORMAL I	mitukero	mitukeru na
	II	mitukenasai	mitukenasaru na
	III	mitukete kudasai	mitukenai de kudasai
	FORMAL	omituke nasaimase	omituke nasaimasu na
Presumptive	INFORMAL I	mitukeyoo	mitukemai
	II	mitukeru daroo	mitukenai daroo
	FORMAL I	mitukemasyoo	mitukemasumai
	II	mitukeru desyoo	mitukenai desyoo
Provisional	INFORMAL	mitukereba	mitukenakereba
	FORMAL	mitukemaseba	mitukemaseñ nara
		mitukemasureba	
Gerund	INFORMAL I	mitukete	mitukenai de
	II		mitukenakute
	FORMAL	mitukemasite	mitukemaseñ de
Past Ind.	INFORMAL	mituketa	mitukenakatta
	FORMAL	mitukemasita	mitukemaseñ desita
Past Presump.	INFORMAL	mituketaroo	mitukenakattaroo
		mituketa daroo	mitukenakatta daroo
	FORMAL	mitukemasitaroo	mitukemaseñ desitaroo
		mituketa desyoo	mitukenakatta desyoo
Conditional	INFORMAL	mituketara	mitukenakattara
	FORMAL	mitukemasitara	mitukemaseñ desitara
Alternative	INFORMAL	mituketari	mitukenakattari
	FORMAL	mitukemasitari	mitukemaseñ desitari

INFORMAL AFFIRMATIVE INDICATIVE

Passive	mitukerareru	*Honorific*	I	omituke ni naru
Potential	mitukerareru		II	omituke nasaru
Causative	mitukesaseru	*Humble*	I	
			II	
Causative Pass.	mitukesaserareru			

175

to return, to retrace one's steps

		AFFIRMATIVE	NEGATIVE
Indicative	INFORMAL	modoru	modoranai
	FORMAL	modorimasu	modorimaseñ
Imperative	INFORMAL I	modore	modoru na
	II	modorinasai	modorinasaru na
	III	modotte kudasai	modoranai de kudasai
	FORMAL	omodori nasaimase	omodori nasaimasu na
Presumptive	INFORMAL I	modoroo	modorumai
	II	modoru daroo	modoranai daroo
	FORMAL I	modorimasyoo	modorimasumai
	II	modoru desyoo	modoranai desyoo
Provisional	INFORMAL	modoreba	modoranakereba
	FORMAL	modorimaseba	modorimaseñ nara
		modorimasureba	
Gerund	INFORMAL I	modotte	modoranai de
	II		modoranakute
	FORMAL	modorimasite	modorimaseñ de
Past Ind.	INFORMAL	modotta	modoranakatta
	FORMAL	modorimasita	modorimaseñ desita
Past Presump.	INFORMAL	modottaroo	modoranakattaroo
		modotta daroo	modoranakatta daroo
	FORMAL	modorimasitaroo	modorimaseñ desitaroo
		modotta desyoo	modoranakatta desyoo
Conditional	INFORMAL	modottara	modoranakattara
	FORMAL	modorimasitara	modorimaseñ desitara
Alternative	INFORMAL	modottari	modoranakattari
	FORMAL	modorimasitari	modorimaseñ desitari

INFORMAL AFFIRMATIVE INDICATIVE

Passive	modorareru	*Honorific*	I	omodori ni naru
			II	omodori nasaru
Potential	modoreru			
		Humble	I	omodori suru
Causative	modoraseru		II	omodori itasu
Causative Pass.	modoraserareru			

TRANSITIVE   *to profit, to make money*

		AFFIRMATIVE	NEGATIVE
Indicative	INFORMAL	mookeru	mookenai
	FORMAL	mookemasu	mookemaseñ
Imperative	INFORMAL I	mookero	mookeru na
	II	mookenasai	mookenasaru na
	III	mookete kudasai	mookenai de kudasai
	FORMAL	omooke nasaimase	omooke nasaimasu na
Presumptive	INFORMAL I	mookeyoo	mookemai
	II	mookeru daroo	mookenai daroo
	FORMAL I	mookemasyoo	mookemasumai
	II	mookeru desyoo	mookenai desyoo
Provisional	INFORMAL	mookereba	mookenakereba
	FORMAL	mookemaseba	mookemaseñ nara
		mookemasureba	
Gerund	INFORMAL I	mookete	mookenai de
	II		mookenakute
	FORMAL	mookemasite	mookemaseñ de
Past Ind.	INFORMAL	mooketa	mookenakatta
	FORMAL	mookemasita	mookemaseñ desita
Past Presump.	INFORMAL	mooketaroo	mookenakattaroo
		mooketa daroo	mookenakatta daroo
	FORMAL	mookemasitaroo	mookemaseñ desitaroo
		mooketa desyoo	mookenakatta desyoo
Conditional	INFORMAL	mooketara	mookenakattara
	FORMAL	mookemasitara	mookemaseñ desitara
Alternative	INFORMAL	mooketari	mookenakattari
	FORMAL	mookemasitari	mookemaseñ desitari

INFORMAL AFFIRMATIVE INDICATIVE

Passive	mookerareru	*Honorific*	I	omooke ni naru
			II	omooke nasaru
Potential	mookerareru			
		Humble	I	
Causative	mookesaseru		II	
Causative Pass.	mookesaserareru			

		AFFIRMATIVE	NEGATIVE
Indicative	INFORMAL	morau	morawanai
	FORMAL	moraimasu	moraimaseñ
Imperative	INFORMAL I	morae	morau na
	II	morainasai	morainasaru na
	III	moratte kudasai	morawanai de kudasai
	FORMAL	omorai nasaimase	omorai nasaimasu na
Presumptive	INFORMAL I	moraoo	moraumai
	II	morau daroo	morawanai daroo
	FORMAL I	moraimasyoo	moraimasumai
	II	morau desyoo	morawanai desyoo
Provisional	INFORMAL	moraeba	morawanakereba
	FORMAL	moraimaseba	moraimaseñ nara
		moraimasureba	
Gerund	INFORMAL I	moratte	morawanai de
	II		morawanakute
	FORMAL	moraimasite	moraimaseñ de
Past Ind.	INFORMAL	moratta	morawanakatta
	FORMAL	moraimasita	moraimaseñ desita
Past Presump.	INFORMAL	morattaroo	morawanakattaroo
		moratta daroo	morawanakatta daroo
	FORMAL	moraimasitaroo	moraimaseñ desitaroo
		moratta desyoo	morawanakatta desyoo
Conditional	INFORMAL	morattara	morawanakattara
	FORMAL	moraimasitara	moraimaseñ desitara
Alternative	INFORMAL	morattari	morawanakattari
	FORMAL	moraimasitari	moraimaseñ desitari

INFORMAL AFFIRMATIVE INDICATIVE

Passive	morawareru	*Honorific*	I	omorai ni naru
			II	omorai nasaru
Potential	moraeru			
		Humble		itadaku
Causative	morawaseru			
Causative Pass.	morawaserareru			

TRANSITIVE   *to request, to seek*

		AFFIRMATIVE	NEGATIVE
Indicative	INFORMAL	motomeru	motomenai
	FORMAL	motomemasu	motomemaseñ
Imperative	INFORMAL I	motomero	motomeru na
	II	motomenasai	motomenasaru na
	III	motomete kudasai	motomenai de kudasai
	FORMAL	omotome nasaimase	omotome nasaimasu na
Presumptive	INFORMAL I	motomeyoo	motomemai
	II	motomeru daroo	motomenai daroo
	FORMAL I	motomemasyoo	motomemasumai
	II	motomeru desyoo	motomenai desyoo
Provisional	INFORMAL	motomereba	motomenakereba
	FORMAL	motomemaseba	motomemaseñ nara
		motomemasureba	
Gerund	INFORMAL I	motomete	motomenai de
	II		motomenakute
	FORMAL	motomemasite	motomemaseñ de
Past Ind.	INFORMAL	motometa	motomenakatta
	FORMAL	motomemasita	motomemaseñ desita
Past Presump.	INFORMAL	motometaroo	motomenakattaroo
		motometa daroo	motomenakatta daroo
	FORMAL	motomemasitaroo	motomemaseñ desitaroo
		motometa desyoo	motomenakatta desyoo
Conditional	INFORMAL	motometara	motomenakattara
	FORMAL	motomemasitara	motomemaseñ desitara
Alternative	INFORMAL	motometari	motomenakattari
	FORMAL	motomemasitari	motomemaseñ desitari

INFORMAL AFFIRMATIVE INDICATIVE

Passive	motomerareru	*Honorific*	I	omotome ni naru
			II	omotome nasaru
Potential	motomerareru			
		Humble	I	omotome suru
Causative	motomesaseru		II	omotome itasu
Causative Pass.	motomesaserareru			

		AFFIRMATIVE	NEGATIVE
Indicative	INFORMAL	motu	motanai
	FORMAL	motimasu	motimaseñ
Imperative	INFORMAL I	mote	motu na
	II	motinasai	motinasaru na
	III	motte kudasai	motanai de kudasai
	FORMAL	omoti nasaimase	omoti nasaimasu na
Presumptive	INFORMAL I	motoo	motumai
	II	motu daroo	motanai daroo
	FORMAL I	motimasyoo	motimasumai
	II	motu desyoo	motanai desyoo
Provisional	INFORMAL	moteba	motanakereba
	FORMAL	motimaseba	motimaseñ nara
		motimasureba	
Gerund	INFORMAL I	motte	motanai de
	II		motanakute
	FORMAL	motimasite	motimaseñ de
Past Ind.	INFORMAL	motta	motanakatta
	FORMAL	motimasita	motimaseñ desita
Past Presump.	INFORMAL	mottaroo	motanakattaroo
		motta daroo	motanakatta daroo
	FORMAL	motimasitaroo	motimaseñ desitaroo
		motta desyoo	motanakatta desyoo
Conditional	INFORMAL	mottara	motanakattara
	FORMAL	motimasitara	motimaseñ desitara
Alternative	INFORMAL	mottari	motanakattari
	FORMAL	motimasitari	motimaseñ desitari

INFORMAL AFFIRMATIVE INDICATIVE

Passive	motareru	*Honorific*	I	omoti ni naru
			II	omoti nasaru
Potential	moteru			
		Humble	I	omoti suru
Causative	motaseru		II	omoti itasu
Causative Pass.	motaserareru			

		AFFIRMATIVE	NEGATIVE
Indicative	INFORMAL	nagareru	nagarenai
	FORMAL	nagaremasu	nagaremaseñ
Imperative	INFORMAL I	nagarero	nagareru na
	II		
	III		
	FORMAL		
Presumptive	INFORMAL I	nagareyoo	nagaremai
	II	nagareru daroo	nagarenai daroo
	FORMAL I	nagaremasyoo	nagaremasumai
	II	nagareru desyoo	nagarenai desyoo
Provisional	INFORMAL	nagarereba	nagarenakereba
	FORMAL	nagaremaseba	nagaremaseñ nara
		nagaremasureba	
Gerund	INFORMAL I	nagarete	nagarenai de
	II		nagarenakute
	FORMAL	nagaremasite	nagaremaseñ de
Past Ind.	INFORMAL	nagareta	nagarenakatta
	FORMAL	nagaremasita	nagaremaseñ desita
Past Presump.	INFORMAL	nagaretaroo	nagarenakattaroo
		nagareta daroo	nagarenakatta daroo
	FORMAL	nagaremasitaroo	nagaremaseñ desitaroo
		nagareta desyoo	nagarenakatta desyoo
Conditional	INFORMAL	nagaretara	nagarenakattara
	FORMAL	nagaremasitara	nagaremaseñ desitara
Alternative	INFORMAL	nagaretari	nagarenakattari
	FORMAL	nagaremasitari	nagaremaseñ desitari

INFORMAL AFFIRMATIVE INDICATIVE

Passive	nagarerareru	*Honorific*	I
			II
Potential	nagarerareru		
		Humble	I
Causative	nagaresaseru		II
Causative Pass.	nagaresaserareru		

		AFFIRMATIVE	NEGATIVE
Indicative	INFORMAL	nagusameru	nagusamenai
	FORMAL	nagusamemasu	nagusamemaseñ
Imperative	INFORMAL I	nagusamero	nagusameru na
	II	nagusamenasai	nagusamenasaru na
	III	nagusamete kudasai	nagusamenai de kudasai
	FORMAL	onagusame nasaimase	onagusame nasaimasu na
Presumptive	INFORMAL I	nagusameyoo	nagusamemai
	II	nagusameru daroo	nagusamenai daroo
	FORMAL I	nagusamemasyoo	nagusamemasumai
	II	nagusameru desyoo	nagusamenai desyoo
Provisional	INFORMAL	nagusamereba	nagusamenakereba
	FORMAL	nagusamemaseba	nagusamemaseñ nara
		nagusamemasureba	
Gerund	INFORMAL I	nagusamete	nagusamenai de
	II		nagusamenakute
	FORMAL	nagusamemasite	nagusamemaseñ de
Past Ind.	INFORMAL	nagusameta	nagusamenakatta
	FORMAL	nagusamemasita	nagusamemaseñ desita
Past Presump.	INFORMAL	nagusametaroo	nagusamenakattaroo
		nagusameta daroo	nagusamenakatta daroo
	FORMAL	nagusamemasitaroo	nagusamemaseñ desitaroo
		nagusamemasita desyoo	nagusamenakatta desyoo
Conditional	INFORMAL	nagusametara	nagusamenakattara
	FORMAL	nagusamemasitara	nagusamemaseñ desitara
Alternative	INFORMAL	nagusametari	nagusamenakattari
	FORMAL	nagusamemasitari	nagusamemaseñ desitari

INFORMAL AFFIRMATIVE INDICATIVE

Passive	nagusamerareru	*Honorific*	I	onagusame ni naru
			II	onagusame nasaru
Potential	nagusamerareru			
		Humble	I	onagusame suru
Causative	nagusamesaseru		II	onagusame itasu
Causative Pass.	nagusamesaserareru			

		AFFIRMATIVE	NEGATIVE
Indicative	INFORMAL	naku	nakanai
	FORMAL	nakimasu	nakimaseñ
Imperative	INFORMAL I	nake	naku na
	II	nakinasai	nakinasaru na
	III	naite kudasai	nakanai de kudasai
	FORMAL	onaki nasaimase	onaki nasaimasu na
Presumptive	INFORMAL I	nakoo	nakumai
	II	naku daroo	nakanai daroo
	FORMAL I	nakimasyoo	nakimasumai
	II	naku desyoo	nakanai desyoo
Provisional	INFORMAL	nakeba	nakanakereba
	FORMAL	nakimaseba	nakimaseñ nara
		nakimasureba	
Gerund	INFORMAL I	naite	nakanai de
	II		nakanakute
	FORMAL	nakimasite	nakimaseñ de
Past Ind.	INFORMAL	naita	nakanakatta
	FORMAL	nakimasita	nakimaseñ desita
Past Presump.	INFORMAL	naitaroo	nakanakattaroo
		naita daroo	nakanakatta daroo
	FORMAL	nakimasitaroo	nakimaseñ desitaroo
		naita desyoo	nakanakatta desyoo
Conditional	INFORMAL	naitara	nakanakattara
	FORMAL	nakimasitara	nakimaseñ desitara
Alternative	INFORMAL	naitari	nakanakattari
	FORMAL	nakimasitari	nakimaseñ desitari

INFORMAL AFFIRMATIVE INDICATIVE

Passive	nakareru	Honorific	I	onaki ni naru
			II	onaki nasaru
Potential	nakeru			
		Humble	I	
Causative	nakaseru		II	
Causative Pass.	nakaserareru			

183

		AFFIRMATIVE	NEGATIVE
Indicative	INFORMAL	nakunaru	nakunaranai
	FORMAL	nakunarimasu	nakunarimaseñ
Imperative	INFORMAL I	nakunare	nakunaru na
	II		
	III		
	FORMAL		
Presumptive	INFORMAL I	nakunaroo	nakunarumai
	II	nakunaru daroo	nakunaranai daroo
	FORMAL I	nakunarimasyoo	nakunarimasumai
	II	nakunaru desyoo	nakunaranai desyoo
Provisional	INFORMAL	nakunareba	nakunaranakereba
	FORMAL	nakunarimaseba	nakunarimaseñ nara
		nakunarimasureba	
Gerund	INFORMAL I	nakunatte	nakunaranai de
	II		nakunaranakute
	FORMAL	nakunarimasite	nakunarimaseñ de
Past Ind.	INFORMAL	nakunatta	nakunaranakatta
	FORMAL	nakunarimasita	nakunarimaseñ desita
Past Presump.	INFORMAL	nakunattaroo	nakunaranakattaroo
		nakunatta daroo	nakunaranakatta daroo
	FORMAL	nakunarimasitaroo	nakunarimaseñ desitaroo
		nakunatta desyoo	nakunaranakatta desyoo
Conditional	INFORMAL	nakunattara	nakunaranakattara
	FORMAL	nakunarimasitara	nakunarimaseñ desitara
Alternative	INFORMAL	nakunattari	nakunaranakattari
	FORMAL	nakunarimasitari	nakunarimaseñ desitari

INFORMAL AFFIRMATIVE INDICATIVE

Passive	nakunarareru	*Honorific*	I	onakunari ni naru
			II	onakunari nasaru
Potential	nakunareru			
		Humble	I	
Causative	nakunaraseru		II	
Causative Pass.	nakunaraserareru			

		AFFIRMATIVE	NEGATIVE
Indicative	INFORMAL	naoru	naoranai
	FORMAL	naorimasu	naorimaseñ
Imperative	INFORMAL I	naore	naoru na
	II	naorinasai	naorinasaru na
	III	naotte kudasai	naoranai de kudasai
	FORMAL	onaori nasaimase	onaori nasaimasu na
Presumptive	INFORMAL I	naoroo	naorumai
	II	naoru daroo	naoranai daroo
	FORMAL I	naorimasyoo	naorimasumai
	II	naoru desyoo	naoranai desyoo
Provisional	INFORMAL	naoreba	naoranakereba
	FORMAL	naorimaseba	naorimaseñ nara
		naorimasureba	
Gerund	INFORMAL I	naotte	naoranai de
	II		naoranakute
	FORMAL	naorimasite	naorimaseñ de
Past Ind.	INFORMAL	naotta	naoranakatta
	FORMAL	naorimasita	naorimaseñ desita
Past Presump.	INFORMAL	naottaroo	naoranakattaroo
		naotta daroo	naoranakatta daroo
	FORMAL	naorimasitaroo	naorimaseñ desitaroo
		naotta desyoo	naoranakatta desyoo
Conditional	INFORMAL	naottara	naoranakattara
	FORMAL	naorimasitara	naorimaseñ desitara
Alternative	INFORMAL	naottari	naoranakattari
	FORMAL	naorimasitari	naorimaseñ desitari

INFORMAL AFFIRMATIVE INDICATIVE

Passive	naorareru	*Honorific*	I	onaori ni naru
			II	onaori nasaru
Potential	naoreru			
		Humble	I	
Causative	naoraseru		II	

Causative Pass.

		AFFIRMATIVE	NEGATIVE
Indicative	INFORMAL	naosu	naosanai
	FORMAL	naosimasu	naosimaseñ
Imperative	INFORMAL I	naose	naosu na
	II	naosinasai	naosinasaru na
	III	naosite kudasai	naosanai de kudasai
	FORMAL	onaosi nasaimase	onaosi nasaimasu na
Presumptive	INFORMAL I	naosoo	naosumai
	II	naosu daroo	naosanai daroo
	FORMAL I	naosimasyoo	naosimasumai
	II	naosu desyoo	naosanai desyoo
Provisional	INFORMAL	naoseba	naosanakereba
	FORMAL	naosimaseba	naosimaseñ nara
		naosimasureba	
Gerund	INFORMAL I	naosite	naosanai de
	II		naosanakute
	FORMAL	naosimasite	naosimaseñ de
Past Ind.	INFORMAL	naosita	naosanakatta
	FORMAL	naosimasita	naosimaseñ desita
Past Presump.	INFORMAL	naositaroo	naosanakattaroo
		naosita daroo	naosanakatta daroo
	FORMAL	naosimasitaroo	naosimaseñ desitaroo
		naosita desyoo	naosanakatta desyoo
Conditional	INFORMAL	naositara	naosanakattara
	FORMAL	naosimasitara	naosimaseñ desitara
Alternative	INFORMAL	naositari	naosanakattari
	FORMAL	naosimasitari	naosimaseñ desitari

INFORMAL AFFIRMATIVE INDICATIVE

Passive	naosareru	*Honorific*	I	onaosi ni naru
			II	onaosi nasaru
Potential	naoseru			
		Humble	I	onaosi suru
Causative	naosaseru		II	onaosi itasu
Causative Pass.	naosaserareru			

		AFFIRMATIVE	NEGATIVE
Indicative	INFORMAL	naraberu	narabenai
	FORMAL	narabemasu	narabemaseñ
Imperative	INFORMAL I	narabero	naraberu na
	II	narabenasai	narabenasaru na
	III	narabete kudasai	narabenai de kudasai
	FORMAL	onarabe nasaimase	onarabe nasaimasu na
Presumptive	INFORMAL I	narabeyoo	narabemai
	II	naraberu daroo	narabenai daroo
	FORMAL I	narabemasyoo	narabemasumai
	II	naraberu desyoo	narabenai desyoo
Provisional	INFORMAL	narabereba	narabenakereba
	FORMAL	narabemaseba	narabemaseñ nara
		narabemasureba	
Gerund	INFORMAL I	narabete	narabenai de
	II		narabenakute
	FORMAL	narabemasite	narabemaseñ de
Past Ind.	INFORMAL	narabeta	narabenakatta
	FORMAL	narabemasita	narabemaseñ desita
Past Presump.	INFORMAL	narabetaroo	narabenakattaroo
		narabeta daroo	narabenakatta daroo
	FORMAL	narabemasitaroo	narabemaseñ desitaroo
		narabeta desyoo	narabenakatta desyoo
Conditional	INFORMAL	narabetara	narabenakattara
	FORMAL	narabemasitara	narabemaseñ desitara
Alternative	INFORMAL	narabetari	narabenakattari
	FORMAL	narabemasitari	narabemaseñ desitari

INFORMAL AFFIRMATIVE INDICATIVE

Passive	naraberareru	*Honorific*	I	onarabe ni naru
			II	onarabe nasaru
Potential	naraberareru			
		Humble	I	onarabe suru
Causative	narabesaseru		II	onarabe itasu
Causative Pass.	narabesaserareru			

		AFFIRMATIVE	NEGATIVE
Indicative	INFORMAL	narau	narawanai
	FORMAL	naraimasu	naraimaseñ
Imperative	INFORMAL I	narae	narau na
	II	narainasai	narainasaru na
	III	naratte kudasai	narawanai de kudasai
	FORMAL	onarai nasaimase	onarai nasaimasu na
Presumptive	INFORMAL I	naraoo	naraumai
	II	narau daroo	narawanai daroo
	FORMAL I	naraimasyoo	naraimasumai
	II	narau desyoo	narawanai desyoo
Provisional	INFORMAL	naraeba	narawanakereba
	FORMAL	naraimaseba	naraimaseñ nara
		naraimasureba	
Gerund	INFORMAL I	naratte	narawanai de
	II		narawanakute
	FORMAL	naraimasite	naraimaseñ de
Past Ind.	INFORMAL	naratta	narawanakatta
	FORMAL	naraimasita	naraimaseñ desita
Past Presump.	INFORMAL	narattaroo	narawanakattaroo
		naratta daroo	narawanakatta daroo
	FORMAL	naraimasitaroo	naraimaseñ desitaroo
		naratta desyoo	narawanakatta desyoo
Conditional	INFORMAL	narattara	narawanakattara
	FORMAL	naraimasitara	naraimaseñ desitara
Alternative	INFORMAL	narattari	narawanakattari
	FORMAL	naraimasitari	naraimaseñ desitari

INFORMAL AFFIRMATIVE INDICATIVE

Passive	narawareru	*Honorific*	I	onarai ni naru
Potential	naraeru		II	onarai nasaru
Causative	narawaseru	*Humble*	I	
			II	
Causative Pass.	narawaserareru			

		AFFIRMATIVE	NEGATIVE
Indicative	INFORMAL	naru	naranai
	FORMAL	narimasu	narimaseñ
Imperative	INFORMAL I	nare	naru na
	II	narinasai	narinasaru na
	III	natte kudasai	naranai de kudasai
	FORMAL	onari nasaimase	onari nasaimasu na
Presumptive	INFORMAL I	naroo	narumai
	II	naru daroo	naranai daroo
	FORMAL I	narimasyoo	narimasumai
	II	naru desyoo	naranai desyoo
Provisional	INFORMAL	nareba	naranakereba
	FORMAL	narimaseba	narimaseñ nara
		narimasureba	
Gerund	INFORMAL I	natte	naranai de
	II		naranakute
	FORMAL	narimasite	narimaseñ de
Past Ind.	INFORMAL	natta	naranakatta
	FORMAL	narimasita	narimaseñ desita
Past Presump.	INFORMAL	nattaroo	naranakattaroo
		natta daroo	naranakatta daroo
	FORMAL	narimasitaroo	narimaseñ desitaroo
		natta desyoo	naranakatta desyoo
Conditional	INFORMAL	nattara	naranakattara
	FORMAL	narimasitara	narimaseñ desitara
Alternative	INFORMAL	nattari	naranakattari
	FORMAL	narimasitari	narimaseñ desitari

INFORMAL AFFIRMATIVE INDICATIVE

Passive	narareru	*Honorific*	I	onari ni naru
			II	onari nasaru
Potential	nareru			
		Humble	I	
Causative	naraseru		II	
Causative Pass.	naraserareru			

		AFFIRMATIVE	NEGATIVE
Indicative	INFORMAL	nasaru	nasaranai
	FORMAL	nasaimasu	nasaimaseñ
Imperative	INFORMAL I	nasai	nasaru na
	II		
	III	nasatte kudasai	nasaranai de kudasai
	FORMAL	nasaimase	nasaimasu na
Presumptive	INFORMAL I	nasaroo	nasarumai
	II	nasaru daroo	nasaranai daroo
	FORMAL I	nasaimasyoo	nasaimasumai
	II	nasaru desyoo	nasaranai desyoo
Provisional	INFORMAL	nasareba	nasaranakereba
	FORMAL	nasaimaseba	nasaimaseñ nara
		nasaimasureba	
Gerund	INFORMAL I	nasatte	nasaranai de
	II		nasaranakute
	FORMAL	nasaimasite	nasaimaseñ de
Past Ind.	INFORMAL	nasatta	nasaranakatta
	FORMAL	nasaimasita	nasaimaseñ desita
Past Presump.	INFORMAL	nasattaroo	nasaranakattaroo
		nasatta daroo	nasaranakatta daroo
	FORMAL	nasaimasitaroo	nasaimaseñ desitaroo
		nasatta desyoo	nasaranakatta desyoo
Conditional	INFORMAL	nasattara	nasaranakattara
	FORMAL	nasaimasitara	nasaimaseñ desitara
Alternative	INFORMAL	nasattari	nasaranakattari
	FORMAL	nasaimasitari	nasaimaseñ desitari

INFORMAL AFFIRMATIVE INDICATIVE

Passive	nasarareru	*Honorific*	I
			II
Potential	nasareru		
		Humble	I
Causative			II

Causative Pass.

to sleep, to recline

		AFFIRMATIVE	NEGATIVE
Indicative	INFORMAL	neru	nenai
	FORMAL	nemasu	nemaseñ
Imperative	INFORMAL I	nero	neru na
	II	nenasai	nenasaru na
	III	nete kudasai	nenai de kudasai
	FORMAL*	oyasumi nasaimase	oyasumi nasaimasu na
Presumptive	INFORMAL I	neyoo	nemai
	II	neru daroo	nenai daroo
	FORMAL I	nemasyoo	nemasumai
	II	neru desyoo	nenai desyoo
Provisional	INFORMAL	nereba	nenakereba
	FORMAL	nemaseba	nemaseñ nara
		nemasureba	
Gerund	INFORMAL I	nete	nenai de
	II		nenakute
	FORMAL	nemasite	nemaseñ de
Past Ind.	INFORMAL	neta	nenakatta
	FORMAL	nemasita	nemaseñ desita
Past Presump.	INFORMAL	netaroo	nenakattaroo
		neta daroo	nenakatta daroo
	FORMAL	nemasitaroo	nemaseñ desitaroo
		neta desyoo	nenakatta desyoo
Conditional	INFORMAL	netara	nenakattara
	FORMAL	nemasitara	nemaseñ desitara
Alternative	INFORMAL	netari	nenakattari
	FORMAL	nemasitari	nemaseñ desitari

INFORMAL AFFIRMATIVE INDICATIVE

Passive	nerareru	*Honorific**	I	oyasumi ni naru
			II	oyasumi nasaru
Potential	nerareru			
		Humble	I	
Causative	nesaseru		II	
Causative Pass.	nesaserareru			

*The formal imperative forms and honorific equivalents for *neru* are the same as those of its synonym *yasumu*.

		AFFIRMATIVE	NEGATIVE
Indicative	**INFORMAL**	nigeru	nigenai
	FORMAL	nigemasu	nigemaseñ
Imperative	**INFORMAL I**	nigero	nigeru na
	II	nigenasai	nigenasaru na
	III	nigete kudasai	nigenai de kudasai
	FORMAL	onige nasaimase	onige nasaimasu na
Presumptive	**INFORMAL I**	nigeyoo	nigemai
	II	nigeru daroo	nigenai daroo
	FORMAL I	nigemasyoo	nigemasumai
	II	nigeru desyoo	nigenai desyoo
Provisional	**INFORMAL**	nigereba	nigenakereba
	FORMAL	nigemaseba	nigemaseñ nara
		nigemasureba	
Gerund	**INFORMAL I**	nigete	nigenai de
	II		nigenakute
	FORMAL	nigemasite	nigemaseñ de
Past Ind.	**INFORMAL**	nigeta	nigenakatta
	FORMAL	nigemasita	nigemaseñ desita
Past Presump.	**INFORMAL**	nigetaroo	nigenakattaroo
		nigeta daroo	nigenakatta daroo
	FORMAL	nigemasitaroo	nigemaseñ desitaroo
		nigeta desyoo	nigenakatta desyoo
Conditional	**INFORMAL**	nigetara	nigenakattara
	FORMAL	nigemasitara	nigemaseñ desitara
Alternative	**INFORMAL**	nigetari	nigenakattari
	FORMAL	nigemasitari	nigemaseñ desitari

INFORMAL AFFIRMATIVE INDICATIVE

Passive	nigerareru	*Honorific*	**I**	onige ni naru
			II	onige nasaru
Potential	nigerareru			
		Humble	**I**	
Causative	nigesaseru		**II**	
Causative Pass.	nigesaserareru			

		AFFIRMATIVE	NEGATIVE
Indicative	INFORMAL	nigiru	nigiranai
	FORMAL	nigirimasu	nigirimaseñ
Imperative	INFORMAL I	nigire	nigiru na
	II	nigirinasai	nigirinasaru na
	III	nigitte kudasai	nigiranai de kudasai
	FORMAL	onigiri nasaimase	onigiri nasaimasu na
Presumptive	INFORMAL I	nigiroo	nigirumai
	II	nigiru daroo	nigiranai daroo
	FORMAL I	nigirimasyoo	nigirimasumai
	II	nigiru desyoo	nigiranai desyoo
Provisional	INFORMAL	nigireba	nigiranakereba
	FORMAL	nigirimaseba	nigirimaseñ nara
		nigirimasureba	
Gerund	INFORMAL I	nigitte	nigiranai de
	II		nigiranakute
	FORMAL	nigirimasite	nigirimaseñ de
Past Ind.	INFORMAL	nigitta	nigiranakatta
	FORMAL	nigirimasita	nigirimaseñ desita
Past Presump.	INFORMAL	nigittaroo	nigiranakattaroo
		nigitta daroo	nigiranakatta daroo
	FORMAL	nigirimasitaroo	nigirimaseñ desitaroo
		nigitta desyoo	nigiranakatta desyoo
Conditional	INFORMAL	nigittara	nigiranakattara
	FORMAL	nigirimasitara	nigirimaseñ desitara
Alternative	INFORMAL	nigittari	nigiranakattari
	FORMAL	nigirimasitari	nigirimaseñ desitari

INFORMAL AFFIRMATIVE INDICATIVE

Passive	nigirareru	*Honorific*	I	onigiri ni naru
			II	onigiri nasaru
Potential	nigireru			
		Humble	I	onigiri suru
Causative	nigiraseru		II	onigiri itasu
Causative Pass.	nigiraserareru			

		AFFIRMATIVE	NEGATIVE
Indicative	INFORMAL	noboru	noboranai
	FORMAL	noborimasu	noborimaseñ
Imperative	INFORMAL I	nobore	noboru na
	II	noborinasai	noborinasaru na
	III	nobotte kudasai	noboranai de kudasai
	FORMAL	onobori nasaimase	onobori nasaimasu na
Presumptive	INFORMAL I	noboroo	noborumai
	II	noboru daroo	noboranai daroo
	FORMAL I	noborimasyoo	noborimasumai
	II	noboru desyoo	noboranai desyoo
Provisional	INFORMAL	noboreba	noboranakereba
	FORMAL	noborimaseba	noborimaseñ nara
		noborimasureba	
Gerund	INFORMAL I	nobotte	noboranai de
	II		noboranakute
	FORMAL	noborimasite	noborimaseñ de
Past Ind.	INFORMAL	nobotta	noboranakatta
	FORMAL	noborimasita	noborimaseñ desita
Past Presump.	INFORMAL	nobottaroo	noboranakattaroo
		nobotta daroo	noboranakatta daroo
	FORMAL	noborimasitaroo	noborimaseñ desitaroo
		nobotta desyoo	noboranakatta desyoo
Conditional	INFORMAL	nobottara	noboranakattara
	FORMAL	noborimasitara	noborimaseñ desitara
Alternative	INFORMAL	nobottari	noboranakattari
	FORMAL	noborimasitari	noborimaseñ desitari

INFORMAL AFFIRMATIVE INDICATIVE

Passive	noborareru	*Honorific*	I	onobori ni naru
			II	onobori nasaru
Potential	noboreru			
		Humble	I	
Causative	noboraseru		II	
Causative Pass.	noboraserareru			

to be left over, to be left behind

			AFFIRMATIVE	NEGATIVE
Indicative	INFORMAL		nokoru	nokoranai
	FORMAL		nokorimasu	nokorimaseñ
Imperative	INFORMAL	I	nokore	nokoru na
		II	nokorinasai	nokorinasaru na
		III	nokotte kudasai	nokoranaide kudasai
	FORMAL		onokori nasaimase	onokori nasaimasu na
Presumptive	INFORMAL	I	nokoroo	nokorumai
		II	nokoru daroo	nokoranai daroo
	FORMAL	I	nokorimasyoo	nokorimasumai
		II	nokoru desyoo	nokoranai desyoo
Provisional	INFORMAL		nokoreba	nokoranakereba
	FORMAL		nokorimaseba	nokorimaseñ nara
			nokorimasureba	
Gerund	INFORMAL	I	nokotte	nokoranai de
		II		nokoranakute
	FORMAL		nokorimasite	nokorimaseñ de
Past Ind.	INFORMAL		nokotta	nokoranakatta
	FORMAL		nokorimasita	nokorimaseñ desita
Past Presump.	INFORMAL		nokottaroo	nokoranakattaroo
			nokotta daroo	nokoranakatta daroo
	FORMAL		nokorimasitaroo	nokorimaseñ desitaroo
			nokotta desyoo	nokoranakatta desyoo
Conditional	INFORMAL		nokottara	nokoranakattara
	FORMAL		nokorimasitara	nokorimaseñ desitara
Alternative	INFORMAL		nokottari	nokoranakattari
	FORMAL		nokorimasitari	nokorimaseñ desitari

INFORMAL AFFIRMATIVE INDICATIVE

Passive	nokorareru	*Honorific*	I	onokori ni naru
			II	onokori nasaru
Potential	nokoreru			
		Humble	I	
Causative	nokoraseru		II	
Causative Pass.	nokoraserareru			

		AFFIRMATIVE	NEGATIVE
Indicative	INFORMAL	nomu	nomanai
	FORMAL	nomimasu	nomimaseñ
Imperative	INFORMAL I	nome	nomu na
	II	nominasai	nominasaru na
	III	noñde kudasai	nomanai de kudasai
	FORMAL	mesiagarimase	mesiagarimasu na
		onomi nasaimase	onomi nasaimasu na
Presumptive	INFORMAL I	nomoo	nomumai
	II	nomu daroo	nomanai daroo
	FORMAL I	nomimasyoo	nomimasumai
	II	nomu desyoo	nomanai desyoo
Provisional	INFORMAL	nomeba	nomanakereba
	FORMAL	nomimaseba	nomimaseñ nara
		nomimasureba	
Gerund	INFORMAL I	noñde	nomanai de
	II		nomanakute
	FORMAL	nomimasite	nomimaseñ de
Past Ind.	INFORMAL	noñda	nomanakatta
	FORMAL	nomimasita	nomimaseñ desita
Past Presump.	INFORMAL	noñdaroo	nomanakattaroo
		noñda daroo	nomanakatta daroo
	FORMAL	nomimasitaroo	nomimaseñ desitaroo
		noñda desyoo	nomanakatta desyoo
Conditional	INFORMAL	noñdara	nomanakattara
	FORMAL	nomimasitara	nomimaseñ desitara
Alternative	INFORMAL	noñdari	nomanakattari
	FORMAL	nomimasitari	nomimaseñ desitari

INFORMAL AFFIRMATIVE INDICATIVE

Passive	nomareru	*Honorific*	mesiagaru	I	onomi ni naru
				II	onomi nasaru
Potential	nomeru				
		Humble	itadaku		
Causative	nomaseru				
Causative Pass.	nomaserareru				

		AFFIRMATIVE	NEGATIVE
Indicative	INFORMAL	noru	noranai
	FORMAL	norimasu	norimaseñ
Imperative	INFORMAL I	nore	noru na
	II	norinasai	norinasaru na
	III	notte kudasai	noranai de kudasai
	FORMAL	onori nasaimase	onori nasaimasu na
Presumptive	INFORMAL I	noroo	norumai
	II	noru daroo	noranai daroo
	FORMAL I	norimasyoo	norumasumai
	II	noru desyoo	noranai desyoo
Provisional	INFORMAL	noreba	noranakereba
	FORMAL	norimaseba	norimaseñ nara
		norimasureba	
Gerund	INFORMAL I	notte	noranai de
	II		noranakute
	FORMAL	norimasite	norimaseñ de
Past Ind.	INFORMAL	notta	noranakatta
	FORMAL	norimasita	norimaseñ desita
Past Presump.	INFORMAL	nottaroo	noranakattaroo
		notta daroo	noranakatta daroo
	FORMAL	norimasitaroo	norimaseñ desitaroo
		notta desyoo	noranakatta desyoo
Conditional	INFORMAL	nottara	noranakattara
	FORMAL	norimasitara	norimaseñ desitara
Alternative	INFORMAL	nottari	noranakattari
	FORMAL	norimasitari	norimaseñ desitari

INFORMAL AFFIRMATIVE INDICATIVE

Passive	norareru	*Honorific*	I	onori ni naru
			II	onori nasaru
Potential	noreru			
		Humble	I	
Causative	noraseru		II	
Causative Pass.	noraserareru			

		AFFIRMATIVE	NEGATIVE
Indicative	INFORMAL	noseru	nosenai
	FORMAL	nosemasu	nosemaseñ
Imperative	INFORMAL I	nosero	noseru na
	II	nosenasai	nosenasaru na
	III	nosete kudasai	nosenai de kudasai
	FORMAL	onose nasaimase	onose nasaimasu na
Presumptive	INFORMAL I	noseyoo	nosemai
	II	noseru daroo	nosenai daroo
	FORMAL I	nosemasyoo	nosemasumai
	II	noseru desyoo	nosenai desyoo
Provisional	INFORMAL	nosereba	nosenakereba
	FORMAL	nosemaseba	nosemaseñ nara
		nosemasureba	
Gerund	INFORMAL I	nosete	nosenai de
	II		nosenakute
	FORMAL	nosemasite	nosemaseñ de
Past Ind.	INFORMAL	noseta	nosenakatta
	FORMAL	nosemasita	nosemaseñ desita
Past Presump.	INFORMAL	nosetaroo	nosenakattaroo
		noseta daroo	nosenakatta daroo
	FORMAL	nosemasitaroo	nosemaseñ desitaroo
		noseta desyoo	nosenakatta desyoo
Conditional	INFORMAL	nosetara	nosenakattara
	FORMAL	nosemasitara	nosemaseñ desitara
Alternative	INFORMAL	nosetari	nosenakattari
	FORMAL	nosemasitari	nosemaseñ desitari

INFORMAL AFFIRMATIVE INDICATIVE

Passive	noserareru	*Honorific*	I	onose ni naru
			II	onose nasaru
Potential	noserareru			
		Humble	I	onose suru
Causative	nosesaseru		II	onose itasu
Causative Pass.	nosesaserareru			

		AFFIRMATIVE	NEGATIVE
Indicative	INFORMAL	nureru	nurenai
	FORMAL	nuremasu	nuremaseñ
Imperative	INFORMAL I	nurero	nureru na
	II		
	III		
	FORMAL		
Presumptive	INFORMAL I	nureyoo	nuremai
	II	nureru daroo	nurenai daroo
	FORMAL I	nuremasyoo	nuremasumai
	II	nureru desyoo	nurenai desyoo
Provisional	INFORMAL	nurereba	nurenakereba
	FORMAL	nuremaseba	nuremaseñ nara
		nuremasureba	
Gerund	INFORMAL I	nurete	nurenai de
	II		nurenakute
	FORMAL	nuremasite	nuremaseñ de
Past Ind.	INFORMAL	nureta	nurenakatta
	FORMAL	nuremasita	nuremaseñ desita
Past Presump.	INFORMAL	nuretaroo	nurenakattaroo
		nureta daroo	nurenakatta daroo
	FORMAL	nuremasitaroo	nuremaseñ desitaroo
		nureta desyoo	nurenakatta desyoo
Conditional	INFORMAL	nuretara	nurenakattara
	FORMAL	nuremasitara	nuremaseñ desitara
Alternative	INFORMAL	nuretari	nurenakattari
	FORMAL	nuremasitari	nuremaseñ desitari

INFORMAL AFFIRMATIVE INDICATIVE

Passive	nurerareru	*Honorific*	I	onure ni naru
			II	onure nasaru
Potential	nurerareru			
		Humble	I	
Causative	nuresaseru		II	
Causative Pass.	nuresaserareru			

		AFFIRMATIVE	NEGATIVE
Indicative	INFORMAL	nuru	nuranai
	FORMAL	nurimasu	nurimaseñ
Imperative	INFORMAL I	nure	nuru na
	II	nurinasai	nurinasaru na
	III	nutte kudasai	nuranai de kudasai
	FORMAL	onuri nasaimase	onuri nasaimasu na
Presumptive	INFORMAL I	nuroo	nurumai
	II	nuru daroo	nuranai daroo
	FORMAL I	nurimasyoo	nurimasumai
	II	nuru desyoo	nuranai desyoo
Provisional	INFORMAL	nureba	nuranakereba
	FORMAL	nurimaseba	nurimaseñ nara
		nurimasureba	
Gerund	INFORMAL I	nutte	nuranai de
	II		nuranakute
	FORMAL	nurimasite	nurimaseñ de
Past Ind.	INFORMAL	nutta	nuranakatta
	FORMAL	nurimasita	nurimaseñ desita
Past Presump.	INFORMAL	nuttaroo	nuranakattaroo
		nutta daroo	nuranakatta daroo
	FORMAL	nurimasitaroo	nurimaseñ desitaroo
		nutta desyoo	nuranakatta desyoo
Conditional	INFORMAL	nuttara	nuranakattara
	FORMAL	nurimasitara	nurimaseñ desitara
Alternative	INFORMAL	nuttari	nuranakattari
	FORMAL	nurimasitari	nurimaseñ desitari

INFORMAL AFFIRMATIVE INDICATIVE

Passive	nurareru	*Honorific*	I	onuri ni naru
Potential	nureru		II	onuri nasaru
Causative	nuraseru	*Humble*	I	onuri suru
Causative Pass.	nuraserareru		II	onuri itasu

200

TRANSITIVE   *to steal*

		AFFIRMATIVE	NEGATIVE
Indicative	INFORMAL	nusumu	nusumanai
	FORMAL	nusumimasu	nusumimaseñ
Imperative	INFORMAL I	nusume	nusumu na
	II	nusuminasai	nusuminasaru na
	III	nusuñde kudasai	nusumanai de kudasai
	FORMAL	onusumi nasaimase	onusumi nasaimasu na
Presumptive	INFORMAL I	nusumoo	nusumumai
	II	nusumu daroo	nusumanai daroo
	FORMAL I	nusumimasyoo	nusumimasumai
	II	nusumu desyoo	nusumanai desyoo
Provisional	INFORMAL	nusumeba	nusumanakereba
	FORMAL	nusumimaseba	nusumimaseñ nara
		nusumimasureba	
Gerund	INFORMAL I	nusuñde	nusumanai de
	II		nusumanakute
	FORMAL	nusumimasite	nusumimaseñ de
Past Ind.	INFORMAL	nusuñda	nusumanakatta
	FORMAL	nusumimasita	nusumimaseñ desita
Past Presump.	INFORMAL	nusuñdaroo	nusumanakattaroo
		nusuñda daroo	nusumanakatta daroo
	FORMAL	nusumimasitaroo	nusumimaseñ desitaroo
		nusuñda desyoo	nusumanakatta desyoo
Conditional	INFORMAL	nusuñdara	nusumanakattara
	FORMAL	nusumimasitara	nusumimaseñ desitara
Alternative	INFORMAL	nusuñdari	nusumanakattari
	FORMAL	nusumimasitari	nusumimaseñ desitari

INFORMAL AFFIRMATIVE INDICATIVE

Passive	nusumareru	*Honorific*	I	onusumi ni naru
			II	onusumi nasaru
Potential	nusumeru			
		Humble	I	
Causative	nusumaseru		II	
Causative Pass.	nusumaserareru			

		AFFIRMATIVE	**NEGATIVE**
Indicative	**INFORMAL**	oboeru	oboenai
	FORMAL	oboemasu	oboemaseñ
Imperative	**INFORMAL I**	oboero	oboeru na
	II	oboenasai	oboenasaru na
	III	oboete kudasai	oboenai de kudasai
	FORMAL	oboe nasaimase	oboe nasaimasu na
Presumptive	**INFORMAL I**	oboeyoo	oboemai
	II	oboeru daroo	oboenai daroo
	FORMAL I	oboemasyoo	oboemasumai
	II	oboeru desyoo	oboenai desyoo
Provisional	**INFORMAL**	oboereba	oboenakereba
	FORMAL	oboemaseba	oboemaseñ nara
		oboemasureba	
Gerund	**INFORMAL I**	oboete	oboenai de
	II		oboenakute
	FORMAL	oboemasite	oboemaseñ de
Past Ind.	**INFORMAL**	oboeta	oboenakatta
	FORMAL	oboemasita	oboemaseñ desita
Past Presump.	**INFORMAL**	oboetaroo	oboenakattaroo
		oboeta daroo	oboenakatta daroo
	FORMAL	oboemasitaroo	oboemaseñ desitaroo
		oboeta desyoo	oboenakatta desyoo
Conditional	**INFORMAL**	oboetara	oboenakattara
	FORMAL	oboemasitara	oboemaseñ desitara
Alternative	**INFORMAL**	oboetari	oboenakattari
	FORMAL	oboemasitari	oboemaseñ desitari

INFORMAL AFFIRMATIVE INDICATIVE

Passive	oboerareru	*Honorific*	**I**	ooboe ni na
			II	ooboe nasar
Potential	oboerareru			
		Humble	**I**	
Causative	oboesaseru		**II**	
Causative Pass.	oboesaserareru			

		AFFIRMATIVE	NEGATIVE
Indicative	INFORMAL	odoroku	odorokanai
	FORMAL	odorokimasu	odorokimaseñ
Imperative	INFORMAL I	odoroke	odoroku na
	II	odorokinasai	odorokinasaru na
	III	odoroite kudasai	odorokanai de kudasai
	FORMAL	oodoroki nasaimase	oodoroki nasaimasu na
Presumptive	INFORMAL I	odorokoo	odorokumai
	II	odoroku daroo	odorokanai daroo
	FORMAL I	odorokimasyoo	odorokimasumai
	II	odoroku desyoo	odorokanai desyoo
Provisional	INFORMAL	odorokeba	odorokanakereba
	FORMAL	odorokimaseba	odorokimaseñ nara
		odorokimasureba	
Gerund	INFORMAL I	odoroite	odorokanai de
	II		odorokanakute
	FORMAL	odorokimasite	odorokimaseñ de
Past Ind.	INFORMAL	odoroita	odorokanakatta
	FORMAL	odorokimasita	odorokimaseñ desita
Past Presump.	INFORMAL	odoroitaroo	odorokanakattaroo
		odoroita daroo	odorokanakatta daroo
	FORMAL	odorokimasitaroo	odorokimaseñ desitaroo
		odoroita desyoo	odorokanakatta desyoo
Conditional	INFORMAL	odoroitara	odorokanakattara
	FORMAL	odorokimasitara	odorokimaseñ desitara
Alternative	INFORMAL	odoroitari	odorokanakattari
	FORMAL	odorokimasitari	odorokimaseñ desitari

INFORMAL AFFIRMATIVE INDICATIVE

Passive	odorokareru	*Honorific*	I	oodoroki ni naru
			II	oodoroki nasaru
Potential	odorokeru			
		Humble	I	
Causative	odorokaseru		II	
Causative Pass.	odorokaserareru			

203

		AFFIRMATIVE	NEGATIVE
Indicative	INFORMAL	odoru	odoranai
	FORMAL	odorimasu	odorimaseñ
Imperative	INFORMAL I	odore	odoru na
	II	odorinasai	odorinasaru na
	III	odotte kudasai	odoranai de kudasai
	FORMAL	oodori nasaimase	oodori nasaimasu na
Presumptive	INFORMAL I	odoroo	odorumai
	II	odoru daroo	odoranai daroo
	FORMAL I	odorimasyoo	odorimasumai
	II	odoru desyoo	odoranai desyoo
Provisional	INFORMAL	odoreba	odoranakereba
	FORMAL	odorimaseba	odorimaseñ nara
		odorimasureba	
Gerund	INFORMAL I	odotte	odoranai de
	II		odoranakute
	FORMAL	odorimasite	odorimaseñ de
Past Ind.	INFORMAL	odotta	odoranakatta
	FORMAL	odorimasita	odorimaseñ desita
Past Presump.	INFORMAL	odottaroo	odoranakattaroo
		odotta daroo	odoranakatta daroo
	FORMAL	odorimasitaroo	odorimaseñ desitaroo
		odotta desyoo	odoranakatta desyoo
Conditional	INFORMAL	odottara	odoranakattara
	FORMAL	odorimasitara	odorimaseñ desitara
Alternative	INFORMAL	odottari	odoranakattari
	FORMAL	odorimasitari	odorimaseñ desitari

INFORMAL AFFIRMATIVE INDICATIVE

Passive	odorareru	*Honorific*	I	oodori ni naru
			II	oodori nasaru
Potential	odoreru			
		Humble	I	
Causative	odoraseru		II	
Causative Pass.	odoraserareru			

		AFFIRMATIVE	NEGATIVE
Indicative	INFORMAL	okiru	okinai
	FORMAL	okimasu	okimaseñ
Imperative	INFORMAL I	okiro	okiru na
	II	okinasai	okinasaru na
	III	okite kudasai	okinai de kudasai
	FORMAL	ooki nasaimase	ooki nasaimasu na
Presumptive	INFORMAL I	okiyoo	okimai
	II	okiru daroo	okinai daroo
	FORMAL I	okimasyoo	okimasumai
	II	okiru desyoo	okinai desyoo
Provisional	INFORMAL	okireba	okinakereba
	FORMAL	okimaseba	okimaseñ nara
		okimasureba	
Gerund	INFORMAL I	okite	okinai de
	II		okinakute
	FORMAL	okimasite	okimaseñ de
Past Ind.	INFORMAL	okita	okinakatta
	FORMAL	okimasita	okimaseñ desita
Past Presump.	INFORMAL	okitaroo	okinakattaroo
		okita daroo	okinakatta daroo
	FORMAL	okimasitaroo	okimaseñ desitaroo
		okita desyoo	okinakatta desyoo
Conditional	INFORMAL	okitara	okinakattara
	FORMAL	okimasitara	okimaseñ desitara
Alternative	INFORMAL	okitari	okinakattari
	FORMAL	okimasitari	okimaseñ desitari

INFORMAL AFFIRMATIVE INDICATIVE

Passive	okirareru	*Honorific*	I	ooki ni naru
			II	ooki nasaru
Potential	okirareru			
		Humble	I	ooki suru
Causative	okisaseru		II	ooki itasu
Causative Pass.	okisaserareru			

		AFFIRMATIVE	NEGATIVE
Indicative	**INFORMAL**	okosu	okosanai
	FORMAL	okosimasu	okosimaseñ
Imperative	**INFORMAL I**	okose	okosu na
	II	okosinasai	okosinasaru na
	III	okosite kudasai	okosanai de kudasai
	FORMAL	ookosi nasaimase	ookosi nasaimasu na
Presumptive	**INFORMAL I**	okosoo	okosumai
	II	okosu daroo	okosanai daroo
	FORMAL I	okosimasyoo	okosimasumai
	II	okosu daroo	okosanai daroo
Provisional	**INFORMAL**	okoseba	okosanakereba
	FORMAL	okosimaseba	okosimaseñ nara
		okosimasureba	
Gerund	**INFORMAL I**	okosite	okosanai de
	II		okosanakute
	FORMAL	okosimasite	okosimaseñ de
Past Ind.	**INFORMAL**	okosita	okosanakatta
	FORMAL	okosimasita	okosimaseñ desita
Past Presump.	**INFORMAL**	okositaroo	okosanakattaroo
		okosita daroo	okosanakatta daroo
	FORMAL	okosimasitaroo	okosimaseñ desitaroo
		okosita desyoo	okosanakatta desyoo
Conditional	**INFORMAL**	okositara	okosanakattara
	FORMAL	okosimasitara	okosimaseñ desitara
Alternative	**INFORMAL**	okositari	okosanakattari
	FORMAL	okosimasitari	okosimaseñ desitari

INFORMAL AFFIRMATIVE INDICATIVE

Passive	okosareru	*Honorific*	**I**	ookosi ni naru
			II	ookosi nasaru
Potential	okoseru			
		Humble	**I**	ookosi suru
Causative	okosaseru		**II**	ookosi itasu
Causative Pass.	okosaserareru			

		AFFIRMATIVE	NEGATIVE
Indicative	INFORMAL	oku	okanai
	FORMAL	okimasu	okimaseñ
Imperative	INFORMAL I	oke	oku na
	II	okinasai	okinasaru na
	III	oite kudasai	okanai de kudasai
	FORMAL	ooki nasaimase	ooki nasaimasu na
Presumptive	INFORMAL I	okoo	okumai
	II	oku daroo	okanai daroo
	FORMAL I	okimasyoo	okimasumai
	II	oku desyoo	okanai desyoo
Provisional	INFORMAL	okeba	okanakereba
	FORMAL	okimaseba	okimaseñ nara
		okimasureba	
Gerund	INFORMAL I	oite	okanai de
	II		okanakute
	FORMAL	okimasite	okimaseñ de
Past Ind.	INFORMAL	oita	okanakatta
	FORMAL	okimasita	okimaseñ desita
Past Presump.	INFORMAL	oitaroo	okanakattaroo
		oita daroo	okanakatta daroo
	FORMAL	okimasitaroo	okimaseñ desitaroo
		oita desyoo	okanakatta desyoo
Conditional	INFORMAL	oitara	okanakattara
	FORMAL	okimasitara	okimaseñ desitara
Alternative	INFORMAL	oitari	okanakattari
	FORMAL	okimasitari	okimaseñ desitari

INFORMAL AFFIRMATIVE INDICATIVE

Passive	okareru	*Honorific*	I	ooki ni naru
			II	ooki nasaru
Potential	okeru			
		Humble	I	ooki suru
Causative	okaseru		II	ooki itasu
Causative Pass.	okaserareru			

		AFFIRMATIVE	NEGATIVE
Indicative	INFORMAL	okureru	okurenai
	FORMAL	okuremasu	okuremaseñ
Imperative	INFORMAL I	okurero	okureru na
	II	okurenasai	okurenasaru na
	III	okurete kudasai	okurenai de kudasai
	FORMAL	ookure nasaimase	ookure nasaimasu na
Presumptive	INFORMAL I	okureyoo	okuremai
	II	okureru daroo	okurenai daroo
	FORMAL I	okuremasyoo	okuremasumai
	II	okureru desyoo	okurenai desyoo
Provisional	INFORMAL	okurereba	okurenakereba
	FORMAL	okuremaseba	okuremaseñ nara
		okuremasureba	
Gerund	INFORMAL I	okurete	okurenai de
	II		okurenakute
	FORMAL	okuremasite	okuremaseñ de
Past Ind.	INFORMAL	okureta	okurenakatta
	FORMAL	okuremasita	okuremaseñ desita
Past Presump.	INFORMAL	okuretaroo	okurenakattaroo
		okureta daroo	okurenakatta daroo
	FORMAL	okuremasitaroo	okuremaseñ desitaroo
		okureta desyoo	okurenakatta desyoo
Conditional	INFORMAL	okuretara	okurenakattara
	FORMAL	okuremasitara	okuremaseñ desitara
Alternative	INFORMAL	okuretari	okurenakattari
	FORMAL	okuremasitari	okuremaseñ desitari

INFORMAL AFFIRMATIVE INDICATIVE

Passive	okurerareru	*Honorific*	I	ookure ni naru
			II	ookure nasaru
Potential	okurerareru			
		Humble	I	
Causative	okuresaseru		II	
Causative Pass.	okuresaserareru			

TRANSITIVE   *to send* (a package), *to escort* (a person)

		AFFIRMATIVE	NEGATIVE
Indicative	INFORMAL	okuru	okuranai
	FORMAL	okurimasu	okurimaseñ
Imperative	INFORMAL I	okure	okuru na
	II	okurinasai	okurinasaru na
	III	okutte kudasai	okuranai de kudasai
	FORMAL	ookuri nasaimase	ookuri nasaimasu na
Presumptive	INFORMAL I	okuroo	okurumai
	II	okuru daroo	okuranai daroo
	FORMAL I	okurimasyoo	okurimasumai
	II	okuru desyoo	okuranai desyoo
Provisional	INFORMAL	okureba	okuranakereba
	FORMAL	okurimaseba	okurimaseñ nara
		okurimasureba	
Gerund	INFORMAL I	okutte	okuranai de
	II		okuranakute
	FORMAL	okurimasite	okurimaseñ de
Past Ind.	INFORMAL	okutta	okuranakatta
	FORMAL	okurimasita	okurimaseñ desita
Past Presump.	INFORMAL	okuttaroo	okuranakattaroo
		okutta daroo	okuranakatta daroo
	FORMAL	okurimasitaroo	okurimaseñ desitaroo
		okutta desyoo	okuranakatta desyoo
Conditional	INFORMAL	okuttara	okuranakattara
	FORMAL	okurimasitara	okurimaseñ desitara
Alternative	INFORMAL	okuttari	okuranakattari
	FORMAL	okurimasitari	okurimaseñ desitari

INFORMAL AFFIRMATIVE INDICATIVE

Passive	okurareru	*Honorific*	I	ookuri ni naru
			II	ookuri nasaru
Potential	okureru			
		Humble	I	ookuri suru
Causative	okuraseru		II	ookuri itasu
Causative Pass.	okuraserareru			

		AFFIRMATIVE	NEGATIVE
Indicative	INFORMAL	omou	omowanai
	FORMAL	omoimasu	omoimaseñ
Imperative	INFORMAL I	omoe	omou na
	II	omoinasai	omoi nasaru na
	III	omotte kudasai	omowanai de kudasai
	FORMAL	oomoi nasaimase	oomoi nasaimasu na
Presumptive	INFORMAL I	omooo	omoumai
	II	omou daroo	omowanai daroo
	FORMAL I	omoimasyoo	omoimasumai
	II	omou desyoo	omowanai desyoo
Provisional	INFORMAL	omoeba	omowanakereba
	FORMAL	omoimaseba	omoimaseñ nara
		omoimasureba	
Gerund	INFORMAL I	omotte	omowanai de
	II		omowanakute
	FORMAL	omoimasite	omoimaseñ de
Past Ind.	INFORMAL	omotta	omowanakatta
	FORMAL	omoimasita	omoimaseñ desita
Past Presump.	INFORMAL	omottaroo	omowanakattaroo
		omotta daroo	omowanakatta daroo
	FORMAL	omoimasitaroo	omoimaseñ desitaroo
		omotta desyoo	omowanakatta desyoo
Conditional	INFORMAL	omottara	omowanakattara
	FORMAL	omoimasitara	omoimaseñ desitara
Alternative	INFORMAL	omottari	omowanakattari
	FORMAL	omoimasitari	omoimaseñ desitari

INFORMAL AFFIRMATIVE INDICATIVE

Passive	omowareru	*Honorific*	I	obosimesu	I	oomoi ni naru
			II		II	oomoi nasaru
Potentiol	omoeru					
		Humble	I	oomoi suru		
Causative	omowaseru		II	oomoi itasu		
Causative Pass.	omowaserareru					

		AFFIRMATIVE	NEGATIVE
Indicative	INFORMAL	oriru	orinai
	FORMAL	orimasu	orimaseñ
Imperative	INFORMAL I	oriro	oriru na
	II	orinasai	orinasaru na
	III	orite kudasai	orinai de kudasai
	FORMAL	oori nasaimase	oori nasaimasu na
Presumptive	INFORMAL I	oriyoo	orimai
	II	oriru daroo	orinai daroo
	FORMAL I	orimasyoo	orimasumai
	II	oriru desyoo	orinai desyoo
Provisional	INFORMAL	orireba	orinakereba
	FORMAL	orimaseba	orimaseñ nara
		orimasureba	
Gerund	INFORMAL I	orite	orinai de
	II		orinakute
	FORMAL	orimasite	orimaseñ de
Past Ind.	INFORMAL	orita	orinakatta
	FORMAL	orimasita	orimaseñ desita
Past Presump.	INFORMAL	oritaroo	orinakattaroo
		orita daroo	orinakatta daroo
	FORMAL	orimasitaroo	orimaseñ desitaroo
		orita desyoo	orinakatta desyoo
Conditional	INFORMAL	oritara	orinakattara
	FORMAL	orimasitara	orimaseñ desitara
Alternative	INFORMAL	oritari	orinakattari
	FORMAL	orimasitari	orimaseñ desitari

INFORMAL AFFIRMATIVE INDICATIVE

Passive	orirareru	*Honorific*	I	oori ni naru
			II	oori nasaru
Potential	orirareru			
		Humble	I	
Causative	orisaseru		II	
Causative Pass.	orisaserareru			

		AFFIRMATIVE	NEGATIVE
Indicative	INFORMAL	osaeru	osaenai
	FORMAL	osaemasu	osaemaseñ
Imperative	INFORMAL I	osaero	osaeru na
	II	osaenasai	osaenasaru na
	III	osaete kudasai	osaenai de kudasai
	FORMAL	oosae nasaimase	oosae nasaimasu na
Presumptive	INFORMAL I	osaeyoo	osaemai
	II	osaeru daroo	osaenai daroo
	FORMAL I	osaemasyoo	osaemasumai
	II	osaeru desyoo	osaenai desyoo
Provisional	INFORMAL	osaereba	osaenakereba
	FORMAL	osaemaseba	osaemaseñ nara
		osaemasureba	
Gerund	INFORMAL I	osaete	osaenai de
	II		osaenakute
	FORMAL	osaemasite	osaemaseñ de
Past Ind.	INFORMAL	osaeta	osaenakatta
	FORMAL	osaemasita	osaemaseñ desita
Past Presump.	INFORMAL	osaetaroo	osaenakattaroo
		osaeta daroo	osaenakatta daroo
	FORMAL	osaemasitaroo	osaemaseñ desitaroo
		osaeta desyoo	osaenakatta desyoo
Conditional	INFORMAL	osaetara	osaenakattara
	FORMAL	osaemasitara	osaemaseñ desitara
Alternative	INFORMAL	osaetari	osaenakattari
	FORMAL	osaemasitari	osaemaseñ desitari

INFORMAL AFFIRMATIVE INDICATIVE

Passive	osaerareru	*Honorific*	I	oosae ni naru
			II	oosae nasaru
Potential	osaerareru			
		Humble	I	oosae suru
Causative	osaesaseru		II	oosae itasu
Causative Pass.	osaesaserareru			

TRANSITIVE   *to teach, to inform*

		AFFIRMATIVE	NEGATIVE
Indicative	INFORMAL	osieru	osienai
	FORMAL	osiemasu	osiemaseñ
Imperative	INFORMAL I	osiero	osieru na
	II	osienasai	osienasaru na
	III	osiete kudasai	osienai de kudasai
	FORMAL	oosie nasaimase	oosie nasaimasu na
Presumptive	INFORMAL I	osieyoo	osiemai
	II	osieru daroo	osienai daroo
	FORMAL I	osiemasyoo	osiemasumai
	II	osieru desyoo	osienai desyoo
Provisional	INFORMAL	osiereba	osienakereba
	FORMAL	osiemaseba	osiemaseñ nara
		osiemasureba	
Gerund	INFORMAL I	osiete	osienai de
	II		osienakute
	FORMAL	osiemasite	osiemaseñ de
Past Ind.	INFORMAL	osieta	osienakatta
	FORMAL	osiemasita	osiemaseñ desita
Past Presump.	INFORMAL	osietaroo	osienakattaroo
		osieta daroo	osienakatta daroo
	FORMAL	osiemasitaroo	osiemaseñ desitaroo
		osieta desyoo	osienakatta desyoo
Conditional	INFORMAL	osietara	osienakattara
	FORMAL	osiemasitara	osiemaseñ desitara
Alternative	INFORMAL	osietari	osienakattari
	FORMAL	osiemasitari	osiemaseñ desitari

INFORMAL AFFIRMATIVE INDICATIVE

Passive	osierareru	*Honorific*	I	oosie ni naru
			II	oosie nasaru
Potential	osierareru			
		Humble	I	oosie suru
Causative	osiesaseru		II	oosie itasu
Causative Pass.	osiesaserareru			

to say (honorific)   TRANSITIVE

		AFFIRMATIVE	NEGATIVE
Indicative	INFORMAL	ossyaru	ossyaranai
	FORMAL	ossyaimasu	ossyaimaseñ
Imperative	INFORMAL I	ossyai	ossyaru na
	II	ossyainasai	ossyainasaru na
	III	ossyatte kudasai	ossyaranai de kudasai
	FORMAL	ossyaimase	ossyaimasu na
Presumptive	INFORMAL I	ossyaroo	ossyarumai
	II	ossyaru daroo	ossyaranai daroo
	FORMAL I	ossyaimasyoo	ossyaimasumai
	II	ossyaru desyoo	ossyaranai desyoo
Provisional	INFORMAL	ossyareba	ossyaranakereba
	FORMAL	ossyaimaseba	ossyaimaseñ nara
		ossyaimasureba	
Gerund	INFORMAL I	ossyatte	ossyaranai de
	II		ossyaranakute
	FORMAL	ossyaimasite	ossyaimaseñ de
Past Ind.	INFORMAL	ossyatta	ossyaranakatta
	FORMAL	ossyaimasita	ossyaimaseñ desita
Past Presump.	INFORMAL	ossyattaroo	ossyaranakattaroo
		ossyatta daroo	ossyaranakatta daroo
	FORMAL	ossyaimasitaroo	ossyaimaseñ desitaroo
		ossyatta desyoo	ossyaranakatta desyoo
Conditional	INFORMAL	ossyattara	ossyaranakattara
	FORMAL	ossyaimasitara	ossyaimaseñ desitara
Alternative	INFORMAL	ossyattari	ossyaranakattari
	FORMAL	ossyaimasitari	ossyaimaseñ desitari

INFORMAL AFFIRMATIVE INDICATIVE

Passive		*Honorific*	I
			II
Potential	ossyareru		
		Humble	I
Causative			II
Causative Pass.			

		AFFIRMATIVE	NEGATIVE
Indicative	INFORMAL	otiru	otinai
	FORMAL	otimasu	otimaseñ
Imperative	INFORMAL I	otiro	otiru na
	II		otinasaru na
	III		otinai de kudasai
	FORMAL		ooti nasaimasu na
Presumptive	INFORMAL I	otiyoo	otimai
	II	otiru daroo	otinai daroo
	FORMAL I	otimasyoo	otimasumai
	II	otiru desyoo	otinai desyoo
Provisional	INFORMAL	otireba	otinakereba
	FORMAL	otimaseba	otimaseñ nara
		otimasureba	
Gerund	INFORMAL I	otite	otinai de
	II		otinakute
	FORMAL	otimasite	otimaseñ de
Past Ind.	INFORMAL	otita	otinakatta
	FORMAL	otimasita	otimaseñ desita
Past Presump.	INFORMAL	otitaroo	otinakattaroo
		otita daroo	otinakatta daroo
	FORMAL	otimasitaroo	otimaseñ desitaroo
		otita desyoo	otinakatta desyoo
Conditional	INFORMAL	otitara	otinakattara
	FORMAL	otimasitara	otimaseñ desitara
Alternative	INFORMAL	otitari	otinakattari
	FORMAL	otimasitari	otimaseñ desitari

INFORMAL AFFIRMATIVE INDICATIVE

Passive	otirareru	*Honorific*	I	ooti ni naru
Potential			II	ooti nasaru
		Humble	I	
Causative	otisaseru		II	
Causative Pass.	otisaserareru			

		AFFIRMATIVE	NEGATIVE
Indicative	INFORMAL	otosu	otosanai
	FORMAL	otosimasu	otosimaseñ
Imperative	INFORMAL I	otose	otosu na
	II	otosinasai	otosinasaru na
	III	otosite kudasai	otosanai de kudasai
	FORMAL	ootosi nasaimase	ootosi nasaimasu na
Presumptive	INFORMAL I	otosoo	otosumai
	II	otosu daroo	otosanai daroo
	FORMAL I	otosimasyoo	otosimasumai
	II	otosu desyoo	otosanai desyoo
Provisional	INFORMAL	otoseba	otosanakereba
	FORMAL	otosimaseba	otosimaseñ nara
		otosimasureba	
Gerund	INFORMAL I	otosite	otosanai de
	II		otosanakute
	FORMAL	otosimasite	otosimaseñ de
Past Ind.	INFORMAL	otosita	otosanakatta
	FORMAL	otosimasita	otosimaseñ desita
Past Presump.	INFORMAL	otositaroo	otosanakattaroo
		otosita daroo	otosanakatta daroo
	FORMAL	otosimasitaroo	otosimaseñ desitaroo
		otosita desyoo	otosanakatta desyoo
Conditional	INFORMAL	otositara	otosanakattara
	FORMAL	otosimasitara	otosimaseñ desitara
Alternative	INFORMAL	otositari	otosanakattari
	FORMAL	otosimasitari	otosimaseñ desitari

INFORMAL AFFIRMATIVE INDICATIVE

Passive	otosareru	*Honorific*	I	ootosi ni naru
Potential	otoseru		II	ootosi nasaru
		Humble	I	ootosi suru
Causative	otosaseru		II	ootosi itasu
Causative Pass.	otosaserareru			

		AFFIRMATIVE	NEGATIVE
Indicative	INFORMAL	owaru	owaranai
	FORMAL	owarimasu	owarimaseñ
Imperative	INFORMAL I	oware	owaru na
	II		
	III		
	FORMAL		
Presumptive	INFORMAL I	owaroo	owarumai
	II	owaru daroo	owaranai daroo
	FORMAL I	owarimasyoo	owarimasumai
	II	owaru desyoo	owaranai desyoo
Provisional	INFORMAL	owareba	owaranakereba
	FORMAL	owarimaseba	owarimaseñ nara
		owarimasureba	
Gerund	INFORMAL I	owatte	owaranai de
	II		owaranakute
	FORMAL	owarimasite	owarimaseñ de
Past Ind.	INFORMAL	owatta	owaranakatta
	FORMAL	owarimasita	owarimaseñ desita
Past Presump.	INFORMAL	owattaroo	owaranakattaroo
		owatta daroo	owaranakatta daroo
	FORMAL	owarimasitaroo	owarimaseñ desitaroo
		owatta desyoo	owaranakatta desyoo
Conditional	INFORMAL	owattara	owaranakattara
	FORMAL	owarimasitara	owarimaseñ desitara
Alternative	INFORMAL	owattari	owaranakattari
	FORMAL	owarimasitari	owarimaseñ desitari

INFORMAL AFFIRMATIVE INDICATIVE

Passive		*Honorific*	I
			II
Potential			
		Humble	I
Causative	owaraseru		II
Causative Pass.	owaraserareru		

		AFFIRMATIVE	NEGATIVE
Indicative	INFORMAL	oyogu	oyoganai
	FORMAL	oyogimasu	oyogimaseñ
Imperative	INFORMAL I	oyoge	oyogu na
	II	oyoginasai	oyoginasaru na
	III	oyoide kudasai	oyoganai de kudasai
	FORMAL	ooyogi nasaimase	ooyogi nasaimasu na
Presumptive	INFORMAL I	oyogoo	oyogumai
	II	oyogu daroo	oyoganai daroo
	FORMAL I	oyogimasyoo	oyogimasumai
	II	oyogu desyoo	oyoganai desyoo
Provisional	INFORMAL	oyogeba	oyoganakereba
	FORMAL	oyogimaseba	oyogimaseñ nara
		oyogimasureba	
Gerund	INFORMAL I	oyoide	oyoganai de
	II		oyoganakute
	FORMAL	oyogimasite	oyogimaseñ de
Past Ind.	INFORMAL	oyoida	oyoganakatta
	FORMAL	oyogimasita	oyogimaseñ desita
Past Presump.	INFORMAL	oyoidaroo	oyoganakattaroo
		oyoida daroo	oyoganakatta daroo
	FORMAL	oyogimasitaroo	oyogimaseñ desitaroo
		oyoida desyoo	oyoganakatta desyoo
Conditional	INFORMAL	oyoidara	oyoganakattara
	FORMAL	oyogimasitara	oyogimaseñ desitara
Alternative	INFORMAL	oyoidari	oyoganakattari
	FORMAL	oyogimasitari	oyogimaseñ desitari

INFORMAL AFFIRMATIVE INDICATIVE

Passive	oyogareru	*Honorific*	I	ooyogi ni naru
			II	ooyogi nasaru
Potential	oyogeru			
		Humble	I	
Causative	oyogaseru		II	
Causative Pass.	oyogaserareru			

		AFFIRMATIVE	NEGATIVE
Indicative	INFORMAL	sagasu	sagasanai
	FORMAL	sagasimasu	sagasimaseñ
Imperative	INFORMAL I	sagase	sagasu na
	II	sagasinasai	sagasinasaru na
	III	sagasite kudasai	sagasanai de kudasai
	FORMAL	osagasi nasaimase	osagasi nasaimasu na
Presumptive	INFORMAL I	sagasoo	sagasumai
	II	sagasu daroo	sagasanai daroo
	FORMAL I	sagasimasyoo	sagasimasumai
	II	sagasu desyoo	sagasanai desyoo
Provisional	INFORMAL	sagaseba	sagasanakereba
	FORMAL	sagasimaseba	sagasimaseñ nara
		sagasimasureba	
Gerund	INFORMAL I	sagasite	sagasanai de
	II		sagasanakute
	FORMAL	sagasimasite	sagasimaseñ de
Past Ind.	INFORMAL	sagasita	sagasanakatta
	FORMAL	sagasimasita	sagasimaseñ desita
Past Presump.	INFORMAL	sagasitaroo	sagasanakattaroo
		sagasita daroo	sagasanakatta daroo
	FORMAL	sagasimasitaroo	sagasimaseñ desitaroo
		sagasita desyoo	sagasanakatta desyoo
Conditional	INFORMAL	sagasitara	sagasanakattara
	FORMAL	sagasimasitara	sagasimaseñ desitara
Alternative	INFORMAL	sagasitari	sagasanakattari
	FORMAL	sagasimasitari	sagasimaseñ desitari

INFORMAL AFFIRMATIVE INDICATIVE

Passive	sagasareru	*Honorific*	I	osagasi ni naru
			II	osagasi nasaru
Potential	sagaseru			
		Humble	I	osagasi suru
Causative	sagasaseru		II	osagasi itasu
Causative Pass.	sagasaserareru			

		AFFIRMATIVE	NEGATIVE
Indicative	INFORMAL	saku	sakanai
	FORMAL	sakimasu	sakimaseñ
Imperative	INFORMAL I	sake	saku na
	II		
	III		
	FORMAL		
Presumptive	INFORMAL I	sakoo	sakumai
	II	saku daroo	sakanai daroo
	FORMAL I	sakimasyoo	sakimasumai
	II	saku desyoo	sakanai desyoo
Provisional	INFORMAL	sakeba	sakanakereba
	FORMAL	sakimaseba	sakimaseñ nara
		sakimasureba	
Gerund	INFORMAL I	saite	sakanai de
	II		sakanakute
	FORMAL	sakimasite	sakimaseñ de
Past Ind.	INFORMAL	saita	sakanakatta
	FORMAL	sakimasita	sakimaseñ desita
Past Presump.	INFORMAL	saitaroo	sakanakattaroo
		saita daroo	sakanakatta daroo
	FORMAL	sakimasitaroo	sakimaseñ desitaroo
		saita desyoo	sakanakatta desyoo
Conditional	INFORMAL	saitara	sakanakattara
	FORMAL	sakimasitara	sakimaseñ desitara
Alternative	INFORMAL	saitari	sakanakattari
	FORMAL	sakimasitari	sakimaseñ desitari

INFORMAL AFFIRMATIVE INDICATIVE

Passive		*Honorific*	I
			II
Potential	sakeru		
		Humble	I
Causative	sakaseru		II
Causative Pass.	sakaserareru		

			AFFIRMATIVE	NEGATIVE
Indicative	INFORMAL		sawagu	sawaganai
	FORMAL		sawagimasu	sawagimaseñ
Imperative	INFORMAL	I	sawage	sawagu na
		II	sawaginasai	sawaginasaru na
		III	sawaide kudasai	sawaganai de kudasai
	FORMAL		osawagi nasaimase	osawagi nasaimasu na
Presumptive	INFORMAL	I	sawagoo	sawagumai
		II	sawagu daroo	sawaganai daroo
	FORMAL	I	sawagimasyoo	sawagimasumai
		II	sawagu desyoo	sawaganai desyoo
Provisional	INFORMAL		sawageba	sawaganakereba
	FORMAL		sawagimaseba	sawagimaseñ nara
			sawagimasureba	
Gerund	INFORMAL	I	sawaide	sawaganai de
		II		sawaganakute
	FORMAL		sawagimasite	sawagimaseñ de
Past Ind.	INFORMAL		sawaida	sawaganakatta
	FORMAL		sawagimasita	sawagimaseñ desita
Past Presump.	INFORMAL		sawaidaroo	sawaganakattaroo
			sawaida daroo	sawaganakatta daroo
	FORMAL		sawagimasitaroo	sawagimaseñ desitaroo
			sawaida desyoo	sawaganakatta desyoo
Conditional	INFORMAL		sawaidara	sawaganakattara
	FORMAL		sawagimasitara	sawagimaseñ desitara
Alternative	INFORMAL		sawaidari	sawaganakattari
	FORMAL		sawagimasitari	sawagimaseñ desitari

INFORMAL AFFIRMATIVE INDICATIVE

Passive	sawagareru	*Honorific* I	osawagi ni naru
		II	osawagi nasaru
Potential	sawageru		
		Humble I	
Causative	sawagaseru	II	
Causative Pass.	sawagaserareru		

sibár.u
to tie up TRANSITIVE

sibari

			AFFIRMATIVE	NEGATIVE
Indicative	INFORMAL		sibaru	sibaranai
	FORMAL		sibarimasu	sibarimaseñ
Imperative	INFORMAL	I	sibare	sibaru na
		II	sibarinasai	sibarinasaru na
		III	sibatte kudasai	sibaranai de kudasai
	FORMAL		osibari nasaimase	osibari nasaimasu na
Presumptive	INFORMAL	I	sibaroo	sibarumai
		II	sibaru daroo	sibaranai daroo
	FORMAL	I	sibarimasyoo	sibarimasumai
		II	sibaru desyoo	sibaranai desyoo
Provisional	INFORMAL		sibareba	sibaranakereba
	FORMAL		sibarimaseba	sibarimaseñ nara
			sibarimasureba	
Gerund	INFORMAL	I	sibatte	sibaranai de
		II		sibaranakute
	FORMAL		sibarimasite	sibarimaseñ de
Past Ind.	INFORMAL		sibatta	sibaranakatta
	FORMAL		sibarimasita	sibarimaseñ desita
Past Presump.	INFORMAL		sibattaroo	sibaranakattaroo
			sibatta daroo	sibaranakatta daroo
	FORMAL		sibarimasitaroo	sibarimaseñ desitaroo
			sibatta desyoo	sibaranakatta desyoo
Conditional	INFORMAL		sibattara	sibaranakattara
	FORMAL		sibarimasitara	sibarimaseñ desitara
Alternative	INFORMAL		sibattari	sibaranakattari
	FORMAL		sibarimasitari	sibarimaseñ desitari

INFORMAL AFFIRMATIVE INDICATIVE

Passive	sibarareru	*Honorific*	I	osibari ni naru
			II	osibari nasaru
Potential	sibareru			
		Humble	I	osibari suru
Causative	sibaraseru		II	osibari itasu
Causative Pass.	sibaraserareru			

		AFFIRMATIVE	NEGATIVE
Indicative	INFORMAL	sikaru	sikaranai
	FORMAL	sikarimasu	sikarimaseñ
Imperative	INFORMAL I	sikare	sikaru na
	II	sikarinasai	sikarinasaru na
	III	sikatte kudasai	sikaranai de kudasai
	FORMAL	osikari nasaimase	osikari nasaimasu na
Presumptive	INFORMAL I	sikaroo	sikarumai
	II	sikaru daroo	sikaranai daroo
	FORMAL I	sikarimasyoo	sikarimasumai
	II	sikaru desyoo	sikaranai desyoo
Provisional	INFORMAL	sikareba	sikaranakereba
	FORMAL	sikarimaseba	sikarimaseñ nara
		sikarimasureba	
Gerund	INFORMAL I	sikatte	sikaranai de
	II		sikaranakute
	FORMAL	sikarimasite	sikarimaseñ de
Past Ind.	INFORMAL	sikatta	sikaranakatta
	FORMAL	sikarimasita	sikarimaseñ desita
Past Presump.	INFORMAL	sikattaroo	sikaranakattaroo
		sikatta daroo	sikaranakatta daroo
	FORMAL	sikarimasitaroo	sikarimaseñ desitaroo
		sikatta desyoo	sikaranakatta desyoo
Conditional	INFORMAL	sikattara	sikaranakattara
	FORMAL	sikarimasitara	sikarimaseñ desitara
Alternative	INFORMAL	sikattari	sikaranakattari
	FORMAL	sikarimasitari	sikarimaseñ desitari

INFORMAL AFFIRMATIVE INDICATIVE

Passive	sikarareru	*Honorific*	I	osikari ni naru
			II	osikari nasaru
Potential	sikareru			
		Humble	I	osikari suru
Causative	sikaraseru		II	osikari itasu
Causative Pass.	sikaraserareru			

to spread out flat (as a quilt)   TRANSITIVE

		AFFIRMATIVE	NEGATIVE
Indicative	INFORMAL	siku	sikanai
	FORMAL	sikimasu	sikimaseñ
Imperative	INFORMAL I	sike	siku na
	II	sikinasai	sikinasaru na
	III	siite kudasai	sikanai de kudasai
	FORMAL	osiki nasaimase	osiki nasaimasu na
Presumptive	INFORMAL I	sikoo	sikumai
	II	siku daroo	sikanai daroo
	FORMAL I	sikimasyoo	sikimasumai
	II	siku desyoo	sikanai desyoo
Provisional	INFORMAL	sikeba	sikanakereba
	FORMAL	sikimaseba	sikimaseñ nara
		sikimasureba	
Gerund	INFORMAL I	siite	sikanai de
	II		sikanakute
	FORMAL	sikimasite	sikimaseñ de
Past Ind.	INFORMAL	siita	sikanakatta
	FORMAL	sikimasita	sikimaseñ desita
Past Presump.	INFORMAL	siitaroo	sikanakattaroo
		siita daroo	sikanakatta daroo
	FORMAL	sikimasitaroo	sikimaseñ desitaroo
		siita desyoo	sikanakatta desyoo
Conditional	INFORMAL	siitara	sikanakattara
	FORMAL	sikimasitara	sikimaseñ desitara
Alternative	INFORMAL	siitari	sikanakattari
	FORMAL	sikimasitari	sikimaseñ desitari

INFORMAL AFFIRMATIVE INDICATIVE

Passive	sikareru	*Honorific*	I	osiki ni naru
			II	osiki nasaru
Potential	sikeru			
		Humble	I	osiki suru
Causative	sikaseru		II	osiki itasu
Causative Pass.	sikaserareru			

		AFFIRMATIVE	NEGATIVE
Indicative	INFORMAL	simaru	simaranai
	FORMAL	simarimasu	simarimaseñ
Imperative	INFORMAL I	simare	simaru na
	II		
	III		
	FORMAL		
Presumptive	INFORMAL I	simaroo	simarumai
	II	simaru daroo	simaranai daroo
	FORMAL I	simarimasyoo	simarimasumai
	II	simaru desyoo	simaranai desyoo
Provisional	INFORMAL	simareba	simaranakereba
	FORMAL	simarimaseba	simarimaseñ nara
		simarimasureba	
Gerund	INFORMAL I	simatte	simaranai de
	II		simaranakute
	FORMAL	simarimasite	simarimaseñ de
Past Ind.	INFORMAL	simatta	simaranakatta
	FORMAL	simarimasita	simarimaseñ desita
Past Presump.	INFORMAL	simattaroo	simaranakattaroo
		simatta daroo	simaranakatta daroo
	FORMAL	simarimasitaroo	simarimaseñ desitaroo
		simatta desyoo	simaranakatta desyoo
Conditional	INFORMAL	simattara	simaranakattara
	FORMAL	simarimasitara	simarimaseñ desitara
Alternative	INFORMAL	simattari	simaranakattari
	FORMAL	simarimasitari	simarimaseñ desitari

INFORMAL AFFIRMATIVE INDICATIVE

Passive		*Honorific*	I
			II
Potential			
		Humble	I
Causative			II
Causative Pass.			

to put away, to pack away   TRANSITIVE

		AFFIRMATIVE	NEGATIVE
Indicative	INFORMAL	simau	simawanai
	FORMAL	simaimasu	simaimaseñ
Imperative	INFORMAL I	simae	simau na
	II	simainasai	simainasaru na
	III	simatte kudasai	simawanai de kudasai
	FORMAL	osimai nasaimase	osimai nasaimasu na
Presumptive	INFORMAL I	simaoo	simaumai
	II	simau daroo	simawanai daroo
	FORMAL I	simaimasyoo	simaimasumai
	II	simau desyoo	simawanai desyoo
Provisional	INFORMAL	simaeba	simawanakereba
	FORMAL	simaimaseba	simaimaseñ nara
		simaimasureba	
Gerund	INFORMAL I	simatte	simawanai de
	II		simawanakute
	FORMAL	simaimasite	simaimaseñ de
Past Ind.	INFORMAL	simatta	simawanakatta
	FORMAL	simaimasita	simaimaseñ desita
Past Presump.	INFORMAL	simattaroo	simawanakattaroo
		simatta daroo	simawanakatta daroo
	FORMAL	simaimasitaroo	simaimaseñ desitaroo
		simatta desyoo	simawanakatta desyoo
Conditional	INFORMAL	simattara	simawanakattara
	FORMAL	simaimasitara	simaimaseñ desitara
Alternative	INFORMAL	simattari	simawanakattari
	FORMAL	simaimasitari	simaimaseñ desitari

INFORMAL AFFIRMATIVE INDICATIVE

Passive	simawareru	*Honorific*	I	osimai ni naru
			II	osimai nasaru
Potential	simaeru			
		Humble	I	osimai suru
Causative	simawaseru		II	osimai itasu
Causative Pass.	simawaserareru			

TRANSITIVE   *to shut*

			AFFIRMATIVE	NEGATIVE
Indicative	INFORMAL		simeru	simenai
	FORMAL		simemasu	simemaseñ
Imperative	INFORMAL	I	simero	simeru na
		II	simenasai	simenasaru na
		III	simete kudasai	simenai de kudasai
	FORMAL		osime nasaimase	osime nasaimasu na
Presumptive	INFORMAL	I	simeyoo	simemai
		II	simeru daroo	simenai daroo
	FORMAL	I	simemasyoo	simemasumai
		II	simeru desyoo	simenai desyoo
Provisional	INFORMAL		simereba	simenakereba
	FORMAL		simemaseba	simemaseñ nara
			simemasureba	
Gerund	INFORMAL	I	simete	simenai de
		II		simenakute
	FORMAL		simemasite	simemaseñ de
Past Ind.	INFORMAL		simeta	simenakatta
	FORMAL		simemasita	simemaseñ desita
Past Presump.	INFORMAL		simetaroo	simenakattaroo
			simeta daroo	simenakatta daroo
	FORMAL		simemasitaroo	simemaseñ desitaroo
			simeta desyoo	simenakatta desyoo
Conditional	INFORMAL		simetara	simenakattara
	FORMAL		simemasitara	simemaseñ desitara
Alternative	INFORMAL		simetari	simenakattari
	FORMAL		simemasitari	simemaseñ desitari

INFORMAL AFFIRMATIVE INDICATIVE

Passive	simerareru	*Honorific*	I	osime ni naru
			II	osime nasaru
Potential	simerareru			
		Humble	I	osime suru
Causative	simesaseru		II	osime itasu
Causative Pass.	simesaserareru			

		AFFIRMATIVE	NEGATIVE
Indicative	INFORMAL	sinu	sinanai
	FORMAL	sinimasu	sinimaseñ
Imperative	INFORMAL I	sine	sinu na
	II	sininasai	sininasaru na
	III	siñde kudasai	sinanai de kudasai
	FORMAL		osini nasaimasu na
Presumptive	INFORMAL I	sinoo	sinumai
	II	sinu daroo	sinanai daroo
	FORMAL I	sinimasyoo	sinimasumai
	II	sinu desyoo	sinanai desyoo
Provisional	INFORMAL	sineba	sinanakereba
	FORMAL	sinimaseba	sinimaseñ nara
		sinimasureba	
Gerund	INFORMAL I	siñde	sinanai de
	II		sinanakute
	FORMAL	sinimasite	sinimaseñ de
Past Ind.	INFORMAL	siñda	sinanakatta
	FORMAL	sinimasita	sinimaseñ desita
Past Presump.	INFORMAL	siñdaroo	sinanakattaroo
		siñda daroo	sinanakatta daroo
	FORMAL	sinimasitaroo	sinimaseñ desitaroo
		siñda desyoo	sinanakatta desyoo
Conditional	INFORMAL	siñdara	sinanakattara
	FORMAL	sinimasitara	sinimaseñ desitara
Alternative	INFORMAL	siñdari	sinanakattari
	FORMAL	sinimasitari	sinimaseñ desitari

INFORMAL AFFIRMATIVE INDICATIVE

Passive	sinareru	*Honorific*	I	onakunari ni naru
			II	onakunari nasaru
Potential	sineru			
		Humble	I	
Causative	sinaseru		II	
Causative Pass.	sinaserareru			

TRANSITIVE   *to believe, to trust*

		AFFIRMATIVE	NEGATIVE
Indicative	INFORMAL	siñziru	siñzinai
	FORMAL	siñzimasu	siñzimaseñ
Imperative	INFORMAL I	siñziro	siñziru na
	II	siñzinasai	siñzinasaru na
	III	siñzite kudasai	siñzinai de kudasai
	FORMAL	osiñzi nasaimase	osiñzi nasaimasu na
Presumptive	INFORMAL I	siñziyoo	siñzimai
	II	siñziru daroo	siñzinai daroo
	FORMAL I	siñzimasyoo	siñzimasumai
	II	siñziru desyoo	siñzinai desyoo
Provisional	INFORMAL	siñzireba	siñzinakereba
	FORMAL	siñzimaseba	siñzimaseñ nara
		siñzimasureba	
Gerund	INFORMAL I	siñzite	siñzinai de
	II		siñzinakute
	FORMAL	siñzimasite	siñzimaseñ de
Past Ind.	INFORMAL	siñzita	siñzinakatta
	FORMAL	siñzimasita	siñzimaseñ desita
Past Presump.	INFORMAL	siñzitaroo	siñzinakattaroo
		siñzita daroo	siñzinakatta daroo
	FORMAL	siñzimasitaroo	siñzimaseñ desitaroo
		siñzita desyoo	siñzinakatta desyoo
Conditional	INFORMAL	siñzitara	siñzinakattara
	FORMAL	siñzimasitara	siñzimaseñ desitara
Alternative	INFORMAL	siñzitari	siñzinakattari
	FORMAL	siñzimasitari	siñzimaseñ desitari

INFORMAL AFFIRMATIVE INDICATIVE

Passive	siñzirareru		*Honorific*	I	osiñzi ni naru
				II	osiñzi nasaru
Potential	siñzirareru				
			Humble	I	osiñzi suru
Causative	siñzisaseru			II	osiñzi itasu
Causative Pass.	siñzisaserareru				

			AFFIRMATIVE	NEGATIVE
Indicative	INFORMAL		siraberu	sirabenai
	FORMAL		sirabemasu	sirabemaseñ
Imperative	INFORMAL	I	sirabero	siraberu na
		II	sirabenasai	sirabenasaru na
		III	sirabete kudasai	sirabenai de kudasai
	FORMAL		osirabe nasaimase	osirabe nasaimasu na
Presumptive	INFORMAL	I	sirabeyoo	sirabemai
		II	siraberu daroo	sirabenai daroo
	FORMAL	I	sirabemasyoo	sirabemasumai
		II	siraberu desyoo	sirabenai desyoo
Provisional	INFORMAL		sirabereba	sirabenakereba
	FORMAL		sirabemaseba	sirabemaseñ nara
			sirabemasureba	
Gerund	INFORMAL	I	sirabete	sirabenai de
		II		sirabenakute
	FORMAL		sirabemasite	sirabemaseñ de
Past Ind.	INFORMAL		sirabeta	sirabenakatta
	FORMAL		sirabemasita	sirabemaseñ desita
Past Presump.	INFORMAL		sirabetaroo	sirabenakattaroo
			sirabeta daroo	sirabenakatta daroo
	FORMAL		sirabemasitaroo	sirabemaseñ desitaroo
			sirabeta desyoo	sirabenakatta desyoo
Conditional	INFORMAL		sirabetara	sirabenakattara
	FORMAL		sirabemasitara	sirabemaseñ desitara
Alternative	INFORMAL		sirabetari	sirabenakattari
	FORMAL		sirabemasitari	sirabemaseñ desitari

INFORMAL AFFIRMATIVE INDICATIVE

Passive	siraberareru	*Honorific*	I	osirabe ni naru
			II	osirabe nasaru
Potential	siraberareru			
		Humble	I	osirabe suru
Causative	sirabesaseru		II	osirabe itasu
Causative Pass.	sirabesaserareru			

TRANSITIVE *to learn about, to know*

		AFFIRMATIVE	NEGATIVE
Indicative	INFORMAL	siru	siranai
	FORMAL	sirimasu	sirimaseñ
Imperative	INFORMAL I	sire	
	II		
	III		
	FORMAL		
Presumptive	INFORMAL I	siroo	sirumai
	II	siru daroo	siranai daroo
	FORMAL I	sirimasyoo	sirimasumai
	II	siru desyoo	siranai desyoo
Provisional	INFORMAL	sireba	siranakereba
	FORMAL	sirimaseba	sirimaseñ nara
		sirimasureba	
Gerund	INFORMAL I	sitte	siranai de
	II		siranakute
	FORMAL	sirimasite	sirimaseñ de
Past Ind.	INFORMAL	sitta	siranakatta
	FORMAL	sirimasita	sirimaseñ desita
Past Presump.	INFORMAL	sittaroo	siranakattaroo
		sitta daroo	siranakatta daroo
	FORMAL	sirimasitaroo	sirimaseñ desitaroo
		sitta desyoo	siranakatta desyoo
Conditional	INFORMAL	sittara	siranakattara
	FORMAL	sirimasitara	sirimaseñ desitara
Alternative	INFORMAL	sittari	siranakattari
	FORMAL	sirimasitari	sirimaseñ desitari

INFORMAL AFFIRMATIVE INDICATIVE

Passive	sirareru	*Honorific*	gozoñzi de irassyaru
Potential	sireru		
		Humble	zoñziru
Causative	siraseru		
Causative Pass.	siraserareru		

			AFFIRMATIVE	NEGATIVE
Indicative	INFORMAL		sizumu	sizumanai
	FORMAL		sizumimasu	sizumìmaseñ
Imperative	INFORMAL	I	sizume	sizumu na
		II	sizuminasai	sizuminasaru na
		III	sizuñde kudasai	sizumanai de kudasai
	FORMAL		osizumi nasaimase	osizumi nasaimasu na
Presumptive	INFORMAL	I	sizumoo	sizumumai
		II	sizumu daroo	sizumanai daroo
	FORMAL	I	sizumimasyoo	sizumimasumai
		II	sizumu daroo	sizumanai daroo
Provisional	INFORMAL		sizumeba	sizumanakereba
	FORMAL		sizumimaseba	sizumimaseñ nara
			sizumimasureba	
Gerund	INFORMAL	I	sizuñde	sizumanai de
		II		sizumanakute
	FORMAL		sizumimasite	sizumimaseñ de
Past Ind.	INFORMAL		sizuñda	sizumanakatta
	FORMAL		sizumimasita	sizumimaseñ desita
Past Presump.	INFORMAL		sizuñdaroo	sizumanakattaroo
			sizuñda daroo	sizumanakatta daroo
	FORMAL		sizumimasitaroo	sizumimaseñ desitaroo
			sizuñda desyoo	sizumanakatta desyoo
Conditional	INFORMAL		sizuñdara	sizumanakattara
	FORMAL		sizumimasitara	sizumimaseñ desitara
Alternative	INFORMAL		sizuñdari	sizumanakattari
	FORMAL		sizumimasitari	sizumimaseñ desitari

INFORMAL AFFIRMATIVE INDICATIVE

Passive	sizumareru	*Honorific*	I	osizumi ni naru
			II	osizumi nasaru
Potential	sizumeru			
		Humble	I	
Causative	sizumaseru		II	
Causative Pass.	sizumaserareru			

		AFFIRMATIVE	NEGATIVE
Indicative	INFORMAL	sodateru	sodatenai
	FORMAL	sodatemasu	sodatemaseñ
Imperative	INFORMAL I	sodatero	sodateru na
	II	sodatenasai	sodatenasaru na
	III	sodatete kudasai	sodatenai de kudasai
	FORMAL	osodate nasaimase	osodate nasaimasu na
Presumptive	INFORMAL I	sodateyoo	sodatemai
	II	sodateru daroo	sodatenai daroo
	FORMAL I	sodatemasyoo	sodatemasumai
	II	sodateru desyoo	sodatenai desyoo
Provisional	INFORMAL	sodatereba	sodatenakereba
	FORMAL	sodatemaseba	sodatemaseñ nara
		sodatemasureba	
Gerund	INFORMAL I	sodatete	sodatenai de
	II		sodatenakute
	FORMAL	sodatemasite	sodatemaseñ de
Past Ind.	INFORMAL	sodateta	sodatenakatta
	FORMAL	sodatemasita	sodatemaseñ desita
Past Presump.	INFORMAL	sodatetaroo	sodatenakattaroo
		sodateta daroo	sodatenakatta daroo
	FORMAL	sodatemasitaroo	sodatemaseñ desitaroo
		sodateta desyoo	sodatenakatta desyoo
Conditional	INFORMAL	sodatetara	sodatenakattara
	FORMAL	sodatemasitara	sodatemaseñ desitara
Alternative	INFORMAL	sodatetari	sodatenakattari
	FORMAL	sodatemasitari	sodatemaseñ desitari

INFORMAL AFFIRMATIVE INDICATIVE

Passive	sodaterareru	*Honorific*	I	osodate ni naru
			II	osodate nasaru
Potential	sodaterareru			
		Humble	I	osodate suru
Causative	sodatesaseru		II	osodate itasu
ausative Pass.	sodatesaserareru			

		AFFIRMATIVE	NEGATIVE
Indicative	INFORMAL	sugiru	suginai
	FORMAL	sugimasu	sugimaseñ
Imperative	INFORMAL I	sugiro	sugiru na
	II	suginasai	suginasaru na
	III	sugite kudasai	suginai de kudasai
	FORMAL	osugi nasaimase	osugi nasaimasu na
Presumptive	INFORMAL I	sugiyoo	sugimai
	II	sugiru daroo	suginai daroo
	FORMAL I	sugimasyoo	sugimasumai
	II	sugiru desyoo	suginai desyoo
Provisional	INFORMAL	sugireba	suginakereba
	FORMAL	sugimaseba	sugimaseñ nara
		sugimasureba	
Gerund	INFORMAL I	sugite	suginai de
	II		suginakute
	FORMAL	sugimasite	sugimaseñ de
Past Ind.	INFORMAL	sugita	suginakatta
	FORMAL	sugimasita	sugimaseñ desita
Past Presump.	INFORMAL	sugitaroo	suginakattaroo
		sugita daroo	suginakatta daroo
	FORMAL	sugimasitaroo	sugimaseñ desitaroo
		sugita desyoo	suginakatta desyoo
Conditional	INFORMAL	sugitara	suginakattara
	FORMAL	sugimasitara	sugimaseñ desitara
Alternative	INFORMAL	sugitari	suginakattari
	FORMAL	sugimasitari	sugimaseñ desitari

INFORMAL AFFIRMATIVE INDICATIVE

Passive		*Honorific*	I	osugi ni naru
			II	osugi nasaru
Potential				
		Humble	I	
Causative			II	
Causative Pass.				

to be superior, to surpass, to excel

			AFFIRMATIVE	NEGATIVE
Indicative	**INFORMAL**		sugureru	sugurenai
	FORMAL		suguremasu	suguremaseñ
Imperative	**INFORMAL I**		sugurero	sugureru na
		II	sugurenasai	sugurenasaru na
		III	sugurete kudasai	sugurenai de kudasai
	FORMAL		osugure nasaimase	osugure nasaimasu na
Presumptive	**INFORMAL I**		sugureyoo	suguremai
		II	sugureru daroo	sugurenai daroo
	FORMAL	**I**	suguremasyoo	suguremasumai
		II	sugureru desyoo	sugurenai desyoo
Provisional	**INFORMAL**		sugurereba	sugurenakereba
	FORMAL		suguremaseba	suguremaseñ nara
			suguremasureba	
Gerund	**INFORMAL I**		sugurete	sugurenai de
		II		sugurenakute
	FORMAL		suguremasite	suguremaseñ de
Past Ind.	**INFORMAL**		sugureta	sugurenakatta
	FORMAL		suguremasita	suguremaseñ desita
Past Presump.	**INFORMAL**		suguretaroo	sugurenakattaroo
			sugureta daroo	sugurenakatta daroo
	FORMAL		suguremasitaroo	sugurenakatta desitaroo
			sugureta desyoo	sugurenakatta desyoo
Conditional	**INFORMAL**		suguretara	sugurenakatta
	FORMAL		suguremasitara	suguremaseñ desitara
Alternative	**INFORMAL**		suguretari	sugurenakattari
	FORMAL		suguremasitari	suguremaseñ desitari

INFORMAL AFFIRMATIVE INDICATIVE

Passive	sugurerareru	*Honorific*	**I**	osugure ni naru
			II	osugure nasaru
Potential	sugurerareru			
		Humble	**I**	
Causative	suguresaseru		**II**	
Causative Pass.	suguresaserareru			

		AFFIRMATIVE	NEGATIVE
Indicative	INFORMAL	suku	sukanai
	FORMAL	sukimasu	sukimaseñ
Imperative	INFORMAL I		
	II		
	III		
	FORMAL		
Presumptive	INFORMAL I	sukoo	sukumai
	II	suku daroo	sukanai daroo
	FORMAL I	sukimasyoo	sukimasumai
	II	suku desyoo	sukanai desyoo
Provisional	INFORMAL	sukeba	sukanakereba
	FORMAL	sukimaseba	sukimaseñ nara
		sukimasureba	
Gerund	INFORMAL I	suite	sukanai de
	II		sukanakute
	FORMAL	sukimasite	sukimaseñ de
Past Ind.	INFORMAL	suita	sukanakatta
	FORMAL	sukimasita	sukimaseñ desita
Past Presump.	INFORMAL	suitaroo	sukanakattaroo
		suita daroo	sukanakatta daroo
	FORMAL	sukimasitaroo	sukimaseñ desitaroo
		suita desyoo	sukanakatta desyoo
Conditional	INFORMAL	suitara	sukanakattara
	FORMAL	sukimasitara	sukimaseñ desitara
Alternative	INFORMAL	suitari	sukanakattari
	FORMAL	sukimasitari	sukimaseñ desitari

INFORMAL AFFIRMATIVE INDICATIVE

Passive		*Honorific*	I
Potential			II
Causative	sukaseru	*Humble*	I
Causative Pass.	sukaserareru		II

			AFFIRMATIVE	**NEGATIVE**
Indicative	**INFORMAL**		sumaseru	sumasenai
	FORMAL		sumasemasu	sumasemaseñ
Imperative	**INFORMAL**	**I**	sumasero	sumaseru na
		II	sumasenasai	sumasenasaru na
		III	sumasete kudasai	sumasenai de kudasai
	FORMAL		osumase nasaimase	osumase nasaimasu na
Presumptive	**INFORMAL**	**I**	sumaseyoo	sumasemai
		II	sumaseru daroo	sumasenai daroo
	FORMAL	**I**	sumasemasyoo	sumasemasumai
		II	sumaseru desyoo	sumasenai desyoo
Provisional	**INFORMAL**		sumasereba	sumasenakereba
	FORMAL		sumasemaseba	sumasemaseñ nara
			sumasemasureba	
Gerund	**INFORMAL**	**I**	sumasete	sumasenai de
		II		sumasenakute
	FORMAL		sumasemasite	sumasemaseñ de
Past Ind.	**INFORMAL**		sumaseta	sumasenakatta
	FORMAL		sumasemasita	sumasemaseñ desita
Past Presump.	**INFORMAL**		sumasetaroo	sumasenakattaroo
			sumaseta daroo	sumasenakatta daroo
	FORMAL		sumasemasitaroo	sumasemaseñ desitaroo
			sumaseta desyoo	sumasenakatta desyoo
Conditional	**INFORMAL**		sumasetara	sumasenakattara
	FORMAL		sumasemasitara	sumasemaseñ desitara
Alternative	**INFORMAL**		sumasetari	sumasenakattari
	FORMAL		sumasemasitari	sumasemaseñ desitari

INFORMAL AFFIRMATIVE INDICATIVE				
Passive	sumaserareru	*Honorific*	**I**	osumase ni naru
			II	osumase nasaru
Potential	sumaserareru			
		Humble		
Causative				

Causative Pass.

*This is the causative form of *sum.u* 'to end' and is given to illustrate the full range of inflection found in this type of derived verb.

		AFFIRMATIVE	NEGATIVE
Indicative	INFORMAL	sumu	sumanai
	FORMAL	sumimasu	sumimaseñ
Imperative	INFORMAL I	sume	sumu na
	II	suminasai	suminasaru na
	III	suñde kudasai	sumanai de kudasai
	FORMAL	osumi nasaimase	osumi nasaimasu na
Presumptive	INFORMAL I	sumoo	sumumai
	II	sumu daroo	sumanai daroo
	FORMAL I	sumimasyoo	sumimasumai
	II	sumu desyoo	sumanai desyoo
Provisional	INFORMAL	sumeba	sumanakereba
	FORMAL	sumimaseba	sumimaseñ nara
		sumimasureba	
Gerund	INFORMAL I	suñde	sumanai de
	II		sumanakute
	FORMAL	sumimasite	sumimaseñ de
Past Ind.	INFORMAL	suñda	sumanakatta
	FORMAL	sumimasita	sumimaseñ desita
Past Presump.	INFORMAL	suñdaroo	sumanakattaroo
		suñda daroo	sumanakatta daroo
	FORMAL	sumimasitaroo	sumimaseñ desitaroo
		suñda desyoo	sumanakatta desyoo
Conditional	INFORMAL	suñdara	sumanakattara
	FORMAL	sumimasitara	sumimaseñ desitara
Alternative	INFORMAL	suñdari	sumanakattari
	FORMAL	sumimasitari	sumimaseñ desitari

INFORMAL AFFIRMATIVE INDICATIVE

Passive	sumareru	*Honorific*	I	osumi ni naru
			II	osumi nasaru
Potential	sumeru			
		Humble	I	
Causative	sumaseru		II	
Causative Pass.	sumaserareru			

		AFFIRMATIVE	NEGATIVE
Indicative	INFORMAL	suru	sinai
	FORMAL	simasu	simaseñ
Imperative	INFORMAL I	siro	suru na
	II	sinasai	sinasaru na
	III	site kudasai	sinai de kudasai
	FORMAL	nasaimase	nasaimasu na
Presumptive	INFORMAL I	siyoo	surumai
	II	suru daroo	sinai daroo
	FORMAL I	simasyoo	simasumai
	II	suru desyoo	sinai desyoo
Provisional	INFORMAL	sureba	sinakereba
	FORMAL	simaseba	simaseñ nara
		simasureba	
Gerund	INFORMAL I	site	sinai de
	II		sinakute
	FORMAL	simasite	simaseñ de
Past Ind.	INFORMAL	sita	sinakatta
	FORMAL	simasita	simaseñ desita
Past Presump.	INFORMAL	sitaroo	sinakattaroo
		sita daroo	sinakatta daroo
	FORMAL	simasitaroo	simaseñ desitaroo
		sita desyoo	sinakatta desyoo
Conditional	INFORMAL	sitara	sinakattara
	FORMAL	simasitara	simaseñ desitara
Alternative	INFORMAL	sitari	sinakattari
	FORMAL	simasitari	simaseñ desitari

INFORMAL AFFIRMATIVE INDICATIVE

Passive	sareru	*Honorific*	nasaru
Potential	dekiru		
		Humble	itasu
Causative	saseru		
Causative Pass.	saserareru		

*This is used to derive verbs from Sino-Japanese nouns. For example, *kekkoñ* ('marriage') plus *su.ru* becomes *kekkoñ-suru* 'to get married.'

		AFFIRMATIVE	NEGATIVE
Indicative	INFORMAL	susumu	susumanai
	FORMAL	susumimasu	susumimaseñ
Imperative	INFORMAL I	susume	susumu na
	II	susuminasai	susuminasaru na
	III	susuñde kudasai	susumanai de kudasai
	FORMAL	osusumi nasaimase	osusumi nasaimasu na
Presumptive	INFORMAL I	susumoo	susumumai
	II	susumu daroo	susumanai daroo
	FORMAL I	susumimasyoo	susumimasumai
	II	susumu desyoo	susumanai desyoo
Provisional	INFORMAL	susumeba	susumanakereba
	FORMAL	susumimaseba	susumimaseñ nara
		susumimasureba	
Gerund	INFORMAL I	susuñde	susumanai de
	II		susumanakute
	FORMAL	susumimasite	susumimaseñ de
Past Ind.	INFORMAL	susuñda	susumanakatta
	FORMAL	susumimasita	susumimaseñ desita
Past Presump.	INFORMAL	susuñdaroo	susumanakattaroo
		susuñda daroo	susumanakatta daroo
	FORMAL	susumimasitaroo	susumimaseñ desitaroo
		susuñda desyoo	susumanakatta desyoo
Conditional	INFORMAL	susuñdara	susumanakattara
	FORMAL	susumimasitara	susumimaseñ desitara
Alternative	INFORMAL	susuñdari	susumanakattari
	FORMAL	susumimasitari	susumimaseñ desitari

INFORMAL AFFIRMATIVE INDICATIVE

Passive	susumareru	*Honorific*	I	osusumi ni naru
			II	osusumi nasaru
Potential	susumeru			
		Humble	I	osusumi suru
Causative	susumaseru		II	osusumi itasu
Causative Pass.	susumaserareru			

TRANSITIVE   *to abandon, to throw away*

		AFFIRMATIVE	NEGATIVE
Indicative	INFORMAL	suteru	sutenai
	FORMAL	sutemasu	sutemaseñ
Imperative	INFORMAL I	sutero	suteru na
	II	sutenasai	sutenasaru na
	III	sutete kudasai	sutenai de kudasai
	FORMAL	osute nasaimase	osute nasaimasu na
Presumptive	INFORMAL I	suteyoo	sutemai
	II	suteru daroo	sutenai daroo
	FORMAL I	sutemasyoo	sutemasumai
	II	suteru desyoo	sutenai desyoo
Provisional	INFORMAL	sutereba	sutenakereba
	FORMAL	sutemaseba	sutemaseñ nara
		sutemasureba	
Gerund	INFORMAL I	sutete	sutenai de
	II		sutenakute
	FORMAL	sutemasite	sutemaseñ de
Past Ind.	INFORMAL	suteta	sutenakatta
	FORMAL	sutemasita	sutemaseñ desita
Past Presump.	INFORMAL	sutetaroo	sutenakattaroo
		suteta daroo	sutenakatta daroo
	FORMAL	sutemasitaroo	sutemaseñ desitaroo
		suteta desyoo	sutenakatta desyoo
Conditional	INFORMAL	sutetara	sutenakattara
	FORMAL	sutemasitara	sutemaseñ desitara
Alternative	INFORMAL	sutetari	sutenakattari
	FORMAL	sutemasitari	sutemaseñ desitari

INFORMAL AFFIRMATIVE INDICATIVE

Passive	suterareru	*Honorific*	I	osute ni naru
			II	osute nasaru
Potential	suterareru			
		Humble	I	osute suru
Causative	sutesaseru		II	osute itasu
Causative Pass.	sutesaserareru			

		AFFIRMATIVE	NEGATIVE
Indicative	**INFORMAL**	suwaru	suwaranai
	FORMAL	suwarimasu	suwarimaseñ
Imperative	**INFORMAL I**	suware	suwaru na
	II	suwarinasai	suwarinasaru na
	III	suwatte kudasai	suwaranai de kudasai
	FORMAL	osuwari nasaimase	osuwari nasaimasu na
Presumptive	**INFORMAL I**	suwaroo	suwarumai
	II	suwaru daroo	suwaranai daroo
	FORMAL I	suwarimasyoo	suwarimasumai
	II	suwaru desyoo	suwaranai desyoo
Provisional	**INFORMAL**	suwareba	suwaranakereba
	FORMAL	suwarimaseba	suwarimaseñ nara
		suwarimasureba	
Gerund	**INFORMAL I**	suwatte	suwaranai de
	II		suwaranakute
	FORMAL	suwarimasite	suwarimaseñ de
Past Ind.	**INFORMAL**	suwatta	suwaranakatta
	FORMAL	suwarimasita	suwarimaseñ desita
Past Presump.	**INFORMAL**	suwattaroo	suwaranakattaroo
		suwatta daroo	suwaranakatta daroo
	FORMAL	suwarimasitaroo	suwarimaseñ desitaroo
		suwatta desyoo	suwaranakatta desyoo
Conditional	**INFORMAL**	suwattara	suwaranakattara
	FORMAL	suwarimasitara	suwarimaseñ desitara
Alternative	**INFORMAL**	suwattari	suwaranakattari
	FORMAL	suwarimasitari	suwarimaseñ desitari

INFORMAL AFFIRMATIVE INDICATIVE

Passive	suwarareru	*Honorific*	**I**	osuwari ni naru
			II	osuwari nasaru
Potential	suwareru			
		Humble	**I**	
Causative	suwaraseru		**II**	
Causative Pass.	suwaraserareru			

		AFFIRMATIVE	NEGATIVE
Indicative	INFORMAL	taberu	tabenai
	FORMAL	tabemasu	tabemaseñ
Imperative	INFORMAL I	tabero	taberu na
	II	tabenasai	tabenasaru na
	III	tabete kudasai	tabenai de kudasai
	FORMAL	mesiagarimase	mesiagarimasu na
Presumptive	INFORMAL I	tabeyoo	tabemai
	II	taberu daroo	tabenai daroo
	FORMAL I	tabemasyoo	tabemasumai
	II	taberu desyoo	tabenai desyoo
Provisional	INFORMAL	tabereba	tabenakereba
	FORMAL	tabemaseba	tabemaseñ nara
		tabemasureba	
Gerund	INFORMAL I	tabete	tabenai de
	II		tabenakute
	FORMAL	tabemasite	tabemaseñ de
Past Ind.	INFORMAL	tabeta	tabenakatta
	FORMAL	tabemasita	tabemaseñ desita
Past Presump.	INFORMAL	tabetaroo	tabenakattaroo
		tabeta daroo	tabenakatta daroo
	FORMAL	tabemasitaroo	tabemaseñ desitaroo
		tabeta desyoo	tabenakatta desyoo
Conditional	INFORMAL	tabetara	tabenakattara
	FORMAL	tabemasitara	tabemaseñ desitara
Alternative	INFORMAL	tabetari	tabenakattari
	FORMAL	tabemasitari	tabemaseñ desitari

INFORMAL AFFIRMATIVE INDICATIVE

Passive	taberareru	*Honorific*	mesiagaru
Potential	taberareru		
		Humble	itadaku
Causative	tabesaseru		
Causative Pass.	tabesaserareru		

-tagár.u   -tagari
*non-first person desiderative suffix**

		AFFIRMATIVE	NEGATIVE
Indicative	INFORMAL	-tagaru	-tagaranai
	FORMAL	-tagarimasu	-tagarimaseñ
Imperative	INFORMAL I		
	II		
	III		
	FORMAL		
Presumptive	INFORMAL I	-tagaroo	-tagarumai
	II	-tagaru daroo	-tagaranai daroⱺ
	FORMAL I	-tagarimasyoo	-tagarimasumai
	II	-tagaru desyoo	-tagaranai desyoo
Provisional	INFORMAL	-tagareba	-tagaranakereba
	FORMAL	-tagarimaseba	-tagarimaseñ nara
		-tagarimasureba	
Gerund	INFORMAL I	-tagatte	-tagaranai de
	II		-tagaranakute
	FORMAL	-tagarimasite	-tagarimaseñ de
Past Ind.	INFORMAL	-tagatta	-tagaranakatta
	FORMAL	-tagarimasita	-tagarimaseñ desita
Past Presump.	INFORMAL	-tagattaroo	-tagaranakattaroo
		-tagatta daroo	-tagaranakatta daroo
	FORMAL	-tagarimasitaroo	-tagarimaseñ desitaroo
		-tagatta desyoo	-tagaranakatta desyoo
Conditional	INFORMAL	-tagattara	-tagaranakattara
	FORMAL	-tagarimasitara	-tagarimaseñ desitara
Alternative	INFORMAL	-tagattari	-tagaranakattari
	FORMAL	-tagarimasitari	-tagarimaseñ desitari

INFORMAL AFFIRMATIVE INDICATIVE

Passive		*Honorific*	I
			II
Potential			
		Humble	I
Causative	-tagaraseru		II

Causative Pass.   -tagaraserareru

**-tagaru* is added to the infinitive of verbs, and like *-masu* does not have any transitive/intransitive bias of its own.

244

		AFFIRMATIVE	**NEGATIVE**
Indicative	**INFORMAL**	tamesu	tamesanai
	FORMAL	tamesimasu	tamesimaseñ
Imperative	**INFORMAL I**	tamese	tamesu na
	II	tamesinasai	tamesinasaru na
	III	tamesite kudasai	tamesanai de kudasai
	FORMAL	otamesi nasaimase	otamesi nasaimasu na
Presumptive	**INFORMAL I**	tamesoo	tamesumai
	II	tamesu daroo	tamesanai daroo
	FORMAL I	tamesimasyoo	tamesimasumai
	II	tamesu desyoo	tamesanai desyoo
Provisional	**INFORMAL**	tameseba	tamesanakereba
	FORMAL	tamesimaseba	tamesimaseñ nara
		tamesimasureba	
Gerund	**INFORMAL I**	tamesite	tamesanai de
	II		tamesanakute
	FORMAL	tamesimasite	tamesimaseñ de
Past Ind.	**INFORMAL**	tamesita	tamesanakatta
	FORMAL	tamesimasita	tamesimaseñ desita
Past Presump.	**INFORMAL**	tamesitaroo	tamesanakattaroo
		tamesita daroo	tamesanakatta daroo
	FORMAL	tamesimasitaroo	tamesimaseñ desitaroo
		tamesita desyoo	tamesanakatta desyoo
Conditional	**INFORMAL**	tamesitara	tamesanakattara
	FORMAL	tamesimasitara	tamesimaseñ desitara
Alternative	**INFORMAL**	tamesitari	tamesanakattari
	FORMAL	tamesimasitari	tamesimaseñ desitari

INFORMAL AFFIRMATIVE INDICATIVE

Passive	tamesareru	*Honorific*	**I**	otamesi ni naru
			II	otamesi nasaru
Potential	tameseru			
		Humble	**I**	otamesi suru
Causative	tamesaseru		**II**	otamesi itasu
Causative Pass.	tamesaserareru			

		AFFIRMATIVE	NEGATIVE
Indicative	INFORMAL	tanomu	tanomanai
	FORMAL	tanomimasu	tanomimaseñ
Imperative	INFORMAL I	tanome	tanomu na
	II	tanominasai	tanominasaru na
	III	tanoñde kudasai	tanomanai de kudasai
	FORMAL	otanomi nasaimase	otanomi nasaimasu na
Presumptive	INFORMAL I	tanomoo	tanomumai
	II	tanomu daroo	tanomanai daroo
	FORMAL I	tanomimasyoo	tanomimasumai
	II	tanomu desyoo	tanomanai desyoo
Provisional	INFORMAL	tanomeba	tanomanakereba
	FORMAL	tanomimaseba	tanomimaseñ nara
		tanomimasureba	
Gerund	INFORMAL I	tanoñde	tanomanai de
	II		tanomanakute
	FORMAL	tanomimasite	tanomimaseñ de
Past Ind.	INFORMAL	tanoñda	tanomanakatta
	FORMAL	tanomimasita	tanomimaseñ desita
Past Presump.	INFORMAL	tanoñdaroo	tanomanakattaroo
		tanoñda daroo	tanomanakatta daroo
	FORMAL	tanomimasitaroo	tanomimaseñ desitaroo
		tanoñda desyoo	tamomanakatta desyoo
Conditional	INFORMAL	tanoñdara	tanomanakattara
	FORMAL	tanomimasitara	tanomimaseñ desitara
Alternative	INFORMAL	tanoñdari	tanomanakattari
	FORMAL	tanomimasitari	tanomimaseñ desitari

INFORMAL AFFIRMATIVE INDICATIVE

Passive	tanomareru	*Honorific*	I	otanomi ni naru
			II	otanomi nasaru
Potential	tanomeru			
		Humble	I	otanomi suru
Causative	tanomaseru		II	otanomi itasu
Causative Pass.	tanomaserareru			

TRANSITIVE   *to enjoy, to take pleasure in*

		AFFIRMATIVE	NEGATIVE
Indicative	INFORMAL	tanosimu	tanosimanai
	FORMAL	tanosimimasu	tanosimimaseñ
Imperative	INFORMAL I	tanosime	tanosimu na
	II	tanosiminasai	tanosiminasaru na
	III	tanosiñde kudasai	tanosimanai de kudasai
	FORMAL	otanosimi nasaimase	otanosimi nasaimasu na
Presumptive	INFORMAL I	tanosimoo	tanosimumai
	II	tanosimu daroo	tanosimanai daroo
	FORMAL I	tanosimimasyoo	tanosimimasumai
	II	tanosimu desyoo	tanosimanai desyoo
Provisional	INFORMAL	tanosimeba	tanosimanakereba
	FORMAL	tanosimimaseba	tanosimimaseñ de
		tanosimimasureba	
Gerund	INFORMAL I	tanosiñde	tanosimanai de
	II		tanosimanakute
	FORMAL	tanosimimasite	tanosimimaseñ de
Past Ind.	INFORMAL	tanosiñda	tanosimanakatta
	FORMAL	tanosimimasita	tanosimimaseñ desita
Past Presump.	INFORMAL	tanosiñdaroo	tanosimanakattaroo
		tanosiñda daroo	tanosimanakatta daroo
	FORMAL	tanosimimasitaroo	tanosimimaseñ desitaroo
		tanosiñda desyoo	tanosimanakatta desyoo
Conditional	INFORMAL	tanosiñdara	tanosimanakattara
	FORMAL	tanosimimasitara	tanosimimaseñ desitara
Alternative	INFORMAL	tanosiñdari	tanosimanakattari
	FORMAL	tanosimimasitari	tanosimimaseñ desitari

INFORMAL AFFIRMATIVE INDICATIVE

Passive	tanosimareru	*Honorific*	I	otanosimi ni naru
			II	otanosimi nasaru
Potential	tanosimeru			
		Humble	I	
Causative	tanosimaseru		II	
Causative Pass.	tanosimaserareru			

247

		AFFIRMATIVE	NEGATIVE
Indicative	**INFORMAL**	taoreru	taorenai
	FORMAL	taoremasu	taoremaseñ
Imperative	**INFORMAL I**	taorero	taoreru na
	II	taorenasai	taorenasaru na
	III	taorete kudasai	taorenai de kudasai
	FORMAL	otaore nasaimase	otaore nasaimasu na
Presumptive	**INFORMAL I**	taoreyoo	taoremai
	II	taoreru daroo	taorenai daroo
	FORMAL I	taoremasyoo	taoremasumai
	II	taoreru desyoo	taorenai desyoo
Provisional	**INFORMAL**	taorereba	taorenakereba
	FORMAL	taoremaseba	taoremaseñ nara
		taoremasureba	
Gerund	**INFORMAL I**	taorete	taorenai de
	II		taorenakute
	FORMAL	taoremasite	taoremaseñ de
Past Ind.	**INFORMAL**	taoreta	taorenakatta
	FORMAL	taoremasita	taoremaseñ desita
Past Presump.	**INFORMAL**	taoretaroo	taorenakattaroo
		taoreta daroo	taorenakatta daroo
	FORMAL	taoremasitaroo	taoremaseñ desitaroo
		taoreta desyoo	taorenakatta desyoo
Conditional	**INFORMAL**	taoretara	taorenakattara
	FORMAL	taoremasitara	taoremaseñ desitara
Alternative	**INFORMAL**	taoretari	taorenakattari
	FORMAL	taoremasitari	taoremaseñ desitari

INFORMAL AFFIRMATIVE INDICATIVE

Passive		*Honorific*	**I**	otaore ni naru
Potential			**II**	otaore nasaru
Causative	taoresaseru	*Humble*	**I**	
Causative Pass.	taoresaserareru		**II**	

TRANSITIVE   *to overthrow, to knock down*

		AFFIRMATIVE	NEGATIVE
Indicative	**INFORMAL**	taosu	taosanai
	FORMAL	taosimasu	taosimaseñ
Imperative	**INFORMAL I**	taose	taosu na
	II	taosinasai	taosinasaru na
	III	taosite kudasai	taosanai de kudasai
	FORMAL	otaosi nasaimase	otaosi nasaimasu na
Presumptive	**INFORMAL I**	taosoo	taosumai
	II	taosu daroo	taosanai daroo
	FORMAL I	taosimasyoo	taosimasumai
	II	taosu desyoo	taosanai desyoo
Provisional	**INFORMAL**	taoseba	taosanakereba
	FORMAL	taosimaseba	taosimaseñ nara
		taosimasureba	
Gerund	**INFORMAL I**	taosite	taosanai de
	II		taosanakute
	FORMAL	taosimasite	taosimaseñ de
Past Ind.	**INFORMAL**	taosita	taosanakatta
	FORMAL	taosimasita	taosimaseñ desita
Past Presump.	**INFORMAL**	taositaroo	taosanakattaroo
		taosita daroo	taosanakatta daroo
	FORMAL	taosimasitaroo	taosimaseñ desitaroo
		taosita desyoo	taosanakatta desyoo
Conditional	**INFORMAL**	taositara	taosanakattara
	FORMAL	taosimasitara	taosimaseñ desitara
Alternative	**INFORMAL**	taositari	taosanakattari
	FORMAL	taosimasitari	taosimaseñ desitari

INFORMAL AFFIRMATIVE INDICATIVE

Passive	taosareru	*Honorific*	**I**	otaosi ni naru
			II	otaosi nasaru
Potential	taoseru			
		Humble	**I**	
Causative	taosaseru		**II**	
Causative Pass.	taosaserareru			

		AFFIRMATIVE	NEGATIVE
Indicative	INFORMAL	tariru	tarinai
	FORMAL	tarimasu	tarimaseñ
Imperative	INFORMAL I		
	II		
	III		
	FORMAL		
Presumptive	INFORMAL I	tariyoo	tarimai
	II	tariru daroo	tarinai daroo
	FORMAL I	tarimasyoo	tarimasumai
	II	tariru desyoo	tarinai desyoo
Provisional	INFORMAL	tarireba	tarinakereba
	FORMAL	tarimaseba	tarimaseñ nara
		tarimasureba	
Gerund	INFORMAL I	tarite	tarinai de
	II		tarinakute
	FORMAL	tarimasite	tarimaseñ de
Past Ind.	INFORMAL	tarita	tarinakatta
	FORMAL	tarimasita	tarimaseñ desita
Past Presump.	INFORMAL	taritaroo	tarinakattaroo
		tarita daroo	tarinakatta daroo
	FORMAL	tarimasitaroo	tarimaseñ desitaroo
		tarita desyoo	tarinakatta desyoo
Conditional	INFORMAL	taritara	tarinakattara
	FORMAL	tarimasitara	tarimaseñ desitara
Alternative	INFORMAL	taritari	tarinakattari
	FORMAL	tarimasitari	tarimaseñ desitari

INFORMAL AFFIRMATIVE INDICATIVE

Passive		*Honorific*	I
			II
Potential			
		Humble	I
Causative			II
Causative Pass.			

TRANSITIVE *to ascertain, to confirm*

		AFFIRMATIVE	NEGATIVE
Indicative	INFORMAL	tasikameru	tasikamenai
	FORMAL	tasikamemasu	tasikamemaseñ
Imperative	INFORMAL I	tasikamero	tasikameru na
	II	tasikamenasai	tasikamenasaru na
	III	tasikamete kudasai	tasikamenai de kudasai
	FORMAL	otasikame nasaimase	otasikame nasaimasu na
Presumptive	INFORMAL I	tasikameyoo	tasikamemai
	II	tasikameru daroo	tasikamenai daroo
	FORMAL I	tasikamemasyoo	tasikamemasumai
	II	tasikameru desyoo	tasikamenai desyoo
Provisional	INFORMAL	tasikamereba	tasikamenakereba
	FORMAL	tasikamemaseba	tasikamemaseñ nara
		tasikamemasureba	
Gerund	INFORMAL I	tasikamete	tasikamenai de
	II		tasikamenakute
	FORMAL	tasikamemasite	tasikamemaseñ de
Past Ind.	INFORMAL	tasikameta	tasikamenakatta
	FORMAL	tasikamemasita	tasikamemaseñ desita
Past Presump.	INFORMAL	tasikametaroo	tasikamenakattaroo
		tasikameta daroo	tasikamenakatta daroo
	FORMAL	tasikamemasitaroo	tasikamemaseñ desitaroo
		tasikameta desyoo	tasikamenakatta desyoo
Conditional	INFORMAL	tasikametara	tasikamenakattara
	FORMAL	tasikamemasitara	tasikamemaseñ desitara
Alternative	INFORMAL	tasikametari	tasikamenakattari
	FORMAL	tasikamemasitari	tasikamemaseñ desitari

INFORMAL AFFIRMATIVE INDICATIVE

Passive	tasikamerareru	*Honorific*	I	otasikame ni naru
			II	otasikame nasaru
Potential	tasikamerareru			
		Humble	I	otasikame suru
Causative	tasikamesaseru		II	otasikame itasu
Causative Pass.	tasikamesaserareru			

		AFFIRMATIVE	NEGATIVE
Indicative	INFORMAL	tasukeru	tasukenai
	FORMAL	tasukemasu	tasukemaseñ
Imperative	INFORMAL I	tasukero	tasukeru na
	II	tasukenasai	tasukenasaru na
	III	tasukete kudasai	tasukenai de kudasai
	FORMAL	otasuke nasaimase	otasuke nasaimasu na
Presumptive	INFORMAL I	tasukeyoo	tasukemai
	II	tasukeru daroo	tasukenai daroo
	FORMAL I	tasukemasyoo	tasukemasumai
	II	tasukeru desyoo	tasukenai desyoo
Provisional	INFORMAL	tasukereba	tasukenakereba
	FORMAL	tasukemaseba	tasukemaseñ nara
		tasukemasureba	
Gerund	INFORMAL I	tasukete	tasukenai de
	II		tasukenakute
	FORMAL	tasukemasite	tasukemaseñ de
Past Ind.	INFORMAL	tasuketa	tasukenakatta
	FORMAL	tasukemasita	tasukemaseñ desita
Past Presump.	INFORMAL	tasuketaroo	tasukenakattaroo
		tasuketa daroo	tasukenakatta daroo
	FORMAL	tasukemasitaroo	tasukemaseñ desitaroo
		tasuketa desyoo	tasukenakatta desyoo
Conditional	INFORMAL	tasuketara	tasukenakattara
	FORMAL	tasukemasitara	tasukemaseñ desitara
Alternative	INFORMAL	tasuketari	tasukenakattari
	FORMAL	tasukemasitari	tasukemaseñ desitari

INFORMAL AFFIRMATIVE INDICATIVE

Passive	tasukerareru	*Honorific*	I	otasuke ni naru
			II	otasuke nasaru
Potential	tasukerareru			
		Humble	I	otasuke suru
Causative	tasukesaseru		II	otasuke itasu
Causative Pass.	tasukesaserareru			

TRANSITIVE   *to fight against, to wage war on, to struggle against*

		AFFIRMATIVE	NEGATIVE
Indicative	INFORMAL	tatakau	tatakawanai
	FORMAL	tatakaimasu	tatakaimaseñ
Imperative	INFORMAL I	tatakae	tatakau na
	II	tatakainasai	tatakainasaru na
	III	tatakatte kudasai	tatakawanai de kudasai
	FORMAL	otatakai nasaimase	otatakai nasaimasu na
Presumptive	INFORMAL I	tatakaoo	tatakaumai
	II	tatakau daroo	tatakawanai daroo
	FORMAL I	tatakaimasyoo	tatakaimasumai
	II	tatakau desyoo	tatakawanai desyoo
Provisional	INFORMAL	tatakaeba	tatakawanakereba
	FORMAL	tatakaimaseba	tatakaimaseñ nara
		tatakaimasureba	
Gerund	INFORMAL I	tatakatte	tatakawanai de
	II		tatakawanakute
	FORMAL	tatakaimasite	tatakaimaseñ de
Past Ind.	INFORMAL	tatakatta	tatakawanakatta
	FORMAL	tatakaimasita	tatakaimaseñ desita
Past Presump.	INFORMAL	tatakattaroo	tatakawanakattaroo
		tatakatta daroo	tatakawanakatta daroo
	FORMAL	tatakaimasitaroo	tatakaimaseñ desitaroo
		tatakatta desyoo	tatakawanakatta desyoo
Conditional	INFORMAL	tatakattara	tatakawanakattara
	FORMAL	tatakaimasitara	tatakaimaseñ desitara
Alternative	INFORMAL	tatakattari	tatakawanakattari
	FORMAL	tatakaimasitari	tatakaimaseñ desitari

INFORMAL AFFIRMATIVE INDICATIVE

Passive	tatakawareru	*Honorific*	I	otatakai ni naru
			II	otatakai nasaru
Potential	tatakaeru			
		Humble	I	
Causative	tatakawaseru		II	
Causative Pass.	tatakawaserareru			

to hit, to slap, to beat　　TRANSITIVE

			AFFIRMATIVE	NEGATIVE
Indicative	INFORMAL		tataku	tatakanai
	FORMAL		tatakimasu	tatakimaseñ
Imperative	INFORMAL	I	tatake	tataku na
		II	tatakinasai	tatakinasaru na
		III	tataite kudasai	tatakanai de kudasai
	FORMAL		otataki nasaimase	otataki nasaimasu na
Presumptive	INFORMAL	I	tatakoo	tatakumai
		II	tataku daroo	tatakanai daroo
	FORMAL	I	tatakimasyoo	tatakimasumai
		II	tataku desyoo	tatakanai desyoo
Provisional	INFORMAL		tatakeba	tatakanakereba
	FORMAL		tatakimaseba	tatakimaseñ nara
			tatakimasureba	
Gerund	INFORMAL	I	tataite	tatakanai de
		II		tatakanakute
	FORMAL		tatakimasite	tatakimaseñ de
Past Ind.	INFORMAL		tataita	tatakanakatta
	FORMAL		tatakimasita	tatakimaseñ desita
Past Presump.	INFORMAL		tataitaroo	tatakanakattaroo
			tataita daroo	tatakanakatta daroo
	FORMAL		tatakimasitaroo	tatakimaseñ desitaroo
			tataita desyoo	tatakanakatta desyoo
Conditional	INFORMAL		tataitara	tatakanakattara
	FORMAL		tatakimasitara	tatakimaseñ desitara
Alternative	INFORMAL		tataitari	tatakanakattari
	FORMAL		tatakimasitari	tatakimaseñ desitari

INFORMAL AFFIRMATIVE INDICATIVE

Passive	tatakareru		*Honorific*	I	otataki ni naru
				II	otataki nasaru
Potential	tatakeru				
			Humble	I	otataki suru
Causative	tatakaseru			II	otataki itasu
Causative Pass.	tatakaserareru				

			TRANSITIVE *to erect*

		AFFIRMATIVE	**NEGATIVE**
Indicative	INFORMAL	tateru	tatenai
	FORMAL	tatemasu	tatemaseñ
Imperative	INFORMAL I	tatero	tateru na
	II	tatenasai	tatenasaru na
	III	tatete kudasai	tatenai de kudasai
	FORMAL	otate nasaimase	otate nasaimasu na
Presumptive	INFORMAL I	tateyoo	tatemai
	II	tateru daroo	tatenai daroo
	FORMAL I	tatemasyoo	tatemasumai
	II	tateru desyoo	tatenai desyoo
Provisional	INFORMAL	tatereba	tatenakereba
	FORMAL	tatemaseba	tatemaseñ nara
		tatemasureba	
Gerund	INFORMAL I	tatete	tatenai de
	II		tatenakute
	FORMAL	tatemasite	tatemaseñ de
Past Ind.	INFORMAL	tateta	tatenakatta
	FORMAL	tatemasita	tatemaseñ desita
Past Presump.	INFORMAL	tatetaroo	tatenakattaroo
		tateta daroo	tatenakatta daroo
	FORMAL	tatemasitaroo	tatemaseñ desitaroo
		tateta desyoo	tatenakatta desyoo
Conditional	INFORMAL	tatetara	tatenakattara
	FORMAL	tatemasitara	tatemaseñ desitara
Alternative	INFORMAL	tatetari	tatenakattari
	FORMAL	tatemasitari	tatemaseñ desitari

INFORMAL AFFIRMATIVE INDICATIVE

Passive	taterareru	*Honorific*	I	otate ni naru
			II	otate nasaru
Potential	taterareru			
		Humble	I	otate suru
Causative	tatesaseru		II	otate itasu
Causative Pass.	tatesaserareru			

		AFFIRMATIVE	NEGATIVE
Indicative	INFORMAL	tatu	tatanai
	FORMAL	tatimasu	tatimaseñ
Imperative	INFORMAL I	tate	tatu na
	II	tatinasai	tatinasaru na
	III	tatte kudasai	tatanai de kudasai
	FORMAL	otati nasaimase	otati nasaimasu na
Presumptive	INFORMAL I	tatoo	tatumai
	II	tatu daroo	tatanai daroo
	FORMAL I	tatimasyoo	tatimasumai
	II	tatu desyoo	tatanai desyoo
Provisional	INFORMAL	tateba	tatanakereba
	FORMAL	tatimaseba	tatimaseñ nara
		tatimasureba	
Gerund	INFORMAL I	tatte	tatanai de
	II		tatanakute
	FORMAL	tatimasite	tatimaseñ de
Past Ind.	INFORMAL	tatta	tatanakatta
	FORMAL	tatimasita	tatimaseñ desita
Past Presump.	INFORMAL	tattaroo	tatanakattaroo
		tatta daroo	tatanakatta daroo
	FORMAL	tatimasitaroo	tatimaseñ desitaroo
		tatta desyoo	tatanakatta desyoo
Conditional	INFORMAL	tattara	tatanakattara
	FORMAL	tatimasitara	tatimaseñ desitara
Alternative	INFORMAL	tattari	tatanakattari
	FORMAL	tatimasitari	tatimaseñ desitari

INFORMAL AFFIRMATIVE INDICATIVE

Passive	tatareru	*Honorific*	I	otati ni naru
			II	otati nasaru
Potential	tateru			
		Humble	I	otati suru
Causative	tataseru		II	otati itasu
Causative Pass.	tataserareru			

TRANSITIVE   *to ask* (a question), *to search for*

			AFFIRMATIVE	NEGATIVE
Indicative	INFORMAL		tazuneru	tazunenai
	FORMAL		tazunemasu	tazunemaseñ
Imperative	INFORMAL	I	tazunero	tazuneru na
		II	tazunenasai	tazunenasaru na
		III	tazunete kudasai	tazunenai de kudasai
	FORMAL		otazune nasaimase	otazune nasaimasu na
Presumptive	INFORMAL	I	tazuneyoo	tazunemai
		II	tazuneru daroo	tazunenai daroo
	FORMAL	I	tazunemasyoo	tazunemasumai
		II	tazuneru desyoo	tazunenai desyoo
Provisional	INFORMAL		tazunereba	tazunenakereba
	FORMAL		tazunemaseba	tazunemaseñ nara
			tazunemasureba	
Gerund	INFORMAL	I	tazunete	tazunenai de
		II		tazunenakute
	FORMAL		tazunemasite	tazunemaseñ de
Past Ind.	INFORMAL		tazuneta	tazunenakatta
	FORMAL		tazunemasita	tazunemaseñ desita
Past Presump.	INFORMAL		tazunetaroo	tazunenakattaroo
			tazuneta daroo	tazunenakatta daroo
	FORMAL		tazunemasitaroo	tazunemaseñ desitaroo
			tazuneta desyoo	tazunenakatta desyoo
Conditional	INFORMAL		tazunetara	tazunenakattara
	FORMAL		tazunemasitara	tazunemaseñ desitara
Alternative	INFORMAL		tazunetari	tazunenakattari
	FORMAL		tazunemasitari	tazunemaseñ desitari

INFORMAL AFFIRMATIVE INDICATIVE

Passive	tazunerareru	*Honorific*	I	otazune ni naru
			II	otazune nasaru
Potential	tazunerareru			
		Humble	I	otazune suru
Causative	tazunesaseru		II	otazune itasu
Causative Pass.	tazunesaserareru			

to help (to do work)   TRANSITIVE

		AFFIRMATIVE	NEGATIVE
Indicative	INFORMAL	tetudau	tetudawanai
	FORMAL	tetudaimasu	tetudaimaseñ
Imperative	INFORMAL I	tetudae	tetudau na
	II	tetudainasai	tetudainasaru na
	III	tetudatte kudasai	tetudawanai de kudasai
	FORMAL	otetudai nasaimase	otetudai nasaimasu na
Presumptive	INFORMAL I	tetudaoo	tetudaumai
	II	tetudau daroo	tetudawanai daroo
	FORMAL I	tetudaimasyoo	tetudaimasumai
	II	tetudau desyoo	tetudawanai desyoo
Provisional	INFORMAL	tetudaeba	tetudawanakereba
	FORMAL	tetudaimaseba	tetudaimaseñ nara
		tetudaimasureba	
Gerund	INFORMAL I	tetudatte	tetudawanai de
	II		tetudawanakute
	FORMAL	tetudaimasite	tetudaimaseñ de
Past Ind.	INFORMAL	tetudatta	tetudawanakatta
	FORMAL	tetudaimasita	tetudaimaseñ desita
Past Presump.	INFORMAL	tetudattaroo	tetudawanakattaroo
		tetudatta daroo	tetudawanakatta daroo
	FORMAL	tetudaimasitaroo	tetudaimaseñ desitaroo
		tetudatta desyoo	tetudawanakatta desyoo
Conditional	INFORMAL	tetudattara	tetudawanakattara
	FORMAL	tetudaimasitara	tetudaimaseñ desitara
Alternative	INFORMAL	tetudattari	tetudawanakattari
	FORMAL	tetudaimasitari	tetudaimaseñ desitari

INFORMAL AFFIRMATIVE INDICATIVE

Passive	tetudawareru	*Honorific*	I	otetudai ni naru
			II	otetudai nasaru
Potential	tetudaeru			
		Humble	I	otetudai suru
Causative	tetudawaseru		II	otetudai itasu
Causative Pass.	tetudawaserareru			

		AFFIRMATIVE	NEGATIVE
Indicative	INFORMAL	tigau	tigawanai
	FORMAL	tigaimasu	tigaimaseñ
Imperative	INFORMAL I		
	II		
	III		
	FORMAL		
Presumptive	INFORMAL I	tigaoo	tigaumai
	II	tigau daroo	tigawanai daroo
	FORMAL I	tigaimasyoo	tigaimasumai
	II	tigau desyoo	tigawanai desyoo
Provisional	INFORMAL	tigaeba	tigawanakereba
	FORMAL	tigaimaseba	tigaimaseñ nara
		tigaimasureba	
Gerund	INFORMAL I	tigatte	tigawanai de
	II		tigawanakute
	FORMAL	tigaimasite	tigaimaseñ de
Past Ind.	INFORMAL	tigatta	tigawanakatta
	FORMAL	tigaimasita	tigaimaseñ desita
Past Presump.	INFORMAL	tigattaroo	tigawanakattaroo
		tigatta daroo	tigawanakatta daroo
	FORMAL	tigaimasitaroo	tigaimaseñ desitaroo
		tigatta desyoo	tigawanakatta desyoo
Conditional	INFORMAL	tigattara	tigawanakattara
	FORMAL	tigaimasitara	tigaimaseñ desitara
Alternative	INFORMAL	tigattari	tigawanakattari
	FORMAL	tigaimasitari	tigaimaseñ desitari

INFORMAL AFFIRMATIVE INDICATIVE

Passive		*Honorific*	I
			II
Potential	tigaeru		
		Humble	I
Causative	tigawaseru		II
Causative Pass.	tigawaserareru		

		AFFIRMATIVE	NEGATIVE
Indicative	INFORMAL	tobu	tobanai
	FORMAL	tobimasu	tobimaseñ
Imperative	INFORMAL I	tobe	tobu na
	II	tobinasai	tobinasaru na
	III	toñde kudasai	tobanai de kudasai
	FORMAL	otobi nasaimase	otobi nasaimasu na
Presumptive	INFORMAL I	toboo	tobumai
	II	tobu daroo	tobanai daroo
	FORMAL I	tobimasyoo	tobimasumai
	II	tobu desyoo	tobanai desyoo
Provisional	INFORMAL	tobeba	tobanakereba
	FORMAL	tobimaseba	tobimaseñ nara
		tobimasureba	
Gerund	INFORMAL I	toñde	tobanai de
	II		tobanakute
	FORMAL	tobimasite	tobimaseñ de
Past Ind.	INFORMAL	toñda	tobanakatta
	FORMAL	tobimasita	tobimaseñ desita
Past Presump.	INFORMAL	toñdaroo	tobanakattaroo
		toñda daroo	tobanakatta daroo
	FORMAL	tobimasitaroo	tobimaseñ desitaroo
		toñda desyoo	tobanakatta desyoo
Conditional	INFORMAL	toñdara	tobanakattara
	FORMAL	tobimasitara	tobimaseñ desitara
Alternative	INFORMAL	toñdari	tobanakattari
	FORMAL	tobimasitari	tobimaseñ desitari

INFORMAL AFFIRMATIVE INDICATIVE

Passive	tobareru	*Honorific*	I	otobi ni naru
			II	otobi nasaru
Potential	toberu			
		Humble	I	
Causative	tobaseru		II	
Causative Pass.	tobaserareru			

TRANSITIVE   *to deliver*

			AFFIRMATIVE	NEGATIVE
Indicative	**INFORMAL**		todokeru	todokenai
	FORMAL		todokemasu	todokemaseñ
Imperative	**INFORMAL**	I	todokero	todokeru na
		II	todokenasai	todokenasaru na
		III	todokete kudasai	todokenai de kudasai
	FORMAL		otodoke nasaimase	otodoke nasaimasu na
Presumptive	**INFORMAL**	I	todokeyoo	todokemai
		II	todokeru daroo	todokenai daroo
	FORMAL	I	todokemasyoo	todokemasumai
		II	todokeru desyoo	todokenai desyoo
Provisional	**INFORMAL**		todokereba	todokenakereba
	FORMAL		todokemaseba	todokemaseñ nara
			todokemasureba	
Gerund	**INFORMAL**	I	todokete	todokenai de
		II		todokenakute
	FORMAL		todokemasite	todokemaseñ de
Past Ind.	**INFORMAL**		todoketa	todokenakatta
	FORMAL		todokemasita	todokemaseñ desita
Past Presump.	**INFORMAL**		todoketaroo	todokenakattaroo
			todoketa daroo	todokenakatta daroo
	FORMAL		todokemasitaroo	todokemaseñ desitaroo
			todoketa desyoo	todokenakatta desyoo
Conditional	**INFORMAL**		todoketara	todokenakattara
	FORMAL		todokemasitara	todokemaseñ desitara
Alternative	**INFORMAL**		todoketari	todokenakattari
	FORMAL		todokemasitari	todokemaseñ desitari

INFORMAL AFFIRMATIVE INDICATIVE

Passive	todokerareru	*Honorific*	I	otodoke ni naru
			II	otodoke nasaru
Potential	todokerareru			
		Humble	I	otodoke suru
Causative	todokesaseru		II	otodoke itasu
Causative Pass.	todokesaserareru			

			AFFIRMATIVE	NEGATIVE
Indicative	INFORMAL		todoku	todokanai
	FORMAL		todokimasu	todokimaseñ
Imperative	INFORMAL I		todoke	todoku na
		II	todokinasai	todokinasaru na
		III	todoite kudasai	todokanai de kudasai
	FORMAL		otodoki nasaimase	otodoki nasaimasu na
Presumptive	INFORMAL I		todokoo	todokumai
		II	todoku daroo	todokanai daroo
	FORMAL	I	todokimasyoo	todokimasumai
		II	todoku desyoo	todokanai desyoo
Provisional	INFORMAL		todokeba	todokanakereba
	FORMAL		todokimaseba	todokimaseñ nara
			todokimasureba	
Gerund	INFORMAL I		todoite	todokanai de
		II		todokanakute
	FORMAL		todokimasite	todokimaseñ de
Past Ind.	INFORMAL		todoita	todokanakatta
	FORMAL		todokimasita	todokimaseñ desita
Past Presump.	INFORMAL		todoitaroo	todokanakattaroo
			todoita daroo	todokanakatta daroo
	FORMAL		todokimasitaroo	todokimaseñ desitaroo
			todoita desyoo	todokanakatta desyoo
Conditional	INFORMAL		todoitara	todokanakattara
	FORMAL		todokimasitara	todokimaseñ desitara
Alternative	INFORMAL		todoitari	todokanakattari
	FORMAL		todokimasitari	todokimaseñ desitari

INFORMAL AFFIRMATIVE INDICATIVE

Passive		*Honorific*	I
			II
Potential	todokeru		
		Humble	I
Causative	todokaseru		II
Causative Pass.	todokaserareru		

262

		AFFIRMATIVE	NEGATIVE
Indicative	INFORMAL	tokeru	tokenai
	FORMAL	tokemasu	tokemaseñ
Imperative	INFORMAL I	tokero	tokeru na
	II		
	III		
	FORMAL		
Presumptive	INFORMAL I	tokeyoo	tokemai
	II	tokeru daroo	tokenai daroo
	FORMAL I	tokemasyoo	tokemasumai
	II	tokeru desyoo	tokenai desyoo
Provisional	INFORMAL	tokereba	tokenakereba
	FORMAL	tokemaseba	tokemaseñ nara
		tokemasureba	
Gerund	INFORMAL I	tokete	tokenai de
	II		tokenakute
	FORMAL	tokemasite	tokemaseñ de
Past Ind.	INFORMAL	toketa	tokenakatta
	FORMAL	tokemasita	tokemaseñ desita
Past Presump.	INFORMAL	toketaroo	tokenakattaroo
		toketa daroo	tokenakatta daroo
	FORMAL	tokemasitaroo	tokemaseñ desitaroo
		toketa desyoo	tokenakatta desyoo
Conditional	INFORMAL	toketara	tokenakattara
	FORMAL	tokemasitara	tokemaseñ desitara
Alternative	INFORMAL	toketari	tokenakattari
	FORMAL	tokemasitari	tokemaseñ desitari

INFORMAL AFFIRMATIVE INDICATIVE

Passive		*Honorific*	I
			II
Potential			
		Humble	I
Causative			II

Causative Pass.

to come to a stop, to stay overnight

			AFFIRMATIVE	NEGATIVE
Indicative	INFORMAL		tomaru	tomaranai
	FORMAL		tomarimasu	tomarimaseñ
Imperative	INFORMAL	I	tomare	tomaru na
		II	tomarinasai	tomarinasaru na
		III	tomatte kudasai	tomaranai de kudasai
	FORMAL		otomari nasaimase	otomari nasaimasu na
Presumptive	INFORMAL	I	tomaroo	tomarumai
		II	tomaru daroo	tomaranai daroo
	FORMAL	I	tomarimasyoo	tomarimasumai
		II	tomaru desyoo	tomaranai desyoo
Provisional	INFORMAL		tomareba	tomaranakereba
	FORMAL		tomarimaseba	tomarimaseñ nara
			tomarimasureba	
Gerund	INFORMAL	I	tomatte	tomaranai de
		II		tomaranakute
	FORMAL		tomarimasite	tomarimaseñ de
Past Ind.	INFORMAL		tomatta	tomaranakatta
	FORMAL		tomarimasita	tomarimaseñ desita
Past Presump.	INFORMAL		tomattaroo	tomaranakattaroo
			tomatta daroo	tomaranakatta daroo
	FORMAL		tomarimasitaroo	tomarimaseñ desitaroo
			tomatta desyoo	tomaranakatta desyoo
Conditional	INFORMAL		tomattara	tomaranakattara
	FORMAL		tomarimasitara	tomarimaseñ desitara
Alternative	INFORMAL		tomattari	tomaranakattari
	FORMAL		tomarimasitari	tomarimaseñ desitari

INFORMAL AFFIRMATIVE INDICATIVE

Passive	tomarareru	*Honorific* I	otomari ni naru
		II	otomari nasaru
Potential	tomareru		
		Humble I	otomari suru
Causative	tomaraseru	II	otomari itasu
Causative Pass.	tomaraserareru		

		AFFIRMATIVE	NEGATIVE
Indicative	INFORMAL	tomeru	tomenai
	FORMAL	tomemasu	tomemaseñ
Imperative	INFORMAL I	tomero	tomeru na
	II	tomenasai	tomenasaru na
	III	tomete kudasai	tomenai de kudasai
	FORMAL	otome nasaimase	otome nasaimasu na
Presumptive	INFORMAL I	tomeyoo	tomemai
	II	tomeru daroo	tomenai daroo
	FORMAL I	tomemasyoo	tomemasumai
	II	tomeru desyoo	tomenai desyoo
Provisional	INFORMAL	tomereba	tomenakereba
	FORMAL	tomemaseba	tomemaseñ nara
		tomemasureba	
Gerund	INFORMAL I	tomete	tomenai de
	II		tomenakute
	FORMAL	tomemasite	tomemaseñ de
Past Ind.	INFORMAL	tometa	tomenakatta
	FORMAL	tomemasita	tomemaseñ desita
st Presump.	INFORMAL	tometaroo	tomenakattaroo
		tometa daroo	tomenakatta daroo
	FORMAL	tomemasitaroo	tomemaseñ desitaroo
		tometa desyoo	tomenakatta desyoo
Conditional	INFORMAL	tometara	tomenakattara
	FORMAL	tomemasitara	tomemaseñ desitara
Alternative	INFORMAL	tometari	tomenakattari
	FORMAL	tomemasitari	tomemaseñ desitari

INFORMAL AFFIRMATIVE INDICATIVE

Passive	tomerareru	*Honorific*	I	otome ni naru
			II	otome nasaru
Potential	tomerareru			
		Humble	I	otome suru
Causative	tomesaseru		II	otome itasu
usative Pass.	tomesaserareru			

		AFFIRMATIVE	NEGATIVE
Indicative	INFORMAL	tooru	tooranai
	FORMAL	toorimasu	toorimaseñ
Imperative	INFORMAL I	toore	tooru na
	II	toorinasai	toorinasaru na
	III	tootte kudasai	tooranai de kudasai
	FORMAL	otoori nasaimase	otoori nasaimasu na
Presumptive	INFORMAL I	tooroo	toorumai
	II	tooru daroo	tooranai daroo
	FORMAL I	toorimasyoo	toorimasumai
	II	tooru desyoo	tooranai desyoo
Provisional	INFORMAL	tooreba	tooranakereba
	FORMAL	toorimaseba	toorimaseñ nara
		toorimasureba	
Gerund	INFORMAL I	tootte	tooranai de
	II		tooranakute
	FORMAL	toorimasite	toorimaseñ de
Past Ind.	INFORMAL	tootta	tooranakatta
	FORMAL	toorimasita	toorimaseñ desita
Past Presump.	INFORMAL	toottaroo	tooranakattaroo
		tootta daroo	tooranakatta daroo
	FORMAL	toorimasitaroo	toorimaseñ desitaroo
		tootta desyoo	tooranakatta desyoo
Conditional	INFORMAL	toottara	tooranakattara
	FORMAL	toorimasitara	toorimaseñ desitara
Alternative	INFORMAL	toottari	tooranakattari
	FORMAL	toorimasitari	toorimaseñ desitari

INFORMAL AFFIRMATIVE INDICATIVE

Passive	toorareru	*Honorific*	I	otoori ni n
Potential	tooreru		II	otoori nas
Causative	tooraseru	*Humble*	I	
			II	
Causative Pass.	tooraserareru			

		AFFIRMATIVE	NEGATIVE
Indicative	INFORMAL	toru	toranai
	FORMAL	torimasu	torimaseñ
Imperative	INFORMAL I	tore	toru na
	II	torinasai	torinasaru na
	III	totte kudasai	toranai de kudasai
	FORMAL	otori nasaimase	otori nasaimasu na
Presumptive	INFORMAL I	toroo	torumai
	II	toru daroo	toranai daroo
	FORMAL I	torimasyoo	torimasumai
	II	toru desyoo	toranai desyoo
Provisional	INFORMAL	toreba	toranakereba
	FORMAL	torimaseba	torimaseñ nara
		torimasureba	
Gerund	INFORMAL I	totte	toranai de
	II		toranakute
	FORMAL	torimasite	torimaseñ de
Past Ind.	INFORMAL	totta	toranakatta
	FORMAL	torimasita	torimaseñ desita
Past Presump.	INFORMAL	tottaroo	toranakattaroo
		totta daroo	toranakatta daroo
	FORMAL	torimasitaroo	torimaseñ desitaroo
		totta desyoo	toranakatta desyoo
Conditional	INFORMAL	tottara	toranakattara
	FORMAL	torimasitara	torimaseñ desitara
Alternative	INFORMAL	tottari	toranakattari
	FORMAL	torimasitari	torimaseñ desitari

INFORMAL AFFIRMATIVE INDICATIVE

Passive	torareru	*Honorific*	I	otori ni naru
			II	otori nasaru
Potential	toreru			
		Humble	I	otori suru
Causative	toraseru		II	otori itasu
Causative Pass.	toraserareru			

		AFFIRMATIVE	NEGATIVE
Indicative	**INFORMAL**	tukamaeru	tukamaenai
	FORMAL	tukamaemasu	tukamaemaseñ
Imperative	**INFORMAL I**	tukamaero	tukamaeru na
	II	tukamaenasai	tukamaenasaru na
	III	tukamaete kudasai	tukamaenai de kudasai
	FORMAL	otukamae nasaimase	otukamae nasaimasu na
Presumptive	**INFORMAL I**	tukamaeyoo	tukamaemai
	II	tukamaeru daroo	tukamaenai daroo
	FORMAL I	tukamaemasyoo	tukamaemasumai
	II	tukamaeru desyoo	tukamaenai desyoo
Provisional	**INFORMAL**	tukamaereba	tukamaenakereba
	FORMAL	tukamaemaseba	tukamaemaseñ nara
		tukamaemasureba	
Gerund	**INFORMAL I**	tukamaete	tukamaenai de
	II		tukamaenakute
	FORMAL	tukamaemasite	tukamaemaseñ de
Past Ind.	**INFORMAL**	tukamaeta	tukamaenakatta
	FORMAL	tukamaemasita	tukamaemaseñ desita
Past Presump.	**INFORMAL**	tukamaetaroo	tukamaenakattaroo
		tukamaeta daroo	tukamaenakatta daroo
	FORMAL	tukamaemasitaroo	tukamaemaseñ desitaroo
		tukamaeta desyoo	tukamaenakatta desyoo
Conditional	**INFORMAL**	tukamaetara	tukamaenakattara
	FORMAL	tukamaemasitara	tukamaemaseñ desitara
Alternative	**INFORMAL**	tukamaetari	tukamaenakattari
	FORMAL	tukamaemasitari	tukamaemaseñ desitari

INFORMAL AFFIRMATIVE INDICATIVE

Passive	tukamaerareru	*Honorific* **I**	otukamae ni naru
		II	otukamae nasaru
Potential	tukamaerareru		
		Humble **I**	
Causative	tukamaesaseru	**II**	
Causative Pass.	tukamaesaserareru		

		AFFIRMATIVE	NEGATIVE
Indicative	INFORMAL	tukareru	tukarenai
	FORMAL	tukaremasu	tukaremaseñ
Imperative	INFORMAL I		
	II		
	III		
	FORMAL		
Presumptive	INFORMAL I	tukareyoo	tukaremai
	II	tukareru daroo	tukarenai daroo
	FORMAL I	tukaremasyoo	tukaremasumai
	II	tukareru desyoo	tukarenai desyoo
Provisional	INFORMAL	tukarereba	tukarenakereba
	FORMAL	tukaremaseba	tukaremaseñ nara
		tukaremasureba	
Gerund	INFORMAL I	tukarete	tukarenai de
	II		tukarenakute
	FORMAL	tukaremasite	tukaremaseñ de
Past Ind.	INFORMAL	tukareta	tukarenakatta
	FORMAL	tukaremasita	tukaremaseñ desita
Past Presump.	INFORMAL	tukaretaroo	tukarenakattaroo
		tukareta daroo	tukarenakatta daroo
	FORMAL	tukaremasitaroo	tukaremaseñ desitaroo
		tukareta desyoo	tukarenakatta desyoo
Conditional	INFORMAL	tukaretara	tukarenakattara
	FORMAL	tukaremasitara	tukaremaseñ desitara
Alternative	INFORMAL	tukaretari	tukarenakattari
	FORMAL	tukaremasitari	tukaremaseñ desitari

INFORMAL AFFIRMATIVE INDICATIVE

Passive		*Honorific*	I	otukare ni naru
			II	otukare nasaru
Potential				
		Humble	I	otukare suru
Causative	tukaresaseru		II	otukare itasu
Causative Pass.	tukaresaserareru			

		AFFIRMATIVE	NEGATIVE
Indicative	**INFORMAL**	tukau	tukawanai
	FORMAL	tukaimasu	tukaimaseñ
Imperative	**INFORMAL I**	tukae	tukau na
	II	tukainasai	tukainasaru na
	III	tukatte kudasai	tukawanai de kudasai
	FORMAL	otukai nasaimase	otukai nasaimasu na
Presumptive	**INFORMAL I**	tukaoo	tukaumai
	II	tukau daroo	tukawanai daroo
	FORMAL I	tukaimasyoo	tukaimasumai
	II	tukau desyoo	tukawanai desyoo
Provisional	**INFORMAL**	tukaeba	tukawanakereba
	FORMAL	tukaimaseba	tukaimaseñ nara
		tukaimasureba	
Gerund	**INFORMAL I**	tukatte	tukawanai de
	II		tukawanakute
	FORMAL	tukaimasite	tukaimaseñ de
Past Ind.	**INFORMAL**	tukatta	tukawanakatta
	FORMAL	tukaimasita	tukaimaseñ desita
Past Presump.	**INFORMAL**	tukattaroo	tukawanakattaroo
		tukatta daroo	tukawanakatta daroo
	FORMAL	tukaimasitaroo	tukaimaseñ desitaroo
		tukatta desyoo	tukawanakatta desyoo
Conditional	**INFORMAL**	tukattara	tukawanakattara
	FORMAL	tukaimasitara	tukaimaseñ desitara
Alternative	**INFORMAL**	tukattari	tukawanakattari
	FORMAL	tukaimasitari	tukaimaseñ desitari

INFORMAL AFFIRMATIVE INDICATIVE

Passive	tukawareru	*Honorific*	I	otukai ni nar
			II	otukai nasaru
Potential	tukaeru			
		Humble	I	otukai suru
Causative	tukawaseru		II	otukai itasu
Causative Pass.	tukawaserareru			

| | | TRANSITIVE | *to attach, to add to, to stick on* |
| | | | |

		AFFIRMATIVE	NEGATIVE
Indicative	INFORMAL	tukeru	tukenai
	FORMAL	tukemasu	tukemaseñ
Imperative	INFORMAL I	tukero	tukeru na
	II	tukenasai	tukenasaru na
	III	tukete kudasai	tukenai de kudasai
	FORMAL	otuke nasaimase	otuke nasaimasu na
Presumptive	INFORMAL I	tukeyoo	tukemai
	II	tukeru daroo	tukenai daroo
	FORMAL I	tukemasyoo	tukemasumai
	II	tukeru desyoo	tukenai desyoo
Provisional	INFORMAL	tukereba	tukenakereba
	FORMAL	tukemaseba	tukemaseñ nara
		tukemasureba	
Gerund	INFORMAL I	tukete	tukenai de
	II		tukenakute
	FORMAL	tukemasite	tukemaseñ de
Past Ind.	INFORMAL	tuketa	tukenakatta
	FORMAL	tukemasita	tukemaseñ desita
Past Presump.	INFORMAL	tuketaroo	tukenakattaroo
		tuketa daroo	tukenakatta daroo
	FORMAL	tukemasitaroo	tukemaseñ desitaroo
		tuketa desyoo	tukenakatta desyoo
Conditional	INFORMAL	tuketara	tukenakattara
	FORMAL	tukemasitara	tukemaseñ desitara
Alternative	INFORMAL	tuketari	tukenakattari
	FORMAL	tukemasitari	tukemaseñ desitari

INFORMAL AFFIRMATIVE INDICATIVE

Passive	tukerareru	*Honorific*	I	otuke ni naru
			II	otuke nasaru
Potential	tukerareru			
		Humble	I	otuke suru
Causative	tukesaseru		II	otuke itasu
Causative Pass.	tukesaserareru			

		AFFIRMATIVE	NEGATIVE
Indicative	INFORMAL	tukiau	tukiawanai
	FORMAL	tukiaimasu	tukiaimaseñ
Imperative	INFORMAL I	tukiae	tukiau na
	II	tukiainasai	tukiainasaru na
	III	tukiatte kudasai	tukiawanai de kudasai
	FORMAL	otukiai nasaimase	otukiai nasaimasu na
Presumptive	INFORMAL I	tukiaoo	tukiaumai
	II	tukiau daroo	tukiawanai daroo
	FORMAL I	tukiaimasyoo	tukiaimasumai
	II	tukiau desyoo	tukiawanai desyoo
Provisional	INFORMAL	tukiaeba	tukiawanakereba
	FORMAL	tukiaimaseba	tukiaimaseñ nara
		tukiaimasureba	
Gerund	INFORMAL I	tukiatte	tukiawanai de
	II		tukiawanakute
	FORMAL	tukiaimasite	tukiaimaseñ de
Past Ind.	INFORMAL	tukiatta	tukiawanakatta
	FORMAL	tukiaimasita	tukiaimaseñ desita
Past Presump.	INFORMAL	tukiattaroo	tukiawanakattaroo
		tukiatta daroo	tukiawanakatta daroo
	FORMAL	tukiaimasitaroo	tukiaimaseñ desitaroo
		tukiatta desyoo	tukiawanakatta desyoo
Conditional	INFORMAL	tukiattara	tukiawanakattara
	FORMAL	tukiaimasitara	tukiaimaseñ desitara
Alternative	INFORMAL	tukiattari	tukiawanakattari
	FORMAL	tukiaimasitari	tukiaimaseñ desitari

INFORMAL AFFIRMATIVE INDICATIVE

Passive		*Honorific*	I	otukiai ni naru
			II	otukiai nasaru
Potential	tukiaeru			
		Humble	I	otukiai suru
Causative	tukiawaseru		II	otukiai itasu
Causative Pass.	tukiawaserareru			

		AFFIRMATIVE	NEGATIVE
Indicative	INFORMAL	tuku	tukanai
	FORMAL	tukimasu	tukimaseñ
Imperative	INFORMAL I	tuke	tuku na
	II		
	III		
	FORMAL		
Presumptive	INFORMAL I	tukoo	tukumai
	II	tuku daroo	tukanai daroo
	FORMAL I	tukimasyoo	tukimasumai
	II	tuku desyoo	tukanai desyoo
Provisional	INFORMAL	tukeba	tukanakereba
	FORMAL	tukimaseba	tukimaseñ nara
		tukimasureba	
Gerund	INFORMAL I	tuite	tukanai de
	II		tukanakute
	FORMAL	tukimasite	tukimaseñ de
Past Ind.	INFORMAL	tuita	tukanakatta
	FORMAL	tukimasita	tukimaseñ desita
Past Presump.	INFORMAL	tuitaroo	tukanakattaroo
		tuita daroo	tukanakatta daroo
	FORMAL	tukimasitaroo	tukimaseñ desitaroo
		tuita desyoo	tukanakatta desyoo
Conditional	INFORMAL	tuitara	tukanakattara
	FORMAL	tukimasitara	tukimaseñ desitara
Alternative	INFORMAL	tuitari	tukanakattari
	FORMAL	tukimasitari	tukimaseñ desitari

INFORMAL AFFIRMATIVE INDICATIVE

Passive		*Honorific*	I	otuki ni naru
			II	otuki nasaru
Potential	tukeru			
		Humble	I	
Causative	tsukaseru		II	
Causative Pass.	tsukaserareru			

		AFFIRMATIVE	NEGATIVE
Indicative	INFORMAL	tukuru	tukuranai
	FORMAL	tukurimasu	tukurimaseñ
Imperative	INFORMAL I	tukure	tukuru na
	II	tukurinasai	tukurinasaru na
	III	tukutte kudasai	tukuranai de kudasai
	FORMAL	otukuri nasaimase	otukuri nasaimasu na
Presumptive	INFORMAL I	tukuroo	tukurumai
	II	tukuru daroo	tukuranai daroo
	FORMAL I	tukurimasyoo	tukurimasumai
	II	tukuru desyoo	tukuranai desyoo
Provisional	INFORMAL	tukureba	tukuranakereba
	FORMAL	tukurimaseba	tukurimaseñ nara
		tukurimasureba	
Gerund	INFORMAL I	tukutte	tukuranai de
	II		tukuranakute
	FORMAL	tukurimasite	tukurimaseñ de
Past Ind.	INFORMAL	tukutta	tukuranakatta
	FORMAL	tukurimasita	tukurimaseñ desita
Past Presump.	INFORMAL	tukuttaroo	tukuranakattaroo
		tukutta daroo	tukuranakatta daroo
	FORMAL	tukurimasitaroo	tukurimaseñ desitaroo
		tukutta desyoo	tukuranakatta desyoo
Conditional	INFORMAL	tukuttara	tukuranakattara
	FORMAL	tukurimasitara	tukurimaseñ desitara
Alternative	INFORMAL	tukuttari	tukuranakattari
	FORMAL	tukurimasitari	tukurimaseñ desitari

INFORMAL AFFIRMATIVE INDICATIVE

Passive	tukurareru	*Honorific*	I	otukuri ni naru
			II	otukuri nasaru
Potential	tukureru			
		Humble	I	otukuri suru
Causative	tukuraseru		II	otukuri itasu
Causative Pass.	tukuraserareru			

		AFFIRMATIVE	NEGATIVE
Indicative	INFORMAL	tumoru	tumoranai
	FORMAL	tumorimasu	tumorimaseñ
Imperative	INFORMAL I	tumore	tumoru na
	II		
	III		
	FORMAL		
Presumptive	INFORMAL I	tumoroo	tumorumai
	II	tumoru daroo	tumoranai daroo
	FORMAL I	tumorimasyoo	tumorimasumai
	II	tumoru desyoo	tumoranai desyoo
Provisional	INFORMAL	tumoreba	tumoranakereba
	FORMAL	tumorimaseba	tumorimaseñ nara
		tumorimasureba	
Gerund	INFORMAL I	tumotte	tumoranai de
	II		tumoranakute
	FORMAL	tumorimasite	tumorimaseñ de
Past Ind.	INFORMAL	tumotta	tumoranakatta
	FORMAL	tumorimasita	tumorimaseñ desita
Past Presump.	INFORMAL	tumottaroo	tumoranakattaroo
		tumotta daroo	tumoranakatta daroo
	FORMAL	tumorimasitaroo	tumorimaseñ desitaroo
		tumotta desyoo	tumoranakatta desyoo
Conditional	INFORMAL	tumottara	tumoranakattara
	FORMAL	tumorimasitara	tumorimaseñ desitara
Alternative	INFORMAL	tumottari	tumoranakattari
	FORMAL	tumorimasitari	tumorimaseñ desitari

INFORMAL AFFIRMATIVE INDICATIVE

Passive		*Honorific*	I
			II
Potential			
		Humble	I
Causative			II

Causative Pass.

		AFFIRMATIVE	NEGATIVE
Indicative	INFORMAL	tutaeru	tutaenai
	FORMAL	tutaemasu	tutaemaseñ
Imperative	INFORMAL I	tutaero	tutaeru na
	II	tutaenasai	tutaenasaru na
	III	tutaete kudasai	tutaenai de kudasai
	FORMAL	otutae nasaimase	otutae nasaimasu na
Presumptive	INFORMAL I	tutaeyoo	tutaemai
	II	tutaeru daroo	tutaenai daroo
	FORMAL I	tutaemasyoo	tutaemasumai
	II	tutaeru desyoo	tutaenai desyoo
Provisional	INFORMAL	tutaereba	tutaenakereba
	FORMAL	tutaemaseba	tutaemaseñ nara
		tutaemasureba	
Gerund	INFORMAL I	tutaete	tutaenai de
	II		tutaenakute
	FORMAL	tutaemasite	tutaemaseñ de
Past Ind.	INFORMAL	tutaeta	tutaenakatta
	FORMAL	tutaemasita	tutaemaseñ desita
Past Presump.	INFORMAL	tutaetaroo	tutaenakattaroo
		tutaeta daroo	tutaenakatta daroo
	FORMAL	tutaemasitaroo	tutaemaseñ desitaroo
		tutaeta desyoo	tutaenakatta desyoo
Conditional	INFORMAL	tutaetara	tutaenakattara
	FORMAL	tutaemasitara	tutaemaseñ desitara
Alternative	INFORMAL	tutaetari	tutaenakattari
	FORMAL	tutaemasitari	tutaemaseñ desitari

INFORMAL AFFIRMATIVE INDICATIVE

Passive	tutaerareru	*Honorific*	I	otutae ni naru
			II	otutae nasaru
Potential	tutaerareru			
		Humble	I	otutae suru
Causative	tutaesaseru		II	otutae itasu
Causative Pass.	tutaesaserareru			

		AFFIRMATIVE	NEGATIVE
Indicative	INFORMAL	tutomeru	tutomenai
	FORMAL	tutomemasu	tutomemaseñ
Imperative	INFORMAL I	tutomero	tutomeru na
	II	tutomenasai	tutomenasaru na
	III	tutomete kudasai	tutomenai de kudasai
	FORMAL	otutome nasaimase	otutome nasaimasu na
Presumptive	INFORMAL I	tutomeyoo	tutomemai
	II	tutomeru daroo	tutomenai daroo
	FORMAL I	tutomemasyoo	tutomemasumai
	II	tutomeru desyoo	tutomenai desyoo
Provisional	INFORMAL	tutomereba	tutomenakereba
	FORMAL	tutomemaseba	tutomemaseñ nara
		tutomemasureba	
Gerund	INFORMAL I	tutomete	tutomenai de
	II		tutomenakute
	FORMAL	tutomemasite	tutomemaseñ de
Past Ind.	INFORMAL	tutometa	tutomenakatta
	FORMAL	tutomemasita	tutomemaseñ desita
Past Presump.	INFORMAL	tutometaroo	tutomenakattaroo
		tutometa daroo	tutomenakatta daroo
	FORMAL	tutomemasitaroo	tutomemaseñ desitaroo
		tutometa desyoo	tutomenakatta desyoo
Conditional	INFORMAL	tutometara	tutomenakattara
	FORMAL	tutomemasitara	tutomemaseñ desitara
Alternative	INFORMAL	tutometari	tutomenakattari
	FORMAL	tutomemasitari	tutomemaseñ desitari

INFORMAL AFFIRMATIVE INDICATIVE

Passive	tutomerareru	*Honorific*	I	otutome ni naru
			II	otutome nasaru
Potential	tutomerareru			
		Humble	I	otutome suru
Causative	tutomesaseru		II	otutome itasu
Causative Pass.	tutomesaserareru			

		AFFIRMATIVE	NEGATIVE
Indicative	INFORMAL	tutumu	tutumanai
	FORMAL	tutumimasu	tutumimaseñ
Imperative	INFORMAL I	tutume	tutumu na
	II	tutuminasai	tutuminasaru na
	III	tutuñde kudasai	tutumanai de kudasai
	FORMAL	otutumi nasaimase	otutumi nasaimasu na
Presumptive	INFORMAL I	tutumɔo	tutumumai
	II	tutumu daroo	tutumanai daroo
	FORMAL I	tutumimasyoo	tutumimasumai
	II	tutumu desyoo	tutumanai desyoo
Provisional	INFORMAL	tutumeba	tutumanakereba
	FORMAL	tutumimaseba	tutumimaseñ nara
		tutumimasureba	
Gerund	INFORMAL I	tutuñde	tutumanai de
	II		tutumanakute
	FORMAL	tutumimasite	tutumimaseñ de
Past Ind.	INFORMAL	tutuñda	tutumanakatta
	FORMAL	tutumimasita	tutumimaseñ desita
Past Presump.	INFORMAL	tutuñdaroo	tutumanakattaroo
		tutuñda daroo	tutumanakatta daroo
	FORMAL	tutumimasitaroo	tutumimaseñ desitaroo
		tutuñda desyoo	tutumanakatta desyoo
Conditional	INFORMAL	tutuñdara	tutumanakattara
	FORMAL	tutumimasitara	tutumimaseñ desitara
Alternative	INFORMAL	tutuñdari	tutumanakattari
	FORMAL	tutumimasitari	tutumimaseñ desitari

INFORMAL AFFIRMATIVE INDICATIVE

Passive	tutumareru	*Honorific*	I	otutumi ni naru
Potential	tutumeru		II	otutumi nasaru
Causative	tutumaseru	*Humble*	I	otutumi suru
			II	otutumi itasu
Causative Pass.	tutumaserareru			

tuzuke

TRANSITIVE   *to continue*

		AFFIRMATIVE	NEGATIVE
Indicative	INFORMAL	tuzukeru	tuzukenai
	FORMAL	tuzukemasu	tuzukemaseñ
Imperative	INFORMAL I	tuzukero	tuzukeru na
	II	tuzukenasai	tuzukenasaru na
	III	tuzukete kudasai	tuzukenai de kudasai
	FORMAL	otuzuke nasaimase	otuzuke nasaimasu na
Presumptive	INFORMAL I	tuzukeyoo	tuzukemai
	II	tuzukeru daroo	tuzukenai daroo
	FORMAL I	tuzukemasyoo	tuzukemasumai
	II	tuzukeru desyoo	tuzukenai desyoo
Provisional	INFORMAL	tuzukereba	tuzukenakereba
	FORMAL	tuzukemaseba	tuzukemaseñ nara
		tuzukemasureba	
Gerund	INFORMAL I	tuzukete	tuzukenai de
	II		tuzukenakute
	FORMAL	tuzukemasite	tuzukemaseñ de
Past Ind.	INFORMAL	tuzuketa	tuzukenakatta
	FORMAL	tuzukemasita	tuzukemaseñ desita
Past Presump.	INFORMAL	tuzuketaroo	tuzukenakattaroo
		tuzuketa daroo	tuzukenakatta daroo
	FORMAL	tuzukemasitaroo	tuzukemaseñ desitaroo
		tuzuketa desyoo	tuzukenakatta desyoo
Conditional	INFORMAL	tuzuketara	tuzukenakattara
	FORMAL	tuzukemasitara	tuzukemasen desitara
Alternative	INFORMAL	tuzuketari	tuzukenakattari
	FORMAL	tuzukemasitari	tuzukemaseñ desitari

INFORMAL AFFIRMATIVE INDICATIVE

Passive	tuzukerareru	*Honorific*	I	otuzuke ni naru
			II	otuzuke nasaru
Potential	tuzukerareru			
		Humble	I	otuzuke suru
Causative	tuzukesaseru		II	otuzuke itasu
Causative Pass.	tuzukesaserareru			

		AFFIRMATIVE	NEGATIVE
Indicative	INFORMAL	tyuui suru	tyuui sinai
	FORMAL	tyuui simasu	tyuui simaseñ
Imperative	INFORMAL I	tyuui siro	tyuui suru na
	II	tyuui sinasai	tyuui sinasaru na
	III	tyuui site kudasai	tyuui sinai de kudasai
	FORMAL	gotyuui nasaimase	gotyuui nasaimasu na
Presumptive	INFORMAL I	tyuui siyoo	tyuui surumai
	II	tyuui suru daroo	tyuui sinai daroo
	FORMAL I	tyuui simasyoo	tyuui simasumai
	II	tyuui suru desyoo	tyuui sinai desyoo
Provisional	INFORMAL	tyuui sureba	tyuui sinakereba
	FORMAL	tyuui simaseba	tyuui simaseñ nara
		tyuui simasureba	
Gerund	INFORMAL I	tyuui site	tyuui sinai de
	II		tyuui sinakute
	FORMAL	tyuui simasite	tyuui simaseñ de
Past Ind.	INFORMAL	tyuui sita	tyuui sinakatta
	FORMAL	tyuui simasita	tyuui simaseñ desita
Past Presump.	INFORMAL	tyuui sitaroo	tyuui sinakattaroo
		tyuui sita daroo	tyuui sinakatta daroo
	FORMAL	tyuui simasitaroo	tyuui simaseñ desitaroo
		tyuui sita desyoo	tyuui sinakatta desyoo
Conditional	INFORMAL	tyuui sitara	tyuui sinakattara
	FORMAL	tyuui simasitara	tyuui simaseñ desitara
Alternative	INFORMAL	tyuui sitari	tyuui sinakattari
	FORMAL	tyuui simasitari	tyuui simaseñ desitari

INFORMAL AFFIRMATIVE INDICATIVE

Passive	tyuui sareru	*Honorific*	I	gotyuui ni naru
Potential	tyuui dekiru		II	gotyuui nasaru
Causative	tyuui saseru	*Humble*	I	gotyuui suru
			II	gotyuui itasu
Causative Pass.	tyuui saserareru			

		AFFIRMATIVE	NEGATIVE
Indicative	INFORMAL	ueru	uenai
	FORMAL	uemasu	uemaseñ
Imperative	INFORMAL I	uero	ueru na
	II	uenasai	uenasaru na
	III	uete kudasai	uenai de kudasai
	FORMAL	oue nasaimase	oue nasaimasu na
Presumptive	INFORMAL I	ueyoo	uemai
	II	ueru daroo	uenai daroo
	FORMAL I	uemasyoo	uemasumai
	II	ueru desyoo	uenai desyoo
Provisional	INFORMAL	uereba	uenakereba
	FORMAL	uemaseba	uemaseñ nara
		uemasureba	
Gerund	INFORMAL I	uete	uenai de
	II		uenakute
	FORMAL	uemasite	uemaseñ de
Past Ind.	INFORMAL	ueta	uenakatta
	FORMAL	uemasita	uemaseñ desita
Past Presump.	INFORMAL	uetaroo	uenakattaroo
		ueta daroo	uenakatta daroo
	FORMAL	uemasitaroo	uemaseñ desitaroo
		ueta desyoo	uenakatta desyoo
Conditional	INFORMAL	uetara	uenakattara
	FORMAL	uemasitara	uemaseñ desitara
Alternative	INFORMAL	uetari	uenakattari
	FORMAL	uemasitari	uemaseñ desitari

INFORMAL AFFIRMATIVE INDICATIVE

Passive	uerareru	*Honorific*	I	oue ni naru
			II	oue nasaru
Potential	uerareru			
		Humble	I	oue suru
Causative	uesaseru		II	oue itasu
Causative Pass.	uesaserareru			

		AFFIRMATIVE	NEGATIVE
Indicative	INFORMAL	ugoku	ugokanai
	FORMAL	ugokimasu	ugokimaseñ
Imperative	INFORMAL I	ugoke	ugoku na
	II	ugokinasai	ugokinasaru na
	III	ugoite kudasai	ugokanai de kudasai
	FORMAL	ougoki nasaimase	ougoki nasaimasu na
Presumptive	INFORMAL I	ugokoo	ugokumai
	II	ugoku daroo	ugokanai daroo
	FORMAL I	ugokimasyoo	ugokimasumai
	II	ugoku desyoo	ugokanai desyoo
Provisional	INFORMAL	ugokeba	ugokanakereba
	FORMAL	ugokimaseba	ugokimaseñ nara
		ugokimasureba	
Gerund	INFORMAL I	ugoite	ugokanai de
	II		ugokanakute
	FORMAL	ugokimasite	ugokimaseñ de
Past Ind.	INFORMAL	ugoita	ugokanakatta
	FORMAL	ugokimasita	ugokimaseñ desita
Past Presump.	INFORMAL	ugoitaroo	ugokanakattaroo
		ugoita daroo	ugokanakatta daroo
	FORMAL	ugokimasitaroo	ugokimaseñ desitaroo
		ugoita desyoo	ugokanakatta desyoo
Conditional	INFORMAL	ugoitara	ugokanakattara
	FORMAL	ugokimasitara	ugokimaseñ desitara
Alternative	INFORMAL	ugoitari	ugokanakattari
	FORMAL	ugokimasitari	ugokimaseñ desitari

INFORMAL AFFIRMATIVE INDICATIVE

Passive	ugokareru	*Honorific*	I	ougoki ni nar
Potential	ugokeru		II	ougoki nasar
Causative	ugokaseru	*Humble*	I	
			II	
Causative Pass.	ugokaserareru			

		AFFIRMATIVE	NEGATIVE
Indicative	INFORMAL	ukabu	ukabanai
	FORMAL	ukabimasu	ukabimaseñ
Imperative	INFORMAL I	ukabe	ukabu na
	II		
	III		
	FORMAL		
Presumptive	INFORMAL I	ukaboo	ukabumai
	II	ukabu daroo	ukabanai daroo
	FORMAL I	ukabimasyoo	ukabimasumai
	II	ukabu desyoo	ukabanai desyoo
Provisional	INFORMAL	ukabeba	ukabanakereba
	FORMAL	ukabimaseba	ukabimaseñ nara
		ukabimasureba	
Gerund	INFORMAL I	ukañde	ukabanai de
	II		ukabanakute
	FORMAL	ukabimasite	ukabimaseñ de
Past Ind.	INFORMAL	ukañda	ukabanakatta
	FORMAL	ukabimasita	ukabimaseñ desita
Past Presump.	INFORMAL	ukañdaroo	ukabanakattaroo
		ukañda daroo	ukabanakatta daroo
	FORMAL	ukabimasitaroo	ukabimaseñ desitaroo
		ukañda desyoo	ukabanakatta desyoo
Conditional	INFORMAL	ukañdara	ukabanakattara
	FORMAL	ukabimasitara	ukabimaseñ desitara
Alternative	INFORMAL	ukañdari	ukabanakattari
	FORMAL	ukabimasitari	ukabimaseñ desitari

INFORMAL AFFIRMATIVE INDICATIVE

Passive	ukabareru	*Honorific*	I	oukabi ni naru
			II	oukabi nasaru
Potential	ukaberu			
		Humble	I	
Causative	ukabaseru		II	
Causative Pass.	ukabaserareru			

		AFFIRMATIVE	NEGATIVE
Indicative	INFORMAL	uketoru	uketoranai
	FORMAL	uketorimasu	uketorimaseñ
Imperative	INFORMAL I	uketore	uketoru na
	II	uketorinasai	uketorinasaru na
	III	uketotte kudasai	uketoranai de kudasai
	FORMAL	ouketori nasaimase	ouketori nasaimasu na
Presumptive	INFORMAL I	uketoroo	uketorumai
	II	uketoru daroo	uketoranai daroo
	FORMAL I	uketorimasyoo	uketorimasumai
	II	uketoru desyoo	uketoranai desyoo
Provisional	INFORMAL	uketoreba	uketoranakereba
	FORMAL	uketorimaseba	uketorimaseñ nara
		uketorimasureba	
Gerund	INFORMAL I	uketotte	uketoranai de
	II		uketoranakute
	FORMAL	uketorimasite	uketorimaseñ de
Past Ind.	INFORMAL	uketotta	uketoranakatta
	FORMAL	uketorimasita	uketorimaseñ desita
Past Presump.	INFORMAL	uketottaroo	uketoranakattaroo
		uketotta daroo	uketoranakatta daroo
	FORMAL	uketorimasitaroo	uketorimaseñ desitaroo
		uketotta desyoo	uketoranakatta desyoo
Conditional	INFORMAL	uketottara	uketoranakattara
	FORMAL	uketorimasitara	uketorimaseñ desitara
Alternative	INFORMAL	uketottari	uketoranakattari
	FORMAL	uketorimasitari	uketorimaseñ desitari

INFORMAL AFFIRMATIVE INDICATIVE

Passive	uketorareru	*Honorific*	I	ouketori ni naru
			II	ouketori nasaru
Potential	uketoreru			
		Humble	I	ouketori suru
Causative	uketoraseru		II	ouketori itasu
Causative Pass.	uketoraserareru			

		AFFIRMATIVE	NEGATIVE
Indicative	INFORMAL	umareru	umarenai
	FORMAL	umaremasu	umaremaseñ
Imperative	INFORMAL I	umarero	umareru na
	II		
	III		
	FORMAL		
Presumptive	INFORMAL I	umareyoo	umaremai
	II	umareru daroo	umarenai daroo
	FORMAL I	umaremasyoo	umaremasumai
	II	umareru desyoo	umarenai desyoo
Provisional	INFORMAL	umarereba	umarenakereba
	FORMAL	umaremaseba	umaremaseñ nara
		umaremasureba	
Gerund	INFORMAL I	umarete	umarenai de
	II		umarenakute
	FORMAL	umaremasite	umaremaseñ de
Past Ind.	INFORMAL	umareta	umarenakatta
	FORMAL	umaremasita	umaremaseñ desita
Past Presump.	INFORMAL	umaretaroo	umarenakattaroo
		umareta daroo	umarenakatta daroo
	FORMAL	umaremasitaroo	umaremaseñ desitaroo
		umareta desyoo	umarenakatta desyoo
Conditional	INFORMAL	umaretara	umarenakattara
	FORMAL	umaremasitara	umaremaseñ desitara
Alternative	INFORMAL	umaretari	umarenakattari
	FORMAL	umaremasitari	umaremaseñ desitari

INFORMAL AFFIRMATIVE INDICATIVE

Passive		*Honorific*	I	oumare ni naru
			II	oumare nasaru
Potential				
		Humble	I	
Causative	umaresaseru		II	
Causative Pass.	umaresaserareru			

*This corresponds to the passive derived form of *um.u* 'to give birth.'

			AFFIRMATIVE	NEGATIVE
Indicative	INFORMAL		uru	uranai
	FORMAL		urimasu	urimaseñ
Imperative	INFORMAL	I	ure	uru na
		II	urinasai	urinasaru na
		III	utte kudasai	uranai de kudasai
	FORMAL		ouri nasaimase	ouri nasaimasu na
Presumptive	INFORMAL	I	uroo	urumai
		II	uru daroo	uranai daroo
	FORMAL	I	urimasyoo	urimasumai
		II	uru desyoo	uranai desyoo
Provisional	INFORMAL		ureba	uranakereba
	FORMAL		urimaseba	urimaseñ nara
			urimasureba	
Gerund	INFORMAL	I	utte	uranai de
		II		uranakute
	FORMAL		urimasite	urimaseñ de
Past Ind.	INFORMAL		utta	uranakatta
	FORMAL		urimasita	urimaseñ desita
Past Presump.	INFORMAL		uttaroo	uranakattaroo
			utta daroo	uranakatta daroo
	FORMAL		urimasitaroo	urimaseñ desitaroo
			utta desyoo	uranakatta desyoo
Conditional	INFORMAL		uttara	uranakattara
	FORMAL		urimasitara	urimaseñ desitara
Alternative	INFORMAL		uttari	uranakattari
	FORMAL		urimasitari	urimaseñ desitari

INFORMAL AFFIRMATIVE INDICATIVE

Passive	urareru		*Honorific*	I	ouri ni naru
				II	ouri nasaru
Potential	ureru				
			Humble	I	ouri suru
Causative	uraseru			II	ouri itasu
Causative Pass.	uraserareru				

TRANSITIVE   *to sing*

		AFFIRMATIVE	NEGATIVE
Indicative	**INFORMAL**	utau	utawanai
	FORMAL	utaimasu	utaimaseñ
Imperative	**INFORMAL I**	utae	utau na
	II	utainasai	utainasaru na
	III	utatte kudasai	utawanai de kudasai
	FORMAL	outai nasaimase	outai nasaimasu na
Presumptive	**INFORMAL I**	utaoo	utaumai
	II	utau daroo	utawanai daroo
	FORMAL I	utaimasyoo	utaimasumai
	II	utau desyoo	utawanai desyoo
Provisional	**INFORMAL**	utaeba	utawanakereba
	FORMAL	utaimaseba	utaimaseñ nara
		utaimasureba	
Gerund	**INFORMAL I**	utatte	utawanai de
	II		utawanakute
	FORMAL	utaimasite	utaimaseñ de
Past Ind.	**INFORMAL**	utatta	utawanakatta
	FORMAL	utaimasita	utaimaseñ desita
Past Presump.	**INFORMAL**	utattaroo	utawanakattaroo
		utatta daroo	utawanakatta daroo
	FORMAL	utaimasitaroo	utaimaseñ desitaroo
		utatta desyoo	utawanakatta desyoo
Conditional	**INFORMAL**	utattara	utawanakattara
	FORMAL	utaimasitara	utaimaseñ desitara
Alternative	**INFORMAL**	utattari	utawanakattari
	FORMAL	utaimasitari	utaimaseñ desitari

INFORMAL AFFIRMATIVE INDICATIVE

Passive	utawareru		*Honorific*	**I** outai ni naru
				II outai nasaru
Potential	utaeru			
			Humble	**I** outai suru
Causative	utawaseru			**II** outai itasu
Causative Pass.	utawaserareru			

		AFFIRMATIVE	NEGATIVE
Indicative	INFORMAL	utu	utanai
	FORMAL	utimasu	utimaseñ
Imperative	INFORMAL I	ute	utu na
	II	utinasai	utinasaru na
	III	utte kudasai	utanai de kudasai
	FORMAL	outi nasaimase	outi nasaimasu na
Presumptive	INFORMAL I	utoo	utumai
	II	utu daroo	utanai daroo
	FORMAL I	utimasyoo	utimasumai
	II	utu desyoo	utanai desyoo
Provisional	INFORMAL	uteba	utanakereba
	FORMAL	utimaseba	utimaseñ nara
		utimasureba	
Gerund	INFORMAL I	utte	utanai de
	II		utanakute
	FORMAL	utimasite	utimaseñ de
Past Ind.	INFORMAL	utta	utanakatta
	FORMAL	utimasita	utimaseñ desita
Past Presump.	INFORMAL	uttaroo	utanakattaroo
		utta daroo	utanakatta daroo
	FORMAL	utimasitaroo	utimaseñ desitaroo
		utta desyoo	utanakatta desyoo
Conditional	INFORMAL	uttara	utanakattara
	FORMAL	utimasitara	utimaseñ desitara
Alternative	INFORMAL	uttari	utanakattari
	FORMAL	utimasitari	utimaseñ desitari

INFORMAL AFFIRMATIVE INDICATIVE

Passive	utareru	*Honorific*	I	outi ni naru
			II	outi nasaru
Potential	uteru			
		Humble	I	outi suru
Causative	utaseru		II	outi itasu
Causative Pass.	utaserareru			

		AFFIRMATIVE	NEGATIVE
Indicative	INFORMAL	wakaru	wakaranai
	FORMAL	wakarimasu	wakarimaseñ
Imperative	INFORMAL I	wakare	
	II		
	III	wakatte kudasai	
	FORMAL		
Presumptive	INFORMAL I	wakaroo	wakarumai
	II	wakaru daroo	wakaranai daroo
	FORMAL I	wakarimasyoo	wakarimasumai
	II	wakaru desyoo	wakaranai desyoo
Provisional	INFORMAL	wakareba	wakaranakereba
	FORMAL	wakarimaseba	wakarimaseñ nara
		wakarimasureba	
Gerund	INFORMAL I	wakatte	wakaranai de
	II		wakaranakute
	FORMAL	wakarimasite	wakarimaseñ de
Past Ind.	INFORMAL	wakatta	wakaranakatta
	FORMAL	wakarimasita	wakarimaseñ desita
Past Presump.	INFORMAL	wakattaroo	wakaranakattaroo
		wakatta daroo	wakararakatta daroo
	FORMAL	wakarimasitaroo	wakaranakatta desitaroo
		wakatta desyoo	wakaranakatta desyoo
Conditional	INFORMAL	wakattara	wakaranakattara
	FORMAL	wakarimasitara	wakarimaseñ desitara
Alternative	INFORMAL	wakattari	wakaranakattari
	FORMAL	wakarimasitari	wakarimaseñ desitari

INFORMAL AFFIRMATIVE INDICATIVE

Passive		*Honorific*	I	owakari ni naru
			II	owakari nasaru
Potential				
		Humble	I	
Causative	wakaraseru		II	
Causative Pass.	wakaraserareru			

		AFFIRMATIVE	NEGATIVE
Indicative	**INFORMAL**	warau	warawanai
	FORMAL	waraimasu	waraimaseñ
Imperative	**INFORMAL I**	warae	warau na
	II	warainasai	warainasaru na
	III	waratte kudasai	warawanai de kudasai
	FORMAL	- owarai nasaimase	owarai nasaimasu na
Presumptive	**INFORMAL I**	waraoo	waraumai
	II	warau daroo	warawanai daroo
	FORMAL I	waraimasyoo	waraimasumai
	II	warau desyoo	warawanai desyoo
Provisional	**INFORMAL**	waraeba	warawanakereba
	FORMAL	waraimaseba	waraimaseñ nara
		waraimasureba	
Gerund	**INFORMAL I**	waratte	warawanai de
	II		warawanakute
	FORMAL	waraimasite	waraimaseñ de
Past Ind.	**INFORMAL**	waratta	warawanakatta
	FORMAL	waraimasita	waraimaseñ desita
Past Presump.	**INFORMAL**	warattaroo	warawanakattaroo
		waratta daroo	warawanakatta daroo
	FORMAL	waraimasitaroo	waraimaseñ desitaroo
		waratta desyoo	warawanakatta desyoo
Conditional	**INFORMAL**	warattara	warawanakattara
	FORMAL	waraimasitara	waraimaseñ desitara
Alternative	**INFORMAL**	warattari	warawanakattari
	FORMAL	waraimasitari	waraimaseñ desitari

INFORMAL AFFIRMATIVE INDICATIVE

Passive	warawareru	*Honorific*	**I**	owarai ni naru
			II	owarai nasaru
Potential	waraeru			
		Humble	**I**	
Causative	warawaseru		**II**	
Causative Pass.	warawaserareru			

		AFFIRMATIVE	NEGATIVE
Indicative	INFORMAL	wasureru	wasurenai
	FORMAL	wasuremasu	wasuremaseñ
Imperative	INFORMAL I	wasurero	wasureru na
	II	wasurenasai	wasurenasaru na
	III	wasurete kudasai	wasurenai de kudasai
	FORMAL	owasure nasaimase	owasure nasaimasu na
Presumptive	INFORMAL I	wasureyoo	wasuremai
	II	wasureru daroo	wasurenai daroo
	FORMAL I	wasuremasyoo	wasuremasumai
	II	wasureru desyoo	wasurenai desyoo
Provisional	INFORMAL	wasurereba	wasurenakereba
	FORMAL	wasuremaseba	wasuremaseñ nara
		wasuremasureba	
Gerund	INFORMAL I	wasurete	wasurenai de
	II		wasurenakute
	FORMAL	wasuremasite	wasuremaseñ de
Past Ind.	INFORMAL	wasureta	wasurenakatta
	FORMAL	wasuremasita	wasuremaseñ desita
Past Presump.	INFORMAL	wasuretaroo	wasurenakattaroo
		wasureta daroo	wasurenakatta daroo
	FORMAL	wasuremasitaroo	wasuremaseñ desitaroo
		wasureta desyoo	wasurenakatta desyoo
Conditional	INFORMAL	wasuretara	wasurenakattara
	FORMAL	wasuremasitara	wasuremaseñ desitara
Alternative	INFORMAL	wasuretari	wasurenakattari
	FORMAL	wasuremasitari	wasuremaseñ desitari

INFORMAL AFFIRMATIVE INDICATIVE

Passive	wasurerareru	*Honorific*	I	owasure ni naru
			II	owasure nasaru
Potential	wasurerareru			
		Humble	I	owasure suru
Causative	wasuresaseru		II	owasure itasu
Causative Pass.	wasuresaserareru			

		AFFIRMATIVE	NEGATIVE
Indicative	INFORMAL	yaku	yakanaı
	FORMAL	yakimasu	yakimaseñ
Imperative	INFORMAL I	yake	yaku na
	II	yakinasai	yakinasaru na
	III	yaite kudasai	yakanai de kudasai
	FORMAL	oyaki nasaimase	oyaki nasaimasu na
Presumptive	INFORMAL I	yakoo	yakumai
	II	yaku daroo	yakanai daroo
	FORMAL I	yakimasyoo	yakimasumai
	II	yaku desyoo	yakanai desyoo
Provisional	INFORMAL	yakeba	yakanakereba
	FORMAL	yakimaseba	yakimaseñ nara
		yakimasureba	
Gerund	INFORMAL I	yaite	yakanai de
	II		yakanakute
	FORMAL	yakimasite	yakimaseñ de
Past Ind.	INFORMAL	yaita	yakanakatta
	FORMAL	yakimasita	yakimaseñ desita
Past Presump.	INFORMAL	yaitaroo	yakanakattaroo
		yaita daroo	yakanakatta daroo
	FORMAL	yakimasitaroo	yakimaseñ desitaroo
		yaita desyoo	yakanakatta desyoo
Conditional	INFORMAL	yaitara	yakanakattara
	FORMAL	yakimasitara	yakimaseñ desitara
Alternative	INFORMAL	yaitari	yakanakattari
	FORMAL	yakimasitari	yakimaseñ desitari

INFORMAL AFFIRMATIVE INDICATIVE

Passive	yakareru	*Honorific*	I	oyaki ni naru
			II	oyaki nasaru
Potential	yakeru			
		Humble	I	oyaki suru
Causative	yakaseru		II	oyaki itasu
Causative Pass.	yakaserareru			

TRANSITIVE   *to stop, to give up* (doing something)

		AFFIRMATIVE	NEGATIVE
Indicative	INFORMAL	yameru	yamenai
	FORMAL	yamemasu	yamemaseñ
Imperative	INFORMAL I	yamero	yameru na
	II	yamenasai	yamenasaru na
	III	yamete kudasai	yamenai de kudasai
	FORMAL	oyame nasaimase	oyame nasaimasu na
Presumptive	INFORMAL I	yameyoo	yamemai
	II	yameru daroo	yamenai daroo
	FORMAL I	yamemasyoo	yamemasumai
	II	yameru desyoo	yamenai desyoo
Provisional	INFORMAL	yamereba	yamenakereba
	FORMAL	yamemaseba	yamemaseñ nara
		yamemasureba	
Gerund	INFORMAL I	yamete	yamenai de
	II		yamenakute
	FORMAL	yamemasite	yamemaseñ de
Past Ind.	INFORMAL	yameta	yamenakatta
	FORMAL	yamemasita	yamemaseñ desita
Past Presump.	INFORMAL	yametaroo	yamenakattaroo
		yameta daroo	yamenakatta taroo
	FORMAL	yamemasitaroo	yamemaseñ desitaroo
		yameta desyoo	yamenakatta desyoo
Conditional	INFORMAL	yametara	yamenakattara
	FORMAL	yamemasitara	yamemaseñ desitara
Alternative	INFORMAL	yametari	yamenakattari
	FORMAL	yamemasitari	yamemaseñ desitari

INFORMAL AFFIRMATIVE INDICATIVE

Passive	yamerareru	*Honorific*	I	oyame ni naru
			II	oyame nasaru
Potential	yamerareru			
		Humble	I	oyame suru
Causative	yamesaseru		II	oyame itasu
Causative Pass.	yamesaserareru			

		AFFIRMATIVE	NEGATIVE
Indicative	INFORMAL	yaru	yaranai
	FORMAL	yarimasu	yarimaseñ
Imperative	INFORMAL I	yare	yaru na
	II	yarinasai	yarinasaru na
	III	yatte kudasai	yaranai de kudasai
	FORMAL	oyari nasaimase	oyari nasaimasu na
Presumptive	INFORMAL I	yaroo	yarumai
	II	yaru daroo	yaranai daroo
	FORMAL I	yarimasyoo	yarimasumai
	II	yaru desyoo	yaranai desyoo
Provisional	INFORMAL	yareba	yaranakereba
	FORMAL	yarimaseba	yarimaseñ nara
		yarimasureba	
Gerund	INFORMAL I	yatte	yaranai de
	II		yaranakute
	FORMAL	yarimasite	yarimaseñ de
Past Ind.	INFORMAL	yatta	yaranakatta
	FORMAL	yarimasita	yarimaseñ desita
Past Presump.	INFORMAL	yattaroo	yaranakattaroo
		yatta daroo	yaranakatta daroo
	FORMAL	yarimasitaroo	yarimaseñ desitaroo
		yatta desyoo	yaranakatta desyoo
Conditional	INFORMAL	yattara	yaranakattara
	FORMAL	yarimasitara	yarimaseñ desitara
Alternative	INFORMAL	yattari	yaranakattari
	FORMAL	yarimasitari	yarimaseñ desitari

INFORMAL AFFIRMATIVE INDICATIVE

Passive	yarareru	*Honorific*	I	oyari ni naru
			II	oyari nasaru
Potential	yareru			
		Humble	I	
Causative	yaraseru		II	
Causative Pass.	yaraserareru			

		AFFIRMATIVE	NEGATIVE
Indicative	INFORMAL	yaseru	yasenai
	FORMAL	yasemasu	yasemaseñ
Imperative	INFORMAL I	yasero	yaseru na
	II	yasenasai	yasenasaru na
	III	yasete kudasai	yasenai de kudasai
	FORMAL	oyase nasaimase	oyase nasaimasu na
Presumptive	INFORMAL I	yaseyoo	yasemai
	II	yaseru daroo	yasenai daroo
	FORMAL I	yasemasyoo	yasemasumai
	II	yaseru desyoo	yasenai desyoo
Provisional	INFORMAL	yasereba	yasenakereba
	FORMAL	yasemaseba	yasemaseñ nara
		yasemasureba	
Gerund	INFORMAL I	yasete	yasenai de
	II		yasenakute
	FORMAL	yasemasite	yasemaseñ de
Past Ind.	INFORMAL	yaseta	yasenakatta
	FORMAL	yasemasita	yasemaseñ desita
Past Presump.	INFORMAL	yasetaroo	yasenakattaroo
		yaseta daroo	yasenakatta daroo
	FORMAL	yasemasitaroo	yasemaseñ desitaroo
		yaseta desyoo	yasenakatta desyoo
Conditional	INFORMAL	yasetara	yasenakattara
	FORMAL	yasemasitara	yasemaseñ desitara
Alternative	INFORMAL	yasetari	yasenakattari
	FORMAL	yasemasitari	yasemaseñ desitari

INFORMAL AFFIRMATIVE INDICATIVE

Passive	yaserareru	*Honorific*	I	oyase ni naru
			II	oyase nasaru
Potential	yaserareru			
		Humble	I	
Causative	yasesaseru		II	
Causative Pass.	yasesaserareru			

		AFFIRMATIVE	NEGATIVE
Indicative	INFORMAL	yasumu	yasumanai
	FORMAL	yasumimasu	yasumimaseñ
Imperative	INFORMAL I	yasume	yasumu na
	II	yasuminasai	yasuminasaru na
	III	yasuñde kudasai	yasumanai de kudasai
	FORMAL	oyasumi nasaimase	oyasumi nasaimasu na
Presumptive	INFORMAL I	yasumoo	yasumumai
	II	yasumu daroo	yasumanai daroo
	FORMAL I	yasumimasyoo	yasumimasumai
	II	yasumu desyoo	yasumanai desyoo
Provisional	INFORMAL	yasumeba	yasumanakereba
	FORMAL	yasumimaseba	yasumimaseñ nara
		yasumimasureba	
Gerund	INFORMAL I	yasuñde	yasumanai de
	II		yasumanakute
	FORMAL	yasumimasite	yasumimaseñ de
Past Ind.	INFORMAL	yasuñda	yasumanakatta
	FORMAL	yasumimasita	yasumimaseñ desita
Past Presump.	INFORMAL	yasuñdaroo	yasumanakattaroo
		yasuñda daroo	yasumanakatta daroo
	FORMAL	yasumimasitaroo	yasumimaseñ desitaroo
		yasuñda desyoo	yasumanakatta desyoo
Conditional	INFORMAL	yasuñdara	yasumanakattara
	FORMAL	yasumimasitara	yasumimaseñ desitara
Alternative	INFORMAL	yasuñdari	yasumimasitari
	FORMAL	yasumimasitari	yasumimaseñ desitari

INFORMAL AFFIRMATIVE INDICATIVE

Passive	yasumareru	*Honorific*	I	oyasumi ni naru
			II	oyasumi nasaru
Potential	yasumeru			
		Humble	I	
Causative	yasumaseru		II	
Causative Pass.	yasumaserareru			

TRANSITIVE . *to hire, to employ*

		AFFIRMATIVE	NEGATIVE
Indicative	INFORMAL	yatou	yatowanai
	FORMAL	yatoimasu	yatoimaseñ
Imperative	INFORMAL I	yatoe	yatou na
	II	yatoinasai	yatoinasaru na
	III	yatotte kudasai	yatowanai de kudasai
	FORMAL	oyatoi nasaimase	oyatoi nasaimasu na
Presumptive	INFORMAL I	yatooo	yatoumai
	II	yatou daroo	yatowanai daroo
	FORMAL I	yatoimasyoo	yatoimasumai
	II	yatou desyoo	yatowanai desyoo
Provisional	INFORMAL	yatoeba	yatowanakereba
	FORMAL	yatoimaseba	yatoimaseñ nara
		yatoimasureba	
Gerund	INFORMAL I	yatotte	yatowanai de
	II		yatowanakute
	FORMAL	yatoimasite	yatoimaseñ de
Past Ind.	INFORMAL	yatotta	yatowanakatta
	FORMAL	yatomasita	yatoimaseñ desita
Past Presump.	INFORMAL	yatottaroo	yatowanakattaroo
		yatotta daroo	yatowanakatta daroo
	FORMAL	yatoimasitaroo	yatoimaseñ desitaroo
		yatotta desyoo	yatowanakatta desyoo
Conditional	INFORMAL	yatottara	yatowanakattara
	FORMAL	yatoimasitara	yatoimaseñ desitara
Alternative	INFORMAL	yatottari	yatowanakattari
	FORMAL	yatoimasitari	yatoimaseñ desitari

INFORMAL AFFIRMATIVE INDICATIVE

Passive	yatowareru	*Honorific*	I	oyatoi ni naru
			II	oyatoi nasaru
Potential	yatoeru			
		Humble	I	oyatoi suru
Causative	yatowaseru		II	oyatoi itasu
Causative Pass.	yatowaserareru			

yob.u
to call TRANSITIVE

		AFFIRMATIVE	NEGATIVE
Indicative	INFORMAL	yobu	yobanai
	FORMAL	yobimasu	yobimaseñ
Imperative	INFORMAL I	yobe	yobu na
	II	yobinasai	yobinasaru na
	III	yoñde kudasai	yobanai de kudasai
	FORMAL	oyobi nasaimase	oyobi nasaimasu na
Presumptive	INFORMAL I	yoboo	yobumai
	II	yobu daroo	yobanai daroo
	FORMAL I	yobimasyoo	yobimasumai
	II	yobu desyoo	yobanai desyoo
Provisional	INFORMAL	yobeba	yobanakereba
	FORMAL	yobimaseba	yobimaseñ nara
		yobimasureba	
Gerund	INFORMAL I	yoñde	yobanai de
	II		yobanakute
	FORMAL	yobimasite	yobimaseñ de
Past Ind.	INFORMAL	yoñda	yobanakatta
	FORMAL	yobimasita	yobimaseñ desita
Past Presump.	INFORMAL	yoñdaroo	yobanakattaroo
		yoñda daroo	yobanakatta daroo
	FORMAL	yobimasitaroo	yobimaseñ desitaroo
		yoñda desyoo	yobanakatta desyoo
Conditional	INFORMAL	yoñdara	yobanakattara
	FORMAL	yobimasitara	yobimaseñ desitara
Alternative	INFORMAL	yoñdari	yobanakattari
	FORMAL	yobimasitari	yobimaseñ desitari

INFORMAL AFFIRMATIVE INDICATIVE

Passive	yobareru	*Honorific*	I	oyobi ni r
			II	oyobi nas
Potential	yoberu			
		Humble	I	oyobi sur
Causative	yobaseru		II	oyobi itas
Causative Pass.	yobaserareru			

		AFFIRMATIVE	NEGATIVE
Indicative	INFORMAL	yomu	yomanai
	FORMAL	yomimasu	yomimaseñ
Imperative	INFORMAL I	yome	yomu na
	II	yominasai	yominasaru na
	III	yoñde kudasai	yomanai de kudasai
	FORMAL	oyomi nasaimase	oyomi nasaimasu na
Presumptive	INFORMAL I	yomoo	yomumai
	II	yomu daroo	yomanai daroo
	FORMAL I	yomimasyoo	yomimasumai
	II	yomu desyoo	yomanai desyoo
Provisional	INFORMAL	yomeba	yomanakereba
	FORMAL	yomimaseba	yomimaseñ nara
		yomimasureba	
Gerund	INFORMAL I	yoñde	yomanai de
	II		yomanakute
	FORMAL	yomimasite	yomimaseñ de
Past Ind.	INFORMAL	yoñda	yomanakatta
	FORMAL	yomimasita	yomimaseñ desita
Past Presump.	INFORMAL	yoñdaroo	yomanakattaroo
		yoñda daroo	yomanakatta daroo
	FORMAL	yomimasitaroo	yomimaseñ desitaroo
		yoñda desyoo	yomanakatta desyoo
Conditional	INFORMAL	yoñdara	yomanakattara
	FORMAL	yomimasitara	yomimaseñ desitara
Alternative	INFORMAL	yoñdari	yomanakattari
	FORMAL	yomimasitari	yomimaseñ desitari

INFORMAL AFFIRMATIVE INDICATIVE

Passive	yomareru	*Honorific*	I	oyomi ni naru
			II	oyomi nasaru
Potential	yomeru			
		Humble	I	oyomi suru
Causative	yomaseru		II	oyomi itasu
Causative Pass.	yomaserareru			

		AFFIRMATIVE	NEGATIVE
Indicative	**INFORMAL**	yorokobu	yorokohanai
	FORMAL	yorokobimasu	yorokobimaseñ
Imperative	**INFORMAL I**	yorokobe	yorokobu na
	II	yorokobinasai	yorokobinasaru na
	III	yorokoñde kudasai	yorokobanai de kudasai
	FORMAL	oyorokobi nasaimase	oyorokobi nasaimasu na
Presumptive	**INFORMAL I**	yorokoboo	yorokobumai
	II	yorokobu daroo	yorokobanai daroo
	FORMAL I	yorokobimasyoo	yorokobimasumai
	II	yorokobu desyoo	yorokobanai desyoo
Provisional	**INFORMAL**	yorokobeba	yorokobanakereba
	FORMAL	yorokobimaseba	yorokobimaseñ nara
		yorokobimasureba	
Gerund	**INFORMAL I**	yorokoñde	yorokobanai de
	II		yorokobanakute
	FORMAL	yorokobimasite	yorokobimaseñ de
Past Ind.	**INFORMAL**	yorokoñda	yorokobanakatta
	FORMAL	yorokobimasita	yorokobimaseñ desita
Past Presump.	**INFORMAL**	yorokoñdaroo	yorokobanakattaroo
		yorokoñda daroo	yorokobanakatta daroo
	FORMAL	yorokobimasitaroo	yorokobimaseñ desitaroo
		yorokoñda desyoo	yorokobanakatta desyoo
Conditional	**INFORMAL**	yorokoñdara	yorokobanakattara
	FORMAL	yorokobimasitara	yorokobimaseñ desitara
Alternative	**INFORMAL**	yorokoñdari	yorokobanakattari
	FORMAL	yorokobimasitari	yorokobimaseñ desitari

INFORMAL AFFIRMATIVE INDICATIVE

Passive	yorokobareru	*Honorific* **I**	oyorokobi ni naru
		II	oyorokobi nasaru
Potential	yorokoberu		
		Humble **I**	oyorokobi suru
Causative	yorokobaseru	**II**	oyorokobi itasu
Causative Pass.	yorokobaserareru		

TRANSITIVE   *to forgive, to permit*

		AFFIRMATIVE	NEGATIVE
Indicative	INFORMAL	yurusu	yurusanai
	FORMAL	yurusimasu	yurusimaseñ
Imperative	INFORMAL I	yuruse	yurusu na
	II	yurusinasai	yurusinasaru na
	III	yurusite kudasai	yurusanai de kudasai
	FORMAL	oyurusi nasaimase	oyurusi nasaimasu na
Presumptive	INFORMAL I	yurusoo	yurusumai
	II	yurusu daroo	yurusanai daroo
	FORMAL I	yurusimasyoo	yurusimasumai
	II	yurusu desyoo	yurusanai desyoo
Provisional	INFORMAL	yuruseba	yurusanakereba
	FORMAL	yurusimaseba	yurusimaseñ nara
		yurusimasureba	
Gerund	INFORMAL I	yurusite	yurusanai de
	II		yurusanakute
	FORMAL	yurusimasite	yurusimaseñ de
Past Ind.	INFORMAL	yurusita	yurusanakatta
	FORMAL	yurusimasita	yurusimaseñ desita
Past Presump.	INFORMAL	yurusitaroo	yurusanakattaroo
		yurusita daroo	yurusanakatta daroo
	FORMAL	yurusimasitaroo	yurusimaseñ desitaroo
		yurusita desyoo	yurusanakatta desyoo
Conditional	INFORMAL	yurusitara	yurusanakattara
	FORMAL	yurusimasitara	yurusimaseñ desitara
Alternative	INFORMAL	yurusitari	yurusanakattari
	FORMAL	yurusimasitari	yurusimaseñ desitari

INFORMAL AFFIRMATIVE INDICATIVE

Passive	yurusareru	*Honorific*	I	oyurusi ni naru
			II	oyurusi nasaru
Potential	yuruseru			
		Humble	I	oyurusi suru
Causative	yurusaseru		II	oyurusi itasu
Causative Pass.	yurusaserareru			

VERBS OF GIVING AND RECEIVING

In Japanese many verbs of giving and receiving have an intrinsic 'directionality' which helps to identify the person performing the act of giving. This is a big help to English-speaking students, because Japanese often omits explicit reference to the subject of a sentence.

The four verbs for giving which occur most often in spoken Japanese are *ageru, yaru, kudasaru,* and *kureru.*

Ageru means 'I (you, he, she, or they) give TO SOMEONE OTHER THAN THE SPEAKER.' Thus *Okane o agemasita.* could mean 'I gave you money,' 'You gave him money,' or 'She gave them money,' but it could not mean 'You (he, she, or they) gave me money.' *Ageru* also has an intrinsic element of politeness to the receiver of the gift, so it is used to describe giving to equals or superiors, or to anyone to whom the speaker wishes to express politeness or respect.

Examples:

Señsei ni agete mo ii desu. 'You may give it to the teacher.'
Moo sukosi agemasyoo ka. 'Shall I give you a little more?'
Okaasañ ni agete kudasai. 'Please give to your mother.'

Yaru too means 'give TO SOMEONE OTHER THAN THE SPEAKER,' but it differs greatly in that it lacks the politeness of *ageru.* Thus it is used to describe giving to an inferior. It is sometimes used for giving to an equal when speaking very plainly and informally, but since such judgments are extremely difficult for students, and since using *yaru* at the wrong time could offend the person one is speaking to or about, they are advised to use *yaru* only when talking about giving things to plants and animals. This is a safe usage, and one which is common in Japan.

Examples:

Imooto ni okasi o takusañ yarimasita. 'I gave a lot of candy to my little sister.' *Sañzi ni inu ni esa o yatta.* 'She fed the dog at three o'clock.' *Taroo wa mada hana ni mizu o yarimaseñ.* 'Taroo has not watered the flowers yet.'

Kudasaru means 'giving BY SOMEONE OTHER THAN THE SPEAKER,' and is usually used to describe giving to the speaker or to a member of the speaker's in-group such as a family member. *Kudasaru* forms a pair with *ageru*, but whereas *ageru* shows politeness to the recipient of the gift, *kudasaru* shows politeness to the giver. It implies that the giver's position is superior to that of the speaker, or that the speaker is showing respect to the giver in order to be polite, as would commonly be done when the giver is present.

Examples:

Akai no o kudasai. 'Please give me the red one.' *Señsei ga kudasatta hoñ desu.* 'It's the book the teacher gave me.' *Hiroko ni mo kudasatta no?* 'You mean you gave some to (my child) Hiroko too?'

Kureru also means 'giving BY SOMEONE OTHER THAN THE SPEAKER' but it implies that the giver is equal or inferior to the receiver, so it is not used when one desires to show politeness or respect to the giver. It is often used when the giver is an institution rather than a person. It is also often used when describing a gift to the speaker by a person of roughly equivalent status who is not present. Though it is sometimes used to mean 'someone (other than the speaker) gives to you,' this usage is best avoided by students because it could give offense if used to the wrong person.

Examples:

Tomodati ga kudamono o kuremasita. 'My friend gave me some fruit.' *Unteñsyu wa oturi mo kurenai de itte simatta.* 'The driver went off without giving me my change.' *Kodomotati ga hañkati o kureta.* 'The kids gave me some handkerchiefs.'

The two common verbs for receiving are *itadaku* and *morau*. *Itadaku* means 'something is received by me or by a member of my in-group such as a close relative.' It is a humble verb which shows deference to the giver by placing the receiver in an inferior position. Therefore, it would not be used for 'you receive' unless the receiver is an inferior member of the speaker's in-group. A mother might say to her small child *Maa señsei ni itadaita no?* 'Did you receive it from your teacher?' when the teacher is present, in order to show respect to the teacher.

Examples:

Okusañ ni kippu o itadaita no de, sibai o mite kimasita. 'We received tickets from your wife, so we went to the play.' *Tomita señsei kara itadaita syasiñ wa doko desu ka.* 'Where is the photo that you received from Professor Tomita?' *Oheñzi o itadaite añsiñ itasimasita.* 'I was relieved to receive your reply.'

Morau lacks the directionality of the verbs discussed above. It can mean 'I, you, he, she, or they receive.' Since it has the standard honorific forms of *omorai ni naru* and *omorai nasaru*, it can be used to express deference or politeness to the receiver. Its humble form is *itadaku*.

Examples:

Tomodati kara iroiro na mono o moraimasita. 'I (you, he, she, they) received all sorts of things from friends.' *Zuibuñ ii tokei o omorai ni narimasita nee.* 'My, you certainly got a nice watch.' *Tanakasañ ni moratta no wa dore desyoo ka.* 'Which is the one that we got from Mr. Tanaka?' *Mada moraimaseñ ka?* 'Haven't you received it yet?' *Miñna nani ka ii mono o morau desyoo.* 'Probably everyone will get something good.'

A thorough grasp of these verbs is required because, in addition to describing the giving and receiving of objects, they are also widely employed in describing actions done for another person's benefit. In this construction the informal gerund of the verb which describes the action is used immediately before the appropriate form of the verb of giving or receiving. We have already encountered this construction in the imperative III in which the gerund is used before the informal imperative form of *kudasaru* to make a polite request. The same directionality applies as did in the giving and receiving of objects. That is, just as *Riñgo o ageta.* means 'Someone gave an apple to someone other than the speaker,' *Riñgo o katte ageta.* means 'Someone bought an apple for someone other than the speaker.' and so on.

Examples:

Kodomodati ni kurisumasu torii o katte yatta. 'We bought a Christmas tree for the children.' *Kanai ga itumo boku no suki na mono o tukutte kureru.* 'My wife always cooks things that I like for me.' *Moo sukosi matte kudasaimaseñ ka.* 'Would

305

you please wait a bit longer for me.' *Okaasama ni oisii okas o motte kite itadakimasita.* 'Your mother brought delicious cake for us.' (Literally 'We received the bringing of delicious cake by your mother.') *Dare mo osiete kuremaseñ desita.* 'Nobody told me.' *Sono hana wa dare ni okutte moraimasita ka* 'Who sent you the flowers?' (Literally 'As for those flowers by whom did you receive the sending?') *Misete agemasyoo ka.** 'Shall I show it to you.'* *Señsei ga nañkai mo setume site kudasaimasita.* 'The teacher explained it to me any number of times.'

A gerund plus *morau* or *itadaku* is also used when one person has another do something for them.
Examples:
Otetudaisañ ni señtakumono o tatañde moraimasita. 'She had the maid fold the laundry.' *Nikuyasañ ni tori no ii tokoro totte oite moratta.* 'I had the butcher save the good part of the chicken for me.' *Señsei ni setumei site itadakimasita.* 'I had the teacher explain it for me.' *Biiru o todokete moraeru de syoo.* 'You can probably have the beer delivered.'

We should also mention that a gerund plus *moraitai* or *itadakitai* constitutes an indirect request meaning 'I want to have something done by someone.' With *itadakitai* it usually mean 'I want to have something done by you.'
Examples:
Dare ka ni tana o tukutte moraitai desu. 'I would like to have someone build me a shelf.' *Isya ni mite moraitai.* 'I want to have the doctor take a look at it.' *Sañzi ni irasite itadakitai desu.* 'I want to have you come at three o'clock.' *Ookiku site moraitai ñ desu.* 'I want to have them enlarge it.'

---

*Since this use of *ageru* implies the doing of a favor, it would not b used to a superior or to someone to whom special politeness or defer ence was intended. Instead, one would use the humble form of th verb describing the action. Thus, a clerk in a department store woul not use this *ageru* construction when addressing a customer, b would say *Omise simasyoo ka.* or *Omise itasimasyoo ka.* for 'Shall show it to you?'

ENGLISH-JAPANESE INDEX

This index includes all of the verbs found in the foregoing tables. Transitive verbs are followed by **T**.

314

INDEX OF VERBS BY GERUND

In the early stages of learning Japanese, students often have trouble in identifying a verb on the basis of its informal gerund. The following index should be of some help in this respect. It lists alphabetically all the informal affirmative gerunds found in the text and gives the citation form of the verb or verbs which correspond to each gerund.

The sound changes which occur when forming the gerund also take place when any suffix beginning with -t is added to the verb stem. Therefore, this index will also help in identifying a verb by its (informal affirmative) past indicative, conditional, or alternative forms. For example: the gerund of a verb whose past indicative is *todoketa* will be *todokete;* that of a verb whose past indicative is *totta* will be *totte*. Consulting our list of gerunds we find that these belong to *todokeru* (p. 261) and *toru* (p. 267), and if we consult the tables for these verbs we will find that, indeed, their past indicative forms are *todoketa* and *totta* respectively.

A

agatte **agaru**
agete **ageru**
aite **aku**
akete **akeru**
akiramete **akirameru**
añnai site **añnai suru**
añsiñ site **añsiñ suru**
aratte **arau**
arawarete **arawareru**
arawasite **arawasu**
aruite **aruku**
asoñde **asobu**
atatamete **atatameru**
atte **aru, au**
atumatte **atumaru**
atumete **atumeru**

ayamatte **ayamaru**
ayatutte **ayaturu**
azukatte **azukaru**
azukete **azukeru**

B

beñkyoo site **beñkyoo suru**

D

daihyoo site **daihyoo suru**
daite **daku**
damasite **damasu**
damatte **damaru**
dasite **dasu**
dekite **dekiru**
dete **deru**

317

E

eñryo site **eñryo suru**
erañde **erabu**
ete **eru**

G

gakkari site **gakkari suru**
gañbatte **gañbaru**

H

haite **haku**
haitte **hairu**
hakatte **hakaru**
hakkeñ site **hakkeñ suru**
hanarete **hanareru**
hanasite **hanasu**
hañtai site **hañtai suru**
haratte **harau**
hataraite **hataraku**
hatumei site **hatumei suru**
hayatte **hayaru**
hazimatte **hazimaru**
hazimete **hazimeru**
hiite **hiku**
hikatte **hikaru**
hirotte **hirou**
homete **homeru**
hosigatte **hosigaru**
hosite **hosu**
huete **hueru**
huite **huku**
hukumete **hukumeru**
huruete **hurueru**
huseide **husegu**
hutotte **hutoru**
hutte **huru**
huyasite **huyasu**
huzakete **huzakeru**

I

ibatte **ibaru**
iinaosite **iinaosu**
iisugite **iisugiru**
ikite **ikiru**
inotte **inoru**
irasite **irasyaru**
irassyatte **irassyaru**
irete **ireru**
isoide **isogu**
itadaite **itadaku**
itañde **itamu**
itasite **itasu**
ite **iru (to exist)**
itte **iku, iru (to be necessary), iu**
iyagatte **iyagaru**
iyasiñde **iyasimu**
izimete **izimeru**

K

kaesite **kaesu**
kaete **kaeru (to change)**
kaette **kaeru (to return)**
kakatte **kakaru**
kakete **kakeru**
kakurete **kakureru**
kakusite **kakusu**
kamatte **kamau**
kañde **kamu**
kanasiñde **kanasimu**
kañgaete **kañgaeru**
kañzite **kañziru**
karakatte **karakau**
karite **kariru**
kasanete **kasaneru**
kaseide **kasegu**
kasite **kasu**

katazukete **katazukeru**
katte **katu, kau**
kawaigatte **kawaigaru**
kawaite **kawaku**
kawakasite **kawakasu**
kawatte **kawaru**
kayotte **kayou**
kazatte **kazaru**
kazoete **kazoeru**
kegasite **kegasu**
kesite **kesu**
kiete **kieru**
kiite **kiku**
kikaete **kikaeru**
kikoete **kikoeru**
kimatte **kimaru**
kimete **kimeru**
kiñzite **kiñziru**
kite **kiru (to wear), kuru**
kitte **kiru (to cut)**
koborete **koboreru**
kobosite **kobosu**
koete **koeru**
komatte **komaru**
koñde **komu**
konoñde **konomu**
kootte **kooru**
koraete **koraeru**
korasimete **korasimeru**
koroñde **korobu**
korosite **korosu**
kosikakete **kosikakeru**
kotaete **kotaeru**
kotonatte **kotonaru**
kotowatte **kotowaru**
kowagatte **kowagaru**
kowarete **kowareru**
kowasite **kowasu**

kudasatte **kudasaru**
kumotte **kumoru**
kurabete **kuraberu**
kurasite **kurasu**
kurete **kureru**
kurikaesite **kurikaesu**
kurusimete **kurusimeru**
kurusiñde **kurusimu**
kurutte **kuruu**   .
kusatte **kusaru**
kuzurete **kuzureru**
kuzusite **kuzusu**

M

magatte **magaru**
magete **mageru**
maitte **mairu**
makasete **makaseru**
makasite **makasu**
makete **makeru**
mamotte **mamoru**
manañde **manabu**
maneite **maneku**
matigaete **matigaeru**
matigatte **matigau**
matomete **matomeru**
matte **matu**
mazete **mazeru**
mesiagatte **mesiagaru**
miete **mieru**
migaite **migaku**
mihatte **miharu**
minogasite **minogasu**
misete **miseru**
mite **miru**
mitomete **mitomeru**
mitukatte **mitukaru**
mitukete **mitukeru**

319

modotte **modoru**
mookete **mookeru**
moratte **morau**
motomete **motomeru**
motte **motu**

N

nagarete **nagareru**
nagusamete **nagusameru**
naite **naku**
nakunatte **nakunaru**
naosite **naosu**
naotte **naoru**
narabete **naraberu**
naratte **narau**
nasatte **nasaru**
natte **naru**
nete **neru**
nigete **nigeru**
nigitte **nigiru**
nobotte **noboru**
nokotte **nokoru**
noñde **nomu**
nosete **noseru**
notte **noru**
nurete **nureru**
nusuñde **nusumu**
nutte **nuru**

O

oboete **oboeru**
odoroite **odoroku**
odotte **odoru**
oite **oku**
okite **okiru**
okosite **okosu**
okurete **okureru**
okutte **okuru**

omotte **omou**
orite **oriru**
osaete **osaeru**
osiete **osieru**
ossyatte **ossyaru**
otite **otiru**
otosite **otosu**
owatte **owaru**
oyoide **oyogu**

S

sagasite **sagasu**
saite **saku**
sawaide **sawagu**
sibatte **sibaru**
siite **siku**
sikatte **sikaru**
simatte **simaru, simau**
simete **simeru**
siñde **sinu**
siñzite **siñziru**
sirabete **siraberu**
site **suru**
sitte **siru**
sizuñde **sizumu**
sodatete **sodateru**
sugite **sugiru**
sugurete **sugureru**
suite **suku**
sumasete **sumaseru**
suñde **sumu**
susuñde **susumu**
sutete **suteru**
suwatte **suwaru**

T

tabete **taberu**
-tagatte **-tagaru**

tamesite **tamesu**
tanoñde **tanomu**
tanosiñde **tanosimu**
taorete **taoreru**
taosite **taosu**
tarite **tariru**
tasukete **tasukeru**
tataite **tataku**
tatakatte **tatakau**
tatete **tateru**
tatte **tatu**
tazunete **tazuneru**
tetudatte **tetudau**
tigatte **tigau**
todoite **todoku**
todokete **todokeru**
tokete **tokeru**
tomatte **tomaru**
tomete **tomeru**
toñde **tobu**
tootte **tooru**
totte **toru**
tuite **tuku**
tukamaete **tukamaeru**
tukarete **tukareru**
tukatte **tukau**
tukete **tukeru**
tukiatte **tukiau**
tukutte **tukuru**
tumotte **tumoru**

tutaete **tutaeru**
tutomete **tutomeru**
tutuñde **tutumu**
tuzukete **tuzukeru**
tyuui site **tyuui suru**

U

uete **ueru**
ugoite **ugoku**
ukañde **ukabu**
uketotte **uketoru**
umarete **umareru**
utatte **utau**
utte **uru, utu**

W

wakatte **wakaru**
waratte **warau**
wasurete **wasureru**

Y

yaite **yaku**
yamete **yameru**
yasete **yaseru**
yasuñde **yasumu**
yatotte **yatou**
yatte **yaru**
yoñde **yobu, yomu**
yorokoñde **yorokobu**
yurusite **yurusu**

NOTES

FOREIGN PHRASE BOOKS Series

Barron's new series gives travelers instant access to the most common idiomatic expressions used during a trip — the kind one needs to know instantly, like "Where can I find a taxi?" and "How much does this cost?"

Organized by situation (arrival, customs, hotel, health, etc.) and containing additional information about pronunciation, grammar, shopping plus special facts about the country, these convenient, pocket-size reference books will be the tourist's most helpful guides.

Special features include a bilingual dictionary section with over 2000 key words, maps of each country and major cities, and helpful phonetic spellings throughout.

Each book paperback, 256 pp., 3¾" x 6"

ARABIC AT A GLANCE, Wise (2979-8) $5.95, Can. $7.95
CHINESE AT A GLANCE, Seligman, Chen (2851-1) $5.95, Can. $7.95
FRENCH AT A GLANCE, Stein (2712-4) $5.95, Can. $7.95
GERMAN AT A GLANCE, Strutz (2714-0) $5.95, Can. $7.95
ITALIAN AT A GLANCE, Costantino (2713-2) $5.95, Can. $7.95
JAPANESE AT A GLANCE, Akiyama (2850-3) $6.95, Can. $9.95
KOREAN AT A GLANCE, Holt (3998-X) $6.95, Can. $9.95
RUSSIAN AT A GLANCE, Beyer (4299-9) $5.95, Can. $7.95
SPANISH AT A GLANCE, Wald (2711-6) $5.95, Can. $7.95

Barron's Educational Series, Inc.
250 Wireless Blvd., Hauppauge, NY 11788
Call toll-free: 1-800-645-3476, in NY: 1-800-257-5729
In Canada: Georgetown Book Warehouse, 34 Armstrong Ave.
Georgetown, Ont. L7G 4R9, Call toll-free: 1-800-247-7160

Books may be purchased at your bookstore, or by mail from Barron's. Enclose check or money order for total amount plus sales tax where applicable and 10% for postage and handling (minimum charge $1.75, Canada $2.00). Prices subject to change without notice.
ISBN PREFIX: 0-8120